D0754506

THE BLACKWELL ENCYCLOPEDIA OF MANAGEMENT

FINANCE

THE BLACKWELL ENCYCLOPEDIA OF MANAGEMENT

SECOND EDITION

Encyclopedia Editor: Cary L. Cooper
Advisory Editors: Chris Argyris and William H. Starbuck

THE BLACKWELL ENCYCLOPEDIA OF MANAGEMENT

SECOND EDITION

FINANCE

Edited by
Ian Garrett
*Manchester Business School,
University of Manchester*

First edition edited by
Dean Paxson and Douglas Wood

Blackwell
Publishing

BLACKWELL PUBLISHING
350 Main Street, Malden, MA 02148–5020, USA
108 Cowley Road, Oxford OX4 1JF, UK
550 Swanston Street, Carlton, Victoria 3053, Australia

First published 1997 by Blackwell Publishers Ltd
Published in paperback in 1999 by Blackwell Publishers Ltd
Second edition published 2005 by Blackwell Publishing Ltd

Library of Congress Cataloging-in-Publication Data

The Blackwell encyclopedia of management. Finance / edited by Ian Garrett.
p. cm.— (The Blackwell encyclopedia of management; v. 4)
Rev. ed. of: The Blackwell encyclopedic dictionary of finance / edited by Dean Paxson and Douglas Wood. c1998.
Includes bibliographical references and index.
ISBN 1-4051-1826-1 (hardcover : alk. paper)
1. Finance—Dictionaries. I. Garrett, Ian. II. Blackwell encyclopedic dictionary of finance.
III. Series.
HD30.15. B455 2005 vol. 4
[HG151]
658'.003 s—dc22
[658.15'. 003]
2004024922

ISBN for the 12–volume set 0-631-23317-2

A catalogue record for this title is available from the British Library.

Set in 9.5 on 11pt Ehrhardt
by Kolam Information Services Pvt. Ltd, Pondicherry, India
Printed and bound in the United Kingdom
by TJ International, Padstow, Cornwall

For further information on
Blackwell Publishing, visit our website:
www.blackwellpublishing.com

Contents

Preface to the First Edition

Although the basic purposes of finance, and the nature of the core instruments used in attaining them, are relatively constant, recent years have seen an explosion in complexity of both products and techniques.

A number of forces are driving this explosion. The first is internationalization encompassing a dramatic growth in the number of countries with stock markets, convertible currencies and a positive regime for foreign investors. For a number of years the more adventurous institutional and private investors have been increasing the proportion of their investments in foreign markets in general and emerging markets in particular in search of growth, higher returns and better diversification. Reflecting this, finance has begun the long process of overhauling the traditionally domestic measurement of risk and return. In the new world order in which the next generation is likely to see an unprecedented transfer of economic power and influence from slow growing developed economies to the high growth tigers in Asia and the Pacific Rim, the ability of financial markets to recognize and accommodate the changes will be a priority.

The second change has come from dramatic falls in the costs of both information and transaction processing. More information is available and it is available more quickly in more places. Improved databases allow sophisticated analysis that would have been impossible a few years ago and data intensive artificial intelligence techniques allow a much richer array of market structures to be considered. The switch to electronic systems of transactions and trading has dramatically lowered costs, allowing increased arbitrage and stimulating the widespread use of complex new derivative products and products offering potentially an infinity of combinations of underlying products. It is no exaggeration to claim that these new techniques and instruments can be used to provide a proxy for any underlying traded instrument.

This power is increasingly used in the marketplace to provide the financial community with new choices, including performance guarantees and indexed products. The development of traded instruments provides an ability to pinpoint exposures precisely and this has lead to a new science of risk management, where the net exposures of a portfolio of risky assets such as securities or bank loans can be estimated and, where required, selectively or completely hedged by buying opposite exposures in the marketplace. Not surprisingly, this encyclopedic dictionary reflects these new techniques which are inexorably creating a world in which financial assets are priced in a seamless global marketplace.

New technology has helped in selecting entries for the dictionary. A word count of titles in finance and business journals was used to identify the frequency with which particular terms appeared and this was used as a primary guide to the priority and length of entries. To accommodate new topics such as real options that are only just emerging into the literature, we also included some entries where interest was growing rapidly towards the end of the search period.

In compiling the dictionary we have been privileged in the support we have received from a wide range of distinguished contributors who have taken the time from a busy programme of research and publication to summarize the often voluminous literature in their specialist areas into an accessible form. Inevitably the technical content of some of the entries reflects the rocket science development in the areas covered, but all entries provide an initial definition and bibliographic references for the less expert.

Finally, we would like to thank Joanne Simpson and Catherine Dowie for their support for this project. The demands of monitoring and recording the progress of contributions as they passed from commissioning through each stage of the editing process to final completion provided an essential foundation to the project.

Dean Paxson
Douglas Wood

Preface to the Second Edition

A large amount of credit for this edition is due to Dean Paxson and the late Douglas Wood for the work they did on the first edition of this volume. Much of what they said in the Preface to the First Edition (above) is true for this edition.

In this volume, I have tried to build on the first edition by including entries that reflect developments and growth in areas such as behavioral finance, asset pricing, and the emergence of nonlinear econometric models. Of course, with a project such as this, there will inevitably be errors of omission, for which I would like to apologise in advance.

I can only echo what Dean Paxson and Douglas Wood said previously: the support from the wide range of distinguished contributors in agreeing to take time out from their schedules to contribute has been exceptional. I would also like to thank Rosemary Nixon and Karen Wilson from Blackwell Publishing for their support and for keeping me on track.

About the Editors

Editor in Chief

Cary Cooper is based at Lancaster University as Professor of Organizational Psychology. He is the author of over 80 books, past editor of the *Journal of Organizational Behavior*, and Founding President of the British Academy of Management.

Advisory Editors

Chris Argyris is James Bryant Conant Professor of Education and Organizational Behavior at Harvard Business School.

William Haynes Starbuck is Professor of Management and Organizational Behavior at the Stern School of Business, New York University.

Volume Editor

Ian Garrett is Professor of Finance at the Manchester School of Accounting and Finance, University of Manchester. Prior to joining Manchester University in 1996, he was a lecturer in the Department of Economics and Finance at Brunel University. His current research interests are in dividend policy, the relationship between spot and derivative markets and their implications for the predictability of mispricing, and the empirical performance of asset pricing models and their ability to explain behavioral anomalies.

Contributors

Reena Aggarwal
Georgetown University

Lakshman A. Alles
Curtin University of Technology

Paul Barnes
Nottingham Trent University

Giovanni Barone-Adesi
Università della Svizzera Italiana

Joyce E. Berg
University of Iowa

Ramaprasad Bhar
University of Technology, Sydney

David Blake
Cass Business School,
City University

John Board
ISMA Centre, Reading University

David Brookfield
University of Liverpool

Frank Byrne
Manchester Business School,
University of Manchester

Peter Byrne
University of Reading

Nusret Cakici
City University of New York

David Camino
Universidad Carlos III de Madrid

Philip Chang
University of Calgary

Derek F. Channon
Late of Imperial College London

Nick Collett
Manchester Business School,
University of Manchester

Oscar Couwenberg
University of Groningen

Susan J. Crain
Southwest Missouri State University

Peter J. DaDalt
Georgia State University

Ian Davidson
Loughborough University

Suresh Deman
Mayo-Deman Associates

Istemi S. Demirag
Queen's University, Belfast

Steven A. Dennis
East Tennessee State University

Athanasios Episcopos
Athens University of Economics and Business

Vihang R. Errunza
McGill University

Ismail Ertürk
Manchester Business School,
University of Manchester

Heber Farnsworth
Washington University in St. Louis

Robert Forsythe
University of Iowa

Ian Garrett
Manchester Business School,
University of Manchester

Gerald T. Garvey
Peter F. Drucker Graduate
School of Management,
Claremont Graduate University

Gordon Gemmill
Warwick Business School,
University of Warwick

Debra A. Glassman
University of Washington

Leslie M. Goldschlager
Monash University

Christian Haefke
Universitat Pompeu Fabra, Spain

Ian R. Harper
Melbourne Business School

Christian Helmenstein
Institute for Advanced Studies, Austria

Stuart Hyde
Manchester Business School,
University of Manchester

Nikunj Kapadia
Stern School of Business,
New York University

Jongchai Kim
Georgia State University

Paul Kofman
Monash University

M. Ameziane Lasfer
Cass Business School, City University

Ricardo Leal
COPPEAD, Brazil

Edward Lee
Manchester Business School,
University of Manchester

Jae Ha Lee
Sungkyunkwan University

Milan Lehocky
Lehman Brothers, London

Joakim Levin
Stockholm School of Economics

Weimin Liu
Manchester Business School,
University of Manchester

Steven V. Mann
University of South Carolina

Sumon C. Mazumdar
Haas School of Business, University of
California, Berkeley

Arie L. Melnik
University of Haifa, Israel

S. Nagarajan
Formerly of University of Hyderabad

Gregory R. Niehaus
Moore School of Business, University of
South Carolina

Jeffry Netter
University of Georgia

Anthony Neuberger
Warwick Business School,
University of Warwick

David P. Newton
Manchester Business School,
University of Manchester

Joseph Ogden
State University of New York at Buffalo

Per Olsson
Fuqua School of Business, Duke University

Katherine O'Sullivan
Manchester Business School,
University of Manchester

Francesco M. Paris
University of Brescia, Italy

Dean A. Paxson
Manchester Business School,
University of Manchester

J. Azevedo Pereira
Manchester Business School,
University of Manchester

Steven Peterson
Virginia Commonwealth University

Steven E. Plaut
University of Haifa, Israel

Sunil Poshakwale
Birmingham Business School,
University of Birmingham

David M. Power
University of Dundee

Vesa Puttonen
Helsinki School of Economics
and Business Administration

Thomas A. Rietz
University of Iowa

Michelle A. Romero
Georgia Institute of Technology

Klaus Sandmann
University of Bonn

Sudipto Sarkar
McMaster University

Charles Schell
University of Northern British Columbia

C. W. Sealey
University of North Carolina at Charlotte

Paul Seguin
Carlson School of Management,
University of Minnesota

Tyler Shumway
University of Michigan Business School

Richard W. Sias
Washington State University

Thomas F. Siems
Federal Reserve Bank of Dallas

Joseph F. Sinkey, Jr.
University of Georgia

Charles Sutcliffe
University of Southampton

Amadou N. R. Sy
International Monetary Fund

Stephen J. Taylor
Lancaster University

David C. Thurston
Henderson State University

Allan Timmermann
University of California, San Diego

A. Tourani-Rad
University of Waikato,
New Zealand

Alexander Triantis
University of Maryland

Ruey S. Tsay
University of Chicago

Nikhil P. Varaiya
San Diego State University

Chris Veld
Tilburg University, The Netherlands

Anne Fremault Vila
Bank of England

Premal Vora
Penn State, Harrisburg

Ed Vos
University of Waikato, New Zealand

C. W. R. Ward
University of Reading

Nick Webber
Cass Business School,
City University

Ivo Welch
Yale School of Management,
Yale University

Jonathon Williams
University of Wales, Bangor

Douglas Wood
Formerly of Manchester Business School,
University of Manchester

agency theory

Steven V. Mann

When human interaction is viewed through the lens of the economist, it is presupposed that all individuals act in accordance with their self-interest. Moreover, individuals are assumed to be cognizant of the self-interest motivations of others and can form unbiased expectations about how these motivations will guide their behavior. Conflicts of interest naturally arise. These conflicts are apparent when two individuals form an agency relationship: one individual (principal) engages another individual (agent) to perform some service on his or her behalf. A fundamental feature of this contract is the delegation of some decision-making authority to the agent. Agency theory is an economic framework employed to analyze these contracting relationships. Jensen and Meckling (1976) present the first unified treatment of agency theory.

Unless incentives are provided to do otherwise or unless they are constrained in some other manner, agents will take actions that are in their self-interest. These actions are not necessarily consistent with the principal's interests. Accordingly, a principal will expend resources in two ways to limit the agent's diverging behavior: (1) structure the contract so as to give the agent appropriate incentives to take actions that are consistent with the principal's interests; (2) monitor the agent's behavior over the contract's life. Conversely, agents may also find it optimal to expend resources to guarantee they will not take actions detrimental to the principal's interests (i.e., bonding costs). These expenditures by principal and/or agent may be pecuniary/non-pecuniary and are the costs of the agency relationship.

Given costly contracting, it is infeasible to structure a contract so that the interests of both the principal and agent are perfectly aligned. Both parties incur monitoring costs and bonding costs up to the point where the marginal benefits equal the marginal costs. Even so, there will be some divergence between the agent's actions and the principal's interests. The reduction in the principal's welfare arising from this divergence is an additional cost of an agency relationship (i.e., "residual loss"). Therefore, Jensen and Meckling (1976) define agency costs as the sum of (1) the principal's monitoring expenditures; (2) the agent's bonding expenditures; and (3) the residual loss.

Barnea, Haugen, and Senbet (1985) divide agency theory into two parts according to the type of contractual relationship examined: the economic theory of agency and the financial theory of agency. The economic theory of agency examines the relationship between a single principal who provides capital and an agent (manager) whose efforts are required to produce some good or service. The principal receives a claim on the firm's end-of-period value. Agents are compensated for their efforts by a dollar wage, a claim on the end-of-period firm value, or some combination of the two.

Two significant agency problems arise from this relationship. First, agents will not put forward their best efforts unless provided the proper incentives to do so (i.e., the incentive problem). Second, both the principal and agent share in the end-of-period firm value and since this value is unknown at the time the contract is negotiated, there is a risk sharing between the two parties (i.e., the risk sharing problem). For example, a contract that provides a constant dollar compensation for the agent (principal) implies that all the risk is borne by the principal (agent).

Contracts that simultaneously solve the incentive problem and the risk-sharing problem are referred to as first-best. First-best contracts provide agents with incentives to expend an optimal amount of effort while producing an optimal distribution of risk between principal and agent. A vast literature examines these issues (e.g., Ross, 1973; Shavell, 1979; Holmstrom, 1979).

The financial theory of agency examines contractual relationships that arise in financial markets. Three classic agency problems are examined in the finance literature: (1) partial ownership of the firm by an owner-manager; (2) debt financing with limited liability; (3) information asymmetry. A corporation is considered to be a nexus for a set of contracting relationships (Jensen and Meckling, 1976). Not surprisingly, conflicts arise among the various contracting parties (manager, shareholder, bondholders, etc.).

When the firm manager does not own 100 percent of the equity, conflicts may develop between managers and shareholders. Managers make decisions that maximize their own utility. Consequently, a partial owner-manager's decisions may differ from those of a manager who owns 100 percent of the equity. For example, Jensen (1986) argues that there are agency costs associated with free cash flow. Free cash flow is discretionary cash available to managers in excess of funds required to invest in all positive net present value projects. If there are funds remaining after investing in all positive present value projects, managers have incentives to misuse free cash flow by investing in projects that will increase their own utility at the expense of shareholders (Mann and Sicherman, 1991).

Conflicts also arise between stockholders and bondholders when debt financing is combined with limited liability. For example, using an analogy between a call option and equity in a levered firm (Black and Scholes, 1973; Galai and Masulis, 1976), one can argue that increasing the variance of the return on the firm's assets will increase equity value (due to the call option feature) and reduce debt value (by increasing the default probability). Simply put, high variance capital investment projects increase shareholder wealth through expropriation from the bondholders. Obviously, bondholders are cognizant of these incentives and place restrictions on shareholder behavior (e.g., debt covenants).

The asymmetric information problem manifests itself when a firm's management seeks to finance an investment project by selling securities (Myers and Majluf, 1984). Managers may possess some private information about the firm's investment project that cannot be credibly conveyed (without cost) to the market due to a moral hazard problem. A firm's securities will command a lower price than if all participants possessed the same information. The information asymmetry can be resolved in principle with various signaling mechanisms. Ross (1977) demonstrates how a manager compensated by a known incentive schedule can use the firm's financial structure to convey private information to the market.

Bibliography

Barnea, A., Haugen, R., and Senbet, L. (1985). *Agency Problems and Financial Contracting*. Englewood Cliffs, NJ: Prentice-Hall.

Black, F., and Scholes, M. (1973). The pricing of options and corporate liabilities. *Journal of Political Economy*, 81, 637–54.

Galai, D., and Masulis, R. (1976). The option pricing model and the risk factor of stock. *Journal of Financial Economics*, 3, 53–82.

Holmstrom, B., (1979). Moral hazard and observability. *Bell Journal of Economics*, 10, 74–91.

Jensen, M., (1986). Agency costs of free cash flow. *American Economic Review*, 76, 323–9.

Jensen, M., and Meckling, W. (1976). Theory of the firm: Managerial behavior, agency costs, and ownership structure. *Journal of Financial Economics*, 3, 306–60.

Mann, S. and Sicherman, N. (1991). The agency costs of free cash flow: Acquisition activity and equity issues. *Journal of Business*, 64, 213–27.

Myers, S., and Majluf, M. (1984). Corporate financing and investment decisions when firms have information that investors do not have. *Journal of Financial Economics*, 13, 187–221.

Ross, S. (1973). The economic theory of agency: The principal's problem. *American Economic Review*, 62, 134–9.

Ross, S. (1977). The determination of financial structure: The incentive signaling approach. *Bell Journal of Economics*, 8, 23–40.

Shavell, S. (1979). Risk-sharing and incentives in the principal–agent relationship. *Bell Journal of Economics*, 10, 55–73 .

arbitrage

see PORTFOLIO THEORY AND ASSET PRICING

arbritrage pricing theory

see PORTFOLIO THEORY AND ASSET PRICING

artificial neural networks

Athanasios Episcopos

Artificial neural networks (ANNs) are learning algorithms in the form of computer programs or hardware. ANNs are characterized by an architecture and a method of training. Network architecture refers to the way processing elements are connected and the direction of the signals exchanged. A processing element or unit is a node where input signals converge and are transformed to outputs via transfer or activation functions. The values of outputs are usually multiplied by weights before they reach another node. The purpose of training is to find optimal values of these weights according to a criterion. In supervised training, inputs are presented to the network and outputs are compared to the desired or target outputs. Weights are then adjusted to minimize an objective function such as the root mean square error, for instance. In unsupervised training, the network itself finds its own optimal parameters.

Although there are several types of neural networks, a simple example of ANN is the multilayer perceptron. The middle sets of units are called hidden layers and the other two input and output layers. The transfer functions in the input and output layers can be identities, and those of the hidden layer are usually sigmoid or hyperbolic tangent functions. These functions map the sum of weighted inputs to the range between zero and one or between minus one and plus one. The flow of signals in the example is unidirectional, giving the name *feedforward* to the whole network. One can have also the output from the network and connect it to the inputs, thus leading to recurrent networks which are useful for time series modeling. Typically, the hidden layers contain several processing elements. Obviously, the outputs are modeled as highly non-linear functions of the original inputs. Thus, it is the architecture of units that allows an ANN to be a universal approximator. In other words an ANN can recover an unknown mapping from the input to the output space as long as it contains enough processing elements (White et al., 1992). The network can be trained with back propagation (Rumelhart and McClelland, 1986), which seeks a minimum in the error function via the gradient descent method. Weights are adjusted in the direction that reduces the value of the error function after each presentation of the input records.

ANNs sometimes share the problem of local minima and the problem of overtraining. Because of the non-linearity involved, the algorithm may not always reach a global minimum. Overtraining refers to the situation where the network literally memorizes the inputs and cannot generalize (predict well) when it is applied to a new set of data. However, there are ways to overcome these problems and ANNs are very useful. In fact, on many occasions they are superior to linear models in terms of prediction accuracy. A correctly trained network should be able to generalize, that is, to recognize patterns in data it has not yet "seen." Although statistical measures such as t-ratios are not available, one can perform sensitivity analysis. This consists of varying one input within a reasonable range and observing how the estimated output function behaves.

Neural networks have been successfully applied in finance and economics, although research in this area is still new. Examples include forecasting security prices, rating bonds, predicting failure of banks or corporate mergers, and conducting portfolio management (Refenes, 1995). Neural networks have been useful in classification because they are often capable of sharply discriminating between classes of inputs (Episcopos, Pericli, and Hu, 1998). In addition, ANNs are useful in uncovering an unknown pricing function (Hutchinson, Lo, and Poggio, 1994). Statistical models and ANNs overlap considerably, but the two sets of models are not identical. White (1989) and Kuan and White (1992) discuss the parallels between statistical or econometric models and feedforward networks. Cheng and Titterington (1994) study ANNs from a statistical perspective, and Ripley (1994) compares standard classification techniques with ANNs. The general literature on ANNs is extensive. Hecht-Nielsen (1990) and Wasserman (1993) are two introductory books. The Internet news group comp.ai. neural_nets is an informative forum for exploring this growing field.

Bibliography

Cheng, B., and Titterington, D. (1994). Neural networks: A review from a statistical perspective. *Statistical Science*, **9**, 2–54.

Episcopos, A., Pericli, and Hu, J. (1998). Commercial mortgage default: A comparison of logit with radial basis function networks. *Journal of Real Estate Finance and Economics*, **17**, 163–78.

Hecht-Nielsen, R. (1990). *Neurocomputing*. Reading, MA: Addison-Wesley.

Hutchinson, J., Lo, A. W., and Poggio, T. (1994). A nonparametric approach to pricing and hedging derivative securities via learning networks. *Journal of Finance*, **49**, 851–89.

Kuan, C., and White, H. (1992). Artificial neural networks: An econometric perspective. *Econometric Reviews*, **13**, 1–91.

Refenes, A. (1995) (ed.). *Neural Networks in the Capital Markets*. New York: John Wiley.

Ripley, B. (1994). Neural networks and related methods for classification. *Journal of the Royal Statistical Society*, **56**, 409–56.

Rumelhart, E., and McClelland, J. (1986). *Parallel Distributed Processing: Explorations in the Microstructure of Cognition*. Cambridge, MA: MIT Press.

Wasserman, P. (1993). *Advanced Methods in Neural Computing*. New York: Van Nostrand Reinhold.

White, A., Gallant, A. R., Hornik, K., Stinchcombe, M., and Wooldridge, J. (1992). *Artificial Neural Networks: Approximation and Learning Theory*. Cambridge, MA: Blackwell.

White, H. (1989). Learning in artificial neural networks: A statistical perspective. *Neural Computation*, **1**, 425–64.

asset allocation

C. W. R. Ward

In the analysis of portfolio management, the initial work of Markowitz (1959) was directed towards finding the optimal weights in a portfolio. It was quickly realized that the decisions involved in building up a portfolio were less frequent than the decisions to modify existing portfolios. This is especially important when analyzing how profitable portfolio managers have been over time. If, for example, a portfolio consists of equities and bonds, some investment managers might be particularly skilled in choosing specific companies in which the portfolio should invest, while others might be able to forecast at which times the portfolio should be more heavily invested in shares. The first type of skill would be classified as being more concerned with portfolio selection, while the latter would be described as connected with timing or asset allocation.

Asset allocation decisions can be further divided. Investors can decide on an *ad hoc* basis to alter their portfolio by changing the weights of the constituent assets as a result of some specific model. For example, forecasting models are used to predict the performance of equities relative to bonds or real estate relative to equities. Dependent on the outcome of these forecasts, the investor will switch into or out of the asset being forecast. Models are used to derive frequent forecasts of one asset against another and to move the portfolio day by day depending on the outcome of the forecasting model. This type of model is sometimes referred to as tactical asset allocation (TAA) and in practice is used in conjunction with some sophisticated trading in derivatives such as options or futures. Instead of buying more shares, this system buys options or futures in an index representing equities. If equities rise in value, so will the options and futures position and the portfolio thereby will increase in value to a greater extent than underlying equities. TAA is used to adjust portfolio exposure to various factors such as interest rates and currency movements as well as overseas investments (Arnott et al., 1989).

An alternative category of asset allocation is the technique of dynamic asset allocation, where there is less emphasis on forecasting which component assets will perform well in the next period and more on setting up a policy by which the portfolio reacts automatically to market movements. This can be organized with the help of options and futures, but can also be carried out by adjusting the weights of the component assets in the light of predetermined rules.

For example, the policy of buying an asset when that asset has performed well in the current period and selling when it has done badly can be carried out in such a way as to provide portfolio insurance (i.e., it protects the portfolio by reducing the exposure to successive falls in the value of one of its constituent assets). An alternative dynamic asset allocation policy is that carried out by rebalancing so as to maintain a reasonably constant proportion in each asset. This involves selling those assets which have just risen in value and selling those assets which have just fallen in value. The two strategies are profitable in different phases of the market. When the market is moving strongly, the insurance policy is most successful. If, however, the market is tending to oscillate without a strong trend, the rebalancing policy works best. These principles are well illustrated in Perold and Sharpe (1988).

Bibliography

Arnott, R. D., Kelso, C. M., Kiscadden, S., and Macedo, R. (1989). Forecasting factor returns: An intriguing possibility. *Journal of Portfolio Management*, 16, 28–35.

Markowitz, H. (1959). *Portfolio Selection: Efficient Diversification of Investments*. New York: John Wiley and Sons.

Perold, A., and Sharpe, W. F. (1988). Dynamic strategies for asset allocation. *Financial Analysts Journal*, **44**, 16–27.

Sharpe, W. F. (1992). Asset allocation: Management style and performance measurement. *Journal of Portfolio Management*, 18, 7–19.

bankruptcy

David Camino

A central tenet in economics is that competition drives markets toward a state of long-run equilibrium in which inefficient firms are eliminated and those remaining in existence produce at a minimum average cost. Consumers benefit from this state of affairs because goods and services are produced and sold at the lowest possible prices. A legal mechanism through which most firms exit the market is generally known as insolvency and/or bankruptcy.

Bankruptcy occurs when the assets of a firm are insufficient to meet the fixed obligations to debtholders and it can be defined in an accounting or legal framework. The legal approach relates outstanding financial obligations to "the fair market value" of the firm's assets, while an accounting bankruptcy would simply be a negative net worth in a conventional balance sheet (Weston and Copeland, 1992). Under bankruptcy laws the firm has the option of either being reorganized as a recapitalized going concern (known as Chapter 11 in the USA or administration in the UK) or being liquidated (Chapter 7 in the USA or liquidation in the UK).

Reorganization means the firm continues in existence and the most informal arrangement is simply to postpone the payment required (known as extension) or an agreement for creditors to take some fraction of what is owed as full settlement (composition). Liquidation, however, occurs as a result of economic distress in the event that liquidation value exceeds the going concern value. Although bankruptcy and liquidation are often confounded in the literature, liquidation (dismantling the assets of the firm and selling them) and bankruptcy (a transfer of ownership from stockholders to bondholders) are really independent events.

The efficient outcome of a good bankruptcy procedure, according to Aghion (1992), should be either of the following:

1 Close the company down and sell the assets for cash or as a going concern, if the present value of expected cash flows is less than outstanding obligations.
2 Reorganize and restructure the company, either through a merger or scaling down or modifying creditors' claims.

Each country has its own insolvency laws, but bankruptcy remedies are very similar in most industrialized nations, incorporating in various ways the economic rationale for fairness among creditors, preservation of enterprise value, providing a fresh start to debtors, and the minimization of economic costs.

There is, however, a widespread dissatisfaction with the existing procedures, as laws have been developed haphazardly with little or almost no economic analysis about how regulations work in practice. Governments and legal structures have not kept pace with the globalization of business and internationalization of financial markets and they have particularly not kept pace in the area of resolving the financial problems of insolvent corporations. For both bankruptcy and insolvency procedures, the key economic issue should be to determine the legal and economic screening processes they provide, and to eliminate only those companies that are economically inefficient and whose resources could be better used in another activity.

Company insolvencies have increased very sharply in the last few years, and currently stand at record levels in many countries. Several factors may severely affect corporate default, and although the combination of recession and high interest rates is likely to have been the main cause of this rise in defaults, the more moderate increases in company failures, which have accompanied more severe downturns in the past, suggest that other factors may also have been important. One important common determinant in companies' failures is the general economic conditions for business; the other is the level of debt. Both capital leverage (debt as a proportion of assets) and income gearing (interest payments as a proportion of income), together with high levels of indebtedness in the economy, may lead to companies' insolvencies.

Recent developments in the theory of finance have considerably advanced our understanding of the nature and role of debt. Debt, unlike any other "commodity," entails a "promise" to pay an amount and the fulfillment of this promise is, by its nature, uncertain. Many of its features, however, can be understood as means of overcoming uncertainty, transaction costs, and incomplete contracts, arising from asymmetric information between the parties concerned.

The risk of bankruptcy and financial distress, however, highlights the fact that conflicts of interest between stockholders and various fixed payment claimants do still exist. These conflicts arise because the firm's fixed claims bear default risk while stockholders have limited liability residual claims and influence the managerial decision process. Bankruptcy procedures often do not work well, because incomplete (private) contracts cannot be reconciled, so laws have to step in. Bankruptcy, as such, does not create wealth transfers to shareholders or undermine the provisions of debt finance, but it creates, due to asymmetric information, a conflict of interest between creditors and shareholders, which harms companies' prospects.

The implications of these conflicts of interest have been explored by a number of researchers, including Jensen and Meckling (1976), Myers (1977), and Masulis (1988). One consistent message in these works is that these conflicts create incentives for stockholders to take actions that benefit themselves at the expense of creditors and that do not necessarily maximize firm value.

Jensen and Meckling (1976) argue that rational investors are aware of these conflicts and the possible actions firms can take against creditors. Thus, when loans are made, they are discounted immediately for the expected losses these anticipated actions would induce. This discounting means that, on average, stockholders do not gain from these actions, but firms consistently suffer by making suboptimal decisions. If the firm is confronted with a choice between investment and debt reduction, it will continue to invest past the efficient point. Then creditors will prefer a debt reduction to investment and, since there are no efficiencies, stockholders must prefer investment.

However, if the actions of the owners (managers or shareholders) are unobservable several complications arise. First, there is asset substitution. Since the owner only benefits from returns in non-default states, risky investments of given mean return will be chosen in preference to safer investments (moral hazard). Owners benefit from the upside gains from high risk investments but do not bear the costs of downside losses. Those are inflicted on creditors rather than shareholders. This is the standard consequence that debt can cause firms to take on uneconomic projects simply to increase risk and shift wealth from creditors to stockholders.

Second, there is underinvestment. Owners do not benefit from the effort that they apply to improve returns in insolvency states. Those accrue for creditors not owners. Since some of the returns to investments accrue to bondholders in bankrupt states, firms may be discouraged from carrying out what would otherwise be profitable investments (Myers, 1977).

Third, there is claim dilution; that is, an incentive for owners to issue debt that is senior to existing debt. Senior debt has priority over existing debt in the event of bankruptcy; it can therefore be issued on more favorable terms than existing debt, which leaves existing creditors' claims intact in the event of bankruptcy.

The literature suggests, therefore, that bankruptcy impediments to pure market solutions are concerned with the free rider and holdout problems caused by the inconsistent incentives arising in a business contract specifying a fixed value payment between debtor and creditor, particularly given limited liability. Limited liability implies moral hazard and adverse selection due to asymmetric information problems.

Consequently, the prospect of corporate insolvency may result in increased borrowing costs and, simultaneously, a reduction in the amount of funds available.

Bibliography

Aghion, P. (1992). The economics of bankruptcy reform. Working paper 0 7530 1103 4. London: London School of Economics.

Akerlof, G. A. (1970). The market for lemons: Quality uncertainty and the market mechanism. *Quarterly Journal of Economics*, **84**, 488–500.

Altman, E. I. (1993). *Corporate Financial Distress and Bankruptcy*. New York: John Wiley

Davis, E. P. (1992). *Debt, Financial Fragility, and Systemic Risk*. Oxford: Clarendon Press.

Jensen, M., and Meckling, W. (1976). Theory of the firm: Managerial behavior, agency costs and ownership structure. *Journal of Financial Economics*, **3**, 305–60.

Masulis, R. W. (1988). *The Debt/Equity Choice*. New York: Ballinger.

Myers, S. C. (1977). Determinants of corporate borrowing. *Journal of Financial Economics*, **4**, 147–75.

Webb, D. (1991). An economic evaluation of insolvency procedures in the United Kingdom: Does the 1986 Insolvency Act satisfy the creditors' bargain? *Oxford Economic Papers*, **42**, 139–57.

Weston, J. F., and Copeland, T. E. (1992). *Managerial Finance*. Orlando, FL: Dryden Press.

White, M. J. (1988). The corporate bankruptcy decision. *Journal of Economic Perspectives*, **3**, 129–51.

banks as barrier options

Francesco M. Paris

A barrier option is an option which is initiated or extinguished if the underlying asset price hits a prespecified value. More specifically, a "down and out call" is a call option expiring worthless as soon as the value of the underlying asset hits a lower bound K, which is usually equal to or less than the option's exercise price, as developed in Merton (1973) and Cox and Rubinstein (1985).

Chesney and Gibson (1993, 1994) applied the down and out call model to the pricing of equity in a levered firm, while Paris (1995, 1996) extended the model to banks and financial intermediaries.

Valuing bank capital as a traditional call option written on the bank assets, with a strike price equal to the total bank deposits, has two main theoretical underpinnings:

1   As soon as the bank asset value declines to the value of the liabilities, the bank capital is worth zero, while the call value is positive, before the option's expiration.
2   In order to maximize the market value of their equity, the bank shareholders systematically choose the most risky projects characterizing the investment opportunity set.

The down and out call approach overcomes both of these problems. The value of the bank capital is:

$$
\begin{aligned}
C_t =& A_t N(x) - B_t N(x - \sigma_t \sqrt{T - t}) \\
& - \left[A_t \left(\frac{A_t}{K} \right)^{-2\xi} N(y) \right. \\
& \left. - B_t \left(\frac{A_t}{K} \right)^{-2\xi+2} N(y - \sigma_t \sqrt{T - t}) \right]
\end{aligned}
$$

where C_t is the current market value of the bank capital, A_t is the stochastic current value of the bank assets, which follow a continuous diffusion process,

$$
\frac{\mathrm{d}A_t}{A_t} = \mu_t \, \mathrm{d}t + \sigma_t \, \mathrm{d}z
$$

where μ_t is the expected instantaneous rate of return of the bank assets, σ_t is the standard deviation of the instantaneous rate of return of the bank assets, z is a standard Wiener process, B_t is the current market value of the bank liabilities, K is the knock out value, assumed to be constant, r is the constant instantaneous risk free-rate of interest, ξ is $r/\sigma_t^2 + 1/2$, and $N(.) = $ the standard normal distribution function

$$
x = \frac{\ln\left(\frac{A_t}{B_t} \right)}{\sigma_t \sqrt{T - t}} + \xi \sigma_t \sqrt{T - t}
$$

$$
y = \frac{\ln\left(\frac{K^2}{A_t B_t} \right)}{\sigma_t \sqrt{T - t}} + \xi \sigma_t \sqrt{T - t}
$$

and goes to zero whenever $A_t \geq K$.

The optimal value of the asset volatility is obtained by setting the partial derivative of the capital value with respect to the bank asset volatility equal to 0:

$$\frac{\partial C_t}{\partial \sigma_t} = \frac{A_t \sqrt{T-t}}{\sqrt{2\pi}} \left[e^{\left(\frac{-y^2}{2}\right)} - \left(\frac{A_t}{K}\right)^{-2\xi} e^{-\frac{y^2}{2}} \right]$$

$$+ \left(\frac{2r}{\sigma_t^3}\right) \ln\left(\frac{A_t}{K}\right) \left(\frac{A_t}{K}\right)^{-2\xi} \left[A_t N(y) \right.$$

$$\left. - B_t \left(\frac{A_t}{K}\right)^2 N(y - \sigma_t \sqrt{T-t}) \right] = 0$$

This equation can be solved numerically. The optimal value of the asset volatility is an increasing function of the bank leverage and a decreasing function of the knock out value K. This result means that the greater the bank's capitalization, the lower the management bias towards the volatility of its investments.

K can be interpreted as a reputational constraint resulting in insolvency if it is violated. It is usually industry specific, even if it could be related to some firm specific feature, like leverage.

This approach to the valuation of bank capital has two fundamental implications: (1) the asset volatility is related to the bank capital structure, meaning that an explicit and positive linkage exists between the two main sources of risk in the bank; and (2) the existence of an optimal asset volatility implies that the bank shareholders may be risk averse instead of risk neutral, as they are traditionally considered in the theoretical literature, eliminating, as a consequence, any behavioral differences among shareholders and bank managers. Distinguishing between a shareholder and a management controlled bank is thus meaningless, to the extent that the utility function of the bank controller is considered.

Paris (1995) applies the down and out call framework to the valuation of bank capital. This approach has two merits.

1 The market value of the bank capital can be easily computed at any time, once the marking to the market of bank assets and liabilities is assumed to be feasible, and a continuous time model of bank monitoring can be implemented. It is worthwhile to stress that frequent, possibly continuous, monitoring is a necessary, if not sufficient, condition for prompt and effective corrective actions by financial regulators, in case of bank problems.

2 The chosen optimal value of the bank asset volatility, if observed by the market, is an effective signal of the true bank capitalization. The important implication is that observing the bank's investment strategy allows the market to evaluate the bank's safety and soundness.

An extension of the down and out call model to any kind of financial intermediary has been applied in Paris (1996) in order to derive relevant properties of alternative regulatory approaches. Once more the optimal intermediary asset volatility is the critical variable determining the intermediary's response to the regulatory provision, in addition to the regulator's action in terms of minimum capital requirement. Moreover, under specific conditions, the same volatility measure can be unambiguously inferred by the market, by simply observing the intermediary's capital ratio.

Bibliography

Chesney, M., and Gibson, R. (1993). The investment policy and the pricing of equity in a levered firm: A reexamination of the contingent claims' valuation approach. *EFA Annual Conference Proceedings*, Copenhagen.

Chesney, M., and Gibson, R. (1994). Option pricing theory, security design and shareholders' risk incentives. *AFFI Annual Conference Proceedings*, Tunis.

Cox, J. C., and Rubinstein, M. (1985). *Options Markets*. Englewood Cliffs, NJ: Prentice-Hall.

Merton, R. C. (1973). Theory of rational option pricing. *Bell Journal of Economics and Management Science*, **4**, 141–83.

Paris, F. M. (1995). An alternative theoretical approach to the regulation of bank capital. University of Brescia Working paper 97.

Paris, F. M. (1996). Modelling alternative approaches to financial regulation. University of Brescia Working paper 103.

behavioral finance

Ian Garrett

Modern finance theory, or what has been referred to as the traditional finance paradigm (Barberis and Thaler, 2003), is based on rational economic agents making rational decisions based on available information, and forming rational expectations about future events. This latter statement means that the subjective distribution of possible outcomes rational agents use in forming their forecasts of future events matches the distribution that the actual outcomes come from. Agents with rational expectations will on average be correct. If agents are rational, and assuming that markets are frictionless, the price of an asset reflects the present value of expected cash flows from that asset; that is, the price of the asset equals its fundamental value. If prices deviate from their fundamental value the mispricing will be profitably exploited by rational agents. If an apparent mispricing, or anomaly, seems to persist, then it may reflect something other than mispricing. For example, Fama and French (1996) show that their three factor asset pricing model explains some of the anomalies, such as the overreaction effect, that the one factor capital asset pricing model cannot explain. In this case, the apparent anomalies seem to have a risk-based explanation.

Behavioral finance, on the other hand, argues that mispricing can be present and persist because of *limits* to arbitrage and psychological biases. Excellent surveys of behavioral finance can be found in Hirshleifer (2001), Daniel, Hirshleifer, and Teoh (2002), and Barberis and Thaler (2003). In the models of behavioral finance, not all agents are fully rational. The result is that if rational and irrational (often known as noise) traders interact, it is possible for irrational traders to have a significant and lasting impact on prices. The reason for this is that while in theory arbitrage is costless (the purchase of the undervalued asset is financed by selling the overvalued asset short, for example) and risk-free, this is typically not the case in practice. If the risks and costs involved with the strategy to exploit the mispricing are perceived to be too high the mispricing will not be exploited (for a discussion of what these risks and costs are, see Barberis and Thaler, 2003). In other words, there are limits to arbitrage or, as Barberis and Thaler (2003) put it, while "prices are right" means there is "no free lunch," "no free lunch" does not mean "prices are right." There are several examples of this in the literature. Lamont and Thaler (2003), for example, examine 3Com's sale of 5 percent of its wholly

owned subsidiary, Palm Inc., and their announced intention to sell the rest within 9 months with 3Com shareholders being given 1.5 shares of Palm. Lamont and Thaler (2003) point out that at the end of the first day of trading after the IPO, the market valuation of 3Com's businesses outside of Palm was −$60 per share, a substantial mispricing of 3Com's shares, yet it persisted for quite some time. Lamont and Thaler (2003) found that there were substantial costs involved in exploiting the mispricing as the demand for Palm shares to short was so high that the supply of Palm's shares to short could not match the demand.

The sources of irrationality that may explain anomalies in stock returns are psychological biases that may arise from what Hirshleifer (2001) terms heuristic simplification, self-deception, and emotional loss of control (for a detailed review, see Hirshleifer, 2001). Heuristic simplification is the situation where, because time and cognitive resources such as memory and attention span are limited, rules of thumb and narrow framing (compartmentalizing problems that perhaps should not be analyzed in isolation) are used in decision-making. When rules of thumb are used out of context or problems are placed too much in isolation, (quite substantial) biases can arise. One example of this is what Thaler (1985) calls mental accounting. This is the situation where individuals keep track of any gains and losses in artificial, separate mental accounts. Narrow framing such as mental accounting may explain such things as the disposition effect (Shefrin and Statman, 1985), whereby investors hold on to loss-making stocks (losers) longer than they should and sell winning stocks before they should (for recent evidence on this, see Odean, 1998). A related concept is that of loss aversion.

Self-deception is the situation where individuals think they are better than they actually are. This leads to overconfidence which, because of biased self-attribution (good outcomes are due to one's own ability, bad outcomes are due to factors outside one's own control), can persist and can cause mispricing. Daniel, Hirshleifer, and Subrahmanyam (2001) derive an asset pricing model which has overconfident traders who trade with risk-averse, rational traders. The presence of overconfident traders, who overreact to information, leads to equilibrium security returns that depend not only on the market β (systematic risk) but also on mispricing, as proxied by such factors as the book-to-market equity ratio. This provides an alternative explanation for the significance of the book-to-market factor in the Fama–French three factor model.

Emotional loss of control relates to, among other things, the effect of mood on decision-making. Unsurprisingly, research has shown that individuals in good moods tend to make more optimistic choices. However, what is interesting is the effect that mood has on individuals' judgments when they lack information and when the judgment is somewhat abstract. The evidence suggests that when people are in bad moods, they tend to be more analytical and critical in their decision-making. However, studies have found that when people are in a good mood, while they show greater mental flexibility and better problem solving capabilities, they are more receptive to weak or neutral arguments. They are also likely to misattribute the source of their feelings. Mood, therefore, influences individuals' assessments of future prospects and their assessment of risk. If the decisions of the marginal trader (i.e., the trader who sets prices) are influenced by mood, then it is not unreasonable to suspect that mood will influence stock returns. Examples of studies that document the impact of mood on stock returns are Kamstra, Kramer, and Levi (2000, 2003) and Hirshleifer and Shumway (2003). Kamstra, Kramer, and Levi (2000) document that daylight saving changes, which disrupt sleep patterns, have a significant impact on stock returns. Moreover, this effect does not appear to be limited to one market. Hirshleifer and Shumway (2003) examine the impact of number of hours of sunshine on stock returns. There is a good deal of evidence in the psychology literature documenting a positive relationship between sunshine and mood. The idea here is that prospects look better when you are in a good mood and if individuals are susceptible to weak or neutral arguments when they are in a good mood they may, in the words of Hirshleifer and Shumway (2003), "incorrectly attribute their good mood to positive economic prospects rather than good weather." In other words,

even though an individual's prospects have not changed, being in an upbeat mood can cast a different light on things. Hirshleifer and Shumway (2003) examine the relationship between excess cloud cover and stock returns worldwide and find that there is a significant negative relationship between excess cloud cover and stock returns: on unusually sunny days, stock returns will increase. Kamstra, Kramer, and Levi (2003) examine the impact of Seasonal Affective Disorder (SAD) on stock returns, while Garrett, Kamstra, and Kramer (2004) examine the impact of SAD on risk. SAD is a condition that is closely linked to depression which affects many people during the seasons of the year in which hours of night are longest. Individuals who suffer from SAD or its milder form, the Winter Blues, become more risk averse as the depression caused by SAD takes hold. If the marginal trader suffers from SAD, or the milder Winter Blues, then one might expect to see a relationship between seasonal patterns in the length of night and stock returns and risk. Kamstra, Kramer, and Levi (2003) document a significant relationship between the length of night and stock returns in several stock markets in both the northern and southern hemispheres, while Garrett, Kamstra, and Kramer (2004) find that the length of night affects the risk premium.

Bibliography

Barberis, N., and Thaler, R. (2003). A survey of behavioral finance. In G. M. Constantinides, M. Harris, and R. Stulz (eds.), *Handbook of the Economics of Finance*. Amsterdam: Elsevier.

Daniel, K., Hirshleifer, D., and Subrahmanyan, A. (2001). Mispricing, covariance risk and the cross-section of security returns. *Journal of Finance*, **56**, 921–65.

Daniel, K., Hirshleifer, D., and Teoh, S. H. (2002). Investor psychology in capital markets: Evidence and policy implications. *Journal of Monetary Economics*, **49**, 139–209.

Fama, E. F., and French, K. R. (1996). Multifactor explanations of asset pricing anomalies. *Journal of Finance*, **51**, 55–84.

Garrett, I., Kamstra, M., and Kramer, L. (2004). Winter blues and time variation in the price of risk. *Journal of Empirical Finance* forthcoming.

Hirshleifer, D. (2001). Investor psychology and asset pricing, *Journal of Finance*, **56**, 1533–97.

Hirshleifer, D., and Shumway, T. (2003). Good day sunshine: Stock returns and the weather. *Journal of Finance*, **58**, 1009–32.

Kamstra, M., Kramer, L., and Levi, M. (2000). Losing sleep at the market: The daylight savings anomaly. *American Economic Review*, **90**, 1005–11.

Kamstra, M., Kramer, L., and Levi, M. (2003). Winter blues: A SAD stock market cycle. *American Economic Review*, **93**, 324–43.

Lamont, O. and Thaler, R. (2003). Can the market add and subtract? Mispricing in tech stock carve-outs. *Journal of Political Economy*, **111**, 227–68.

Odean, T. (1998). Are investors reluctant to realize their losses? *Journal of Finance*, **53**, 1775–98.

Shefrin, H., and Statman, M. (1985). The disposition to sell winners too early and ride losers too long. *Journal of Finance*, **40**, 777–90.

Thaler, R. (1985). Mental accounting and consumer choice. *Marketing Science*, **4**, 119–214.

bid–ask spread

Steven V. Mann

Security dealers maintain a continuous presence in the market and stand ready to buy and sell securities immediately from impatient sellers and buyers. Dealers are willing to buy securities at a price slightly below the perceived equilibrium price (i.e., bid price) and sell securities immediately at a price slightly above the perceived equilibrium price (i.e., ask price). Of course, buyers and sellers of securities could wait to see if they can locate counterparties who are willing to sell or buy at the current equilibrium price. However, there are risks associated with patience. The equilibrium price may change "adversely" in the interim such that it is either higher or lower than the dealer's current bid or ask quotes. Thus, the willingness of traders to transact at a price that differs from the perceived equilibrium price compensates market makers, in part, for the risks of continuously supplying patience to the market. Although the dealers' willingness to post bid and ask quotes springs from their self-interest, their actions generate a positive externality of greater liquidity for the market as a whole.

In general, the bid–ask spread compensates the dealer/market makers for three costs that attend their function of providing liquidity. These costs include order processing costs, inventory control costs, and adverse selection costs. The order processing costs include maintaining a continuous presence in the market and the administrative costs of exchanging titles (Demsetz, 1968). The inventory control costs are incurred because the dealer holds an undiversified portfolio (Amihud and Mendelson, 1986; Ho and Stoll, 1980). The adverse selection costs compensate the dealer for the risk of trading with individuals who possess superior information about the security's equilibrium price (Copeland and Galai, 1983; Glosten and Milgrom, 1985).

A dealer's quote has two component parts. The first part is the bid and ask prices. The second part is the quotation size which represents the number of shares dealers are willing to buy (sell) at the bid (ask) price. A dealer's quote can be described as an option position (Copeland and Galai, 1983): the bid and ask price quotes are a pair of options of indefinite maturity written by the dealer. A put (call) option is written with a striking price equal to the bid (ask) price. The quotation size is the number of shares dealers are willing to buy (sell) at the bid (ask) price. Simply put, the quotation size represents the number of put (call) options written with a striking price equal to the bid (ask) price.

In the parlance of options, the dealer's position is a short strangle. A strangle consists of a call and a put on the same stock with the same expiration date and different striking prices. The call (put) has a striking price (below) the current stock price. Dealers are short a strangle since they write both options. If one assumes the dealer's bid and ask prices bracket the market's estimate of the stock's current equilibrium price, the analogy is complete.

Bibliography

Amihud, Y., and Mendelson, H. (1986). Asset pricing and the bid–ask spread. *Journal of Financial Economics*, **17** (2), 223–49.

Copeland, T., and Galai, D. (1983). Information effects on the bid–ask spread. *Journal of Finance*, **38** (5), 1457–69.

Demsetz, H. (1968). The cost of transacting. *Quarterly Journal of Economics*, **82** (1), 33–53.

Glosten, L. and Milgrom, P. (1985). Bid, ask and transaction prices in a specialist market with heterogeneously informed traders. *Journal of Financial Economics*, **14** (1), 71–100.

Ho, T., and Stoll, H. (1980). On dealer markets under competition. *Journal of Finance*, **35** (2), 259–67.

Black–Scholes

Gordon Gemmill

This is a famous equation for determining the price of an option, first discovered in 1972 by Fischer Black of Goldman Sachs and Myron Scholes of the University of Chicago and published in Black and Scholes (1973). The unique insight of this research was to use arbitrage in solving the option-pricing problem. Black and Scholes reasoned that a position which involved selling a call option and buying some of the underlying asset could be made risk free. It would be a hedged position and, as such, should pay the risk free rate on the net investment. Using continuous-time mathematics they were able to solve for the call price from the equation for the hedged position. This resulted in an equation for the value of a European option (i.e., one which cannot be exercised before maturity) which did not need to take account of the attitude to risk of either the buyer or seller.

The equation (expressed for a call option) is:

$$c = SN(d_1) - Ee^{-rt}N(d_2)$$

where c is the call price, S is the asset price, $N(x)$ is a normal distribution probability, E is the exercise price, r is the interest rate in continuous form, and t is years to maturity.

The $N(d_1)$ and $N(d_2)$ values, which are probabilities from the normal distribution, have values for d_1 and d_2 calculated as follows:

$$d_1 = \frac{\log(S/E) + rt + 0.5\sigma^2 t}{\sigma\sqrt{t}}$$

and

$$d_2 = d_1 - \sigma\sqrt{t}$$

where σ is the standard deviation of returns on the asset per annum.

In the equation, the value of a call option depends on five variables: the asset price (S), the exercise price (E), the continuous interest rate (r), the time to maturity (t), and the standard deviation of returns on the asset (σ) (which is usually known as the volatility). Of these five variables, only the volatility is unknown and needs to be forecast to the maturity of the option. The call price in the equation is a weighted function of the asset price (S) and the present value of the exercise price (Ee^{-rt}). The weights are respectively $N(d_1)$, which is the hedge ratio or "delta" of the option, and $N(d_2)$, which is the probability that the option matures in the money.

Many academic papers have proposed more complicated models, only to conclude that the simple Black–Scholes model can be modified to give almost equally good results. Several assumptions are necessary to derive the model, but it is surprisingly robust to small changes in them. The first assumption is that the asset price follows a random walk with drift. This means that the asset price is lognormally distributed and so returns on the asset are normally distributed. This assumption is widely used in financial models. The second assumption is that the distribution of returns on the asset has a constant volatility. This assumption is clearly wrong and use of the model depends crucially on forecasting volatility for the period to maturity of the option. The third assumption is that there are no transaction costs, so that the proportions of the asset and option in the hedged portfolio may be continuously adjusted without incurring huge costs. This assumption sounds critical, but it is relatively unimportant in liquid markets. The fourth assumption is that interest rates are constant, which is not correct but is of little importance since option prices are not very sensitive to interest rates. The fifth assumption is that there are no dividends on the asset, which once again is unrealistic, but modification of the model to accommodate them is relatively simple (e.g., Black, 1975).

While most of the theoretical results in finance have not had any impact on practitioners, the Black–Scholes model is universally known and used. The existence of the equation has facilitated the development of markets in options, both on-exchange (beginning with the Chicago Board Options Exchange in 1973) and over the counter. Without the equation, there could not have been such rapid growth in the use of derivative assets over the last 30 years. Many derivative assets might even not exist.

Bibliography

Black, F. (1975). Fact and fantasy in the use of options. *Financial Analysts Journal*, 31, 36–41, 61–72.

Black, F., and Scholes, M. (1973). The pricing of options and corporate liabilities. *Journal of Political Economy*, 81, 637–59.

capital asset pricing model

see PORTFOLIO THEORY AND ASSET PRICING

capital structure

David P. Newton

Capital structure is the mixture of securities issued by a company to finance its operations. Companies need real assets in order to operate. These can be tangible assets, such as buildings and machinery, or intangible assets, such as brand names and expertise. To pay for the assets, companies raise cash not only via their trading activities but also by selling financial assets, called securities, financial instruments, or contingent claims. These securities may be classified broadly as either equity or debt (though it is possible to create securities with elements of both). Equity is held as shares of stock in the company, whereby the company's stock holders are its owners. If the company's trading activities are sufficiently successful, the value of its owners' equity increases. Debt may be arranged such that repayments are made only to the original holder of the debt, or a "bond" may be created which can be sold on, thus transferring ownership of future repayments to new bondholders.

Capital structure can be changed by issuing more debt and using the proceeds to buy back shares, or by issuing more equity and using the proceeds to buy back debt. The question then arises: Is there an optimal capital structure for a company? The solution to this question, for the restricted case of "perfect markets," was given by Modigliani and Miller (1958), whose fame is now such that they are referred to in finance textbooks simply as MM. A perfect market is

one in which there are neither taxes nor brokerage fees and the numbers of buyers and sellers are sufficiently large, and all participants are financially sufficiently small relative to the size of the market that trading by a single participant cannot affect the market prices of securities. MM's "first proposition" states that the market value of any firm is independent of its capital structure. This may be considered as a law of conservation of value: the value of a company's assets is unchanged by the claims against them. It means that in a perfect and rational market a company would not be able to gain value simply by recombining claims against its assets and offering them in different forms. Modigliani and Miller (1961) likewise deduced that whether or not cash was disbursed as dividends was irrelevant in a perfect market.

MM's first proposition relies on investors being able to borrow at the same interest rate as companies; if they cannot, then companies can increase their values by borrowing. If they can, then there is no advantage to investors if a company borrows more money, since the investors could, if they wished, borrow money themselves and use the money to buy extra shares of stock in the company. The investors would then have to pay interest on the cash borrowed, as would the company, but will benefit from holding more equity in the company, resulting in the same overall benefit to the investor.

An analogy which has been used for this proposition is the sale of milk and its derivative products (see Ross, Westerfield, and Jaffe, 1988). Milk can be sold whole or it can be split into cream and low cream milk. Suppose that splitting (or recombining) the milk costs virtually nothing and that you buy and sell all three products through a broker at no cost. Cream can be sold at a high price in the market and so by splitting off the cream from your milk you might appear to be able to gain wealth. However, the low cream milk remaining will be less valuable than the original, full cream milk – a buyer has a choice in the market between full cream milk and milk with its cream removed; offered both at the same price, he would do best to buy full cream milk, remove its cream and sell it himself. Trading in the perfect market would act so as to make the combined price of cream and low cream milk in the perfect market the same as the price of full cream milk (conservation of value). If, for example, the combined price dropped below the full cream price then traders could recombine the derivative products and sell them at a profit as full cream milk.

What was considered perplexing, before Modigliani–Miller, is now replaced by a strong and simple statement about capital structure. This is very convenient because any supposed deviations can be considered in terms of the weakening of the assumptions behind the proposition. Obvious topics for consideration are the payment of brokers' fees, taxes, the costs of financial distress, and new financial instruments (which may stimulate or benefit from a temporarily imperfect market). New financial instruments may create value if they offer a service not previously available but required by investors. This is becoming progressively harder to achieve; but even if successful, the product will soon be copied and the advantage in the market will be removed. Charging of brokers' fees simply removes a portion of the value and (as long as the portion is small) this is not a major consideration, since we are concerned with the merits of different capital structures rather than the costs of conversion. Taxes, however, can change the result significantly: interest payments reduce the amount of corporation tax paid and so there is a tax advantage, or "shield," given to debt compared with equity. When modified to include corporate taxes, MM's proposition shows the value of a company increasing linearly as the amount of debt is increased (Brealey and Myers, 1991). This would suggest that companies should try to operate with as much debt as possible. The fact that very many companies do not do this motivates further modifications to theory: inclusion of the effect of personal tax on shareholders and inclusion of the costs of financial distress. Miller (1977) has argued that the increase in value caused by the corporate tax shield is reduced by the effect of personal taxes on investors. In addition, the costs of financial distress increase with added debt, so that the value of the company is represented by the following equation, in which PV denotes present value:

value of company = value if all equity financed $+ PV$ (tax shield) $- PV$ (costs of financial distress)

As debt is increased, the corporate tax shield increases in value, but the probability of financial distress increases, thus increasing the present value of the costs of financial distress. The value of the company is maximized when the present value of tax savings on additional borrowing only just compensates for increases in the present value of the costs of financial distress.

One element of financial distress can be bankruptcy. It is generally the case throughout the world's democracies that shareholders have limited liability. Although shareholders may seem to fare badly by receiving nothing when a company is declared bankrupt, their right simply to walk away from the company with nothing is actually valuable, since they are not liable personally for the company's unpaid debts. Short of bankruptcy there are other costs, including those caused by unwillingness to invest and shifts in value engineered between bondholders and shareholders, which increase with the level of debt. Holders of corporate debt, as bonds, stand to receive a maximum of the repayments owed; shareholders have limited liability, suffer nothing if the bondholders are not repaid, and benefit from all gains in value above the amount owed to bondholders. Therefore, if a company has a large amount of outstanding debt it can be to the shareholders' advantage to take on risky projects which may give large returns, since this is essentially a gamble using bondholders' money. Conversely, shareholders may be unwilling to provide extra equity capital, even for sound projects. Thus a company in financial distress may suffer from a lack of capital expenditure to renew its machinery and underinvestment in research and development. Even if a company is not in financial distress, it can be put into that position by management issuing large amounts of debt. This devalues the debt already outstanding, thus transferring value from bondholders to shareholders. Interesting examples of this are to be found in leveraged buyouts (LBOs), perhaps the most famous being the attempted management buyout of R. J. R. Nabisco in the 1980s (Burrough and Helyar, 1990). Top management in R. J. R. Nabisco were, of course, trying to become richer by their actions – an extreme example of so-called agency costs, whereby managers do not act in the shareholders' interest but seek extra benefits for themselves.

There is, finally, no simple formula for the optimum capital structure of a company. A balance has to be struck between the tax advantages of corporate borrowing (adjusted for the effect of personal taxation on investors) and the costs of financial distress. This suggests that companies with strong, taxable profits and valuable tangible assets should look towards high debt levels, but that currently unprofitable companies with intangible and risky assets should prefer equity financing. This approach is compatible with differences in debt levels between different industries, but fails to explain why the most successful companies within a particular industry are often those with low debt. An attempt at an explanation for this is a "pecking order" theory (Myers, 1984). Profitable companies generate sufficient cash to finance the best projects available to management. These internal funds are preferred to external financing since issue costs are thus avoided, financial slack is created, in the form of cash, marketable securities, and unused debt capacity, which gives valuable options on future investment, and the possibly adverse signal of an equity issue is avoided.

Bibliography

Brealey, R. A., and Myers, S. C. (1991). *Principles of Corporate Finance*, 4th edn. New York: McGraw-Hill.
Burrough, B., and Helyar, J. (1990). *Barbarians at the Gate: The Fall of R. J. R. Nabisco*. London: Arrow Books.
Miller, M. (1977). Debt and taxes. *Journal of Finance*, **32**, 261–76.
Modigliani, F., and Miller, M. (1958). The cost of capital, corporation finance and the theory of investment. *American Economic Review*, **48**, 261–97.
Modigliani, F., and Miller, M. (1961). Dividend policy, growth and the valuation of shares. *Journal of Business*, **34**, 411–33.
Myers, S. C. (1984). The capital structure puzzle. *Journal of Finance*, **39**, 575–92.
Ross, S. A., Westerfield, R. W., and Jaffe, J. F. (1988). *Corporate Finance*, 3rd edn. Chicago: University of Chicago Press, 434–5.

catastrophe futures and options

Steven V. Mann and Gregory R. Niehaus

Catastrophe futures and options are derivative securities whose payoffs depend on insurers' underwriting losses arising from natural catastrophes (e.g., hurricanes). Specifically, the payoffs are derived from an underwriting loss ratio that measures the extent of the US insurance industry's catastrophe losses relative to premiums earned for policies in some geographical region over a specified time period. The loss ratio is multiplied by a notional principal amount to obtain the dollar payoff for the contract. The Chicago Board of Trade (CBOT) introduced national and regional catastrophe insurance futures contracts and the corresponding options on futures in 1992.

Insurers/reinsurers can use catastrophe futures and options to hedge underwriting risk engendered by catastrophes (Harrington, Mann, and Niehaus, 1995). For example, when taking a long position, an insurer implicitly agrees to buy the loss ratio index at a price equal to the current futures price. Accordingly, a trader taking a long catastrophe futures position when the futures price is 10 percent commits to paying 10 percent of the notional principal in exchange for the contract's settlement price. If the futures loss ratio equals 15 percent of the notional principal there is a 5 percent profit. Conversely, if the settlement price is 5 percent at expiration, the trader pays 10 percent and receives 5 percent of the notional principal for a 5 percent loss. The CBOT catastrophe futures contracts have a notional principal of US$25,000.

Prior to the expiry of the contract, the futures price reflects the market's expectation of the futures loss ratio. As catastrophes occur or conditions change so as to make their occurrence more likely (e.g., a shift in regional weather patterns), the futures price will increase. Conversely, if expected underwriting losses from catastrophes decrease, the futures price will decrease. Given that the futures price reflects the futures loss ratio's expected value, an insurer can take a long futures position when a contract begins to trade at a relatively low futures price. Then, if an unusual level of catastrophe losses occurs, the settlement price will rise above the established futures price and the insurer will profit on the futures position and thus offset its higher than normal catastrophe losses.

Call and put options on catastrophe futures contracts are also available. A futures call (put) option allows the owner to assume a long (short) position in a futures contact with a futures price equal to the option's exercise price. For example, consider a call option with an exercise price of 40 percent. If the futures price rises above 40 percent, the call option can be exercised which establishes a long futures position with an embedded futures price of 40 percent. If the futures price is less than 40 percent at expiration, the call option will expire worthless.

Catastrophe futures and options are an innovative way for insurers to hedge underwriting risk arising from catastrophes. In essence, the catastrophe derivatives market is a secondary market competing with the reinsurance market for trading underwriting risk.

Bibliography

Harrington, S. E., Mann, S. V., and Niehaus, G. R. (1995). Insurer capital structure decisions and the viability of insurance derivatives. *Journal of Risk and Insurance*, **62**, 483–508.

commodity futures volatility

Susan J. Crain and Jae Ha Lee

The definition of a commodity (by the Commodity Futures Trading Commission) includes all goods, articles, services, rights, and interest in which contracts for future delivery are dealt. However, another approach extracts the financial instruments (interest rate, equity, and foreign currency), leaving those assets more commonly referred to as commodities, that is agricultural (such as grains and livestock), metals (such as copper and platinum), and energy (such as crude oil and natural gas).

Early studies of commodity futures identified several factors that have an impact on volatility, including effects due to contract maturity, contract month, seasonality, quantity, and loan rate. For the contract maturity theory, Samuelson (1965) suggested that futures contracts close to maturity exhibit greater volatility than futures contracts away from maturity. The intuition for this idea is that contracts far from maturity incorporate a greater level of uncertainty to be resolved and therefore react weakly to information. On the other hand, the nearer contracts tend to respond more strongly to new information to achieve the convergence of the expiring futures contract price to the spot price.

The seasonality theory is also grounded in the resolution of uncertainty, but is approached by Anderson and Danthine (1980) in the framework of the simultaneous determination of an equilibrium in the spot and futures markets based on supply and demand. As explained by Anderson (1985), during the production period, supply and demand uncertainty are progressively resolved as random variables are realized and publicly observed. Thus, *ex ante* variance of futures price is shown to be high (low) in periods when a relatively large (small) amount of uncertainty is resolved. For agricultural commodities, particularly the grains, crucial phases of the growing cycle tend to occur at approximately the same time each year, leading to a resolution of production uncertainty that follows a strong seasonal pattern. Seasonality on the demand side is explained on the basis of substitute products, which also exhibit production seasonalities. Under the general heading of "seasonality" are various studies of such aspects as month-of-the-year effect, day-of-the-week effect, and turn-of-the-year effect.

The contract month effect explained by Milonas and Vora (1985) suggests that an old crop contract should exhibit higher variability than a new crop contract due to delivery problems (squeezes) when supply is low.

Quantity and loan rate effects are an artifact of the government farm programs. Government involvement in price support and supply control in the grain market can have an impact on volatility as follows. A major component of price support is the loan, whereby a producer who participates may obtain a loan at the predetermined loan rate (dollars per bushel) regardless of the cash market price. If cash prices do not rise above the loan rate plus storage and interest costs, the producer forfeits the grain to the government to satisfy the loan. As a result, the program tends to put a floor on the cash and futures price near the loan rate and thus, as prices decline to the loan rate level, price volatility should decline. Additionally, when production and ending inventories are relatively large (quantity effect), the cash and futures prices have a tendency to be supported by the loan program, and once again, volatility should decrease.

Several empirical tests of these hypotheses have been conducted, of which we will mention only a few. First, Anderson (1985) tests the seasonality and maturity effects theories for nine commodities including five grains, soybean oil, livestock, silver, and cocoa. Employing both non-parametric and parametric tests, he finds that the variance of futures price changes is not constant and that the principal predictable factor is seasonality with maturity effects as a secondary factor. Milonas (1986) finds evidence of the contract maturity effect in agriculturals, financials, and metals markets, which shows that the impact of a vector of known or unknown variables is progressively increasing as contract maturity approaches. Gay and Kim (1987) confirm day-of-the-week and month-of-the-year effects by analyzing a 29-year history of the Commodity Research Bureau (CRB) futures price index. This index is based on the geometric average of 27 commodities using prices from all contract maturities of less than 12 months for each commodity. Kenyon et al. (1987) incorporate four factors into a model to estimate the volatility of futures prices (seasonal effect, futures price level effect, quantity effect, and loan rate effect). Test results of the model in three grain markets support the loan rate hypothesis, while the quantity effect was insignificant. Once again, seasonality effects are supported.

Crain and Lee (1996) also study the impact of government farm programs on futures volatility. The test period covers 43 years (1950–93) with 13 pieces of legislation and concentrates on the wheat market. Patterns of changes in futures and spot price volatility are linked to major program provision changes, such as allotments, loan rates, and the conservation reserve. Three sub-periods of distinguishable volatility magnitudes seem to exist with the discernible patterns explained as follows. Mandatory allotments contribute to low volatility, voluntary allotments and low loan rates contribute to higher volatility, and both market-driven loan rates and conservation reserve programs induce lower levels of volatility. Seasonality is also confirmed in this study, but the seasonality effects do not seem to be as important as farm program impacts. Additionally, there is evidence of changing seasonality patterns over the three defined sub-periods.

Another issue addressed in Crain and Lee (1996) concerns the price discovery role of futures markets. In particular, the wheat futures market has carried out this role by transferring volatility to the spot market. This is consistent with previous studies in other markets, such as equity, interest rate, and foreign exchange markets. Also, there is some evidence that the causal relationship has been affected by the farm programs.

Bibliography

Anderson, R. W. (1985). Some determinants of the volatility of futures prices. *Journal of Futures Markets*, **5**, 331–48.

Anderson, R. W., and Danthine, J. P. (1980). The time pattern of hedging and the volatility of futures prices. Center for the Study of Futures Markets CSFM Working Paper Series 7.

Crain, S. J., and Lee, J. H. (1996). Volatility in wheat spot and futures markets, 1950–1993: Government farm programs, seasonality, and causality. *Journal of Finance*, **51**, 325–44.

Gay, G. D., and Kim, T. (1987). An investigation into seasonality in the futures market. *Journal of Futures Markets*, **7**, 169–81.

Kenyon, D., Kling, K., Jordan, J., Seale, W., and McCabe, N. (1987). Factors affecting agricultural futures price variance. *Journal of Futures Markets*, **7**, 169–81.

Milonas, N. T. (1986). Price variability and the maturity effect in futures markets. *Journal of Futures Markets*, **6**, 443–60.

Milonas, N. T., and Vora, A. (1985). Sources of non-stationarity in cash and futures prices. *Review of Research in Futures Markets*, **4**, 314–26.

Samuelson, P. A. (1965). Proof that properly anticipated prices fluctuate randomly. *Industrial Management Review*, **6**, 41–9 .

conditional CAPM

see PORTFOLIO THEORY AND ASSET PRICING

conditional performance evaluation

Heber Farnsworth

Conditional performance evaluation refers to the measurement of performance of a managed portfolio taking into account the information that was available to investors at the time the returns were generated. An example of an unconditional measure is Jensen's alpha based on the capital asset pricing model (CAPM). Unconditional measures may assign superior performance to managers who form dynamic strategies using publicly available information. Since any investor could have done the same (because the information is public) it is undesirable to label this as superior performance. In addition, the distribution of returns on assets which managers invest in is known to change as the public information changes.

Recent empirical work has found that incorporating public information variables such as dividend yields and interest rates is important in explaining expected returns. Conditional performance evaluation brings these insights to the portfolio performance problem. For instance, Ferson and Schadt (1996) assume that the beta conditional on a vector Z_{t-1} of information variables has a linear functional form:

$$\beta_p(Z_{t-1}) = \beta_{0,p} + B_p' z_{t-1}$$

where z_{t-1} is a vector of deviations of Z_{t-1} from its mean vector. The coefficient $\beta_{0,p}$ is an average beta, and the vector B_p measures the response of the conditional beta to the information variables.

Applying this model of conditional beta to Jensen's alpha regression equation yields the following model for conditional performance evaluation:

$$r_{p,t} = \alpha_p + \beta_{0,p} r_{b,t} + B_p'(z_{t-1} r_{b,t}) + \varepsilon_t$$

where the α_p can now be interpreted as a conditional alpha. Ferson and Schadt find that the

inclusion of conditioning information changes inferences slightly in that the distribution of alphas seems to shift to the right, the region of superior performance. This can be easily extended to the case of a model with multiple factors (perhaps motivated by the APT) by including the cross products of each benchmark with the information variables.

Christopherson, Ferson, and Glassman (1996) make the additional extension of allowing the conditional alpha to vary with the information variables. They model alpha as a linear function of z_{t-1}

$$\alpha_p(Z_{t-1}) = \alpha_{0,p} + A_p' z_{t-1}$$

which generates the modified model

$$r_{p,t} = \alpha_{0,p} + A_p' z_{t-1} + \beta_{0,p} r_{b,t} + B_p'(z_{t-1} r_{b,t}) + \epsilon_t$$

They find that conditional models seem to have more power to detect persistence of performance relative to unconditional models.

Chen and Knez (1996) extend the theory of performance evaluation to the case of general asset pricing models. Modern asset pricing theory identifies models on the basis of the stochastic discount factors (SDFs) which they imply. For any asset pricing model, the SDF is a scalar random variable m_{t+1} such that for any claim which provides a (random) time $t+1$ payoff of V_{t+1} the price of the claim at time t is given by

$$p_t = E(m_{t+1} V_{t+1} | \Omega_t) = 1$$

where $_t$ is the public information set at time t. Suppose that there are N assets available to investors and that prices are non-zero. Since m_{t+1} is the same for all assets we have that

$$E(m_{m+1} R_{t+1} | \Omega_t) = 1$$

where R_{t+1} is the vector of primitive asset gross returns (payoffs divided by price) and 1 is an N-vector of ones.

Let R_p denote the gross return on a portfolio formed of the primitive assets. R_p may be expressed as $x'R$ where x is a vector of portfolio weights. These weights may change over time according to the information available to the person who manages the portfolio. Suppose that this person has only public information. Then we can write $x(\Omega_t)$ to indicate this dependence on the public information set. Such a portfolio must satisfy

$$E(m_{t+1}x(\Omega_t)'R_{t+1}|\Omega_t) = x(\Omega_t)'1 = 1$$

since x depends only on Ω_t and the elements of x sum to one.

Since performance evaluation is involved with identifying managers who form portfolios using superior information (which is not in Ω_t at time t) it is natural to speak of abnormal performance as a situation in which the above does not hold. In particular, define the alpha of a fund as

$$\alpha_{p,t} \equiv E(m_{t+1}R_{p,t+1}|\Omega_t) - 1$$

If we choose predetermined information variables Z_{t-1} as above and assume that these variables are in Ω_{t-1}, we can apply the law of iterated expectations to both sides of the above equation to obtain a conditional alpha measure of performance. Unconditional performance evaluation amounts to taking the unconditional expectation.

Farnsworth et al. (1996) empirically investigate several conditional and unconditional formulations of m_{t+1}, including an SDF version of the CAPM, various versions of multifactor models where the factors are specified to be economic variables, the numeraire portfolio of Long (1990), and a primitive efficient SDF which is the payoff on a portfolio which is constructed to be mean–variance efficient (this case is also examined in Chen and Knez, 1996). Their results showed that inferences based on the SDF formulation of the CAPM differ from those obtained using Jensen's alpha approach even though the same market index was used.

Whether these results show that the SDF framework is superior is still an open question. Future research should try to determine if SDF models are better at pricing portfolios which are known to use only public information. If they do not, then another reason must be found for the difference. It does appear that inclusion of conditioning information sharpens inferences on

performance. Future work may help determine what information specifically should be included in order to perform conditional performance evaluation.

Bibliography

Chen, Z., and Knez, P. J. (1996). Portfolio performance measurement: Theory and applications. *Review of Financial Studies*, 9, 511–55.

Christopherson, J. A., Ferson, W. E., and Glassman, D. A. (1996). Conditioning manager alphas on economic information: Another look at the persistence of performance. University of Washington working paper.

Farnsworth, H. K., Ferson, W. E., Jackson, D., Todd, S., and Yomtov, B. (1996). Conditional performance evaluation. University of Washington working paper.

Ferson, W. E., and Schadt, R. W. (1996). Measuring fund strategy and performance in changing economic conditions. *Journal of Finance*, 51, 425–62.

Long, J. B. (1990). The numeraire portfolio. *Journal of Financial Economics*, **26**, 29–70.

consolidation

David P. Newton

Because of their separate legal status, a parent company and its subsidiaries keep independent accounts and prepare separate financial statements. However, investors are interested in the financial performance of the combined group and so this is reported as the group's "consolidated" or "group" financial statements, which present the financial accounts as if they were from a single company.

Companies within a group often do business with one another. Raw materials and finished goods may be bought and sold between companies in a group; cash may also be lent by the parent company in order to finance operations or capital investments. These transactions appear in the financial accounts of both parties but need to be eliminated in the consolidated accounts; if not, then the combined companies would appear to have been carrying on more business than was actually the case. For example, suppose a subsidiary is lent US$1 million by its parent via a note payable. The balance sheets of the two companies would contain these lines:

Parent company   Subsidiary company
Balance sheet   Balance sheet
Assets   Liabilities
Notes receivable   Notes payable
   US$1 m   US$1 m

In forming the consolidated accounts, these transactions would be entered for elimination on a work sheet in some fashion, such as the following:

Notes payable (subsidiary)   US $1 m
Notes receivable (parent)   US $1 m

to eliminate inter-company receivable and payable.

A parent company need not own 100 percent of a subsidiary in order to maintain control of it. In acquiring a new subsidiary company, the parent need only obtain more than half of the voting stock of the acquired company. The parent then has what is called a majority interest while the other owners have a minority interest. Elimination in the consolidated accounts is then carried out in proportion to ownership. This can be illustrated as follows for the balance sheet:

Predator company buys 80 percent of Prey company (as voting shares of stock)

Predator has US$1,000,000 of stock and US$800,000 of retained earnings
Prey has US$100,000 of stock and US$50,000 of retained earnings
Predator records the acquisition as:

Investment in prey   US$120,000
Cash   US$120,000

to record the acquisition of 80 percent of Prey.

The eliminations needed in preparing the consolidated accounts could be achieved as shown in table 1.

The minority interest is recorded as shown in table 2.

Thus, the controlling stockholders of the combined companies have US$1,800,000 of equity and outside stockholders of the prey subsidiary have US$30,000 of equity.

Table 2   Recording of minority interest

Shareholders' equity	
Minority interest in prey	$30,000
Common stock	$1,000,000
Retained earnings	$800,000
	$1,830,000

Table 1   Preparing consolidated accounts

	Predator	Prey	Debit	Credit	Consolidated
Cash	$250,000	$20,000			$270,000
Accounts receivable	$500,000	$20,000			$520,000
Inventories	$730,000	$30,000			$760,000
Investment in acquired company	$120,000			$120,000	
Property, plant and equipment	$1,700,000	$180,000			$1,880,000
	$3,300,000	$250,000		$120,000	$3,430,000
Accounts payable	$300,000	$50,000			$350,000
Bonds payable	$1,200,000	$50,000			$1,250,000
Common stock of acquiring company	$1,000,000				$1,000,000
Common stock of acquired company		$100,000	$80,000		
			$20,000		
Retained earnings of acquiring company	$800,000				$800,000
Retained earnings of acquired company		$50,000	$40,000		
			$10,000		
Minority interest in acquired company				$30,000	$30,000
	$3,300,000	$250,000	$150,000	$30,000	$3,430,000

If a subsidiary is formed by acquisition, this can be treated in the stockholders' books by two alternative accounting methods, called purchase and pooling of interests. The purchase method requires the assets of the acquired company to be reported in the books of the acquiring company at their fair market value. The price actually paid will often be greater than the fair market value of the assets of the acquired company, since the value of the company lies in its trading capability, not simply in the resale value of its fixed assets. Therefore, the financial accounting quantity called goodwill is created, equal to the excess of the purchase price over the sum of the fair market values of the assets acquired. Goodwill can be amortized over a period of years (this does not mean that the tax authorities in a particular country will allow tax deductions on these amortization expenses). In contrast, using pooling of interests, no goodwill is created and the assets of both companies are combined in new books at the same values as recorded in their separate books; the total recorded assets and the total equity are unchanged.

It is useful to know what differences arise from the use of these alternative financial accounting treatments. In purchase accounting, amortization of goodwill reduces income shown on the stockholders' books. Also, the assets of the acquired company are put on the stockholders' books at the fair market value. Depreciation expense is increased, again lowering the income reported compared with pooling. However, the cash flows on acquisition are not affected by the choice of financial accounting method and so neither the net present value of the acquisition nor taxes are affected.

consumption CAPM

see PORTFOLIO THEORY AND ASSET PRICING

contingent claims

Suresh Deman

A contingent claims market can be understood by comparing it with betting in a horse race. The state of the world corresponds to how the various horses will place, and a claim corresponds to a bet that a horse will win. If your horse comes in, you get paid in proportion to the number of tickets you purchased. But *ex ante* you do not know which state of the world will occur. The only way to guarantee payment in all states of the world is to bet on all the horses.

The state preference model is an alternative way of modeling decision under uncertainty. Consumers trade contingent claims, which are rights to consumption, if and only if a particular state of the world occurs. In the insurance case, in one state of the world the consumer suffers a loss and in the other, they do not; however, *ex ante* they do not know which state will occur, but want to be sure to have consumption goods available in each state.

In a corporate context, Deman (1994) identified basically two theories of takeovers: (1) AGENCY THEORY, and (2) incomplete contingent claims market. The latter theory hypothesizes that takeovers result from the lack of a complete state-contingent claims market. The main argument can be summarized briefly. If complete state-contingent claims markets exist, then shareholders' valuations of any state distribution of returns are identical (because of one price for every state-contingent claim) and hence, they agree on a value-maximizing production plan. However, in the absence of complete-state contingent claims markets, any change in technologies (i.e., a change in the state distribution of payoffs) is not, in general, valued identically by all shareholders. Thus, majority support for such a change in plan may be lacking. Takeover is a contingent contract which enables a simultaneous change in technologies and portfolio holdings.

Merton (1990) describes some commercial examples of contingent claims which include futures and options contracts based on commodities, stock indices, interest rates, and exchange rates, etc. Other examples are Arrow–Debreu (AW) securities, which play a crucial role in general equilibrium theory (GE), and options. Under AW conditions, the pricing of contingent claims is closely related to the optimal solutions to portfolio planning problems. Thus, contingent claims analysis (CCA) plays a central role in achieving its results by integrating the option-pricing theory with the optimal portfolio planning problem of agents under uncertainty.

One of the salient features of CCA is that many of its valuation formulae are by and large or completely independent of agents' preferences and expected returns, which are sometimes referred to as risk neutral valuation relationships. Contributions to CCA have adopted both continuous and multiperiod discrete time models. However, most of them are dominated by continuous time, using a wide range of sophisticated mathematical techniques of stochastic calculus and martingale theory. There are several other facets of contingent claims, such as the option price theory of Black and Scholes (1973) and Merton (1977), general equilibrium and pricing by arbitrage illustrated in Cox, Ingersoll, and Ross (1981), and transaction costs in Harrison and Kreps (1979). CCA, from its origin in option pricing and valuation of corporate liabilities, has become one of the most powerful analysis tools of intertemporal GE theory under uncertainty.

Bibliography

Black, F., and Scholes, M. S. (1973). The pricing of options and corporate liabilities. *Journal of Political Economy*, **81**, 637–59.

Cox, J. C., Ingersoll, J. E., and Ross, S. A. (1981). The relationship between forward prices and future prices. *Journal of Financial Economics*, **9**, 321–46.

Deman, S. (1994). The theory of corporate takeover bids: A subgame perfect approach. *Managerial Decision Economics*, Special Issue on Aspects of Corporate Governance, **15**, 383–97.

Harrison, J. M., and Kreps, D. M. (1979). Martingale and arbitrage in multi-period securities markets. *Journal of Economic Theory*, **20**, 381–408.

Merton, R. C. (1977). On the pricing of contingent claims and the Modigliani–Miller theorem. *Journal of Financial Economics*, **5**, 241–9.

Merton, R. C. (1990). *Continuous-Time Finance*. Cambridge, MA: Blackwell.

convenience yields

Milan Lehocky

The notion of convenience yields was first introduced by Kaldor (1939) as the value of physical goods, held in inventories resulting from their inherent consumption use, which accrues only to the owner of the physical commodity and must be deducted from carrying costs. Similarly, Brennan and Schwartz (1985) define the convenience yield as the flow of services that accrues to an owner of the physical commodity but not to an owner of a contract for future delivery of the commodity. These benefits of holding physical stocks often stem from local shortages, and the ability to keep the production process running (Cho and McDougall, 1990). Working (1949) showed that the convenience yield can assume various levels over time, especially for seasonal commodities like wheat. He argued that when inventory levels are high the convenience derived from holding an additional unit of the physical good is small and can be zero or even negative. On the other hand, when inventory levels are low, the convenience yield can be significant.

The notion of convenience yields has become an integral part in explaining the term structure of commodity futures prices. The risk premium theory as advanced by Keynes (1923), Hicks (1938), and Cootner (1960) relates futures prices to anticipated future spot prices, arguing that speculators bear risks and must be compensated for their risk bearing services in the form of a discount (normal backwardation). The theory of storage as proposed by Kaldor (1939), Working (1948, 1949), Telser (1958), and Brennan (1958) postulates that the return from purchasing a commodity at time t and selling it forward for delivery at time T, should be equal to the cost of storage (interest forgone, warehousing costs, insurance) minus a convenience yield. In absolute values this relationship can formally be expressed as:

$$F(S, t, T) = Se^{r(T-t)} + w_{T-t} - \delta_{T-t} \qquad (1)$$

where $Se^{r(T-t)}$ is the current spot compounded at the risk free rate, w_{T-t} is storage costs, and δ_{T-t} is the convenience yield.

An alternative expression for the futures price can be obtained by stating the storage costs and convenience yield as a constant proportion per unit of the underlying commodity:

$$F(S, t, T) = Se^{(r+w-\delta)(T-t)} \qquad (2)$$

In contrast to Keynes's risk premium theory, the theory of storage postulates an intertemporal relationship between spot and futures prices which could be referred to as "normal contango." Abstracting from the convenience yield, the futures price would be an upwardly biased estimator of the spot price. In this case storers would be compensated for holding the commodity in their elevators. However, the theory of storage predicts that the higher the possibility of shortages in the respective commodity, the higher the convenience yield will be, and positive amounts of the commodity will be stored even if the commodity could be sold for higher spot prices. This observation is referred to as inverse-carrying charge (Working, 1948).

Both theories have been subject to empirical studies. Empirical studies of Keynes's risk premium theory have been ambiguous. Evidence supporting the risk premium theory has been found by Houthakker (1961, 1968, 1982), Cootner (1960), and Bodie and Rosansky (1980). However, Telser (1958) and Dusak (1973) could not find evidence of a systematic risk premium in commodity markets. Early attempts to test the theory of storage were conducted by Telser (1958) and Brennan (1958) relating inventory data to convenience yields for several commodities. These "direct tests" suffer from the difficulty of obtaining, defining, and measuring inventory data. Fama and French (1987) propose "indirect test" strategies, building on the variation of differences in spot and futures prices (the basis). The logic of the indirect testing methodology is based on the proposition that when inventories are low (i.e., the convenience yield is high, negative basis) demand shocks for the commodity produce small changes in inventories, but large changes in the convenience yield and the interest adjusted basis. In this case, following Samuelson's (1965) proposition, the spot prices should change more than futures prices and the basis should exhibit more variability than when inventory levels are high. Hence, negative carry is associated with low inventory levels. Alternatively, if the variation of spot and futures prices is nearly equal when the basis is positive, it can be concluded that positive carrying costs are associated with high inventory levels. This reasoning should hold in particular for commodities with significant per unit storage costs. Fama and French (1987) find significantly differing basis standard deviations across the 21 commodity groups studied. Basis variability is highest for commodities with significant per unit storage costs (wood and animal products) and lowest for precious metals. This finding is consistent with the theory of storage.

More recent studies of the intertemporal relationship of futures prices incorporating convenience yields have been carried out in the context of pricing contingent claims by arbitrage. The most prominent authors to apply continuous time stochastic models to the pricing of commodity contingent claims are Brennan and Schwartz (1985), Gibson and Schwartz (1990a, 1990b, 1991), Brennan (1991), Gabillon (1991), and Garbade (1993). Typically, the analysis starts off by assuming an exogenously given geometric Brownian motion process for the spot price relative changes of the commodity:

$$\frac{dS}{S} = \mu \, dt + \sigma_S \, dz_S \qquad (3)$$

where σ_S is the instantaneous standard deviation of the spot price, μ is the expected drift of the spot price over time, and dz_S is the increment of a Wiener process with zero mean and unit variance. Further assuming a constant deterministic relationship between the spot price and the convenience yield (net of cost-of-carry) $\delta(S) = \delta S$, Brennan and Schwartz (1985) employ a simple arbitrage argument in order to derive a partial differential equation which must be satisfied by the futures price:

$$(r - \delta)SF_S - F_\tau + \frac{1}{2}F_{SS}\sigma_S^2 S^2 = 0 \qquad (4)$$

where subscripts denote partial derivatives and with the futures price at maturity satisfying the boundary condition $F(S,0) = S$. One possible solution to this partial differential equation is the well-known relationship between the futures and spot price as mentioned above:

$$F(S, \delta, \tau) = Se^{(r-\delta)\tau} \qquad (5)$$

where τ denotes the time to maturity of the futures contract and δ denotes the convenience yield net of storage costs. Note that equation (5) is independent of the stochastic process of the spot price. From a theoretical point of view the derivation of the futures price under the constant and deterministic convenience yield assumption is associated with the problem that only parallel shifts in the term structure can be modeled, since both spot and futures prices in equation (5) have equal variance. This is inconsistent with Samuelson's (1965) proposition of decreasing volatility of futures prices over time to delivery or settlement.

Brennan (1991) estimates and tests alternative functions and stochastic processes for convenience yield and its dependence on price and time. Both Brennan (1991) and Gibson and Schwartz (1990a, 1991) present stochastic two-factor models of the term structure of commodity and oil futures prices respectively, incorporating an "autonomous" stochastic process for the convenience yield. The process governing the convenience yield changes is modeled as an Ornstein-Uhlenbeck process with Gaussian variance. An analysis of the time series properties of the convenience yields is presented in Gibson and Schwartz (1991), who find support for a mean-reverting pattern in the convenience yield series. The system of stochastic processes can then be represented by the following equations:

$$\frac{\mathrm{d}S}{S} = \mu \, \mathrm{d}t + \sigma_S \, \mathrm{d}z_S \tag{6a}$$

$$\mathrm{d}\delta = k(\hat{\delta} - \delta) \, \mathrm{d}t + \sigma_\delta \, \mathrm{d}z_\delta \tag{6b}$$

with $\mathrm{d}z_s \mathrm{d}z_\delta = \rho \mathrm{d}t$, where ρ denotes the correlation coefficient between the increments of the two stochastic processes, k is the speed of adjustment, and $\hat{\delta}$ denotes the long-run mean of the convenience yield process.

Abstracting from interest rate uncertainty and applying Ito's lemma, it can be shown that under the same arbitrage assumptions made in the one-factor model the futures price must satisfy the following partial differential equation:

$$\frac{1}{2}F_{SS}S^2\sigma_S^2 + \frac{1}{2}F_{\delta\delta}\sigma_b^2 + F_{S\delta}S\rho\sigma_S\sigma_\delta + F_S(r - \delta)$$
$$+ F_\delta\left[k(\hat{\delta} - \delta) - \lambda\sigma_\delta\right] - F_\tau = 0 \tag{7}$$

subject to the boundary condition $F(S,\delta,0) = S$, where λ denotes the market price per unit of convenience yield risk. Gibson and Schwartz (1990a, 1990b) solve this partial differential equation numerically and obtain values for crude oil futures and futures options under the appropriate boundary conditions. Both Brennan (1991) and Gibson and Schwartz (1990) report that the accuracy of commodity futures pricing relative to the simple continuous compounding model can be enhanced by adding a mean-reverting convenience yield as a second stochastic variable. Although the Brennan and Gibson and Schwartz models are consistent with Samuelson's decreasing volatility pattern, the convenience yield is specified independently of the spot price of oil, which implies that although the spot price of oil is stable, the convenience yield tends to a long-run mean level. Based on this critical remark, Gabillon (1991) proposes an alternative two-state variable stochastic model, where the system of stochastic processes consists of the current spot price of oil and the long-term price of oil. Gabillon uses the ratio of current spot price to long-term price and time to maturity in order to determine the convenience yield level. According to this model, the current term structure of futures prices depends on the relative level of the spot price. Garbade (1993) presents an alternative two-factor arbitrage free model of the term structure of crude oil futures prices, with the term structure fluctuating around some "normal shape" in a mean-reverting manner, abstracting from the convenience yield.

More empirical and theoretical work is necessary in order to shed light on the relative pricing efficiency of alternative models of the term structure of commodity futures prices. In particular, shortcomings in the appropriate modeling of the convenience yield process and its distributional properties, as well as its relation to the spot price of oil, are still unresolved. Moreover, current research has not addressed problems associated with the assumption of constant spot price volatilities and interest rates. The assumption of constant interest rates might not be warranted, especially in the long run. Potential corporate finance applications have been discussed by Gibson and Schwartz (1991) in the case of long-term oil linked bonds. Other useful applications might concern the valuation of long-term delivery contracts and the hedging of such commitments with respect to both price and convenience yield risk.

Bibliography

Bodie, Z., and Rosansky, V. I. (1980). Risk and return in commodity futures. *Financial Analysts Journal*, **36**, 27–39.

Brennan, M. J. (1958). The supply of storage. *American Economic Review*, **48**, 50–72.

Brennan, M. J. (1991). The price of convenience and the valuation of commodity contingent claims. In D. Lund and B. Öksendal (eds.), *Stochastic Models and Option Values*. Amsterdam: North-Holland, 135–57.

Brennan, M. J., and Schwartz, E. S. (1985). Evaluating natural resource investments. *Journal of Business*, **58**, 135–57.

Cho, D. W., and McDougall, G. S. (1990). The supply of storage in energy futures markets. *Journal of Futures Markets*, **10**, 611–21.

Cootner, P. (1960). Returns to speculators: Telser versus Keynes. *Journal of Political Economy*, **68**, 396–418.

Dusak, K. (1973). Futures trading and investor's returns: An investigation of commodity market risk premiums. *Journal of Political Economy*, **81**, 1387–406.

Fama, E. F. and French, K. R. (1987). Commodity futures prices: Some evidence on forecast power, premiums, and the theory of storage. *Journal of Business*, **60**, 55–74.

Gabillon, J. (1991). The term structure of oil futures prices. Working Paper M17, Oxford Institute of Energy Studies.

Garbade, K. D. (1993). A two-factor, arbitrage-free, model of fluctuations in crude oil futures prices. *Journal of Derivatives*, **1**, 86–97.

Gibson, R., and Schwartz, E. S. (1990a). Stochastic convenience yield and the pricing of oil contingent claims. *Journal of Finance*, **45**, 959–76.

Gibson, R., and Schwartz, E. S. (1990b). The pricing of crude oil futures options contracts. UCLA working paper.

Gibson, R., and Schwartz, E. S. (1991). Valuation of long-term oil linked assets. In D. Lund and B. Öksendal (eds.), *Stochastic Models and Option Values*. Amsterdam: North-Holland, 73–102.

Hicks, J. R. (1938). *Value and Capital*. Oxford: Clarendon Press.

Houthakker, H. S. (1961). Systematic and random elements in short-term price movements. *American Economic Review, Papers and Proceedings*, **51**, 164–72.

Houthakker, H. S. (1968). Normal backwardation. In J. N. Wolfe (ed.), *Value, Capital and Growth*. Edinburgh: Edinburgh University Press.

Houthakker, H. S. (1982). The extension of futures trading to the financial sector. *Journal of Banking and Finance*, **6**, 37–47.

Kaldor, N. (1939). Speculation and economic stability. *Review of Economic Studies*, 7, 1–27.

Keynes, J. M. (1923). Some aspects of commodity markets. In *The Collected Writings of John Maynard Keynes*, Vol. 12. London: Macmillan.

Samuelson, P. A. (1965). Proof that properly anticipated prices fluctuate randomly. *Industrial Management Review*, **6**, 41–9.

Telser, L. (1958). Futures trading and the storage of cotton and wheat. *Journal of Political Economy*, **66**, 233–55.

Working, H. (1948). Theory of the inverse carrying charge in futures markets. *Journal of Farm Economics*, **30**, 1–28.

Working, H. (1949). The theory of price of storage. *American Economic Review*, **39**, 1254–62.

convertibles

Chris Veld

A convertible is a bond with an option for the holder to exchange the bond into "new" shares of common stock of the issuing company under specified terms and conditions. These include the conversion period and the conversion ratio. The conversion period is the period during which the bond may be converted into shares. The conversion ratio is the number of shares received per convertible. The conversion price, which is the effective price paid for the common stock, is the ratio of the face value of the convertible and the conversion ratio. Convertibles almost always have a call provision built in. Special types of convertibles are mandatory convertible bonds, exchangeable bonds, and LYONS.

A convertible is much like a bond with a warrant attached. However, this concept is not very useful for valuation purposes. An important problem is that the exercise price of the warrant (the conversion price) is paid by surrendering the accompanying bond. Therefore the exercise price changes through time. The fact that most convertibles are callable creates another valuation problem. Brennan and Schwartz (1980) have developed a model which takes all these factors into account.

Motives for the issuance of convertibles can be divided into traditional and modern. Traditional motives are that convertibles are (1) a deferred sale of stock at an attractive price and (2) a cheap form of capital (Brigham, 1966). These motives are criticized by Brennan and Schwartz (1988). The first motive is based on the fact that normally the conversion price is above the market price of the underlying stock at the issuance date. However, the conversion price should in fact be compared to the underlying stock price at the exercise date. If the underlying stock price is higher than the conversion price, the company suffers an opportunity loss. If it is lower than the conversion price, the conversion right will not be exercised. The second motive is based on the fact that the coupon rate of a convertible is lower than the coupon rate of an ordinary bond. However, if the cost of the conversion right is taken into account it can be demonstrated that the cost of convertibles is relatively high (for a numerical example, see Veld, 1992). The cost of convertibles is neither a reason to issue, nor a reason to refrain from issuing convertibles. Its cost is just an adequate compensation for the risk involved in its investment.

Modigliani and Miller have demonstrated that in perfect markets the financing decision of the firm is irrelevant for its market value. Therefore, modern motives for the issuance of convertibles are based on market imperfections. Brennan and Schwartz (1988) argue that convertibles are relatively insensitive to the risk of the issuing company. If the risk increases, the value of the bond part decreases, but the value of the warrant part increases, because the value of a warrant is an increasing function of the volatility. This makes it easier for bond issuers and purchasers to come to terms when they disagree about the riskiness of the firm. Because of the insensitivity towards risk, convertibles may result in lower agency costs between share and bondholders. Bondholders are less concerned about the possibility that shareholders attract risky projects. Because of their conversion right they also participate in the value created if risky projects are undertaken (Green, 1984). Other motives, based on imperfections, include the reduction of flotation costs compared to the case where the firm raises debt now and equity later, and the possibility to "polish" the company's financial accounts by recording the con-

vertible as debt on the balance sheet (Veld, 1992).

With regard to the optimal moment to call convertibles, Ingersoll (1977) has demonstrated that this moment occurs when the conversion value (the value of the common stock to be received in the conversion exchange) equals the call price. However, in an empirical study he finds that in practice the calls show a delay. On average the conversion value of the bonds was 43.9 percent above the call price.

EXCHANGEABLE BONDS

An exchangeable bond may be converted into existing shares of the same or an alternative company. It is much like a convertible, except that in a convertible, the bond may be converted into "new" shares. Analogously, the conversion right of an exchangeable bond is equivalent to a covered warrant. An example of a large issue of exchangeable debt is the IBM US$300 million offering in January 1986, which is convertible into the common stock of Intel Corporation. An analysis of exchangeable debt is made by Ghosh, Varma, and Woolridge (1990).

LYONS

Liquid yield option notes (LYONS) are zero-coupon, callable, puttable convertibles. This security was created by Merrill Lynch in 1985. It was first issued by Waste Management Inc. in spring 1985. A number of subsequent issues were made in the United States. McConnell and Schwartz (1986) have developed a valuation model, which takes all the above mentioned characteristics of LYONS into account.

MANDATORY CONVERTIBLE BONDS

Mandatory convertible bonds are convertibles which may be converted during the conversion period and which are automatically converted at the end of the conversion period.

Bibliography

Brennan, M. J., and Schwartz, E. S. (1980). Analyzing convertible bonds. *Journal of Financial and Quantitative Analysis*, **4**, 907–29.

Brennan, M. J., and Schwartz, E. S. (1988). The case for convertibles. *Journal of Applied Corporate Finance*, summer, 55–64.

Brigham, E. F. (1966). An analysis of convertible debentures: Theory and some empirical evidence. *Journal of Finance*, **21**, 35–54.

Ghosh, C., Varma, R., and Woolridge, J. R. (1990). An analysis of exchangeable debt offers. *Journal of Financial Economics*, **19**, 251–63.

Green, R. C. (1984). Investment incentives, debt, and warrants. *Journal of Financial Economics*, **13**, 115–36.

Ingersoll, J. (1977). An examination of corporate call policies on convertible securities. *Journal of Finance*, **32**, 463–78.

McConnell, J. J., and Schwartz, E. S. (1986). LYON taming. *Journal of Finance*, **41**, 561–76.

Veld, C. (1992). *Analysis of Equity Warrants as Investment and Finance Instruments*. Tilburg: Tilburg University Press.

corporate governance

Gerald T. Garvey

The firm is a nexus of contracts, and the corporation is a firm whose equity claims have limited liability and are generally traded on liquid markets. Corporate governance refers to the rules, procedures, and administration of the firm's contracts with its shareholders, creditors, employees, suppliers, customers, and sovereign governments. Governance is legally vested in a board of directors who have a fiduciary duty to serve the interests of the corporation rather than their own interests or those of the firm's management (see Clark, 1985).

The apparent simplicity of this description disguises two key problems which have stimulated most popular and academic interest in corporate governance. First, what exactly is meant by the interests of the corporation, given that a corporation is not an individual? Second, the courts' ability to enforce the vague notion of fiduciary duty is limited at best (Romano, 1991). What other forces exist to motivate self-interested directors and managers to serve corporate interests?

One way in which financial economists have answered both questions is to maintain that corporate interests are identical to the wealth of shareholders, and that directors and managers are motivated to serve these interests by incentive pay, by their own shareholdings and reputational concerns, and by the threat of takeover.

This approach must, however, be supplemented by the recognition that in some firms the costs and benefits of corporate decisions are also borne by parties such as creditors and long-term employees. We conclude that the most promising areas for further research are based on the recognition that the optimal governance structure varies widely across corporations, depending on the relative importance of these various claims on its cash flows (for a more extensive survey, see Garvey and Swan, 1994).

GOVERNANCE AND PERFORMANCE

The question of most immediate relevance to researchers and commentators is how governance affects firm performance and, in particular, whether firms perform better when shareholders' interests are likely to be dominant. Such firms are identified in the empirical literature either by the proportion of outsiders who serve on the board of directors, or by the linkage between chief executive officer (CEO) wealth and the wealth of shareholders. Evidence on the role of outside board members is provided by Rosenstein and Wyatt (1990), who find that the appointment of outsiders to the board is associated with a stock price increase, and by Weisbach (1988), who finds that outsider-dominated boards are more likely to dismiss the CEO for poor share price performance. Evidence on the performance effects of CEO incentives can be found in DeFusco, Johnson, and Zorn (1990), who document an increase in the share price of firms which introduce stock option or ownership plans, and in McConnell and Servaes (1990), who find a positive relationship between the percentage of shares owned by managers and board members and firms' market-to-book values.

This type of evidence is not as useful as it might appear. In particular, it does not establish that firms should increase outside board membership or CEO incentive pay as advocated by the American Law Institute (1982). First, an increase in the stock price could be driven by wealth transfers rather than efficiency gains. Indeed, DeFusco, Johnson, and Zorn (1990) found that the increase in share price was also associated with a decline in the value of the firm's outstanding debt. Second, even if the share price were a reliable guide to performance, compensation and board structures are not chosen randomly as required by the performance studies. A recent study by Agrawal and Knoeber (1994) attempts to account for the endogeneity of compensation and board structure, and comes to the provocative conclusion that many firms have too many rather than too few outside members on their boards. To disentangle these effects, we need to understand more about the effects of various governance mechanisms and how they relate to a firm's unique environment and strategies.

Governance and Behavior

A less obvious but arguably more useful research strategy is to examine how different governance mechanisms affect the firm's behavior rather than its performance. While this approach cannot tell us whether actions such as the dismissal of a CEO or rejection of a takeover bid are optimal for the firm in question, it is an essential input into any understanding of optimal governance structures.

The most robust finding is that changes in control due to takeover or insolvency bring dramatic changes in firm personnel and strategy. Gilson and Vetsuypens (1993) document that CEO and board member turnover increases radically in the event the firm goes into financial distress. Martin and McConnell (1991) present similar findings for a hostile takeover. These findings suggest if nothing else that incumbent managers and board members will take steps to avoid takeover or insolvency, either by increasing the firm's cash flows or by some less productive avenue.

The importance of the takeover threat depends not only on the slack to be found in the target firm, but also on the premium that must be paid by a bidder. Grossman and Hart (1980) show that collective choice problems between target shareholders can greatly increase this premium, thereby deterring many takeovers. Stulz, Walkling, and Song (1990) find evidence that the severity of this problem differs across firms, and is mitigated when a firm's shares are concentrated in the hands of financial institutions. Brickley, Lease, and Smith's (1994) study of voting on anti-takeover amendments provides further evidence of the rich differences

that exist between firms. They find that only those institutional shareholders who have no obvious business ties to the firm are willing to oppose management sponsored anti-takeover amendments. Such heterogeneity leads naturally to our final question: How are these differences adapted to the different environments of firms?

Governance Structures and Environments

Governance mechanisms are not cost free. Any party who would oversee management must bear the direct costs of monitoring and the indirect costs of bearing firm risk. Demsetz and Lehn (1985) were the first to explicitly recognize these costs and ask how governance characteristics vary with the attributes of each firm's environment. They found that shareholdings were less concentrated in larger firms, in regulated firms, and in firms whose profits were more predictable. Garen (1994) finds that such firms also tend to exhibit less incentive pay for the CEO, because the benefits of oversight and incentive alignment are smaller relative to their costs for such firms.

Areas for Further Research

The ambiguous results of the performance studies summarized above suggest that corporate performance cannot be reliably increased simply by adding outsiders to the board of directors or by increasing the CEO's stockholdings. Future research efforts are better devoted to understanding why and how governance structures differ across firms. Studies such as Kaplan (1994) provide useful evidence on how Japanese and German firms differ from their US counterparts. Other differences that merit further study include the liquidity of the stock market (Bhide, 1993) and the importance of employee claims on the firm's future cash flows (Garvey and Swan, 1992).

Bibliography

Agrawal, A., and Knoeber, C. R. (1994). Firm performance and control mechanisms to control agency problems between managers and shareholders. Working paper, Wharton School, University of Pennsylvania.

American Law Institute (1982). *Principles of Corporate Governance and Structure: Restatement and Recommendations*. Philadelphia, PA: American Law Institute.

Bhide, A. (1993). The hidden costs of stock market liquidity. *Journal of Financial Economics*, **34**, 31–51.

Brickley, J., Lease, R., and Smith, C. W. (1994). Corporate voting: Evidence from charter amendment proposals. *Journal of Corporate Finance*, **1**, 5–32.

Clark, R. (1985). Agency costs versus fiduciary duties. In J. A. Pratt and R. Zeckhauser (eds.), *Principals and Agents: The Structure of Business*. Boston, MA: Harvard Business School Press, 55–79.

DeFusco, R., Johnson, R., and Zorn, T. (1990). The effect of executive stock option plans on stockholders and bondholders. *Journal of Finance*, **45**, 617 27.

Demsetz, H., and Lehn, K. (1985). The structure of corporate ownership: Causes and consequences. *Journal of Political Economy*, **93**, 1155–77.

Garen, J. (1994). Executive compensation and principal–agent theory. *Journal of Political Economy*, **102**, 1175–99.

Garvey, G. T., and Swan, P. L. (1992). Optimal capital structure for a hierarchical firm. *Journal of Financial Intermediation*, **2**, 376–400.

Garvey, G. T., and Swan, P. L. (1994). The economics of corporate governance: Beyond the Marshallian firm. *Journal of Corporate Finance*, **1**, 139–74.

Gilson, S. C., and Vetsuypens, M. R. (1993). CEO compensation in financially distressed firms: An empirical analysis. *Journal of Finance*, **48**, 425–58.

Grossman, S., and Hart, O. D. (1980). Takeover bids, the freerider problem, and the theory of the corporation. *Bell Journal of Economics*, **11**, 42–64.

Jensen, M. C. (1986). Agency costs of free cash flow, corporate finance and takeovers. *American Economic Review*, **76**, 323–9.

Kaplan, S. (1994). Top executive rewards and firm performance: A comparison of Japan and the United States. *Journal of Political Economy*, **102**, 510–46.

McConnell, J. J., and Servaes, H. (1990). Additional evidence on equity ownership and corporate value. *Journal of Financial Economics*, **27**, 595–612.

Martin, K., and McConnell, J. (1991). Corporate performance, corporate takeovers and management turnover. *Journal of Finance*, **46**, 671–87.

Romano, R. (1991). The shareholder suit: Litigation without foundation? *Journal of Law, Economics, and Organization*, **7**, 55–88.

Rosenstein, S., and Wyatt, J. G. (1990). Outside directors, board independence, and shareholder wealth. *Journal of Financial Economics*, **27**, 175–91.

Stulz, R., Walkling, R., and Song, M. H. (1990). The distribution of target ownership and the division of gains in successful takeovers. *Journal of Finance*, **45**, 817–34.

Weisbach, M. S. (1988). Outside directors and CEO turnover. *Journal of Financial Economics*, **20**, 431–60.

corporate takeover language

Suresh Deman

The word takeover is used as a generic term to refer to any acquisition through a tender offer. It is a straightforward transaction in which two firms decide to combine their assets either in a friendly or unfriendly manner under established legal procedures.

A *friendly takeover* is sometimes referred to as a merger or synergistic takeover; it occurs when an acquiring firm (referred to as the bidder or raider) and a target firm agree to combine their businesses to realize the benefits. Synergistic gains can accrue to the corporation from consolidation of research and development labs or of market networks. Merger proposals require the approval of the managers (board of directors) of the target corporation.

Hostile takeovers are also called disciplinary takeovers in the literature. The purpose of such takeovers seems to be to correct the non-value maximizing practices of managers of the target corporations. Takeover proposals do not need the approval of the managers of the target corporation. In fact, they are made directly to the shareholders of the target.

A *tender offer* is an offer by a bidder or raider directly to shareholders to buy some or all of their shares for a specified price during a specified time. Unlike merger proposals, any tender offers for takeovers are made and successfully executed over the expressed objections of the target management.

Prior to the 1960s, the so-called *intra-firm* tender offer was used exclusively to acquire shares in the issuer's repurchase program. The separation of ownership and control in large corporations led to the development of the *inter-firm* tender offer as an important vehicle and became a popular mechanism for transfer of ownership.

An *any-or-all* tender offer is where the bidder or raider will buy any tendered shares of the target corporation as long as the conditions of minimum number of tendered shares are met to insure majority control after the offer.

In a *conditional* tender offer the raider specifies a maximum number of shares to be purchased in addition to the minimum required.

If the bid is oversubscribed, the tendered share becomes subject to pro-rationing. This tender offer is further subdivided into two-tier negotiated, non-negotiated, and partial tender offers.

A *two-tier* tender offer is a takeover offer that provides a cash and non-cash price in two steps. In the first step, there is a cash price offer for sufficient shares to obtain control of the corporation, then in the second step, a lower non-cash (securities) price is offered for the remaining shares.

A *pure partial* tender offer is defined as one in which there is no announced second-tier offer during the tender offer and no clean-up merger or tender offer closely following the execution of the tender offer. Partial offers are commonly used for less than 50 percent control of ownership in the corporation.

In a *negotiated* two-tier tender offer the bidder or raider, at the time of the first-tier offer, agrees with target management on the terms of the subsequent merger. By contrast, in a *non-negotiated* two-tier tender offer no terms are agreed to at the time of the original offer for control of the corporation. This lies between the pure partial offer and non-negotiated two-tier tender offer.

The raider or bidder is the person(s) or corporation who identifies the potential target and attempts to take over. The target is the potential corporation at which the takeover attempt is directed.

If the number of shares tendered in a takeover bid are more than required by their conditional offer (i.e., if the bid is oversubscribed) then the raider will buy the same proportion of shares from everyone who tendered; this is known as pro-rationing.

The *dilution factor* is the extent to which the value of minority shareholders is diluted after the takeover of a corporation. It is prohibited by the Securities and Exchange Commission. But it is argued that it is necessary to create a divergence between the value of the target corporation to its shareholders and the value to the raider or the bidder to overcome the free-rider problem.

The *crown jewel* is the most valued asset held by an acquisition target, and divestiture of this asset is frequently a sufficient defense to discourage takeover of the corporation.

A *fair price amendment* requires supermajority approval of non-uniform, or two-tier, tender offers. Takeover bids not approved by the board of directors can be avoided by a uniform bid for less than all outstanding shares (if the bid is oversubscribed, it is subjected to pro-rationing).

Golden parachutes are provisions in the employment contracts of top-level executives that provide for severance pay or other compensation should they lose their job as a result of a hostile takeover.

Greenmail is the premium paid by a targeted company to a raider or bidder in exchange for their acquired shares of the targeted company.

Leveraged buyout is the purchase of publicly owned company stock by the incumbent management with a portion of the purchase price financed by outside investors. The company is delisted and public trading in the stock ceases.

A *lockup defense* gives a friendly party (i.e., white knight) the right to purchase assets of the corporation, in particular the crown jewel, thus discouraging a takeover attempt by the raider.

The term *maiden* is sometimes used to refer to the company at which the takeover is directed by the raider or bidder (i.e., target).

A *poison pill* is used as a takeover defense by the incumbent management; it gives stockholders other than those involved in a hostile takeover the right to purchase securities at a very favorable price in the event of a takeover bid.

A *proxy contest* involves the solicitation of stockholder votes generally for the purpose of electing a slate of directors in competition with the current directors to change the composition.

Shark repellant is an anti-takeover corporate charter amendment such as staggered terms for directors, supermajority requirement for approving merger, or mandate that bidders pay the same price for all shares in a buyout.

A *standstill agreement* is a contract in which a raider or corporation agrees to limit its holdings in the target corporation and not make a takeover attempt.

A successful raider who, once the target is acquired, sells off some of the assets of the target company to destroy its original entity, is known as a *stripper*.

A *targeted repurchase* is a repurchase of common stock from an individual holder or a tender repurchase that excludes an individual holder. The former is the most frequent form of greenmail, while the latter is a common defensive tactic against takeover.

A *white knight* is a merger partner solicited by management of a target corporation who offers an alternative merger plan to that offered by the raider which protects the target company from the takeover.

A *kick in the pants* is new information that induces the incumbent management to implement a higher-valued strategy on its own.

Sitting on the gold mine is where the dissemination of the new information prompts the market to revalue previously "undervalued" target shares.

In a *management buyout* a management team within a corporation or division purchases that corporation from its current owners, thus becoming owner managers. It is prevalent in both the private and public sectors and is one means by which privatization may take place.

cost of capital

M. Ameziane Lasfer

The cost of capital is the rate of return that investors in the market require in order to participate in the financing of an investment. The cost of capital is the rate used by managers of value-maximizing firms to discount the expected cash flows in capital budgeting. The investment projects which offer expected returns greater than the cost of capital are accepted because they generate positive net present values (NPV), while projects with expected returns lower than the cost of capital should be rejected. Thus, the cost of capital is the hurdle rate used to evaluate proposed investment projects.

When the project is marginal and does not significantly shift the risk profile of the firm, the cost of capital can be computed as the weighted average costs of the various sources of finance. In the case where the firm is financed by debt and equity, the weighted average cost of capital (WACC) is computed as follows:

$$WACC = r_D(1 - \tau_c)\frac{D}{V} + r_E\frac{E}{V} \qquad (1)$$

where r_D is the cost of debt finance, τ_c is the marginal corporation tax rate, r_E is the cost of equity finance, D is the market value of debt, E is the market value of equity, and V is the market value of the firm (i.e., $E + D$). In principle, each project should be valued at its own cost of capital to reflect its level of risk. However, in practice, it is difficult to estimate project-by-project cost of capital. Instead, the firm's overall weighted average cost of capital is used as a benchmark and then adjusted for the degree of the specific risk of the project.

The cost of capital can also be regarded as the rate of return that a business could earn if it chooses another investment with equivalent risk. The cost of capital is, in this case, the opportunity cost of the funds employed as the result of an investment decision. For value maximizing firms, the cost of capital is the opportunity cost borne by various investors who choose to invest in the proposed project and not in other securities and, thus, it is estimated as the expected rates of return in the securities market. For regulated companies, the cost of capital can be used as a target fair rate of return.

Modigliani and Miller (1958) show that, in a world of perfect capital markets and no taxes (i.e., τ_c in equation (1) is zero), the cost of capital of a firm is independent of the type of securities used to finance the project or the capital structure of the firm. The main argument advocated is that as debt is substituted for equity, the cost of the remaining equity increases but the overall cost of capital, r_0, is kept constant:

$$r_E = r_0 + (1 - r_D)\frac{D}{E} \qquad (2)$$

When taxes are introduced, Modigliani and Miller (1963) show that firms will prefer debt to equity finance because of the tax shields associated with the company's borrowing plans. However, Miller (1977) demonstrated that the value of corporate interest tax shields can be completely offset by the favorable treatment of equity income to investors and, as result, the firm's cost of capital is independent of its financing method.

The current main problems associated with the cost of capital relate to the estimation of the components of the WACC. While r_D can be proxied by the average interest rate paid by the firm on its loans, τ_c should be the marginal not the standard corporation tax rate. Lasfer (1995) showed that in the UK the effective corporation tax rates vary significantly from one firm to another and that a large number of companies are tax exhausted and do have lower debt in their capital structure compared to taxpaying firms. Thus the net tax advantages to corporate borrowing are unknown unless one computes the effective tax rate for each individual company.

The cost of equity, r_E, can be based on the capital asset pricing model (CAPM) and computed as:

$$r_E = r_f + \beta(r_m - r_f) \tag{3}$$

where β is the risk measure and $(r_m - r_f)$ is the risk premium on the overall stock market, r_m, relative to the risk-free rate of return, r_f. However, the validity of this formulation has been the subject of severe empirical criticisms (Fama and French, 1992). Stulz (1995a) argues that the cost of equity capital should be estimated using the global rather than the local CAPM because capital markets are integrated. This method involves an estimation of a global market portfolio and for countries that are only partially integrated in international capital markets, the computation of the cost of capital may not be possible.

The traditional formulation of the WACC assumes that managers are value maximizers. Recent evidence provides a challenge to this assumption and argues that managers do not act to maximize shareholder wealth but, instead, maximize their own utility. In this case the WACC should be modified to account for the agency costs of managerial discretion. Stulz (1995b) defined the agency cost adjusted cost of capital by incorporating into the discount rate the impact of agency costs in the same way that the WACC approach incorporates in the cost of capital the tax shield of debt. However, it is not clear whether, in investment decisions, managers should adjust the discount rate or the expected cash flows. Moreover, the agency costs of managerial discretion depend on a firm's capital structure, dividend policy, and other firm specific factors which might be difficult to value. Furthermore, the above measurements can be difficult because they involve measuring expectations by market participants which are not directly measurable. In practice, the "true" cost of capital is likely to be unobservable.

Bibliography

Fama, E. F., and French K. R. (1992). The cross-section of expected stock returns. *Journal of Finance*, **47**, 427–66.

Lasfer, M. A. (1995). Agency costs, taxes and debt: The UK evidence. *European Financial Management*, 1, 265–85.

Miller, M. H. (1977). Debt and taxes. *Journal of Finance*, 32, 261–76.

Modigliani, F., and Miller, M. H. (1958). The cost of capital, corporate finance, and the theory of investment. *American Economic Review*, **48**, 261–97.

Modigliani, F., and Miller, M. H. (1963). The cost of capital, corporate finance, and the theory of investment: A correction. *American Economic Review*, **53**, 433–43.

Stulz, R. (1995a). The cost of capital in internationally integrated markets. *European Financial Management*, 1, 11–22.

Stulz, R. (1995b). Does the cost of capital differ across countries? An agency perspective. Keynote address prepared for the fourth meeting of the European Financial Management Association, London, June.

data-mining in finance

Allan Timmermann

Suppose that a regression of stock returns on some variable, X, yields an estimate with a t-statistic of 2.1. Does this mean that stock returns are predictable? Comparing the t-value to the critical values of the standard normal distribution, stock returns would appear to be predictable as the coefficient estimate is statistically significant at standard levels. Suppose, however, that both X and some other variable, Z, were considered as predictor variables and that the t-value of 2.1 is the highest of the t-values from two models. Whether or not, at 2.1, the largest of the two t-values is statistically significant depends on their correlation, which is typically unknown.

This example illustrates two important points. First, data-mining is a problem because the data was used to formulate the hypothesis of interest ("variable X forecasts stock returns"). If the researcher *ex-ante* had (theoretical) reason to believe that X should predict stock returns, data-mining would not have constituted a problem (because Z would not then have been considered). Second, data-mining occurs when what is genuinely a joint or multiple hypothesis testing problem (that the largest t-value from two correlated regressions exceeds a certain value) is treated as a single hypothesis testing problem. Data-mining can thus be viewed as the distortion of critical levels of a hypothesis test that has been subject to pre-testing.

In general, data-mining occurs when a given set of data is used more than once to choose a theory or select a model and test the resulting specification. This is a widespread problem. Theory often is vague about the functional form or exact identity of variables entering into financial models. As a result, many empirical relations were initially established from apparent empirical regularities and were not predicted *ex ante* by theory. If not accounted for, this practice can generate serious biases in statistical inference. In the limited sample sizes often encountered in financial studies, systematic patterns and apparently significant relations are bound to occur if the data are analyzed with sufficient intensity.

Like many of the social sciences, finance predominantly studies non-experimental data and thus does not have the advantage of being able to test hypotheses independently of the data that gave rise to them in the first instance. If the data are experimental, data-mining is likely to be less of an issue unless it is very costly to generate new data. This is because new data can readily be generated to test the hypothesis formed on the basis of the original data set.

Researchers in finance have long been aware of the potential dangers of data-mining. For example, Merton (1987: 107) poses the question: "Is it reasonable to use the standard t-statistic as a valid measure of significance when the test is conducted on the same data used by many earlier studies whose results influenced the choice of theory to be tested?" Data-mining biases have been quantified in studies such as Lo and MacKinlay (1990) and have been described in mainstream books on investing and forecasting.

Although data-mining is by no means unique to financial studies, there are several reasons why it may be particularly important in finance. At face value, the efficient market hypothesis – that asset returns net of trading costs and risk premia are unpredictable – is one of the most concrete and directly testable hypotheses in the social sciences. This theory, which has been subject to countless studies, apparently rules out that *any* variable be able to predict asset returns. The degree of data-mining can be expected to increase with the number of studies simply because each study may introduce new predictor variables. Data with important outliers, such as those observed in stock market returns, may also be particularly prone to data-mining biases. If enough economic models are studied, by pure chance some of them are likely to outperform a given benchmark by any economic or statistical criterion. For example, a variable that took an unusual value around the stock market crash of October 19, 1987 *could* have been used to construct a trading rule that would outperform the market index in a longer sample simply because of the significance of this single observation.

Several cross-validation methods have been devised to deal with data-mining. In cross-sectional studies, part of the cross-sectional sample can be retained for validation after a hypothesis has been formulated. This method only works, of course, provided that the researcher avoids repeatedly testing the first-stage theory against the validation sample. Furthermore, if the hold-out sample is strongly correlated with the original sample, statistical tests on the hold-out sample need not behave in line with standard assumptions. Cross-validating by separately considering the returns on portfolios from different industries or countries can be misleading because of the high correlation between such portfolios' returns and the resulting dependence between the test statistics computed on seemingly different samples (c.f. Foster, Smith, and Whaley, 1997).

For time-series data, it is more common to use an initial (in-sample) part of the data to determine the functional form and estimate the parameters of the model that is then tested on the remaining (out-of-sample) data. While this practice can be used to control for data-mining, it also introduces questions about how to split the full sample into the in-sample and out-of-sample periods. It may also lead to a severe loss in statistical power (i.e., the ability to reject a false null hypothesis, when compared to the alternative of using the full sample to test the model). This is a particular problem when dealing with monthly or quarterly data where the sample is generally quite small.

The strategy of avoiding data-mining by using a hold-out sample requires strong stationarity assumptions insuring that the same data generating process stays in effect over the full sample. As a case in point, suppose that stock returns could have been predicted up to, say, 1975 by means of some variable whose identity was published in that year as a result of which it subsequently failed to have any predictive power. Using data up to 1975 as the in-sample period may then correctly lead the researcher to form the hypothesis that the variable predicted stock returns. However, when tested on post-1975 data, the hypothesis would be rejected. This obviously does not constitute a test of whether predictability was present prior to 1975.

A very different strategy is to directly account for the specification search that preceded the discovery of the "best" model. This is the approach suggested by White (2000) and exploited in a study of the profitability of technical trading rules by Sullivan, Timmermann, and White (1999). To demonstrate this approach, suppose that each of $k = 1, \ldots, l$ models produces a sequence of forecasts. To account for dependencies across models, a test procedure must consider the distribution of the $l \times 1$ performance statistic

$$\bar{f} = T^{-1} \sum_{t=1}^{T} \hat{f}_{t+1},$$

where T is the length of the assessment period and $\hat{f}_{t+1}$ is the vector of observed performance measures each of which may depend on a set of recursively updated parameter estimates. The elements $f_{k,t+1}$ of f_{t+1} measure the performance of the individual models $k = 1, \ldots, l$ relative to a given benchmark (e.g., returns on the market portfolio). Often, the null hypothesis is that the best model is not capable of outperforming the benchmark:

$$H_0: \max_{k=1,\ldots l} \{E(f_k^*)\} \leq 0,$$

where $E\{f_k^*\}$ is the expected performance evaluated at the probability limit of the parameters underlying the kth model. Under a broad set of assumptions and under the element of H_0 least favorable to the alternative,

$$\max_{k=1,\ldots l} n^{1/2} \bar{f}_k \xrightarrow{d} \max_{k=1,\ldots,l} \{\Psi_k\},$$

where $\Psi \sim N(0,\Omega)$ is an $l \times 1$ multivariate normally distributed random vector with elements Ψ_k with covariance matrix Ω, and $\xrightarrow{d}$ denotes convergence in distribution. If only a single model is considered, then its performance measure would follow an asymptotic normal distribution. Suppose, however, that the best model has been selected from a universe of l candidate models, all of which may be correlated. Then its p-value should be evaluated based on the maximum value drawn from an l-dimensional normal distribution with mean zero and a covariance matrix reflecting the correlations across the included models' performances. In practice, this often means using much larger critical values than if only a single model had been investigated.

How likely is it then that established empirical findings in finance could be due to data-mining? This is difficult to answer in general. However, there are several questions in finance where data-mining is likely to have played a role. In the case of predictability of stock market returns, the ability of technical trading rules is a prime example, since there is little or no theory to suggest that technical trading rules should be able to forecast stock returns. The design of technical trading rules must therefore be data-based, essentially driven by a search for empirical "regularities." Sullivan, Timmermann, and White (1999) investigate almost 8,000 technical trading rules and find that, over the last part of their sample, the best technical trading rule is capable of producing superior performance of almost 10 percent per year and has a p-value of 0.04 when considered in isolation. However, when account is made for the fact that this trading rule is drawn from a wide universe of rules, the effective data-snooping-adjusted p-value is actually 0.90. An even bigger contrast occurs from considering model performance based on the Sharpe ratio criterion: here the snooping-adjusted and unadjusted p-values are 0.99 and 0.00, respectively.

Bibliography

Foster, F. D., Smith, T., and Whaley, R. E. (1997). Assessing goodness-of-fit of asset pricing models: The distribution of the maximal R^2. *Journal of Finance*, **52**, 591–607.

Lo, A. W., and MacKinlay, A. C. (1990). Data-mining biases in tests of financial asset pricing models. *Review of Financial Studies*, **3**, 431–67.

Merton, R. (1987). On the state of the efficient market hypothesis in financial economics. In R. Dornbusch, S. Fischer, and J. Bossons (eds.), *Macroeconomics and Finance: Essays in Honor of Franco Modigliani*. Cambridge, MA: MIT Press, 93–124.

Sullivan, R., Timmermann, A., and White, H. (1999). Data-mining, technical trading rule performance, and the bootstrap. *Journal of Finance*, **54**, 1647–91.

White, H. (2000). A reality check for data-mining. *Econometrica*, **68**, 1097–126.

debt swaps

Sudipto Sarkar

Debt swap is a generic term for an exchange of debt with some other asset. Examples of debt swaps include the convertible bond, in which a debt–equity swap is initiated by the bondholder, and the debt–equity swap pioneered by Salomon Brothers in the USA in the early 1980s, when corporations replaced over US$10 billion of debt with US$7 billion of new equity. The latter, however, disappeared after 1984, probably because the tax-related incentive ceased to exist (Hand, 1989).

The most significant application of debt swaps has been in international finance, particularly as a mechanism for solving the debt servicing problems of less developed countries (LDCs). The LDC debt crisis exploded in 1982 with Mexico defaulting on its loan payments, followed by other defaults, mostly Latin American. The creditors were generally international (largely US) commercial banks. Among the various solutions proposed, the most popular were market-based strategies like debt buybacks and various debt swaps such as debt for debt and debt for equity.

In a debt for debt swap, the creditor bank exchanges its outstanding loans for US dollar-denominated bonds issued by the LDC's central bank. These bonds are known as Brady bonds after the US Treasury Secretary Nicholas Brady, architect of the Brady Plan of 1989 to deal with the debt crisis. The Brady Plan was the first to accept debt reduction as necessary for a permanent solution; therefore, Brady bonds have longer maturities and lower coupons than the original loans. However, they have certain attractive features such as liquidity, collateralization, and rolling guarantees. The liquidity is a result of an active secondary market, with a volume of US$100 billion in mid-1994. Most Brady bonds also have collateralization of principal and immediate coupons, the collateral usually being US Treasury instruments of the appropriate maturity, and paid for partly by World Bank and IMF loans and partly from the LDC's own reserves. The interest guarantees are rolled forward continuously. Because of this collateral backing, Brady bonds are normally senior to other LDC loans.

A debt–equity swap is an exchange of outstanding LDC debt for an equity stake in a private corporation in the LDC, as follows: LDC debt is purchased on the secondary market from the bank at the market price, usually at a discount from face value by a multinational corporation (MNC). The MNC then trades the debt claim to the LDC's central bank for the full face value in the local currency (less the central bank's cut), which it then invests in a local company, very often a newly privatized corporation. The investment in local equity must be maintained for a minimum number of years.

The advantage for the MNC is that the investment is made at a significant discount, since the discounts prevailing in the market can be quite high. The LDC's advantage is that the swap reduces external debt with no outflow of foreign currency, and external debt is replaced by foreign direct investment. The swap converts foreign debt into foreign equity; this is equivalent, in a corporate finance setting, to reducing leverage and thereby improving credit rating. Another potential benefit is the increased efficiency resulting from privatization which often accompanies the debt swap. In the USA, the Federal Reserve Bank amended Regulation K in 1986 to allow commercial banks to make investments through debt swaps. This led to many banks taking equity positions in LDCs, and had a significant positive effect on commercial bank stocks (Eyssell, Fraser, and Rangan, 1989).

A disadvantage for the LDC is that its liquidity position might worsen by allowing direct foreign investment through swaps instead of fresh capital inflows. The swaps may be subsidizing foreign investments that would have been carried out anyway, and not generating any additional investment. Furthermore, swaps can actually reduce investment in the LDC through their effect on interest rates, inflation, and other macroeconomic variables. For the creditor banks, there is the usual moral hazard problem; by encouraging swaps, they may be helping reduce the value of the debt by providing incentives to debtor countries to delay repayments.

There is a small theoretical literature on the analysis of debt–equity swaps. The seminal paper is Helpman (1989), which derived conditions under which a swap will not be Pareto improving (strictly preferred by all participants), and also showed that a swap may actually reduce investment in the LDC. Errunza and Moreau (1989) showed that, with homogeneous expectations, swaps are not Pareto improving even in the presence of informational asymmetries; they might, however, be Pareto improving with heterogeneous expectations. For valuation purposes, it has been demonstrated (Blake and Pradhan, 1991) that a debt swap is equivalent to the conversion of convertible bonds to equity, with the addition of exchange rate risk. However, the fact that the equity investment must be maintained for a number of years significantly reduces the swap value.

Debt–equity swaps have been the most important type of debt reduction instrument, accounting for over US$35 billion (or almost 40 percent of the total volume of debt conversions of all types) from 1985 to 1993. Since the establishment of the first institutionalized debt–equity swap program in Chile in 1985, it has become an integral part of external debt management and reduction. It started slowly with conversions worth US$500 million in 1985, and peaked in 1992 with a volume of US$9.2 billion. After 1992, there was a decline in the volume, partly because market discounts on LDC debt were much smaller (Collyns et al., 1992).

How effective was the debt conversion program in resolving the debt crisis? One point of view is that it was very successful, and "Latin American borrowers have recovered from the debt crisis" (World Bank, 1994–5). At the other extreme, some believe that the program has not tackled the root causes of the debt problem. A report by Larrain and Velasco (1990) on Chile, which had the most ambitious swap program, suggests that the contribution of debt–equity swaps to real investment in Chile has been moderate at best. Although it did contribute to the amelioration of Chile's debt burden, the program came nowhere near offering a permanent solution. Bartolini (1990) has concluded, based on numerical simulations with reasonable parameter values, that a much larger fraction of debt forgiveness is required (about 60 percent, instead of the 30 percent envisaged by the Brady Plan) for a sustainable long-term solution.

Although it is true that there has been substantial LDC debt reduction and credit rating improvement, it is too early to make a definitive assessment. The Mexican peso crisis of 1994 indicates that the market remains very volatile and vulnerable to shocks. Defaults do occur, albeit on a smaller scale, such as the Alto Parana corporation of Argentina in 1995. External debt has also risen to dangerous levels in many LDCs, with total debt estimated at US\$1,945 billion by end-1994 compared to US\$1,369 at end-1987. Debt overhang remains a serious problem for the international banking sector; however, we are likely to be better prepared for the next crisis because banks have become more circumspect in their lending activities.

Bibliography

Bartolini, L. (1990). Waiting to lend to borrowers with limited liability. Working paper, Department of Economics, Princeton University.

Blake, D., and Pradhan, M. (1991). Debt–equity swaps as bond conversions: Implications for pricing. *Journal of Banking and Finance*, 15, 29–41.

Collyns, C., Clark, J., Fledman, R., Mansur, A., Mylonas, P., Parker, K., Prowse, S., Rennhack, R., Szymczak, P., and Pauly, L. W. (1992). *Private Market Financing for Developing Countries*. Washington, DC: International Monetary Fund.

Errunza, V. R., and Moreau, A. F. (1989). Debt for equity swaps under a rational expectations equilibrium. *Journal of Finance*, 45, 663–80.

Eyssell, T. H., Fraser, D. R., and Rangan, N. K. (1989). Debt–equity swaps, Regulation K, and bank stock returns. *Journal of Banking and Finance*, 13, 853–68.

Hand, J. R. M. (1989). Did firms undertake debt equity swaps for an accounting paper profit or true financial gains? *Accounting Review*, 44, 587–623.

Helpman, E. (1989). The simple analytics of debt–equity swaps. *American Economic Review*, 79, 440–51.

Larrain, F., and Velasco, A. (1990). Can swaps solve the debt crisis? Lessons from the Chilean experience. Princeton Studies in International Finance Report No. 69, Princeton University.

Remolona, E. M., and Roberts, D. L. (1986). Loan swaps and the LDC debt problem. Research Paper No. 8615, Federal Reserve Bank of New York.

World Bank (1994–5). *World Debt Tables: External Finance for Developing Countries*. Washington, DC: World Bank.

deposit insurance

Steven A. Dennis and David C. Thurston

The essential functions of a bank are to loan funds and serve as a riskless depository, paying interest on deposits. A riskless environment is particularly important to small investors, given their greater information and surveillance costs. Diamond and Dybvig (1983) show that the contract between the depository institutions and depositors is very delicate, using a game theoretic approach to show that this contract is prone to bank runs. That is, as a depositor, there is an incentive to get in line first, even if you believe the bank to be sound, because a run by other depositors may cause the bank to become insolvent. The depositor at the back of the line is likely to lose. To be a "safe haven" for depositors, the insurance of deposits (implicit or explicit) by a third party, a guarantor, is required. To be credible, the guarantor of deposit insurance must have taxing power. Deposit insurance removes the incentive for bank runs.

There has been a dramatic increase in our understanding of the value of deposit insurance to the bank and correspondingly, the cost of deposit insurance to the guarantor (the Federal Deposit Insurance Corporation (FDIC) in the United States) in the last two decades. An important issue in deposit insurance is the ability to incorporate theoretical developments in the field to the actual pricing of deposit insurance by the FDIC. In many cases, the theoretical developments have largely been ignored by the FDIC's politics. Although there are still issues which remain unresolved in the theoretical pricing of deposit insurance, we understand the basic mechanics from which the ultimate model must come.

VALUING DEPOSIT INSURANCE AS A PUT OPTION

The pioneering work in the pricing of deposit insurance comes from Merton (1977), who identifies an "isomorphic" correspondence between deposit insurance and common stock put options. Merton works in the BLACK–SCHOLES (1973) framework of constant interest rates and volatility for expositional convenience. In Merton's (1977) model, a depository institution borrows money by issuing a single homogeneous debt issue as a pure discount bond. The bank promises to pay a total of B dollars to depositors at maturity. If V denotes the value of the bank's assets, the payoff structure of the payment guarantee (deposit insurance) to the guarantor at the maturity date if the face value of the debt exceeds the bank's assets is: $-(B - V(T))$, while if the value of the banks assets equals or exceeds the face value of the debt, the payoff is zero. In either case the payoff may be expressed as: $\max(B - V(T),0)$. Providing deposit insurance can be viewed as issuing a put option on the value of the bank's assets with an exercise price equal to the face value of the bank's outstanding debt. Assuming V follows a geometric Brownian motion, and the original assumptions of Black–Scholes, valuation of the deposit insurance as a put option follows from Black–Scholes. The value of deposit insurance is:

$$Be^{-rT}\Phi(x + \sigma\sqrt{T}) - V\Phi(x) \quad (1)$$

where

$$x = \frac{\log(B/V) - (r + \sigma_V^2/2)T}{\sigma_V\sqrt{T}}$$

Φ is the cumulative normal distribution, σ_V is the instantaneous standard deviation of V, and r is the instantaneous spot rate.

EMPIRICAL METHODOLOGY

Though the Merton (1977) model describes the pricing of deposit insurance, empirical and practical applications of his model require two important variables that are unknown: the value of

the bank's assets and the volatility of returns on those assets. In this regard, Marcus and Shaked (1984) and Ronn and Verma (1986) attempt to estimate these unknown inputs from observable data. Ronn and Verma (1986) note an important contribution from Black–Scholes: the equity of the bank, E, can be viewed as a call option on the value of the bank's assets. This provides one equation with two unknown parameters: the value of the bank's assets and the volatility of returns on those assets. Moreover, Ronn and Verma employ Merton's (1974) equation relating the volatility of returns on equity to the volatility of returns on assets. This provides a two-equation system:

$$E = V\Phi(y) - Be^{-rT}\Phi(y - \sigma_V\sqrt{T}) \quad (2)$$

where

$$y = \frac{\log(V/B) + (r + \sigma_V^2/2)T}{\sigma_V\sqrt{T}}$$

and

$$\sigma_E = \left(\frac{\partial E}{\partial V} \cdot \frac{V}{E}\right)\sigma_V \quad (3)$$

which can be solved simultaneously for the two unknown parameters. These two papers led to numerous empirical studies examining the over- or underpricing of deposit insurance by the FDIC. Work on the determination of the two unknown parameters in deposit insurance pricing by Duan (1994) suggests that the Ronn and Verma methodology is flawed, in that equation (3) is derived from equation (2) under the assumption of constant volatility of equity. Duan (1994) suggests that if bank assets are assumed to follow a process with constant variance (as Merton, 1977, assumes) and bank equity is a call option on bank assets, bank equity must have a non-constant variance. This presents two empirical problems. First, one cannot sample bank equity returns for estimates of bank equity volatility because equity volatility is stochastic. Second, Merton's (1974) equation relating equity volatility to asset volatility assumes equity volatility is constant and therefore cannot be employed.

Duan (1994) offers an alternative methodology which overcomes some of the shortcomings of the Ronn and Verma (1986) approach. Duan (1994) suggests that the unobserved series of market value of assets and the volatility of assets of the bank can be estimated using a time series of equity values of the bank. Equation (3) relating the value of assets and asset volatility to equity values can be transformed in such a way that the value of assets is written in terms of the equity value of the bank and the volatility of assets. Estimation is then carried out on a transformed log-likelihood function of the time series of equity values. This estimation technique provides estimates for the mean return and volatility of a bank's assets.

STOCHASTIC INTEREST RATES AND VOLATILITY

Although we have come a long way in the pricing of deposit insurance, there are still many issues which are unresolved. An important consideration is the value of extending Merton's (1977) model to a stochastic interest rate environment. Duan, Moreau, and Sealey (1995) have empirically tested the effect of stochastic interest rates on deposit insurance using Vasicek's (1977) model and find that the inclusion of stochastic interest rates has a significant impact on deposit insurance. Au, Dennis, and Thurston (1995) directly incorporate the bank's duration gap into the put option's total volatility. They price the deposit insurance put option following Merton's (1973) generalization of Black Scholes and model interest rate dynamics following the no-arbitrage-based Heath, Jarrow, and Morton (HJM) (1992) model. The HJM paradigm provides a number of important benefits for modeling interest rate dynamics, as it avoids the specification of the market price of risk, allows a wide variety of volatility functions, and easily allows for multiple factors for interest rate shocks.

Another important issue in deposit insurance pricing is the ability of the bank to change the volatility of its assets over time. For instance, as a bank approaches failure, bank management may have incentives to increase the riskiness of its portfolio because bank management reaps the rewards of a successful outcome, while the FDIC pays for an unsuccessful outcome. Work such as that by Boyle and Lee (1996) has developed theoretical extensions to the model to account for stochastic volatility.

FDIC's CLOSURE POLICY AND NON-TRADABLE ASSETS

Additionally, the Merton (1977) model does not account for the closure policy of the insuring agency. Ronn and Verma (1986) alter Merton's (1977) model to allow for forbearance on the part of the insuring agent. Forbearance essentially allows the bank to operate with negative net worth. However, the exact amount of forbearance is debatable. Moreover, although some forbearance may be granted, there is some limit at which the FDIC will close the bank. Therefore, perhaps a more appropriate method of modeling the deposit insurance put option is to value it as a down-and-out barrier option, wherein, once a certain level of asset value is exceeded, the bank is closed. Recent papers have begun to examine this question.

Finally, and importantly, an unresolved issue is the appropriateness of Merton's (1977) model in light of the fact that the assets of the bank are non-tradable. For the isomorphic correspondence between stock options and deposit insurance to hold, one must be able to achieve the riskless hedge, which requires the ability to trade in the underlying.

FDIC AND CONTINUING DEVELOPMENTS

Though there are currently limitations in the theoretical pricing of deposit insurance, our knowledge is much greater than it was 20 years ago. Such a guarantee is costly, as is obvious from the failure of FSLIC, the Savings and Loan deposit insuring agency. The cost of the guarantee is increasing in the debt level of the bank and the riskiness of the bank's assets. However, the FDIC has largely ignored theoretical developments, maintaining a constant premium of deposit insurance (per dollar of deposits) regardless of individual bank characteristics. Kendall and Levonian (1991) show that even a dichotomous grouping of banks on individual characteristics improves upon the FDIC's current policy. It is therefore troublesome that the FDIC would continue to ignore the developments in the area.

Bibliography

Au, K. T., Dennis, S. A., and Thurston, D. C. (1995). The deposit insurance fund and the regulation of interest rate and credit risks at depository institutions. Working paper series, University of New South Wales.

Black, F., and Scholes, M. (1973). The pricing of options and corporate liabilities. *Journal of Political Economy*, 81, 637–54.

Boyle, P., and Lee, I. (1996). Deposit insurance with changing volatility: An application of exotic options. *Journal of Financial Engineering*.

Diamond, D., and Dybvig, P. (1983). Bank runs, deposit insurance, and liquidity. *Journal of Political Economy*, 91, 501–19.

Duan, J. C. (1994). Maximum likelihood estimation using price data of the derivative contract. *Mathematical Finance*, 4, 155–67.

Duan, J. C., Moreau, A. F., and Sealey, C. W. (1995). Deposit insurance and bank interest rate risk: Pricing and regulatory implications. *Journal of Banking and Finance*, 19, 1091–108.

Heath D., Jarrow, R., and Morton, A. (1992). Bond pricing and the term structure of interest rates: A new methodology for contingent claims valuation. *Econometrica*, 60, 77–105.

Kendall, S., and Levonian, M. (1991). A simple approach to better deposit insurance pricing. *Journal of Banking and Finance*, 15, 999–1018.

Marcus, A., and Shaked, I. (1984). The valuation of FDIC deposit insurance using option-pricing estimates. *Journal of Money, Credit, and Banking*, 16, 446–60.

Merton, R. (1973). The theory of rational option pricing. *Bell Journal of Economics and Management Science*, 4, 141–83.

Merton, R. (1974). On the pricing of corporate debt: The risk structure of interest rates. *Journal of Finance*, 29, 449–70.

Merton, R. (1977). The analytic derivation of the cost of deposit insurance and loan guarantees: An application of modern option pricing theory. *Journal of Banking and Finance*, 1, 3–11.

Ronn, E., and Verma, A. (1986). Pricing risk-adjusted deposit insurance: An option-based model. *Journal of Finance*, 41, 871–95.

Vasicek, O. (1977). An equilibrium characterization of the term structure. *Journal of Financial Economics*, 5, 177–88.

discounted cash flow models

Per Olsson and Joakim Levin

Discounted cash flow (DCF) models are used to determine the present value (PV) of an asset by discounting all future incremental cash flows, C_t, pertaining to the asset at the appropriate discount rate r_t:

$$PV = \sum_{t=1}^{T} \frac{C_t}{(1 + r_t)^t}$$

Present value analysis (originating from Fisher, 1930) using DCF models is widely used in the process of deciding how the company's resources should be committed across its lines of businesses (i.e., in the appraisal of projects). The typical application of a DCF model is the calculation of an investment's net present value (NPV), obtained by deducting the initial cash outflow from the present value. An investment with positive NPV is considered profitable. The NPV rule is often heralded as the superior investment decision criterion (Brealey and Myers, 1991). Since present values are additive, the DCF methodology is quite general and can be used to value complex assets as well. Miller and Modigliani (1961), in their highly influential article, note that the DCF approach can be "applied to the firm as a whole which may be thought of in this context as simply a large, composite machine." They continue by using different DCF models for valuation of shares in order to show the irrelevance of dividend policy. The DCF approach is also the standard way of valuing fixed income securities (e.g., bonds and preferred stocks) (Myers, 1984).

Option pricing models can in a sense be viewed as another sub-family of DCF models, since the option value may be interpreted as the present value of the estimated future cash flows generated by the option. Since the estimation procedures for options' future cash flows are derived from a specific and mathematically more advanced theory (introduced for finance purposes by Black and Scholes, 1973), option pricing theory is usually treated separately from other types of DCF modeling.

Myers (1984) identifies four basic problems in applying a DCF model to a project: (1) estimating the discount rate; (2) estimating the project's future cash flows; (3) estimating the project's impact on the firm's other assets' cash flows; and (4) estimating the project's impact on the firm's future investment opportunities.

When estimating the discount rate one must bear in mind that any future cash flow, be it from a firm, from an investment project, or from any asset, is more or less uncertain and hence always involves risk. It is often recommended to adjust for this by choosing a discount rate that reflects the risk and discounting the expected future cash flows. A popular model for estimating the appropriate risk adjusted discount rate (i.e., the cost of capital) is the capital asset pricing model (CAPM) by Sharpe (1964), where the discount rate is determined by adding a risk premium to the risk-free interest rate. The risk premium is calculated by multiplying the asset's sensitivity to general market movements (its beta) to the market risk premium. However, the empirical validity of CAPM is a matter of debate. Proposed alternatives to the single-factor CAPM include different multifactor approaches based on Ross's (1977) arbitrage pricing model. Fama and French (1993) identify five common risk factors in returns on stocks and bonds that can be used for estimating the cost of capital.

Different procedures for estimating future cash flows are normally required, depending on which type of asset is being valued. The Copeland, Koller, and Murrin (1994) DCF model for equity valuation provides a practical way of determining the relevant cash flows in company valuation. By forecasting a number of financial ratios and economic variables, the company's future balance sheets and income statements are predicted. From these predictions, the expected free cash flows (i.e., cash not retained and reinvested in the business) for future years are calculated. The sum of the discounted free cash flows for all coming years is the company's asset value, from which the present market value of debts is deducted to arrive at a valuation of the equity.

Irrespective of asset type, cash flows should normally be calculated on an after-tax basis and with a treatment of inflation that is consistent with the discount rate (i.e., a nominal discount rate requires cash flows in nominal terms) (Brealey and Myers, 1991). It is also important to insure that all cash flow effects are brought into the model – including effects on cash flows from other assets influenced by the investment.

An intelligent application of DCF should also include an estimation of the impact of today's investments on future investment opportunities. One example is valuation of equity in companies with significant growth opportunities. The growth opportunities can be viewed as a portfolio of options for the company to invest in second stage, and even later stage, projects. Also research and development and other intangible assets can, to a large part, be viewed as

options (Myers, 1984). Another example concerns the irreversible character of many capital investments. When the investment itself can be postponed, there is an option to wait for more (and better) information. Ideas such as these are exploited in Dixit and Pindyck (1994), where it is shown how the complete asset value, including the value from these different types of opportunities, can be calculated using option pricing techniques or dynamic programming.

Bibliography

Black, F., and Scholes, M. (1973). The pricing of options and corporate liabilities. *Journal of Political Economy*, 81, 637–59.

Brealey, R. A., and Myers, S. C. (1991). *Principles of Corporate Finance*, 4th edn. New York: McGraw-Hill.

Copeland, T., Koller, T., and Murrin, J. (1994). *Valuation: Measuring and Managing the Value of Companies*, 2nd edn. New York: John Wiley.

Dixit, A. K., and Pindyck, R. S. (1994). *Investment Under Uncertainty*. Princeton, NJ: Princeton University Press.

Fama, E. F., and French, K. R. (1993). Common risk factors in stock and bond returns. *Journal of Financial Economics*, 33, 3–56.

Fisher, I. (1930) [1965]. *The Theory of Interest*. New York: Augustus M. Kelley.

Miller, M. H., and Modigliani, F. (1961). Dividend policy, growth, and the valuation of shares. *Journal of Business*, 34, 411–33.

Myers, S. C. (1984). Finance theory and financial strategy. *Interfaces*, 14, 126 37.

Ross, S. A. (1977). Return, risk and arbitrage. In I. Friend and J. L. Bicksler (eds.), *Risk and Return in Finance*. Cambridge, MA: Ballinger.

Sharpe, W. (1964). Capital asset prices: A theory of market equilibrium under conditions of risk. *Journal of Finance*, 19, 425–42.

disinvestment decisions

Peter J. DaDalt

Disinvestment represents a subset of the universe of restructuring strategies available to firms. Restructuring encompasses a range of initiatives, some of which include changes in the ownership and financing structure. The term *disinvestment* as used here is restricted to decisions which involve only changes in asset structure. From a balance sheet perspective, we restrict the term to transactions immediately involving changes in the composition of assets rather than transactions also involving changes in financing and ownership structure. In this framework, sell-offs (including both divestitures and liquidations), plant closings, and abandonments are considered disinvestments, whereas spin-offs, split-offs, and equity carve outs are not.

Among voluntary disinvestment decisions, the most frequent transactions are sell-offs, where one asset is substituted for cash or securities. The subsequent use of the proceeds is related to the type of disinvestment decision. In the extreme case, voluntary liquidations of firms are transactions where sell-offs generate cash, and the residual cash is distributed to stockholders after all other obligations have been met. More frequently, firms sell only a portion of the firm's assets in a transaction known as a divestiture. The discussion that follows focuses on the issues surrounding divestitures only.

The earliest empirical study examining the divestiture of corporate assets was conducted by Boudreaux (1975). This study found there "was an unusually positive price movement in a firm's common stock" for the three months previous through the month following announcement of divestiture. This foundational work provided the first evidence that divestment decisions could be shareholder wealth enhancing.

The first published studies using contemporary statistical techniques were by Alexander, Benson, and Kampmeyer (1984) and Jain (1985). Using event-study methodology, Alexander, Benson, and Kampmeyer (1984) found positive abnormal returns to sellers over a number of intervals. Jain (1985) found similar results, and also found evidence that buyers also gained (although, as in mergers, not to the extent that sellers did).

There are many possible driving forces motivating divestiture decisions. Perhaps the most widely cited is that of "efficient redeployment." This concept (closely related to the concept of synergy in mergers) implies that asset sales need not be a zero-sum game between the seller and acquirer. In this paradigm, the selling firm may not have sufficient resources or complementary assets to extract the full potential of the asset under question. By selling the asset to another firm having these missing attributes, the asset increases in value. This implies the possibility of both parties benefiting from the transaction. Evidence in support of mutually beneficial transactions has been found in a number of studies (Jain, 1985; Sicherman and Pettway, 1992).

The strongest evidence that gains to divesting firms accrue from perceptions of potential synergies (as opposed to some "information effect") comes from Hite, Owers, and Rogers (1987). They examined both partial sell-offs and total liquidations. In their liquidation sample, average abnormal returns to selling firms were 33 percent. In the partial sell-off sample, Hite, Owers, and Rogers (1987) examined both completed transactions and those which were announced but subsequently canceled. They found that divesting firms' gains upon announcement were maintained only if the transaction was actually consummated.

Related to the efficient redeployment motive is the divestment of unrelated business units. The potentially negative effects for shareholders of acquirers purchasing firms in unrelated lines of business is well known. Firms' diversification-related investments in areas outside their core business areas generally provide more benefit to managers than to shareholders. Divesting these unrelated assets limits the potential agency costs and results in increased focus of managerial and financial resources. John and Ofek (1995) provide evidence that focus-increasing divestitures of unrelated operations result in higher announcement returns.

The financing hypothesis (as formalized in Lang, Stultz, and Poulsen, 1995) contends that asset sales are often used to provide sources of capital. When financial constraints limit firms' effective access to traditional capital markets, asset sales may be the only feasible source of financing available. However, knowledge of the firm's financial condition prior to the asset sale significantly affects the relative bargaining positions (and hence the relative gains) of the transacting firms. Firms with recent bond downgrades in the period prior to asset sales are often forced to sell at a bargain price. This results in a larger share of any redeployment gains going to the acquiring firm (Sicherman and Pettway, 1992).

Finally, current research indicates that asset sales may be driven by the presence and resolution of informational asymmetries. In the presence of informational asymmetry between corporate insiders and the market regarding the true value of the firm's assets in place, asset sales may be the only feasible means of raising capital while avoiding the mispricing problems detailed in Myers and Majluf (1984). The firm may be able to credibly convey private information regarding individual corporate assets to potential buyers. Additionally, if the market rationally expects the firm to sell its most overpriced asset (and therefore to retain its most undervalued assets), asset sales may provide sufficient information for the market to resolve the undervaluation of the firm's remaining operations. DaDalt et al. (1996) found that divesting firms with potentially high levels of information asymmetry (those not followed by security analysts) have announcement period returns several times greater than firms followed by one or more analysts.

Bibliography

Alexander, G. J., Benson, P. G., and Kampmeyer, J. M. (1984). Investigating the valuation effects of announcements of voluntary corporate selloffs. *Journal of Finance*, **29**, 503–17.

Boudreaux, K. J. (1975). Divestiture and share price. *Journal of Financial and Quantitative Analysis*, **10**, 619–26.

DaDalt, P. J., McManus, G. V., Owers, J. E., and Zimmerman, O. V. (1996). The informational context of divestiture announcements: An empirical investigation. Unpublished manuscript, Georgia State University.

Hite, G. L., Owers, J. E., and Rogers, R. C. (1987). The market for interfirm asset sales: Partial sell-offs and total liquidations. *Journal of Financial Economics*, **8**, 229–52.

Jain, P. (1985). The effect of voluntary sell-off announcements on shareholder wealth. *Journal of Finance*, **40**, 209–24.

John, K., and Ofek, E. (1995). Asset sales and increase in focus. *Journal of Financial Economics*, **37**, 105–26.

Lang, L., Stultz, R. L., and Poulsen, A. B. (1995). Asset sales, firm performance, and the agency costs of managerial discretion. *Journal of Financial Economics*, **37**, 3–37.

Myers, S. C., and Majluf, N. S. (1984). Corporate financing and investment decisions when firms have information that investors do not have. *Journal of Financial Economics*, **13**, 187–221.

Sicherman, N. W., and Pettway, R. F. (1992). Wealth effects for buyers and sellers of the same divested assets. *Financial Management*, **21**, 119–28.

dividend growth model

Paul Barnes

One of the simplest stock valuation models is the dividend growth model, often attributed to Gordon (1962). For instance, suppose that a firm pays dividends once a year and that after one year, when that dividend is paid, the stockholder plans to sell the investment. The value of the stock, P_0, at the beginning of the year will be

$$P_0 = \frac{E(d_1) + E(P_1)}{1 + k} \tag{1}$$

where $E(P_1)$ is the estimate of the value of the stock at the end of the year and $E(d_1)$ is the estimate of the dividend per stock paid then, and k is the discount rate for that firm based upon its level of risk. This model may be extended to take into account the permanent nature of the firm and the fact that the stock owner is uncertain as to when he or she intends to sell the stock. Thus

$$P_0 = \frac{E(d_1)}{1 + k} + \cdots + \frac{E(d_n)}{(1 + k)^n} \tag{2}$$

where $E(d_n)$ is the dividend expected at the end of year n. Now, if it is assumed that the dividend per stock is constant

$$P_0 = d_1 \left(\frac{1}{1 + k} + \cdots + \frac{1}{(1 + k)^n} \right) \tag{3}$$

If equation (3) is multiplied by $(1 + k)$ and this is subtracted from equation (3) then

$$P_0 \times k = d_1 - \frac{1}{(1 + k)^n} \tag{4}$$

As n approaches infinity then the last term on the right-hand side of equation (4) approaches zero. Therefore

$$P_0 = \frac{d_1}{k} \tag{5}$$

It should not be thought that this model assumes that the investor holds the stock for an infinite period of time! After whatever period the stock is held for, it will be purchased by another whose valuation is based upon holding it for another finite period and who in turn will sell it on to another who will similarly hold it, and so on. The effect of this is that the stock is held by a series of owners for a period approaching infinity and the price at which it passes between them reflects the infinite time horizon of that dividend stream. Thus, this model is not sensitive to how long the present stockholder intends to hold the stock.

The main problems with this simple dividend model are the assumption of constant d and k over an infinite time horizon, and their estimation. An assumption of a constant growth in dividends may easily be incorporated into the model. Let the annual growth in dividends grow at a compound rate, g. Thus

$$P_0 = \frac{D_0(1+g)}{1+k} + \cdots + \frac{D_0(1+g)^n}{(1+k)^n} \quad (6)$$

Multiplying equation (6) by $(1+k)/(1+g)$ and subtracting equation (6) from it gives

$$\frac{P_0(1+k)}{(1+g)} - P_0 = D_0\left(1 - \frac{(1+g)^n}{(1+k)^n}\right) \quad (7)$$

If $k > g$ and as $D_1 = D_0(1+g)$ the right-hand side of equation (7) simplifies to D_1. Thus

$$P_0 = \frac{D_1}{k-g} \quad (8)$$

Models have been developed to vary some of the above assumptions. For example, Fuller and Hsia (1984) have developed a three-step dividend growth rate model which assumes that the "middle step" growth rate g_2 is exactly half way between the other two. This is

$$P_0 = [D_0/(k - g_3)][(1 + g_3) + H(g_1 - g_3)] \quad (9)$$

where D_0 is the current dividend per share, g_1 is the growth rate in phase 1, g_2 is the growth rate in phase 2, g_3 is the long-run growth rate in the final phase, and $H = (A + B)/2$ where A is the number of years in phase 1 and B is the end of phase 2.

Say the present dividend is 1.00, and that its growth is 12 percent but declining in a linear fashion until it reaches 8 percent at the end of ten years. Because the total above-normal growth is ten years, H is five years. Thus

$$P_0 = [1/(0.14 - 0.08)] \times$$
$$[(1.08 + 5(0.12 - 0.08)] = 21.33 \quad (10)$$

A surprising variable to be included in these models is the dividend per share. This may be adjusted to include the firm's reported earnings per share. Consider the firm's sources and application of funds statement:

$$y_t + e_t + r_t = d_t + i_t \quad (11)$$

where y_t is the firm's reported earnings, e_t is the firm's new external funds received during the period, r_t is the depreciation charged for the period, d_t is the dividend paid during the period, and i_t is the amount of new investment made during the period. It will be seen that the firm's economic (or Hicksian) income also equals its dividend, that is

$$y_t + e_t + r_t - i_t = d_t \quad (12)$$

It should not be thought that the results of these models will necessarily coincide with market values. The user may have quite different expectations. They may be useful, therefore, to quantify the effect of different forecasts. They may also be used to compute forecasts and expectations built into existing stock prices.

Bibliography

Fuller, R. J., and Hsia, C. (1984). A simplified common stock valuation model. *Financial Analysts Journal*, **40**, 49–56.

Gordon, M. J. (1962). *The Investment, Financing and Valuation of the Corporation*. Homewood, IL: Irwin.

dividend policy

Ian Davidson and Nick Webber

Dividends are the reward to shareholders for supplying capital to the firm. Without the payment of dividends, shares would have no value.

Only the promise of future dividends gives value to shares, and therefore under conventional valuation arguments (Williams, 1938) fluctuations in the value of a share are brought about by changes in investors' expectations about the value of the future dividend stream. Dividends, which are payable in cash (or sometimes optionally in shares – "stock dividends"), are set at the discretion of directors, usually on a biannual (UK) or quarterly (USA) basis. The key question is how the directors should set the level of current dividend, or plan future dividend policy, so as to maximize the value of the firm and hence maximize returns to the firm's owners, the shareholders.

There are two main approaches to explaining the dividend decision. The first starts from the theoretical result that, under perfect market assumptions, both managers and shareholders should be indifferent to the size of the current dividend announcement (Miller and Modigliani, 1961). The various assumptions that lead to this conclusion can be examined and relaxed, leading to a deeper appreciation of the determinants of the dividend level in practice. The second approach starts from the empirical observation that directors have a profound reluctance to decrease the dividend over time (this is certainly true in nominal terms; however, real decreases, such as would be caused by holding the dividend constant, are much more frequent). Investors, while accepting that earnings levels may fluctuate in the short term, seem to be strongly averse to any signal that the underlying level or trend of earnings may be unsustainable. A reduction in dividend, it is argued, has particularly unambiguous information content (however, see Taylor, 1979) and is viewed as strong evidence that managers believe earning levels cannot be maintained, and has a profound effect on the market's perception of the value of the company. A possible additional consequence is the increased threat of replacement of management through, for example, takeover activity or other means. Consequently, managers may go to exceptional lengths to avoid a reduction in dividend. The corollary is that an increase in dividend should only be made if managers believe the new level is sustainable. These behavioral influences give some predictability to the current dividend based on knowledge of current earnings and past dividends (the "partial adjustment" model of Lintner, 1956). However, attempts to establish a link empirically between current dividend changes and future earnings changes (the signaling hypothesis) have not been convincing, despite the plausibility of the theoretical arguments.

Dividend Irrelevancy

Miller and Modigliani (1961) demonstrated that in ideal circumstances the level of a firm's dividend would not affect the value of the firm, with shareholders being indifferent to an announcement of low or high levels of dividend. The assumptions underpinning this result hinge around the notion that company value depends solely upon the investment opportunities available to it, and that finance for investment is always available. In effect, for a given set of investment opportunities, the firm can raise sufficient capital (internally and externally) to fund both its investment program and its dividend. This result is closely related to the theoretical position established by Miller and Modigliani (1961) that under a similar set of idealized assumptions, company value is unaffected by the mix of equity and debt used to finance it.

Of course, the world does not always obey the theoretical assumptions, and many caveats modify the Miller and Modigliani proposition. From the perspective of shareholders, "irrelevance" implies that they are indifferent between receiving returns as dividends or as capital gains. For a given investment program, a lower dividend implies a greater capital gain and a higher dividend implies a lower capital gain; the overall returns being equivalent in either case. In practice, the tax regime may favor one form of return over another. An investor who is taxed on dividend income, but not on capital gains, will prefer a low dividend policy provided the capital gain reflects the full amount of the retention, and vice versa (short-term capitalization evidence suggesting this is not the case is provided by Elton and Gruber, 1970, and a consistent longer-term analysis is found in Auerbach, 1979). For a company, retained earnings may be taxed differently to distributed earnings (as was the case in the UK in the 1950s), leading to different corporate tax bills under different dividend policies. Assuming that this is not the case, then a company that is acting in the best interests of its shareholders will choose the dividend policy that minimizes the total tax bill of its shareholders. However, under a classical tax system such as that operated in the USA, this would seem to suggest that no dividends would be paid at all, since the effective rate of tax on capital gains is less than that on income! Even under the comparative neutrality of an imputation tax system as used in the UK, Australasia, and elsewhere, shareholders may not be indifferent between dividend returns and returns taken as capital gains. Mallin's (1993) evidence of the take up of stock dividends in the UK shows that on average shareholders elect to take only about 5 percent of dividend in stock form, implying that income returns are generally preferred to capital gain.

From the perspective of a firm's management, an essential component of the irrelevance view is that investment decisions should not be affected by dividend policy. This amounts to asking two questions. First, is there any discernible evidence that internal investment is affected by dividend levels, and second, is there any evidence that the rates of return generated by employing different forms of finance are different? The answer to the first question depends on whether an investigation is carried out in cross-section (where, following Dhrymes and Kurz (1967), an interactive effect is generally supported) or in time series (where, following Fama (1974), it is not), so this question is not yet resolved. In a situation of market-induced capital rationing, were this situation to exist, it is accepted that investment choices would be heavily influenced by the quantity of retained earnings. Dividend policy would directly impact upon investment policy and the Miller–Modigliani proposition would not apply.

One of the main issues surrounding the second question is the hypothesis that management uses retained earnings inefficiently (Baumol et al., 1970, provide some evidence, although their methodology is problematic). A firm's management that pays a low dividend in order to invest retained earnings avoids the costs and the scrutiny that comes with attempting to raise capital in the market. There is a direct financial cost involved in going to the market to raise capital, and indirect costs may be incurred in facilitating the monitoring expected. Avoidance of the discipline of the market leaves management more latitude to enjoy "perquisites" (management perks), with a consequential increase in agency costs which high dividend levels would avoid.

Conclusion

There is no single theory to explain a firm's dividend policy or to determine an optimal level for the firm's dividend. Empirical studies give contradictory evidence, but from a practical viewpoint managers seem to attempt to maintain a particular payout ratio, tempered by a great reluctance to reduce the dividend from last year's (nominal) level.

Dividend levels as a whole may be paradoxically high. For example, why do many firms incur unnecessary issue and transactions costs by paying dividends and at the same time seek new equity capital – in the case of a rights issue from the same shareholders as receive the dividend? The cross-sectional evidence suggests in addition that high dividend levels may be damaging to a firm's investment program. Despite these inefficiencies shareholders seem to prefer the cash-in-hand of immediate high dividends (together with the discipline this imposes on management) to the uncertain promise of higher dividends in the future.

Bibliography

Auerbach, A. J. (1979). Share valuation and corporate equity policy. *Journal of Public Economics*, 11, 291–305.

Baumol, W. J., Heim, P., Malkiel, B. G., and Quandt, R. E. (1970). Earnings retention, new capital, and the growth of the firm. *Review of Economics and Statistics*, 52, 345–55.

Black, F. (1976). The dividend puzzle. *Journal of Portfolio Management*, 2, 5–8.

Dhrymes, P. J., and Kurz, M. (1967). Investment, dividend and external finance behavior of firms. In R. Ferber (ed.), *Determinants of Investment Behavior*. New York: National Bureau of Economic Research, 427–67.

Elton, E. J., and Gruber, M. J. (1970). Marginal stockholder tax rates and the clientele effect. *Review of Economics and Statistics*, 52, 68–74.

Fama, E. F. (1974). The empirical relationship between the dividend and investment decisions of firms. *American Economic Review*, 64, 304–18.

Feldstein, M., and Green, J. (1983). Why do companies pay dividends? *American Economic Review*, 73, 17–30.

Gordon, M. J. (1962). *The Savings, Investment and Valuation of the Corporation*. Homewood, IL: Richard Irwin.

Lintner, J. (1956). Distribution of incomes of corporations among dividends, retained earnings, and taxes. *American Economic Review*, **46**, 97–113.

Mallin, C. A. (1993). Stock dividends: The implications for the corporate and private sectors. *Stock Exchange Quarterly*, winter, 21–4.

Miller, M. H., and Modigliani, F (1961). Dividend policy, growth and the valuation of shares. *Journal of Business*, **34**, 411–33.

Taylor, P. A. (1979). The information content of dividends hypothesis: Back to the drawing board? *Journal of Business Finance and Accounting*, **6**, 495–526.

Williams, J. B. (1938). *The Theory of Investment Value*. Amsterdam: North Holland.

electronic banking

Jonathon Williams

Electronic banking is a generic term encompassing the use of increasingly sophisticated, computer-based technologies for delivering, transferring, recording, and developing banking and related financial services. Payments, funds transfers, and related services are generally regarded as the core elements of electronic banking, but the wider meaning of electronic banking also covers back-office functions like bank accounting and management information systems (MIS). These kinds of innovations in the financial services industry are stimulated generally by market and regulatory forces. Market forces include technology, interest rate risk, and competition for customers. Regulatory forces include reregulation and capital adequacy supervisory requirements.

The main innovation to date has been the application of electronic funds transfer (EFT) systems. Paper-based payment systems are characterized by relatively low fixed cost but high variable cost (reflecting the labor-intensive nature of such operations). EFT systems offer banks three major incentives: (1) the opportunity to reduce their volumes of staff and paper and, hence, to control costs; (2) protect and increase market share; and (3) generate new revenues. EFT systems offer potential scale economies where the marginal cost per transaction may decline as the volume of transactions increases, and their variable cost is low although the fixed cost component is relatively high (Lewis and Davis, 1987).

In today's deregulated markets, technological comparative advantage is one key to bank success. The diffusion of electronic banking services, however, is a long-term process; this kind of diffusion tends to begin in the wholesale markets before spreading to retail (Sinkey, 1992). An innovation time lag exists between the conception of an idea and the collective acceptance by consumers of the final product. Acceptance of an innovation involves customers changing their payment habits. Given the slow nature of this process, the spread of electronic banking at the retail level has been relatively slow, except in the case of automated teller machines (ATMs).

Technology is altering the face of modern banking. Automated accounting and processing systems have modernized back-office functions, while EFT systems are differentiating front-end operations; office staff now have more time to develop customer relationships and at the same time cross-sell bank products and services. EFT systems comprise an increasing amount of services. Perhaps the most transparent are ATMs, which provide an extension of credit and other typical branching functions on a 24-hour basis. ATMs have an added strategic advantage: they may be located inside or outside a branch (for example, in remote and/or popular areas), offering opportunities for market segmentation (Gardener and Molyneux, 1993; Lipis, Marshall, and Linker, 1985). With today's technical infrastructure, cardholders of different types can access domestic and international ATM networks. Indeed, technology is freeing the customer from the need to enter branches, thereby reducing banks' need for a comprehensive branch network. Table 1 highlights the global growth in the number of ATM machines and EFTPOS terminals between 1989 and 1993 (BIS, 1993).

Electronic point-of-sale (POS) systems allow the buyer of goods and services to have his or her bank account debited at purchase by the seller

Table 1 The spread of electronic banking

	Cash dispensers and ATMs per 1 million inhabitants		EFTPOS terminals per 1 million inhabitants	
	1989	1993	1989	1993
Belgium	92	119	2477	5246
France	231	325	2842	7435
Germany	148	308	174	344
Italy	135	266	178	1350
Japan	627	935	14	168
UK	275	321	1311	3780
USA	306	367	200	759

through the use of a terminal which activates an EFT system. France and Belgium have made the greatest provision of this service in Europe. In the USA there has been a threefold increase in the number of terminals, but the total number available per million inhabitants is much lower than in France, Belgium, Italy, and the UK. In 1993 there were 128 million debit cards in use in Belgium, France, Germany, Italy, the Netherlands, Spain, and the UK, twice the number of credit cards (56 million) and store cards (44.6 million) (Farbrother, 1994).

Table 2 illustrates the numbers of different cards held per thousand persons (BIS, 1994). Cards have evolved from just providing a cash function to dispensing travelers checks or

Table 2 The number of cards (1993, per 1,000 inhabitants)

Country	Cards with a cash function	Cards with a credit/ debit function	Cards with a cheque guarantee	Retailers' cards
Belgium	823	835	531	99
France	378	372	3	n/a
Germany	n/a	552	442	n/a
Italy	197	285	29	n/a
Japan	2145	1769	n/a	425
UK	1196	876	756	146
USA	n/a	n/a	n/a	2070

cinema tickets (this is so-called smart-card technology). Credit cards extend credit to the holder who must reconcile expenditures within a given period or else face interest charges on the remaining balance. The creditor has virtually instant access to funds when purchases are made by debit card. Charge cards are also operated by retailers; this raises the notion that banks are becoming disenfranchised as non-banks enter the electronic financial services market and/or form ties with existing banks. Banks have begun investing in smart-card technology. Based on microchip technology, smart cards offer potentially better card authentication and cardholder verification systems, thereby helping to tackle cardholder fraud. In France, for example, domestic fraud levels are at an all-time low of 0.05 percent of card payment turnover compared to a European average of 0.15 percent. Farbrother (1994) estimates that out of a total of 42.5 million cards in issue in France, 23 million are smart cards; the number of smart cards in operation in other European countries is found to be negligible.

Retail bank customers can undertake a variety of banking services through home and office banking facilities (commonly referred to as HOBS). HOBS enable "customers to access cash management services, balance enquiries, funds transfer, bill payment and so on with the use of a TV screen, personal computer or variable-tone, push-button telephone" (Gardener and Molyneux, 1993). Home banking, a recent innovation, is particularly popular in Belgium and France. Some systems operate on a 24-hour basis via digital or voice recognition; recently, some UK banks have began to staff their telephone-based systems. Other electronic delivery systems include telebanking and videotex. Technology provides banks with masses of data. Banks have not been slow in creating customer information files (CIFs) for the purposes of cross-selling; more recently, database marketing strategies have enabled banks to further segment their customer base (Gardener and Molyneux, 1993).

Payments systems in most developed countries share some common characteristics (Sinkey, 1992). Wholesale (large value) and retail systems (small value) can be differentiated; electronic and paper-based systems operate concurrently; and domestic and international services are provided. Furthermore, certain linkages exist: international transactions tend to be wholesale and electronic based; wholesale operations are notably electronic based; and retail transactions are usually paper based and relatively costly. These relationships are illustrated by the following facts: in the UK there are four interbank funds transfer systems currently in operation. Two deal with electronic payments; retail banking transactions are provided by BACS Ltd (Bankers' Automated Clearing Services), while wholesale transfers are provided by CHAPS (clearing house automated payment system). In 1993 CHAPS handled 11 million transactions at a value of US$35,353 billion. BACS handled 1,903 million transactions worth US$1,256 billion. These data are common across Europe (BIS, 1993).

International transactions between banks are electronically handled via the Society for Worldwide Interbank Financial Telecommunication (SWIFT) network. BIS (1993) defines SWIFT as "a cooperative organization created and owned by banks that operates a network which facilitates the exchange of payment and other financial messages between financial institutions . . . throughout the world. A SWIFT payment message is an instruction to transfer funds; the exchange of funds (settlement) subsequently takes place over a payment system or through correspondent banking relationships."

Future bank delivery systems will be electronic at both retail and wholesale levels. Scale economies are expected to generate efficiencies and the provision of services at least cost. EFT payments systems have been likened to monopolistic utilities, in that implementing an optimal pricing rule is not straightforward (Revell, 1983). Fixed costs, including the purchase of hardware and the programming of computer software, are relatively high. Marginal costs per transaction are low (average cost declines as the volume of transactions increases), but a marginal pricing rule does not cover fixed costs. Average cost pricing leads to inefficient production. An alternative is to price by average cost (covering fixed costs) and set the transaction cost at or near marginal cost (encouraging efficient usage of the system).

All payments systems provide a joint service to payer and payee; because of jointness in production and consumption, simple pricing rules are insufficient to cover all costs. This raises the issue of whether banks should use explicit pricing (by product) or implicit pricing (cross-subsidization). The market segmentation hypothesis favors explicit pricing because of (1) the need of banks to generate efficiency gains, and (2) the growing importance of fee income as a source of revenue, especially in the face of thinner interest margins. Banks also face extensive marketing and continuing education costs; there is the additional cost of security. Yet banks must price fully both electronic and paper delivery services if they are to persuade consumers to change to the more cost-effective EFT systems.

The users of payments systems typically require two fundamental services: efficiency and safety. Global electronic systems such as SWIFT link the world's major financial institutions. The risks involved in the evolution and advance of payments systems in general are of great concern to national and global regulatory bodies. The structural shift towards electronic banking has concentrated risk, with respect to time rather than space (Revell, 1983).

A major policy concern for regulators of payments systems is the threat of systemic risk (Borio and Van den Bergh, 1993). This may occur when a counterparty in trouble sets off a kind of "chain reaction" (or "contagion" effect) in the system as other counterparties seek to protect themselves through attempts to close their exposed positions. Regulators seek to prevent systemic risk through various supervisory practices. Although supervision is largely country specific, regulators in the past two decades have increasingly emphasized international cooperation and international risk reduction as major priorities. This action has been fueled by (1) increasing volumes putting payments systems under greater strain; (2) the complexity of financial transactions and the application of different rules for segments of the same deal; and (3) the increased risk-taking behavior exhibited by banks operating in a globalized, competitive environment.

There are three major types of risk associated with large-value EFT systems. Borio and Van den Bergh (1993) explain the intricate relationship between these risks. The key concern in large-value interbank funds transfer systems is the risk of a settlement failure (settlement risk). A settlement failure implies a liquidity shortfall for other participants (liquidity risk). It also typically involves a loss on outstanding contracts (credit risk), whose size and distribution depend on the structure of underlying obligations, the methods of dealing with the liquidity shortfall, and legal arrangements.

Attempts are being made by regulators to encourage participants to monitor, limit, and control their risks. In the UK, for example, efforts to limit settlement risk have been built into CHAPS. Settlement banks in the CHAPS system guarantee final settlement to the payee once an incoming message is accepted. If the sending bank does not settle at the end of the day, payment has to be made by the recipient settlement bank. This has given rise to daylight exposures, or overdrafts, between settlement banks. In 1992, settlement banks were permitted to limit their bilateral exposure to other settlement banks. Furthermore, greater risk reduction was made possible in 1993 through the introduction of net sender limits subject to guidelines set by the CHAPS and Town Company.

Should inbuilt mechanisms fail, reliance for support falls on the shoulders of the central bank. The Bank of England, for example, bears the (liquidity) risk that a settlement bank may be unable to fund its overall debit position at the close of business. Other efforts are currently under way to reduce risk. A central monitoring system has been established by the CHAPS inspectorate. Also, it is proposed to convert CHAPS into a real-time gross settlement system. Banks can control customer credit risk by giving customers intra-day limits, applying individual authorization to each payment, and by monitoring intra-day exposures via online real-time accounting. Competitive pressures, however, may reduce the effectiveness of monitoring.

Bibliography

BIS (1993). *Payments Systems in the Group of Ten Countries*. Basle: Bank for International Settlements.
BIS (1994). *Statistics on Payments Systems in the Group of Ten Countries*. Basle: Bank for International Settlements.
Booth, G. (1994–5). Hole in the wallet. *Banking Technology*, Dec./Jan.,18–22.
Borio, C. E. V., and Van den Bergh, P. (1993). The nature and management of payment system risks: An international perspective. Economic Papers, No. 36. Bank for International Settlements.
Farbrother, R. (1994). Deliver the goods. *The Banker*, **144**, 75–7.
Gardener, E. P. M., and Molyneux, P. (1993). *Changes in Western European Banking*. New York: Unwin Hyman.
Lewis, M. K. and Davis, K. T. (1987). *Domestic and International Banking*. Hemel Hempstead: Philip Allan.
Lipis, A. H., Marshall, T. R., and Linker, J. H. (1985). *Electronic Banking*. New York: John Wiley.
Revell, J. R. S. (1983). *Banking and Electronic Fund Transfers*. Paris: OECD.
Sinkey, J. F., Jr. (1992). *Commercial Bank Financial Management*. New York: Macmillan.
Warley, P. (1994). Take a long view. *The Banker*, **144**, 32–3.

electronic payments systems

Leslie M. Goldschlager and Ian R. Harper

An electronic payments system is one in which financial transactions are conducted via computer and electronic communications devices, without the need to transfer any physical token. It is the lack of a physical representation of money, such as coins or paper or some other physical commodity, which characterizes electronic payments systems. Instead, money is represented in purely electronic form, typically as various patterns of "bits" (i.e., zeros and ones) in a computer's memory or inside a packet of information in transit between two computers.

We can distinguish two major categories of electronic payments. The first is a direct transfer in which the transaction amount is immediately debited from the electronic account of the payer and credited to the electronic account of the payee. The two accounts can be in quite different banks at different geographic locations. An important requirement for direct transfers is that the payer's account should contain a balance at least equal to the transaction amount at the time the transaction takes place. Otherwise, the transaction is repudiated. In other words, direct transfers do not create additional credit. An increasingly widespread example of direct transfers is electronic funds transfer at point of sale (EFTPOS), a process allowing instant payment directly from deposit balances using a debit card.

The second type of electronic payment is the credit card or "pay later" approach. This is similar to the direct transfer except that additional credit is extended at the time of the transaction. This places an obligation upon the payer to repay the credit at a later date. Credit card transactions may be denied when the credit card operator refuses to extend further credit.

An important characteristic of electronic transactions is the degree of privacy extended to the transacting parties. The degree of privacy depends upon any additional information which might be recorded. Examples include the time of the transaction and the identity of the two parties.

Although in principle there are many combinations of recorded information and therefore many degrees of privacy achievable, two major cases occur in practice. They are "complete information" and "complete privacy." Typical debit card and credit card operations belong to the former, since the card operator records a large amount of information including the identity of both parties and, often, the type of goods or services which were bought.

In the non-electronic payments world, complete privacy is most commonly exemplified by cash transactions. An emerging electronic equivalent to cash is the stored-value or smart card. This is a "pay before" approach. Cards are charged with value electronically using an integrated circuit chip embedded within the card. The stored value may then be drawn down at will by the user to effect purchases. The smart-card transaction preserves the privacy of the transacting parties. Neither the identity of the payer and the payee nor any transaction detail is recorded.

It is estimated that at least 75 percent of all transactions are less than US$2.00 in value. For this reason, the number of cash-based transactions vastly exceeds the number of other transaction types at the current time. It is believed that at least 10 percent of all transactions are currently electronic. The figures are quite different when measured by value rather than volume. It is estimated that 90 percent (by value) of transactions are currently executed by check or by electronic means.

Accurate estimates of the cost of operating the cash-based payments system are difficult to come by. One estimate from the UK suggests that the cost of transporting cash exceeds 2 billion annually. To this must be added the cost of storage and security, and the cost of maintaining the quality of the note supply through regular sorting and reissue.

The greatest driving force behind the expansion of electronic payments systems is the low transaction cost which is achievable. The cost per transaction of using a credit card is estimated to be in the range US$0.80 to US$2.50, that of a debit card US$0.50 to US$1.00, and that of a smart card US$0.05 to US$0.15.

For debit and credit cards, verification of credit or funds availability is undertaken prior to completing the transaction. Such a requirement is informationally demanding, and hence more expensive than the transaction cost for smart cards. The higher transaction cost for credit cards results from the costs of assessing creditworthiness, of debt collection, and of provision for bad debts. The marginal cost of using a stored-value card is at least 70 percent less than the cheapest card-based alternative.

Plastic cards are not the only embodiment of electronic payments systems. As the general public's access to computer networks such as the Internet increases, more financial transactions will be carried out directly over the networks, with no physical cards required. This technological trend will herald a further reduction in electronic transaction costs.

Electronic payments systems have made rapid advances in recent years, and their application has become increasingly widespread. As the cost of computers and electronic communications continues to fall, and the volume of electronic payments continues to increase, the marginal cost of electronic payments will fall compared to the marginal cost of cash-based transactions. This will further fuel the acceleration of electronic payments systems.

To the extent that cashless means of payment reduce transaction costs, resource savings will be realized which will, over time, add to national wealth. Resources released from the production and distribution of currency become available for more productive uses.

Perhaps of greater significance for overall resource allocation is the fact that the use of electronic payments systems can be explicitly costed. Faced with a clearer picture of the cost of using the payment system, transaction by transaction, agents can be expected to economize on their consumption of payments services. In addition, financial institutions will be in a better position to unbundle services and attach explicit prices to the payments component. This in turn encourages the production of payment services only up to the point where marginal benefit equals marginal cost.

The chief implications of electronic payments systems for financial institutions are (1) the ability to dispense with vaults, security screens, cash trucks, and the like; and (2) the need to compete in the provision of payments services with a range of non-financial institutions, including telecommunications companies, department stores, and supermarkets.

More so than is the case already, financial institutions will depend upon information technology to produce their services. Accordingly, their main competitors are likely to arise in the information and telecommunications industries.

The cash-based payments system is owned and operated in most countries monopolistically by the central bank. Central banks earn profits by issuing currency, which pays no interest, and purchasing interest-bearing assets with the proceeds. Perhaps the most direct implication of a general move to cashless payments is the loss of these "seigniorage" profits. Governments may seek to replace this source of revenue by levying transaction taxes on the use of the electronic payments system.

An important economic implication of electronic payments technology is that the central bank's currency monopoly will no longer be effective, since people have access to a perfect substitute in the form of smart cards. The advent of smart cards could stimulate a return to privately issued currency, something not observed since the early years of the twentieth century.

These considerations raise the policy issues of who should have the right to issue electronic money and under what regulatory conditions. With the advent of new payments technologies, it is time to review and overhaul the traditional role of central banks in the provision of payments services.

Bibliography

BIS (1989). *Payment Systems in Eleven Developed Countries*. Basle: Bank for International Settlements.

Carmichael, J., and Harper, I. R. (1994). Implementing monetary policy in a deregulated financial system: A study of the Australian official short-term money markets. Working Paper No. 1, Melbourne Business School, University of Melbourne.

Clarke, R. (1994). The multi-function smart-card pilot project of the Swiss PTT, 1985–93. Research report, Research Programme in Supra-Organizational Systems, Department of Commerce, Australian National University.

Goldschlager, L. M., and Baxter, R. (1994). The loans standard model of credit money. *Journal of Post Keynesian Economics*, **16** (3), 453–77.

Harper, I. R. (1984). Some speculation on the long-term implications of financial deregulation and innovations. *Economic Papers*, **3**, 1–8.

Harper, I. R., and Leslie, P. (1995). Electronic payments systems and their economic implications. *Policy*, 23–8.

Humphrey, D. B., and Berger, A. N. (1989). Market failure and resource use: Economic incentives to use different payment instruments. In D. B. Humphrey (ed.), *The US Payment System: Efficiency, Risk and the Role of the Federal Reserve*. Boston, MA: Kluwer Academic Publishers.

Kirkman, P. (1987). *Electronic Funds Transfer Systems*. Oxford: Blackwell.

Martin, C. D., and Weingarten, F. (1991). The less-cash/less-check society: Banking in the informational age. In E. H. Solomon (ed.), *Electronic Money Flows: The Molding of a New Financial Order*. Dordrecht: Kluwer Academic Publishers.

Moore, L. K. S. (1991). Money in the third millennium. In E. H. Solomon (ed.), *Electronic Money Flows: The Molding of a New Financial Order*. Dordrecht: Kluwer Academic Publishers.

Neumann, M. (1992). Seigniorage in the United States: How much does the US government make from money production? *Federal Reserve Bank of St. Louis Review*, 29–40.

Solomon, E. H. (1991). Today's money: Image and reality. In E. H. Solomon (ed.), *Electronic Money Flows: The Molding of a New Financial Order*. Dordrecht: Kluwer Academic Publishers.

Stone, B. K. (1989). The electronic payment industry: Change barriers and success requirements from a market segments perspective. In D. B. Humphrey (ed.), *The US Payment System: Efficiency, Risk and the Role of the Federal Reserve*. Boston, MA: Kluwer Academic Publishers.

Wilmot, R. (1994). Retail banking in the year 2000: Who will be the provider? Video presentation, OASIS Group.

embedded inflation

Lakshman A. Alles and Ramaprasad Bhar

A theory of the relationship between interest rates and expected inflation is contained in the well-known hypothesis expounded by Irwin Fisher (1930). According to the Fisher hypothesis, the nominal interest rate determined by the market is made up of the expected real rate and a premium for the expected inflation rate. Furthermore, changes in nominal interest rates over time adjust to changes in expected inflation while the expected real rate remains constant. More than 75 years after it was first enunciated, the Fisher hypothesis continues to be regarded as a major paradigm in economic theory.

Despite its wide acceptance by the economic community, empirical support for the Fisher hypothesis has been mixed. Initial support was provided by Fama (1975), who showed that if the expected real rate is assumed to be constant, the nominal rate has a roughly one to one correspondence with the inflation rate. Subsequent researchers have, however, challenged the assumption of a constant real rate and provided alternative interpretations for the time-varying behavior of the expected real rate. For example, Nelson and Schwert (1977) show that Fama's empirical evidence is also consistent with a process in which the real rate follows a random walk. Further evidence that the *ex ante* real rate follows a non-stationary stochastic process which is therefore inconsistent with Fama's assumption of a constant real rate is provided by Cheung (1993). Carmichael and Stebbing (1983) present arguments against the Fisher hypothesis; they refer to an "inverted Fisher hypothesis," according to which the expected after-tax real rate on financial assets moves inversely in a one to one correspondence with expected inflation, while the nominal rate remains constant over the long run. Thus, while the challenges to the constant expected real rate assumption appear to be strong, the theoretical explanation for the interest rate–inflation rate relationship is still an unsettled issue.

While the exact nature of the interest rate–inflation rate relationship is being debated, many of the competing theories acknowledge the notion that the nominal rate and future inflation rates have some systematic relationship. Empir-
ical researchers have recognized that any such systematic relationship has useful practical implications, since the nominal interest rate observed in the market can then be used to derive information on the market's assessment of future inflation. Mishkin (1990) formulated a model for deriving information on future inflation changes from the yield spread of the term structure rather than from the interest rate of a single instrument. If the term spread has information on future inflation, Mishkin's model is very appealing because the term structure is readily observable and lends itself as a very convenient forecasting tool. Mishkin's formulation is based on a combination of the Fisher equation with the rational expectations hypothesis. It says that the spread between the long and short rate is directly related to the expected inflation differential between the corresponding long and short horizon. He refers to the derived relation between the term spread and future inflation rates as the "inflation-change equation," which he uses in a regression framework as a forecasting equation. The intuition for the relation between the term spread and future inflation can also be seen in a different light. Previous research has provided evidence of a relationship between the term structure and future interest rates based on the expectations theory, as in Fama (1984). A second set of relationships exists between interest rates and future inflation, which we alluded to in the first paragraph. If these two relationships are combined, the relation between the term structure and future inflation can be viewed as the indirect link in a chain that links the term structure to changes in interest rates and changes in interest rates to future inflation.

Mishkin's tests of his "inflation-change equation" are based on US markets. He found that when the yield spread is constructed from the short end of the term structure (that is, from yields of less than six months maturity), the yield spread provides no information on changes in future inflation rates. However, spreads constructed from maturities beyond nine months do have the ability to predict changes in inflation rates. On a similar note, Mishkin and Simon (1994) report on the existence of a Fisher effect in Australia. Using cointegration-based analysis they find no evidence of a short-run Fisher effect: short-run changes in interest rates do not indicate inflationary expectations. They find evidence, however, that longer-run levels of short-term interest rates reflect inflationary expectations.

In deriving his regression model, Mishkin imposes the restriction that the spread of the real term structure is held constant over time. But if the expected real rate is time varying, as argued in the literature cited above, the real term spread may not necessarily be a constant over time. Alles and Bhar (1995) modify Mishkin's forecasting model by allowing the real term spread to vary over time in a random fashion. They then use the Kalman filter technique to estimate the model using Australian data. The Kalman filter commonly refers to estimation of state-space models where there are two parts: the transition equation and the measurement equation. The transition equation describes the evolution of the state variables (i.e., the parameters) and the measurement equation describes how the observations are actually generated from the state variables. Regression estimates for each time period in this case are based upon previous periods' estimates and data up to and including the current time period. In their Kalman filter model, Alles and Bhar (1995) specify a simple stochastic model for the expected real rate spread – the random walk. Such a specification is consistent with the arguments of Nelson and Schwert (1977) and the evidence provided by Cheung (1993). Alles and Bhar (1995) further consider the possibility that the parameter estimate of the regressor may not be constant and also may vary with time. To allow for such a variation they introduce a further modification to the inflation estimation model by allowing the parameter estimate of the yield spread to vary with time in accordance with the random walk model.

The results of the Alles and Bhar (1995) paper include a comparative evaluation of the forecasting ability of different formulations of the inflation change equation and an assessment of the efficacy of the constant real rate assumption in the forecasting equation. They show that the Kalman filter estimations in all cases present significantly reduced sum-of-square residuals, suggesting the suitability of such models in capturing the time-varying dynamics of the system. This establishes the fact that the real rate is not constant over the period analyzed. A similar result has also been specified by Cheung (1993). However, when the coefficient of the yield spread is allowed to vary as a random walk, the coefficients lose significance, suggesting the inappropriateness of such a formulation.

Bibliography

Alles, L., and Bhar, R. (1995). The information on inflation in the Australian term structure. Working paper, School of Economics and Finance, Curtin University of Technology.

Carmichael, J., and Stebbing, P. (1983). Fisher's paradox and the theory of interest. *American Economic Review*, 83, 619–30.

Cheung, U. Y. (1993). Short-term interest rates as predictors of inflation revisited: A signal extraction approach. *Applied Financial Economics*, 3, 113–18.

Fama, E. F. (1975). Short-term interest rates as predictors of inflation. *American Economic Review*, 65, 269–82.

Fama, E. F. (1984). The information in the term structure. *Journal of Financial Economics*, 13, 509–28.

Fisher, I. (1930). *The Theory of Interest*. New York: Macmillan.

Mishkin, F. (1990). What does the term structure tell us about future inflation? *Journal of Monetary Economics*, 25, 59–80.

Mishkin, F., and Simon, J. (1994). An empirical examination of the Fisher effect in Australia. Discussion Paper 9410, Reserve Bank of Australia.

Nelson, C. R., and Schwert, G. W. (1977). Short-term interest rates as predictors of inflation: On testing the hypothesis that the real rate of interest is constant. *American Economic Review*, 67, 478–86.

equity premium, the equity premium puzzle, and the risk-free rate puzzle

Ian Garrett

The equity premium is simply the return on the stock market in excess of the risk-free rate. The equity premium puzzle stems from the consumption CAPM and was identified by Mehra and Prescott (1985). Assuming that investors have time-separable preferences and constant relative risk aversion, and assuming that gross returns and consumption are jointly lognormally distributed, then from the consumption CAPM, expected returns can be written as

$$E_t(r_{it+1}) = -\ln\delta + \gamma E_t(\Delta c_{t+1})$$
$$-\frac{1}{2}(\sigma_i^2 + \gamma^2\sigma_c^2 - 2\gamma\sigma_{ic}) \quad (1)$$

where r_{it} is the natural log return on asset i, δ is a discount factor, γ is the coefficient of relative risk aversion, c_t is log consumption, σ_i^2 and σ_c^i are the variances of returns and consumption growth respectively, and σ_{ic} is the covariance between returns and consumption growth. The equity premium puzzle is given observed average stock returns, consumption growth and the covariance of stock returns with consumption growth, the value of γ required to fit the equity premium is far too high. There are several possible explanations for this. Related to this is the risk-free rate puzzle (Weil, 1989). Since the variance of the risk-free rate and its covariance with consumption growth are zero (1) becomes

$$r_{ft+1} = -\ln\delta - \frac{\gamma^2\sigma_c^2}{2} + \gamma E_t(\Delta c_{t+1}) \quad (2)$$

For ease of exposition, take unconditional expectations of (2) to give

$$E(r_{ft}) = -\ln\delta - \frac{\gamma^2\sigma_c^2}{2} + \gamma g_c \quad (3)$$

where g_c is the average consumption growth rate. The risk-free rate puzzle is given observed average short-term real interest rates, observed average consumption growth and the average standard deviation of consumption growth, even small values of γ imply a *negative* rate of time preference. Further, if consumption growth is positive, the risk-free rate is low and there is a positive rate of time preference, very risk averse investors would want to borrow. However, a low risk-free rate is only possible in equilibrium if investors have a negative rate of time preference which *reduces* their desire to borrow.

Bibliography

Mehra, R., and Prescott, E. (1985). The equity premium: A puzzle. *Journal of Monetary Economics*, **15**, 145–62.

Weil, P. (1989). The equity premium puzzle and the risk-free rate puzzle. *Journal of Monetary Economics*, **24**, 401–21.

ethics in finance

Douglas Wood

Ethics in finance is concerned with the issue of how criteria reflecting the general good and in excess of formal legal or contractual obligations are incorporated into corporate financial decisions. Key areas of application are in remuneration and conduct of agents, informational asymmetry and disclosure, and the degree to which ethical considerations are priced in capital markets and in companies' internal investment evaluations.

Ethical concerns have a long history in finance, both theoretical, as exemplified in the writings of Adam Smith, the father of the market economy (Smith, 1976), and practical, as evidenced by eighteenth- and nineteenth-century Quaker businesses such as Cadbury's, Clarks, or Rowntrees, renowned for the cradle to grave care shown for employees. Although traditionally motivated by religious beliefs, the ethical stance of modern day businesses is more likely to be motivated by concerns over the environment, justice, equal opportunities, and human and animal rights. Anita Roddick's Body Shop is particularly active in pursuing such issues.

Ethical concerns are somewhat at variance with finance theory, which rests on a core assumption of profit maximization or the maximization of shareholder value. In practice many companies adopt policies that appear to sacrifice profits for other objectives, including esteem or reputation, public duty or responsibility, or to reflect a corporate culture in which no advantage is sought which would impose undue losses on stakeholders such as customers, suppliers, or employees, who have no contractual power to enforce such consideration.

Proof that ethical behavior is inconsistent with the various versions of the wealth maximization paradigm used in finance is more elusive. If businesses frequently sacrifice available profit opportunities in recognition of the losses they imply for other parties, or preempt shareholders' choice by distributing shareholders' funds to charitable causes or disadvantaged suppliers, then profit maximization seems implausible as the only or even main element in the objective function. But ethical behavior may not result solely from altruism. It is possible that an ethical stance is simply another dimension in the competitive armory alongside marketing, new technology, or cost management. Volvo's investment in car safety in excess of regulatory and legal requirements (and in excess of plausible estimates of likely benefit) may have been prompted by concern for human life, but equally may have been motivated by a long-sighted strategy to gain competitive advantage (and home market protection) by anticipating rather than resisting standards that now have legal force. A water supply company overhauling its supply network may consider it ethical to use BATNIEC (best available technology not involving excessive cost) as an investment criterion rather than CATNIP (cheapest available technology not involving prosecution), but whether this involves any loss of shareholder wealth depends on contingencies such as the speed with which regulations are tightened and long-term maintenance costs.

Even those companies run by Quaker philanthropists might in the same way realistically expect to recoup the cost of generous employee conditions in higher retention and productivity. Even the British companies taking pride in not paying an invoice before receipt of three reminders and a telephone call might eventually realize that they are paying for the lost interest and administration cost in less competitive supply prices.

Ethics are important in a major area in finance: agency theory (Jensen and Meckling, 1976). Agent–principal problems are widespread in finance because financial management and intermediation provide fertile grounds for conflicts of interest. Creating incentive structures for agents that reward them for optimizing outcomes for the principals or owners is difficult, and monitoring and controlling agents is expensive. An ethical agent exceeding contractual and legislative requirements may derive business advantage as a result of administrative savings for all parties. Not surprisingly, professions such as lawyers and accountants emphasize codes of ethical conduct in recognition of the almost total trust clients have to invest in them.

Asymmetry of information is another fertile area for ethical concerns. Asymmetry occurs between firms and their customers, investors and their companies, and employers and their employees, with complex signaling used alongside formal reporting to convey information. Maintaining dividends to counteract the negative impact of a temporary profit reduction is one common example. If investors were not convinced that this maintenance was ethical, rather than reflecting the directors' best estimate of the sustainable dividend level for their company, the exercise would be pointless.

The ethics of agents and intermediaries are crucial to the operations of financial markets. Agents such as investment banks, stockbrokers, or company managers have an information advantage relative to their principals which they could use to secure excessive and perhaps hidden benefits. A particular concern has been the justification for the terms and conditions of directors of public companies who effectively set not only their own salaries but also bonuses, option packages, and long-term rolling contracts. Since the directors of the institutional shareholders who effectively control public companies enjoy similar privileges, the scope for unethical behavior is wide. Not only are directors' emoluments outside shareholders' control, but they may also install further "poison pill" defenses to deter reform by outside takeover.

The relation to agency and information asymmetry problems might be to increase the use of performance-based pay, but this also raises ethical concerns where the agent is then encouraged to distort the incentive scheme, perhaps by putting losses into a suspense account or by misleading customers in order to get a sale. The result is a discernible move to legislate for greater accountability and disclosure of intermediaries' commissions and company directors' emoluments which previously were hidden from principals. There is also a noticeable trend to formalizing ethical behavior, both through adoption of codes of practice and customer charters by individual institutions and by self-regulating industry associations.

Policing ethical standards, though, is difficult. The consequences of many ethical defaults are ambiguous and they impose diffuse costs on an industry or community rather than on identifiable parties. As a result, unethical behavior appears victimless and even where ethical behavior is enforced by legal sanctions, as for example in the case of insider trading, proving that privileged information has been exploited by company officers or their professional advisors is difficult, and successful prosecutions are rare. Other legislation designed to reinforce ethical standards covering money laundering or international bribery (the US Foreign Corrupt Practices Act) seem to have left business as usual, with private banking a flourishing area, reinforcing the point (Grant, 1991) that legal structures can be manipulated to facilitate unethical behavior. Bankruptcy law, originally designed to facilitate orderly repayment of obligations and to protect employees, is now frequently used to evade liabilities.

High ethical standards in finance can both help and handicap markets. Historically, the high moral hazards of the emerging banking and insurance markets could only be handled by impeccable ethical standards. Lloyds of London, based on unlimited mutual liability, relied on full disclosure of all material facts, underlined by the slogan "my word is my bond." For banks, the standing of directors as "fit and proper" in the eyes of the governor of the Bank of England was as important as a bank's balance sheet. On the other hand, modern derivatives markets only flourished when ethical aversion to speculative trading receded (Raines and Leathers, 1994).

This suggests that ethical behavior is strongest in close knit markets where loss of reputation among customers would produce irretrievable business damage. With a move to globalized rather than local markets and transaction-based rather than relationship-based culture, ethical feedback is weaker and it is indicative that mutual structure in insurance, banking, and savings and loan operations are being transformed into profit-oriented quoted companies operating with formal regulatory structures.

Whether because of declining ethical standards or greater awareness by customers, in recent years there has been a major increase in compliance costs as regulators have sought to modify information asymmetry and agency problems in a range of activities, including sales of financial products, securities transactions, and exploitation of market power, especially by utilities. Although compliance is intended to achieve broadly ethical objectives, the main thrust of

regulation is on training, qualifications, and procedures rather than performance indicators.

Whether regulation removes ethical dilemmas in finance is arguable. Precisely defining what is acceptable, the minimum amount of reserves needed to safeguard bank deposits invested in a particular class of risk asset, or what must be disclosed under accounting standards, may provide institutions with more certainty about acceptable boundaries and hence result in lower standards. Smith's (1992) vigorous criticisms of accountants' exploitation of existing discretion resulted in an overdue reduction in accountants' powers to issue the kind of favorable interpretations where a transaction was exceptional when it made a loss but non-exceptional when profitable.

The growing interest in ethical behavior is also a reflection of a growing militancy by interest groups, which in practice means companies and their officers act in a near altruistic way because their power and wealth make them natural targets. Shell's decision to take the financially attractive option of sinking the Brent Spar rig may or may not have reflected the best scientific advice, but was rapidly reversed by the imminent losses threatened by a consumer boycott of their products. Banks' liquidations of insolvent businesses or building societies repossessing homes are routinely criticized on the grounds that they can afford the losses better than their clients and that the external costs, in terms of knock-on effect on family, community, and indirectly the tax and welfare system, are likely to be substantial.

The main defense for companies is to introduce new standards of observance of environmental and other sensitive areas such as animal rights, backed with high levels of disclosure. It is evident that poor disclosure, whether of commissions, directors' remuneration packages, or the benzene content of bottled water, is increasingly a primary indicator of ethical malpractice.

Private shareholders do have an alternative route of influence and that is to invest in companies (or in mutual funds) which explicitly reject environmentally or ethically sensitive areas of activity. Areas of concern would typically be material exposure to oppressive regimes (with South Africa a *cause célèbre* in apartheid years), producing armaments or military sup-

Table 1   Avoidance and returns

	Environmental avoidance	Ethical avoidance	5-year returns (%)
Friends Provident Stewardship Fund	3	5	50.1
Jupiter Merlin Ecology Fund	5	5	38.1
CIS Environ Trust	2	2	67.8
Scottish Equitable Ethical Unit Trust	0	5	56.7
TSB Environmental Investor Fund	3	0	41.8
FT All Shares			63.8

Source: Holden Meehan, *Sunday Times*, May 21, 1995, p. 43.

plies, producing or selling tobacco and liquor, participating in the nuclear industry or in industries and firms with poor records for prosecution on environmental, safety, product quality grounds, or for misrepresentation and malpractice in selling.

The financial performance of ethical firms or collective investments provides a partial answer to whether there is any conflict between ethical standards and wealth maximization, although many problems of methodology are unresolved. McGuire, Sungren, and Schnewwis (1988) claimed that ethical behavior produced competitive returns, but the study had poor controls for size and industry membership effects. This is important, since the process of screening to avoid particular ethical concerns generally excludes a high proportion of large multibusiness firms, so ethical portfolios are biased towards smaller, riskier firms expected in any event to earn higher returns.

Nor is there a clear measure of ethical strictness. An investment portfolio can be measured fairly straightforwardly for avoidance – in effect, on the percentage of investment in the portfolio which does not have a given exposure – and some typical avoidance and return results are shown in table 1. These indicate that the higher the avoidance (and hence the more restrictions on the portfolio managers) the lower the returns.

Although avoidance measures are easy to calculate, they cover only the negative aspects of ethical performance. Since total avoidance is available through, for example, mortgage-backed securities, investors logically are as concerned about positive objectives as negative. The Co-operative Insurance Society's Environ Trust scores low on avoidance because it invests in companies contributing solutions in environmentally hazardous area or in companies judged as benefiting the general population in an oppressive regime.

Ultimately, if any market includes ethical and ethics-indifferent investors the efficient markets hypothesis would predict that arbitrage by ethics-indifferent investors would eliminate any significant positive (or negative) excess returns in ethical securities. This is illustrated by the Maxus Investment Group, which established an unethical fund in the USA specifically targeting companies with interests in tobacco, gambling, and pornography. The more interesting long-term question is whether an ethical stance increasingly constitutes new and valuable information because it tracks the risk to future profits, as legislation backed policies such as "polluter pays" redirect external costs to the company responsible.

Bibliography

Grant, C. (1991). Friedman fallacies. *Journal of Business Ethics*, **10**, 907–14.

Jensen, M. C., and Meckling, W. (1976). Theory of the firm: Managerial behavior, agency costs and ownership structure. *Journal of Financial Economics*, **3**, 305–60.

McGuire, J. B., Sungren, A., and Schnewwis, T. (1988). Corporate social responsibility and firm financial performance. *Academy of Management Journal*, **31**, 197–204.

Mallin, C. A., Saadouni, B., and Briston, R. J. (1995). The financial performance of ethical investment funds. *Journal of Business Finance and Accounting*, **22**, 483–96.

Raines, J. P., and Leathers, C. G. (1994). Financial derivative instruments and social ethics. *Journal of Business Ethics*, **13**, 197–204.

62   eurocredit markets

Smith, A. (1976). *The Theory of Moral Sentiments*, ed. D. D. Raphael and A. L. MacFie. Oxford: Clarendon Press.

Smith, T. (1992). *Accounting for Growth*. London: Random House.

Sparkes, R. (1995). Providing evidence of good consistent performance in ethical investment. In *The Ethical Investor*. New York: Harper Collins, 102–13.

eurocredit markets

Arie L. Melnik and Steven E. Plaut

During the past decades various international financial markets have grown very rapidly. This growth was accompanied by changes in the process of international financial intermediation (Bloch, 1989; Courtadon, 1985; Miller, 1986). Our purpose here is to survey some of the recent developments in the international credit market. Specifically, we will review some of the regulatory changes that had an impact on international financial markets and describe the trend towards securitization.

DEREGULATION

During the first half of the 1980s several major countries liberalized the way in which their financial markets were regulated. The trend towards deregulation enhanced the integration between the international Euromarket and the national markets of the countries involved (Herring, 1985; McRae, 1985; BIS, 1986). The most noteworthy liberalization measures were undertaken in the USA, but other major countries complemented the trend with their own deregulation. In the early 1980s the UK and Japan abolished restrictions on capital outflows, while West Germany liberalized capital inflows. The integration between the US short-term loan markets and the corresponding euromarkets was aided by US deregulation of domestic interest rate ceilings. A similar effect occurred in France, where banks were permitted to sell foreign currency-denominated CDs.

More recently, many regulations with respect to market participation were liberalized. In Japan, the access of non-resident borrowers to the domestic issue market and the euroyen bond markets has been eased. In Germany, foreign-owned banking entities were allowed to manage euro-DM bond issues. Market integration was aided by the abolition in the USA, UK, France, and Germany of withholding taxes on interest payments to non-residents. The outcome of these developments has been an increasing convergence between domestic and euromarket rates and a growing internationalization of securities markets. One immediate outcome is to link the capital markets more closely to the foreign exchange markets. One example is bonds with currency conversion options (or with dual currency features) that offer a combination of a capital-market asset and a foreign exchange option contract. The tendency to deregulate financial institutions also increased the number of participants in international financial markets.

THE SECURITIZATION OF DEBT

A major recent trend in the international financial market has been the shift of credit flows from bank lending to marketable debt instruments. According to Walter (1988) and Melnik and Plaut (1991), this "securitization" contributed to the liquidity and marketability of debt instruments. The securitization trend has been fostered by the maturing of the eurobond markets, which became broader and more homogeneous, and developed standardized trading practices. It is now common practice to issue bonds through multinational syndicats with well-developed placing power.

The secondary market for eurobonds has grown rapidly. It is relatively free of official regulation and operates through standard clearing mechanisms producing low-cost dealing and delivery. The organization of short-term securities markets is less clearly defined, but the development of new forms of back-up facilities and note issuance facilities (NIFs) is creating access to funds for many new borrowers. The development of both markets was aided by the deregulations that took place in several major countries over the past decades.

In the early 1980s NIFs and euro-commercial paper became an important form of short-term credits, while bonds and floating rate notes (FRNs) accounted for most of the securitized long-term credits. New issue activity rose by close to 400 percent between 1983 and 1993. FRNs range between 12–30 percent of new short-term credit volume. The FRNs introduced new types of interest pricing formulas. A number of issues have contained maximum and minimum interest rates (capped and collared FRNs), either over the life of the instrument or beginning two or three years from original issuance. An interesting feature since 1985 has been the issuance of perpetual FRNs by banks and financial institutions, which must be converted into equity in case of solvency problems.

The fixed-rate sector has grown relatively slowly. It has made increasing use of special features to compensate for lack of attractiveness. Bonds were issued with warrants, some for further issues of bonds, others for shares. This has been particularly popular for euroyen issues. Convertible bonds have been issued for years in international markets, but recently gained market share. Partly paid-up bonds were also issued, which allowed purchasers to defer the payment of principal for some months.

Market Participants

An important outcome of deregulation is the increasing role of foreign banks in national markets. These banks have become major participants in wholesale money markets. Foreign banks have internationalized domestic financial activity by expanding business abroad. An interesting example is the underwriting of securities by banking subsidiaries whose head offices are prohibited from engaging in such activities in their countries of origin.

The international loan market is extremely large. Over 1,200 banks from 50 countries are active in various areas of the eurocredit market. The banks serve three essential economic functions. First, they allocate international funds from surplus units to deficit units. Second, they provide liquidity. Third, the international credit market provides a hedging device for interest rate and foreign exchange exposures. The trend towards securitization appears to be a pattern of providing these three functions in a more cost-efficient manner.

Unlike the situation in various domestic markets, direct participation by commercial banks in the international securities markets as issuers, dealers, underwriters, and investors is very common. The blurring of distinctions between banks, securities brokers, and other financial institutions is manifested in the international credit market. Banks are able to become dealers in the wholesale paper markets of the world either directly or through international subsidiaries. On the other side, investment bankers have also redirected their activities towards more involvement in the international markets. Since they were initially smaller than the universal banks that dominate in Europe, they grew through a series of mergers which led to the disappearance of many institutions, but strengthened the remaining firms.

Securitization of loans by packaging them into marketable instruments has only recently begun to have an impact on the international markets. A few packages of mortgages originating in the USA have recently been funded through eurobond issues. US mortgage-backed securities often include swap components contracted in the euromarket. In the UK, specialized institutions have begun to issue mortgage-backed FRNs aimed at the international investor.

Outright sales of loans by banks, not involving packaging into securities, have also expanded rapidly. This eurolending market may be viewed as a supplement to the market for loan syndications. Banks have also attempted to increase the marketability of their international assets. The two main innovations are the trading of claims on sovereign debtors and a more aggressive selling of participations in syndicated loans. Banks have sought to market their claims on problem debtor countries. Most outright loan sales appear to have been concentrated in higher-quality loans.

In recent years the number of participants in international syndicated loans has increased due to the "repackaging" of loans. The sale of participations, or "subparticipations," is done through assignment and novation. Assignment is based on the creation of transferable loan instruments. Novation involves the replacement of one obligation by the creation of an entirely new one. Both instruments entail the setting up of a register in which transfers of ownership are recorded. Transferability provides the syndicated credit with some of the attributes of securities together with the flexibility and liquidity features of NIFs.

Bibliography

BIS (1986). *Recent Innovations in International Banking*. Basle: Bank for International Settlements.

Bloch, E. (1989). *Inside Investment Banking*, 2nd edn. Homewood, IL: Dow-Jones Irwin.

Courtadon, C. L. (1985). The competitive structure of the eurobond underwriting industry. Salomon Brothers Center Monograph, New York University.

Herring, R. (1985). The interbank market. In P. Savona and G. Sutija (eds.), *Eurodollars and International Banking*. Basingstoke: Macmillan.

McRae, H. (1985). *Japan's Role in the Emerging Global Securities Market*. New York: Group of Thirty.

Melnik, A., and Plaut, S. E. (1991). The short-term eurocredit market. Salomon Brothers Center Monograph, New York University.

Miller, M. H. (1986). Financial innovation: The last twenty years and the next. *Journal of Financial and Quantitative Analysis*, **21**, 459–69.

Walter, I. (1988). *Global Competition in Financial Services*. Cambridge, MA: Ballinger–Harper and Row.

event studies

J. Azevedo Pereira

The term "event study" describes an empirical research design widely used in finance and accounting. Event studies employ a common general methodology aimed at studying the impact of specified economic or financial events on security market behavior. The occurrence of an event is used as the sampling criterion and the objective of the research is to identify information flows and market behavior both before and after the event. Although some event studies have examined the volatility of returns and patterns of trading volume surrounding events (for a review, see Yadav, 1992), most studies have focused on an event and its impact on the market prices of securities. Price-based event studies were originally designed to test the semi-strong form of the efficient market hypothesis (Fama et al., 1969), with the expectation that efficiency would be reflected in a full and immediate response to the new information conveyed by the event. In the mid-1970s a new type of price-based approach was developed (Mandelker, 1974; Dodd and Ruback, 1977) called value event studies; their main aim was not to study market efficiency but to examine the impact of

events on the market value of specific companies (or groups of companies).

The scope of events studied ranges from firm-specific incidents (e.g., announcements of stock splits, or changes in dividend policy) to more general phenomena such as regulatory changes or economic shocks. Analysis occurs over "event windows" or test periods when evidence of abnormal behavior in the market is sought. Such abnormality occurs relative to behavior during an estimation or benchmark period, which is used to estimate the benchmark for the expected behavior of a parameter around the event. Abnormality can occur in the form of abnormal returns, abnormal trading volumes, or changes in the levels of the volatility of returns. The research methodologies used in each case are similar, differing only in respect of evaluating criterion. Accordingly, the brief description that follows will take into account only the general price-based event studies.

Formally, abnormal return is the difference between the actual and expected return during the test period:

$$AR_{it} = R_{it} - R_{it}^*$$

where AR_{it} is the abnormal return on security i during period t, R_{it} the actual return on security i during period t, and R_{it}^* is the expected return on security i during period t. Several alternatives exist to determine the expected return. The market model approach uses a regression analysis (usually OLS) to estimate the security returns as a function of the market index during the estimation period and then uses this model in conjunction with the actual market return during the test period to calculate the expected return. In this case, the classic configuration of the expected return generating model is the following (Fama et al., 1969):

$$R_{it}^* = \alpha_i + \beta_i R_{mt} + u_{it} \text{ for } t = 1, 2, \ldots, T$$

where R_{mt} is the return on the market index for period t (systematic component of return), α_i is the intercept coefficient and β_i is the slope coefficient for security i, u_{it} is the zero mean disturbance term for the return on security i during period t (unsystematic component of return), and T is the number of (sub-)periods during the benchmark period.

The model does not imply the acceptance of any explicit assumptions about equilibrium prices. This fact, and the specific design characteristics, which allow for an easy and powerful statistical treatment, constitute the main reasons for its wide popularity. The alternative mean adjusted method assumes that the best predictor for a security's return is given by historic performance. This assumption implies that each security's expected return is a constant given by its average return during the estimation period:

$$R_{it}^* = \frac{1}{T} \sum_{t=1}^{T} R_{it}$$

where R_{it} is the return on security i over the T (sub-)periods of the estimation interval.

The market adjusted return method assumes that the expected market return constitutes the best predictor for each security's market performance. The market return on the index during the test period is then the predicted return for each security:

$$R_{it}^* = R_{mt}$$

Finally, CAPM-based benchmarks define the expected return of each security as a function of its systematic risk or β and of the market price of risk, effectively the difference between the return on the market index and the return on the risk-free security:

$$R_{it}^* = R_{ft} + \beta_i (R_{mt} - R_{ft})$$

where R_{ft} is the risk-free rate of return during period t and β_i is the systematic risk of the security i (previously estimated with reference to the market index).

A variant of this approach uses a control portfolio benchmark, under which the expected return of a specific security or group of securities is given by the expected return of a portfolio with the same β.

The estimation of expected returns is usually considered the main source of variations in event study methodology. Other aspects of the methodology are (1) the reference basis used to calculate the returns (logarithmic or discrete); (2) the measurement interval (the more common are monthly, weekly, or daily returns); (3) treatment of disturbances during the event window; (4) the duration of the event window; and (5) the choice of market index (where used).

To reflect the uncertain holding period pre- and post-event, it is usual to present the abnormal return in both periodic return form and as cumulative abnormal returns (CAR). The hypothesis normally tested then becomes whether CARs during the test period are significantly different from zero.

Some of the recent developments in event studies are (1) the application of the methodology to the market for debt securities (Crabbe and Post, 1994); (2) the study of the likely implications of non-constant volatility on abnormal return estimates (Boehmer, Musumeci, and Poulsen, 1991); (3) the employment of non-parametric tests of abnormal returns when the usual assumption of normally distributed returns seems problematic (Corrado, 1989); and (4) the implementation of multiple regression approaches based on the application of joint generalized least squares (GLS) techniques (Bernard, 1987).

The volume of event study literature has grown significantly in recent years and shows every sign of continued expansion. At the theoretical level, two topics for continuing research are the control for extra market effects in the securities return generating processes, and the handling of statistical problems caused by samples of thinly traded securities. At the empirical level, the great challenge is accounting for the observed abnormal returns.

Bibliography

Bernard, V. L. (1987). Cross-sectional dependence and problems in inference in market-based accounting research. *Journal of Accounting Research*, **25**, 1–48.

Boehmer, E., Musumeci, J., and Poulsen, A. B. (1991). Event-study methodology under conditions of event-induced variance. *Journal of Financial Economics*, **30**, 253–72.

Brown, S. J., and Warner, J. B. (1980). Measuring security price performance. *Journal of Financial Economics*, 8, 205–58.

Brown, S. J., and Warner, J. B. (1985). Using daily stock returns: The case of event studies. *Journal of Financial Economics*, **14**, 3–32.

Corrado, C. J. (1989). A non-parametric test for abnormal security-price performance in event studies. *Journal of Financial Economics*, 23, 385–95.

Crabbe, L., and Post, M. A. (1994). The effect of a rating downgrade on outstanding commercial paper. *Journal of Finance*, 49, 39–56.

Dodd, P., and Ruback, R. (1977). Tender offers and stockholder returns: An empirical analysis. *Journal of Financial Economics*, 5, 351–73.

Fama, E. F., Fisher, L., Jensen, M., and Roll, R. (1969). The adjustment of stock prices to new information. *International Economic Review*, 10, 1–21.

Mandelker, G. (1974). Risk and return: The case of merging firms. *Journal of Financial Economics*, 1, 303–36.

Salinger, M. (1992). Value event studies. *Review of Economics and Statistics*, 74, 671–7.

Strong, N. (1992). Modeling abnormal returns: A review article. *Journal of Business Finance and Accounting*, 19, 533–53.

Yadav, P. K. (1992). Event studies based on volatility of returns and trading volume: A review. *British Accounting Review*, 24, 157–85.

exotic options

Dean A. Paxson

Exotic options are possibly defined as all options that are not "vanilla" options, with a predefined (or constant) exercise price and time to expiration, and where there is one underlying asset. Thus, exotic options may have uncertain exercise prices, expiration times, and several underlying assets, which may not follow lognormal or normal diffusion processes.

Characteristic exotic options include Asian options, where the exercise price and/or the underlying asset is an average of prices defined over some time period; barrier options, where the option is initiated or extinguished if the asset price hits a specific, predetermined level; chooser options, where the holder has the choice after a number of days whether to hold a call or a put on the underlying asset; compound options, which are options on options; and lookback options, where the call option holder has the right to buy/sell at the minimum/maximum price recorded over the option lifetime. Perhaps the primary identifying characteristic of exotic options is that the field is particularly fertile for combinations and permutations of the generic exotic types, and options involving innovative characteristics, ideal for creative artists.

The valuation of exotic options is sometimes simply through building blocks of vanilla-type options, perhaps with the asset-price volatility modified (as in Margrabe, 1978), or averaged, as in Asian options. Some illustrations are provided below for such building-block approaches, involving closed-form solutions for barriers, choosers, and lookbacks. Otherwise, the path-dependent options such as barriers and lookbacks, the multivariate spread and correlation products, and the nested options, such as complex choosers and compounded options, are valued through numerical methods, including Monte Carlo simulations, lattice methods, and explicit and implicit finite differences.

BRIEF HISTORY OF THEORY AND PRACTICE

Being first in exotic-option theory is alleged of many authors, including Merton (1973), who values a "down and out" barrier option. Earlier, Cox and Miller (1965) provided solutions for homogeneous diffusion processes with absorbing barriers, and there were many predecessors. Margrabe (1978) provided a simple valuation for an option to exchange one asset for another, now used for spread options. Geske (1979) valued compound options, while Goldman, Sosin, and Gatto (1979) provided the valuation methodology for lookback options, without regret, buying at the low and selling at the high.

The Rubinstein (1991) working paper has been widely circulated and published, along with many other authors. Thus, exotic options are no longer so "strikingly unusual or colorful in appearance or effect," as finance textbooks such as Gemmill (1993) provide solutions and illustrations.

The use of exotic options is largely anecdotal, since only a few exotics have been exchange traded. No doubt there were many embedded options in contracts and bonds, such as the publicly traded Petro-Lewis 9 percent guaranteed oil-indexed notes issued in April 1981 which had contingent interest based on lookback Asian barrier features, prior to the academic and investment banking "discoveries" of exotics in the late 1980s.

Perhaps a distinguishing feature of exotics is that options may and are designed to suit almost any conceivable or desired payoff structure for an investor, or for a producer/consumer who seeks a complex, customized hedge for commodity, interest rate, equity, currency, or other asset/liability exposure.

BARRIER OPTIONS

An extinguish (or absorbing) barrier option is a vanilla option from the contract date until (or if) the underlying asset hits a predetermined level, and the option is "knocked out." Thus, the potential time of the option is uncertain and is no greater than a vanilla option with the same original time to expiration. An exercisable (or knock in) option is activated only when the barrier has been hit. In both cases, when the barrier is hit, either the option expires or is exercised or the then time to expiration is specified.

There are a wide variety of barrier options, including the simple knockouts, such as down and out call, down and out put, up and out call, and up and out put; the knockups, down and in call, down and in put, up and in call, and up and in put; and other combinations, such as the knockout must be both up and down or either up and down (double barriers); or there are a specified number of partial sufficient, or necessary, barriers for knockout or knockin.

A simple valuation of down and in call barriers (without any rebates) is:

$$\text{Call}_{D,I} = Se^{-\delta T}(H/S)^{2\lambda}N(y) \\ - Xe^{-rT}(H/S)^{2\lambda-2}N(y - \sigma\sqrt{T})$$

where

$$\lambda = (r - \delta + \sigma^2/2)/\sigma^2 \\ y = \ln[H^2/(SX)]/\sigma\sqrt{T} + \lambda\sigma\sqrt{T}$$

and S is the underlying asset, T is the time to expiration (if barrier not hit), r is the riskless rate, X is the exercise price, H is the barrier, is the underlying asset payout rate, δ is the volatility of underlying asset, and N is the cumulative normal distribution; then

$$\text{Call}_{D,O} = \text{Call (Vanilla)} - \text{Call}_{D,I}$$

With these building blocks, plus a few additions, Rich (1994) shows how to construct a long menu of barriers.

CHOOSER OPTIONS

A curious convention is that choosers are options for the undecided, or "as you like it" options. For payment today, the holder has the right (and requirement) to choose, after t days, whether to hold a call or put on the underlying asset. This enables the investor to establish a long position in volatility, but unlike a vanilla straddle or strangle, the investor is forced to abandon one option at the decision or choice date.

If the call and put have a common exercise price and (initially) remaining time to expiration, the chooser payoff is:

$$\text{MAX}[C(X, T - t), P(X, T - t)]$$

where $C(X,T - t)$ is the value of a call option and $P(X,T - t)$ is the value of a put option.

If t_1 is the time of required choice, and S_1 is the asset price at t_1, the European put-call parity theorem implies:

$$\text{MAX}[C, (C - S_1e^{-\delta(T-t_1)} + Xe^{-r(T-t_1)})] \\ = C(X, T) + \text{MAX}[0, Xe^{-(r-\delta)(T-t_1)} - S_1]$$

or

$$= C(X, T) + \text{MAX}[0, Xe^{-r(T-t_1)} - S_1e^{-\delta(T-t_1)}]$$

which is the same as a call option with maturity $e^{-\delta(T-t)}1$ put options with $Xe^{-(r-\delta)(T-t)}1$ and maturity t_1.

This package has the same value as:

$$Se^{-\delta(T-t)}N(a) - Xe^{-r(T-t)}N(a - \sigma\sqrt{T}) \\ - Se^{-\delta(T-t)}N(-b) + Xe^{-r(T-t)}N(-b + \sigma\sqrt{t_1})$$

where

$$a = [\ln(Se^{-\delta(T-t)}/Xe^{-r(T-t)}) \div \sigma\sqrt{T}] + \frac{1}{2}\sigma\sqrt{T}$$

$$b = [\ln(Se^{-\delta(T-t)}/Xe^{-r(T-t)}) \div \sigma\sqrt{t_1}] + \frac{1}{2}\sigma\sqrt{t_1}$$

LOOKBACK OPTIONS

The lookback option is termed an option for investing without any regrets, or always buying at the low and/or selling at the high, or for investors without any market-timing ability.

While the option holder is guaranteed the "best" price over a specified period, the disadvantage is the high cost, compared to a plain vanilla option.

The payoff from a lookback call is: MAX (0, $S_T - S_{\min}$) and the initial value is:

$$Se^{-\delta T}N(a_1) - Se^{-\delta T}\frac{\sigma^2}{2(r - \delta)}$$
$$* N(-a_1) - S_{\min}e^{-rT}[N(a_2)$$
$$- \frac{\sigma^2}{2(r - \delta)}e^{Y_1}N(-a_3)]$$

where $S^{\min}$ is the minimum value achieved to date (Gemmill, 1993) and

$$a_1 = \frac{\ln(S/S_{\min}) + (r - \delta + \sigma^2/2)T}{\sigma\sqrt{T}}$$

$$a_2 = a_1 - \sigma\sqrt{T}$$

$$a_3 = \frac{\ln(S/S_{\min}) + (-r + \delta + \sigma^2/2)T}{\sigma\sqrt{T}}$$

$$Y_1 = -\frac{2(r - \delta - \sigma^2/2)\ln(S/S_{\min})}{\sigma^2}$$

RESEARCH AND PRACTICAL ISSUES

Exotic options may be adapted to suit a wide variety of investment objectives and exposures, often derived directly from the solutions provided for certain types of partial differential equations. However, with complexity, both the assumed usage and conceivable dynamic hedging processes may become problematical. Since exotics are by definition innovative, new exotic formations and combinations should be a growing industry. Plausible exotics may cover all sorts of distribution functions, chapters of texts on probability and measure, and STOCHASTIC PROCESSES, including fat tails (see FAT TAILS IN FINANCE), and extremes, incorporating stochastic volatility, correlation, and discontinuities.

Bibliography

Cox, D. R., and Miller, H. D. (1965). *The Theory of Stochastic Processes*. London: Chapman and Hall.

Gemmill, G. (1993). *Options Pricing*. London: McGraw-Hill.

Geske, R. (1979). The valuation of compound options. *Journal of Financial Economics*, 7, 63–81.

Goldman, M. B., Sosin, H. B., and Gatto, M. A. (1979). Path dependent options: "Buy at the low, sell at the high." *Journal of Finance*, 34, 1111–27.

Margrabe, W. (1978). The value of an option to exchange one asset for another. *Journal of Finance*, 33, 177–86.

Merton, R. C. (1973). The theory of rational option pricing. *Bell Journal of Economics*, 4, 141–83.

Rich, D. R. (1994). The mathematical foundations of barrier option-pricing theory. *Advances in Futures and Options Research*, 7, 267–311.

Rubinstein, M. (1991). Exotic options. Working paper, University of California.

expectations

Suresh Deman

Expectations arise when economic agents make decisions in a world involving uncertainty. If we were living in a world of perfect information with unbounded rationality, the notion of expectation would be irrelevant. However, the reality of the world is much more complex than captured by theoretical models. The concept of expectations, like love, has many splendorous dimensions. In finance and economics, its applications include the theories of intertemporal consumption, labor supply decisions, theory of firm's pricing, sale, investment or inventory decisions, theories of insurance, financial markets, and search behavior, signaling, AGENCY THEORY, and corporate takeovers, etc. In fact, expectations are implicit in the study of all behavioral models.

The use of expectations appears to be similar in all academic disciplines. However, there are some important distinctions. For example, the term "expectations" used in economics does not necessarily conform to the term "expectations" used in the statistical theory of probability. Linear utility functions exhibit risk-neutral behavior and may give rise to models in which agents care only about the mathematical expectations of variables. In the models in finance, mathematical expectations of returns on various assets are equalized. Quadratic expected utility functions may also produce a model in which mathematical expectations become important.

The concept of expectations has a wide range of applications in economics, business, and finance. Simple expectations proxies are proposed by Fisher (1930), and a variation on Fisher's expectation mechanism of adaptive expectations is given by Cagan (1956). Alternatives to adaptive expectations are regressive expectations, expectations of experts, rational expectations versus mechanical expectation proxies, mathematical expectations, etc. In fact, expectations are the reality of modeling of stochastic processes. One of the most useful applications of expectations in economic and finance is expected utility theory. According to the expected utility hypothesis, individual decision-makers possess a "Von Neumann–Morgenstern utility function" defined over every conceivable outcome. Individuals faced with alternative risky "lotteries" over these outcomes will choose that prospect which maximizes the expected value of utility function $\{Ui\}$.

The expected utility hypothesis can be applied to a variety of situations because the outcomes of "lotteries" could be alternative wealth levels, multidimensional commodity bundles, time streams of consumption, or even qualitative consequences (e.g., a trip to Pink City Jaipur), etc. Most research in the economics of uncertainty and all applied research in the field of optimal trade, investment, or search under uncertainty, is carried out in the framework of expected utility. In Arrow–Debreu general equilibrium theory, the expected utility model proceeds by specifying a set of objects of choice. It is assumed that the individual possesses a preference ordering over these objects (in the sense that one object is preferred to another if, and only if, it is assigned a higher value by this preference function) which can be represented by a real valued function $V(.)$.

The expected utility model (under uncertainty) differs from the theory of choice over non-stochastic commodity bundles in two important ways. First, in the expected utility model, choice is made under uncertainty; the objects of choice are not deterministic outcomes, but rather probability distributions over the outcomes. Second, unlike the non-stochastic case, the expected utility model imposes a very specific restriction on the functional form of the preference function $V(.)$. Mathematically speaking, the hypothesis that the preference function $V(.)$ takes the form of a statistical expectation is equivalent to the condition that it be "linear in

the probabilities." In the Von Neumann–Morgenstern utility function, this assumption is a primary feature of the expected utility model and provides the basis for many of its observable implications and predictions.

At this stage, it is important to distinguish between the preference function $V(.)$ and the Von Neumann–Morgenstern utility function $U(.)$ of an expected utility maximizer, particularly with respect to the mistaken belief that expected utility preferences are somehow "cardinal" in a sense that is not represented by preferences over non-stochastic commodity bundles. An expected utility function $V(.)$ is "ordinal" because it may be subject to any increasing transformation without affecting the validity of the representation. One important property stems from the above characterization of utility function that $U(x)$ be an increasing function of x. Rothschild and Stiglitz (1970, 1971) have generalized the notion of a mean preserving increase in risk to density functions or cumulative distribution functions. The algebraic condition for risk aversion generalizes to the condition that $U''(x) < 0$ for all x which implies that the Von Neumann–Morgenstern utility function $U(.)$ is concave.

Arrow (1971) and Pratt (1964) have contributed a great deal to the analytical capabilities of the expected utility model for the study of behavior under uncertainty. They showed that the "degree" of concavity of the Von Neumann–Morgenstern utility function can be used to provide a measure of an expected utility maximizer's degree of risk aversion. The curvature measure of $R(x) - U''(x)/U'(x)$ is known as the Arrow–Pratt index of absolute risk aversion. The certainty equivalence and asset demand conditions makes the Arrow–Pratt measure an important result in expected utility theory. Ross (1981) gave an alternative and stronger formulation of comparative risk aversion. According to Hey (1979), the application of the expected utility model extends to virtually all branches of economic theory, but much of the flavor of these can be sensed from Arrow's (1971) analysis of the portfolio problem. If $R(x)$ is a decreasing (increasing) function of the individual's wealth level x, then it would mean that an increase in initial wealth will always increase (decrease) the demand for the risky asset if, and only if, $U(.)$

exhibits "decreasing (increasing) absolute risk aversion in wealth."

Finally, we focus on axiomatic developments in expected utility theory. There exist quite a few formal axiomatizations of the expected utility model in different contexts in Von Neumann and Morgenstern (1944), Marschak (1950), Herstein and Milnor (1953), and Savage (1954). Most of these axiomatizations proceed by specifying an outcome space and postulating that the individual's preferences over probability distributions on the outcome space satisfy the following four axioms: completeness, transitivity, continuity, and the independence axiom. It is beyond the scope of this short piece to provide a derivation and explanation of these axioms and sketch a proof. Researchers have begun to develop alternative formulations of expected utility models by taking into account first order stochastic dominance preference and risk aversion.

Bibliography

Arrow, K. J. (1971). *Essays in the Theory of Risk-Bearing.* Chicago: Markham.

Cagan, P. (1956). The monetary dynamics of hyperinflation. In M. Friedman (ed.), *Studies in the Quantity Theory of Money.* Chicago: University of Chicago Press.

Debreu, G. (1959). *Theory of Value.* New York: Wiley.

Fisher, I. (1930). *The Theory of Interest.* New York: Macmillan.

Herstein, I., and Milnor, J. (1953). An axiomatic approach to measurable utility. *Econometrica*, **21**, 291–7.

Hey, J. (1979). *Uncertainty in Microeconomics.* Oxford: Martin Robinson.

Marschak, J. (1950). Rational behavior, uncertain prospects, and measurable utility. *Econometrica*, **18**, 111–41.

Pratt, J. (1964). Risk aversion in the small and in the large. *Econometrica*, **32**, 122–36.

Ross, S. (1981). Some stronger measures of risk aversion in the small and in the large with applications. *Econometrica*, **49**, 621–38.

Rothschild, M., and Stiglitz, J. (1970). Increasing risk I: A definition. *Journal of Economic Theory*, **2**, 225–43.

Rothschild, M. and Stiglitz, J. (1971). Increasing risk II: Its economic consequences. *Journal of Economic Theory*, **3**, 66–84.

Savage, L. (1954). *The Foundations for Statistics.* New York: John Wiley.

Von Neumann, J., and Morgenstern, O. (1944). *The Theory of Games and Economic Behavior*, 1st edn. Princeton, NJ: Princeton University Press.

experimental asset markets

Steven Peterson

Experimental asset markets are multiple-period laboratory double-auction markets utilizing human subjects who trade asset units with fundamental values determined by well-defined (perhaps stochastic) dividend streams. Traders' monetary payoffs are typically tied to individual performance (e.g., traders attempt to maximize earnings in the form of per share dividend payments and capital gains). The seminal work on double auction design was due to Smith (1962). Methodological precepts, which govern virtually all current experimental asset market designs, originated with Smith (1982).

Essentially, experimental asset markets were developed to investigate and test various hypotheses which followed from the theory of efficient markets. In particular, attention has centered on various predictions concerning market efficiency in the presence of rational expectations. These include tests for the existence of both weak-form and strong-form efficiency (i.e., asset prices reflect all public and private information, respectively), along with the ability of the market to both disseminate and aggregate diverse private information, as well as the study of individual expectation formation. As such, a fundamental cornerstone of the research investigates the diffusion of information in the market in the presence of trader uncertainty.

In general, the multiple period setting of asset markets presents several sources of trader uncertainty. Uncertainty may derive from diverse expectations among traders concerning the movement of future prices conditional on a distribution governing states of the world such as dividend payout. Uncertainty may also present itself in the form of private information concerning trader type (e.g., assets have differing valuations depending on trader-type endowments). Otherwise, uncertainty emanates from individual differences in home-grown expectations governing the expectation formation process and uncertainty regarding the future movements of prices. It is the assumptions regarding the formation of expectations that discriminate between competing models of asset valuation. As such, the object of investigation is to observe individual decision-making in an environment in which uncertainty generated by the diversity of states and trader types is the experimental control.

Early laboratory studies examined whether asset markets were informationally efficient, and presented results which indicated that market efficiency is generally robust to information asymmetries. Controlling for trader type uncertainty, Forsythe, Palfrey, and Plott (1982) present evidence indicating convergence to strong-form efficiency. Essentially, the design consisted of repeated two-period asset markets with trader type uncertainty (i.e., share value was private information and differed in each period for each trader type). Two types of equilibria are possible: a naive equilibrium which results when traders value assets based solely on their private information regarding dividend values and a full information, and rational equilibrium which results from the dissemination of otherwise private information into the market. It is the rational equilibrium that the market converged to in repeated sessions and, hence, generated support for strong-form market efficiency. Plott and Sunder (1982) examined essentially the same issue but in the presence of state uncertainty in which dividend payout followed a probability distribution and certain traders were given more information than others regarding payout states. The experimental evidence showed that the market reveals insider information; market prices converge quickly to a fully revealing rational expectations equilibrium.

Extensions followed. Forsythe and Lundholm (1990) examine information aggregation rather than information dissemination in a series of experiments looking at whether markets are capable of efficiently aggregating a highly diverse, but sufficient, body of information. The issue here, as above, is whether traders can form inferences about market fundamentals through an examination of publicly available information on bids, asks, and contracts. They conclude that, in the presence of diverse private information, trading experience and complete information are jointly sufficient to generate a rational equilibrium. Copeland and Friedman (1987, 1991) extend the analysis in an examination of the sequential revelation of private information to uninformed traders.

Other asset market experiments differ markedly in their designs and investigative intent. Smith, Suchanek, and Williams (1988) utilize a multi-period finite horizon model with state uncertainty regarding dividend payout, but with no private information beyond individual endowments, to examine bubble behavior (e.g., market prices that deviate from fundamentals). Traders' one-period ahead forecasts of market prices were simultaneously solicited to test various theories of expectation formation. Market prices were observed repeatedly to exhibit bubble–crash behavior and expectation formation was best characterized as adaptive (not rational) in character. What caused these bubbles is not clear. Speculative behavior is theoretically impossible in finite horizon experiments. Other explanations, however, suggest these bubbles occur due to incomplete learning. Subsequent experiments did indicate that expectations do converge to rational expectations as traders gain experience, and prices tended to vary little relative to fundamentals.

Other experiments have examined the efficiency of dividend signals by measuring the noise content of the signal but still leave the dividend puzzle an unresolved issue. Still others have altered the finite dimensionality of the design to test for the presence of speculative behavior. These designs essentially involve a probabilistic horizon in which subsequent trading periods occur conditional on the outcome of a random draw. In such cases, the (known) probability of continuing serves the same function as the discount rate in conventional asset valuation mathematics. These experiments show definite evidence of speculative bubbles which occur despite the absence of private information. As such, the concept of market efficiency is not yet a resolved issue. In addition, investigators have designed asset market experiments to examine the issue of form versus substance; that is, whether traders prefer one asset over another because form matters even though both assets are substantively identical in terms of fundamental value. The evidence at this point is inconclusive, but the research is important nevertheless, because should form matter, then asset values may be more than merely functions of discounted dividend streams.

Experimental asset markets are an invaluable research resource since they permit the investigator to extract a sufficient level of institutional detail necessary to an examination of the research objective and abstract away unnecessary sources of noise. At the same time, the experimental designs allow one to exercise the necessary level of control through a judicious choice of structural designs and parameterizations in order to collect data necessary for strong statistical tests of underlying hypotheses.

Bibliography

Copeland, T. E., and Friedman, D. (1987). The effect of sequential information arrival on asset prices: An experimental study. *Journal of Finance*, **42**, 763–97.

Copeland, T. E., and Friedman, D. (1991). Partial revelation of information in experimental asset markets. *Journal of Finance*, **46**, 265–95.

Forsythe, R., and Lundholm, R. (1990). Information aggregation in an experimental market. *Econometrica*, **58**, 309–47.

Forsythe, R., Palfrey, T. R., and Plott, C. R. (1982). Asset valuation in an experimental market. *Econometrica*, **50**, 537–82.

Plott, C. R., and Sunder, S. (1982). Efficiency of experimental security markets with insider information: An application of rational expectations models. *Journal of Political Economy*, **90**, 663–98.

Smith, V. L. (1962). An experimental study of competitive market behavior. *Journal of Political Economy*, **70**, 111–37.

Smith, V. L. (1982). Microeconomic systems as an experimental science. *American Economic Review*, **72**, 923–55.

Smith, V. L., Suchanek, G. L., and Williams, A. W. (1988). Bubbles, crashes and endogenous expectations in experimental spot asset markets. *Econometrica*, **56**, 1119–51.

F

Fama-French Three Factor Model

see PORTFOLIO THEORY AND ASSET PRICING

fat tails in finance

Paul Kofman

Fat tails refer to the excessive probability of "extreme" observations in a distribution. Natural disasters are a fact of life. They tend to have dreadful consequences, but fortunately, occur very rarely. Except for the occasional last-minute warning, they also have the nasty habit of being unpredictable. However, that does not imply that their probability is zero. Financial disasters are rather similar. Stock market crashes, oil crises, and exchange rate collapses occasionally remind us that there is a very relevant probability of observing extreme values. The magnitude of the fall out from such disasters explains the attention they attract, which is disproportionate to their supposedly minute probabilities of occurrence. Actuarial studies have acknowledged this fact for a long time. Estimating the probability of ruin is one of the major tasks new actuaries have to learn.

Attracted by expected payoffs, investors in financial markets are often lured into investing in high-risk assets. The downside risk is then managed or even fully covered by installing safeguards, such as stop loss or limit orders. As long as the market moves smoothly this does indeed guarantee a well-timed exit from an adverse market. However, it is well known that markets occasionally jump, sometimes excessively. In such situations, a market could suffocate from the accumulation of exit orders. While recently introduced circuit breakers provide market makers and brokers with valuable time to realign their positions, they do not offer similar protection for small investors. For them, it is crucial to have at least some probabilistic idea of these "catastrophes." Estimating these probabilities based on the past worst experience is not a good idea. The fact that probabilistically some observations occur on average only once every decade, or once every hundred years or more, indicates that so far we might have been just lucky in not observing a worse crash.

To specify these extreme probabilities, the finance literature usually prefers a "normal" stochastic process, like a Brownian motion, or a lognormal distribution with autoregressive conditional heteroskedasticity (ARCH) errors. That may be valid in a risk-neutral environment, but for the risk-averse investor an implied disaster probability of virtually zero might be fatal. Empirically, we know that financial prices do not at all behave like they are normally distributed. The pioneering studies by Mandelbrot (1963) and Fama (1963) acknowledge the fact that the observed fat tails are not well captured by normal distributions. Therefore, the Pareto or sum stable distributions (including the normal as a special case) have been suggested as a likely alternative. Cornew, Town, and Crowson (1984) give empirical applications for different distributions nested within this class. Praetz (1972) and Blattberg and Gonedes (1974) proposed yet another class of distributions that had one major advantage over the Paretian class. The Student-t, while still being fat tailed, has a finite variance unlike the Paretian. This fits better with the assumptions underlying asset pricing models.

An alternative model that also retains the finite variance property is given by Engle's (1982) ARCH process for normally distributed innovations in asset prices. Instead of focusing on the unconditional distribution, ARCH specifies a conditional distribution for the variance. However, the apparent popularity of these models for describing the clusters in volatility falls short when evaluating their excess kurtosis capacity. A second normality preserving approach is given by the mixtures-of-distributions hypothesis (Tauchen and Pitts, 1983). But due to the necessary specification of a mixing process, or variable, this approach tends to be difficult to implement.

ESTIMATION PROCEDURES

The first step one should consider before engaging in any formal estimation is a simple plot of the empirical cumulative distribution function of variable X, versus a comparable (standardized by mean and variance) normal cumulative distribution. One can immediately observe the amount of excessive empirical "frequency" at the lower or upper tail. Combined with more than normal probability in the center of the distribution, this phenomenon is known as leptokurtosis. Kurtosis (K) values exceeding 3, which is the normal value, point toward fat-tailed distributions. Unfortunately, a single extreme value may dramatically inflate the value of K. Formal testing of normality is based on two common tests. The Jarque–Bera (JB) test for normality uses both K and the measure for skewness (the normal being a symmetric non-skewed distribution): high values of JB point towards rejection of normality. Unfortunately, this test does not help us any further to indicate what an appropriate distribution would be.

A more enlightening insight may be obtained by focusing exclusively on the tails and plotting the "extreme" empirical quantiles versus different theoretical quantiles. For these different theoretical distributions, we can then apply a goodness-of-fit test:

$$GF = \sum_{i=1}^{k} \frac{(O_i - E_i)^2}{E_i} \qquad (1)$$

where we split the empirical frequency distribution into k quantiles and compare the observed frequency per quantile (O_i) with the theoretically expected frequency for that quantile(E_i). This KS test is chi-squared distributed with $k - 1$ degrees of freedom.

RESIDUAL LIFE AND DURATION MODELS

The first formal model we discuss is usually encountered in the actuarial literature, where the concept of "mean residual life" $e(.)$ is specified as follows:

$$e(x) = E(X - x | X \geq x)$$
$$= \int_x^{\infty} (q - x) \frac{f(q)}{\int_x^{\infty} f(q) \mathrm{d}q} \qquad (2)$$

This $e(x)$ is the complete expectation of "life." Obviously, life can be interpreted as the remaining tail size of X given that X is larger than some prespecified level x. This exceedance function can then take several shapes depending on different underlying distributions $F(x)$, the probability density function of X. The empirical $e^*(x)$ is a simple averaging process:

$$e_m(X_{(i)}) = \frac{1}{m-1} \sum_{i=1}^{m-1} X_{(i)} - X_{(m)} \qquad (3)$$

where the subscript (i) relates to the ordered observations X_i, in descending order. The next step then consists of fitting theoretical $e(.)$ to the $e^*(m)$ (.). Two techniques are typically used: either maximum likelihood estimation, or a minimizing distance measure (minimizing the distance between the empirical $F^*(x)$ and the theoretical $F(x)$, as in the GF test). Failure time or duration models are very similar to these residual life models. They also condition on a prespecified high level x, and then fit different distributions to the remaining tail. For that purpose, a derived probability function, the so-called survival function $S(x) = 1 - F(x)$, is used. After fitting $S(x)$, we can specify an inverse survival function which generates quantiles $Z(a)$ that are exceeded by X with some prespecified probability a.

These fitting techniques have a drawback: if the distributions are not nested, or they do not have a finite variance, they are no longer valid. The next tool avoids that problem.

EXTREME VALUE MODELS

A stationary time series $X_1, X_2, \ldots, X_n$ of independent and identically distributed random variables has some unknown distribution function $F(x)$. The probability that the maximum M_n of the first n random variables is below some prespecified level is given as:

$$P(M_n \leq x) = F^n(x) \qquad (4)$$

Even though we do not know which F applies, extreme value theory shows that after suitable normalization, this maxima distribution converges asymptotically to a limit-law extreme value distribution $G(x)$. $G(x)$ can be of three types where the main feature of distinction is the speed by which its tails decline. If they decline exponentially, the domain of attraction is given by a Gumbel distribution (encompassing the exponential and normal distributions). If, on the other hand, they decline by a power (hence much slower), the domain of attraction is given by Fréchet distributions (encompassing fat-tailed Paretian and Student-t distributions). In the likely latter case, we can estimate the tail shape parameter based on a sequence of the largest order statistics $X(i)$ – the ordered empirical maxima. The Hill (1975) estimator:

$$\hat{\alpha} = \left[\frac{1}{m-1} \sum_{i=1}^{m-1} \ln\left(X_{(i)}\right) - \ln\left(X_{(m)}\right) \right]^{-1} \qquad (5)$$

uses m as the number of order statistics considered to be the tail in the sample. The choice of m is the controversial part of this procedure. Including too many observations from the center of the distribution will lead to an increase in bias, while restricting too much will lead to an undesirable efficiency loss. So far, no undisputed procedure has been developed to estimate m. (For a number of m-estimators, see Kalb, Kofman, and Vorst, 1996.) Fortunately, for financial applications, choosing m is less relevant, given the very long time series. The availability of transaction prices has even further alleviated this problem.

With the chosen m, we can proceed with equation (5) and, based on the α-estimate, discriminate among a wide class of (not necessarily nested) distributions. For the Paretian distributions to be acceptable, α (their characteristic exponent) should be less than two. For values of α exceeding two, the Student-t distributions are more likely (where α equals the degrees of freedom). For α approaching infinity, this im-

plies a normal distribution. Having an estimate for this tail parameter, we can also calculate exceedance quantiles:

$$\hat{x}_p = \frac{\left(\frac{m}{2n(p)}\right)^{1/\hat{\alpha}} - 1}{1 - 2^{-1/\hat{\alpha}}} [X_{(n-m/2)} - X_{(n-m)}] \\ + X_{(n-m/2)} \qquad (6)$$

where tail parameter α has been obtained above, and p is some chosen probability. Since we are interested in threshold levels x_p for which $1 - F(x_p) = p$, being extremely small (in fact $p < 1/n$), the empirical distribution function is no longer of use. Extreme value theory, however, does allow probability statements beyond this p-limit, by extrapolating the empirical distribution function based on the estimated tail shape. Hence, we can even make "precise" statements on the probability of so far not observed catastrophic observations.

The major advantage of extreme value distributions is that they are limit distributions. This implies that regardless of the data generating $F(x)$, for large values of m, they become good approximations. If $F(x)$ were known, of course, the use of limiting distributions should be avoided. In that case the true distribution of extremes is known as well.

In conducting tail analysis, we often assume that the extreme observations are independently and identically distributed. However, it is well known that clusters occur in both small values and large values. The ARCH models are especially designed to capture this phenomenon. In principle, however, each of the above mentioned tail approaches can be adapted to cover clustering effects. One attractive "mixing" approach is given by the EM models.

Mixtures modeling by expectation maximization (EM) analysis Kalb, Kofman, and Vorst (1996) develop a novel approach where the extreme value method is combined with an EM algorithm to capture potential mixtures of distributions. Since maximum likelihood is generally preferred as the statistically most efficient approach, we would like to incorporate its application while acknowledging the non-nesting problems. A two-stage procedure is proposed where the discrimination among classes of distributions is conducted by extreme value estimation. This results in a tail parameter which indicates the appropriate class. The second stage then exploits this information by further refining the parameter estimates (plus additional characterizing parameters) by maximum likelihood estimation. We use the extreme value distribution class as input in the likelihood function, and reestimate its parameters. This will also provide a check on the appropriateness of the chosen m. If the updated tail parameter differs too much from the extreme value stage, one has to rethink the choice of m, and repeat the first stage. The extended parameter set in the second stage allows for incorporating particular anomalies in the tail observations like size clustering. The actuarial application given in Kalb, Kofman, and Vorst (1996) can easily be adjusted to also allow for temporal clustering effects that are typical for financial time series.

SOME EMPIRICAL FINDINGS

The empirical evidence based on residual life models seems restricted to actuarial applications giving mixed results (see Hogg and Klugman, 1983). Increasing "residual lives" either indicate a Paretian distribution, or perhaps a Weibull or lognormal distribution. Fitting is performed by maximum likelihood, after which a likelihood ratio test can be used to discriminate among these distributions.

Extreme value estimates　Since the residual life plots are rather restricted, we may resort to more powerful discerning techniques. Extreme value theory has by now been applied to many financial time series. Examples are Jansen and de Vries (1991) for stock returns, and Koedijk, Schafgans, and de Vries (1990) for exchange rates. Empirical evidence for exchange rates points towards extremely fat-tailed Paretian distributions. This is even true for fixed exchange rates, perhaps due to the inevitable occasional devaluations.

Consequences of fat-tailedness　When we know (or have an estimate for) the tail probabilities, how can we usefully apply them? First of all, we have to be sure that our probability estimates have a low standard error. Both exaggerating and underestimating extreme risk could be very costly. The following applications will briefly indicate why it is important to optimally deter-

mine the tails. Obviously, probability statements do not help us in forecasting asset prices (except perhaps in option pricing), nor do they indicate when a particularly large observation is going to occur. It does help, however, to attach appropriate probabilities of occurrence to these observations, and act accordingly in trading off expected returns against risk.

Risk specification　Asset pricing, be it in a CAPM, APT, or even option-pricing setting, is usually performed with a mean–variance framework in mind. This utility maximizing approximation does not leave room for higher order moments (i.e., it ignores the risk captured by the tails of the distribution). Safety-first models, as proposed in the 1950s by Roy (1952), do allow this risk to enter the portfolio decision process. In De Haan et al. (1994) it is shown how extreme value theory can be used to assist in comparing portfolio classes based on prespecified risk probabilities (p) and accompanying exceedance quantile as derived from equation (6) above.

Limits and other (temporary) trading suspensions　The stock market crashes in the late 1980s led to a demand for smoother news absorption mechanisms in times of extreme price changes. Circuit breakers became the latest regulatory fad, but these were already preceded on most commodity exchanges by price limits. Whereas price limits are more rigid, and therefore potentially more distorting, they clearly outperform circuit breakers as far as small investors are concerned. Since an exchange would like to distort the trading process as little as possible, how should it set a price limit or a circuit breaker invoking price change? Obviously, this problem translates into specifying an appropriate p in (6) and then calculating the accompanying quantile. If we look at the exchanges where price limits have been operational, it is obvious that a very small p has supposedly been selected.

Margins　In Kofman (1993), the extreme value theory has been applied to a futures margins setting. To protect the integrity of the exchange, clearing houses usually require a specified percentage level of the contract value to be maintained in a margin deposit by traders on the exchange. These margins are then passed on (marked up) to final customers. Since margins have to be maintained daily (and sometimes even more frequently), the optimal margin level should be sufficient to cover a prespecified maximum (extreme) price change, a level which is only exceeded with, for example, 0.01 percent probability. Obviously, both the clearing house and the traders want to keep margins as low as possible to attract a maximum order flow, while securing the exchange's financial viability.

Bid–ask spreads Market makers quote bid–ask spreads (*see* BID–ASK SPREAD) to get compensation for the cost of generating market liquidity. This cost component can be split into three parts: a risk of holding temporary open positions, a risk of asymmetric information, and normal order processing costs. In highly competitive markets, the latter component will typically dominate the size of the spread. However, in small illiquid markets the other two components become dominant. Both of these are directly related to the risk of sudden large price changes. A rational market maker should then incorporate these extremal probabilities in optimally setting the spread. In Kofman and Vorst (1994) these tail probabilities are estimated from *Bund* futures transaction returns. It seems that market makers are well compensated for the actual risk they incur in holding open positions. This may, however, be a characteristic of a highly liquid market (in this case LIFFE, in London) and for small, illiquid exchanges these risks can be expected to be much higher.

Thresholds Before the demise of the European Monetary System in 1992, currency speculators could take almost riskless futures and/or forward positions in EMS currencies if interest rates were out of line with covered interest parity. Compulsory monetary interventions guaranteed effective price limits. The newly proposed target zones, which allow occasional exceedances, may change all that. The occasional exceedances will induce excessive fat-tailedness in the exchange rate returns distribution, as was observed in Koedijk, Schafgans, and de Vries (1990). These sudden jump probabilities can then no longer be neglected.

This short list of applications in finance illustrates the importance of appropriate inference on the shape of the tail of asset price (or its return) distributions. The tools introduced above are (relatively) easy to apply and should be considered before deciding to enter promising high yield markets. Arbitrage tells us that every excess return has its price in risk; maybe these excesses do not always compensate for the ultimate, extreme, risk.

Bibliography

Blattberg, R., and Gonedes, N. (1974). A comparison of the stable and Student distributions as statistical models for stock prices. *Journal of Business*, **47**, 244–80.

Cornew, R. W., Town, D. E., and Crowson, L. D. (1984). Stable distributions, futures prices, and the measurement of trading performance. *Journal of Futures Markets*, **4**, 531–57.

De Haan, L., Jansen, D. W., Koedijk, K., and de Vries, C. G. (1994). Safety first portfolio selection, extreme value theory and long run asset risks. In J. Galambos, J., Lechner, and E. Simiu (eds.), *Extreme Value Theory and Applications*. Dordrecht: Kluwer Academic Publishers.

Engle, R. F. (1982). Autoregressive conditional heteroscedasticity with estimates of the variance of United Kingdom inflations. *Econometrica*, **50**, 987–1007.

Fama, E. F. (1963). Mandelbrot and the stable Paretian hypothesis. *Journal of Business*, **36**, 420–9.

Hill, B. M. (1975). A simple general approach to inference about the tail of a distribution. *Annals of Statistics*, **3**, 1163–73.

Hogg, R. V., and Klugman, S. A. (1983). On the estimation of long tailed skewed distributions with actuarial applications. *Journal of Econometrics*, **23**, 91–102.

Jansen, D. W., and de Vries, C. G. (1991). On the frequency of large stock returns: Putting booms and busts into perspective. *Review of Economics and Statistics*, **73**, 18–24.

Kalb, G. R. J., Kofman, P., and Vorst, T. C. F. (1996). Mixtures of tails in clustered automobile collision claims. *Insurance: Mathematics and Economics*, **18**, 89–107.

Koedijk, K., Schafgans, M., and de Vries, C. G. (1990). The tail index of exchange rate returns. *Journal of International Economics*, **29**, 93–108.

Kofman, P. (1993). Optimizing futures margins with distribution tails. *Advances in Futures and Options Research*, **6**, 263–78.

Kofman, P., and Vorst, T. C. F. (1994). Tailing the bid–ask spread. Working paper 10/94, Monash University.

Mandelbrot, B. (1963). The variation of certain speculative prices. *Journal of Business*, **36**, 394–419.

Praetz, P. (1972). The distribution of share price changes. *Journal of Business*, **47**, 49–55.

Roy, A. D. (1952). Safety first and the holding of assets. *Econometrica*, **20**, 431–49.

Tauchen, G. E., and Pitts, M. (1983). The price variability–volume relationship on speculative markets. *Econometrica*, **51**, 485–505.

financial distress

Oscar Couwenberg

A firm is considered in financial distress when its cash flow is not sufficient to cover current obligations. Firms need not be declared bankrupt at the moment this situation occurs. In most European countries and in the United States, creditors can only ask the court to invoke the "bankruptcy" procedure when the firm cannot pay debts due (*see* BANKRUPTCY). If the firm has some cash reserves left, or sells off some assets, it may yet be able to evade bankruptcy.

The concept of insolvency is also used by economists to characterize firms in financial distress. Insolvency can be defined as the situation where the firm has a negative economic net worth. It may, however, still be able to pay current obligations.

Once a firm is in financial distress the issue becomes how this distress situation should be resolved. To resolve the financial problems the firm can restructure assets or liabilities and both can be done informally (i.e., without invoking the bankruptcy procedure) or by means of a formal bankruptcy. Table 1 gives the methods associated with each of these types of restructuring.

A firm restructures its assets to free up cash flow. This can take the form of a sale of assets, a reduction in the labor force, a reduction in capital spending, research, and development. Asquith, Gertner, and Scharfstein (1994) find that asset sales and capital expenditure reductions play an important role in the restructuring of companies. After these asset sales, these firms have a lower chance of going bankrupt, compared to firms that do not sell assets. The findings of Asquith, Gertner, and Scharfstein (1994) point to the fact that most companies use the proceeds from the asset sales to pay off (senior) debt. However, it need not be the stockholders that gain the most from these asset sales. The asset base of the firm diminishes and this eliminates equity's option on any future increase in asset values. According to Brown, James, and Mooradian (1994), for this reason financially distressed firms reinvesting the proceeds of asset sales in their firm show higher average abnormal returns than those firms paying down debt.

Although empirical studies shed light on what happens to firms that restructure their assets informally, relatively little is known about firms that liquidate under the bankruptcy code (Chapter 7 in the USA). One prominent difference with informal asset restructuring is that in bankruptcy the liquidation of the firm is not carried out by management, but by an outsider appointed by the court. The associated loss of control makes the asset sale under bankruptcy law far less attractive to management and shareholders.

The other option for the firm to resolve financial distress is to restructure the liabilities, informally or formally. Gilson, John, and Lang (1990) find that the average length of time is shorter and that direct costs are lower for informal reorganizations than for formal procedures. They also find that in informal workouts stockholders gain on average a 41 percent increase in stock value, while the firms that failed in their attempt and ended in bankruptcy showed a −40 percent abnormal return over the restructuring period. Part of this difference may be attributable to differences in operating performance, but it also reflects the cost savings associated with an informal reorganization. Although these cost savings raise a firm's value relative to its value in bankruptcy, the firm participants must agree unanimously how to distribute this value. Hold-out problems and free-riding by atomistic debtholders, information asymmetries between management and creditors, and conflicting

Table 1   The methods to resolve financial distress

	Asset restructuring	*Financial restructuring*
Informal restructuring	Merge/sell off assets	Informal workout
Formal restructuring	Liquidation in bankruptcy	Formal reorganization in bankruptcy

coalitions may lead to the breakdown of the informal reorganization. Gilson, John, and Lang (1990) find that firms with more intangible assets, more bank debt relative to public debt, and fewer (distinct classes of) lenders have a higher chance of successfully completing an informal workout.

The alternative to the informal workout is formal reorganization under bankruptcy law. Most of the research in this area concentrates on the Chapter 11 procedure in the US bankruptcy code. Important issues addressed are the costs associated with the procedure and the violation of the absolute priority rule (APR).

The costs of financial distress are categorized as direct and indirect costs. The direct costs are the sums paid to the lawyers and advisors to the firms. The indirect costs are the costs associated with the disruption of the normal business activities due to the financial problems. Warner (1977), Altman (1984), and Weiss (1990) show that the direct costs range between 3–5 percent of the market value of the firm, measured at the year end prior to bankruptcy. Incorporating the indirect costs into these estimates is problematic. Altman (1984) estimates total bankruptcy costs (i.e., direct and indirect costs) as 8–12 percent of total firm value for retailers and 16 percent for industrial firms. Haugen and Senbet (1978) argue that these costs can be evaded by buying up all financial claims of the firm on the capital market, thus capping the total costs of bankruptcy. However, it was only after the leveraged buy out (LBO) period of the 1980s that the active market in distressed securities that makes this kind of informal restructuring possible developed.

The second issue, the violation of the APR, addresses the redistribution of wealth in bankruptcy. Weiss (1990), Franks and Torous (1989, 1994), and Eberhart, Moore, and Roenfeldt (1990) show that not only in Chapter 11, but also in informal workouts, the APR is violated. This rule asserts that junior claimants (including equity) may only receive financial consideration when more senior creditors are paid in full. The idea behind this rule is that the seniority of claims, as written in financial contracts, should be honored in bankruptcy. If these contract terms are not held up in bankruptcy, then junior claimants have the incentive to use the bankruptcy procedure to expropriate wealth from senior creditors. The reason for this expropriation lies in the formal procedure that gives junior claimants bargaining power over senior creditors. However, all parties know before they enter into a financial contract what to expect in bankruptcy, and credit terms are set accordingly. Altman (1993) argues that it should be these credit terms that should be honored. If the absolute priority doctrine is used, then some parties receive windfall profits.

This debate over priority rules and the costs associated with the violation of such a rule has not yet been settled. Another unresolved issue concerns the efficiency of bankruptcy rules. For instance, it is not clear whether Chapter 11 keeps too many firms alive that should have been liquidated. A promising area of research that could also shed light on the efficiency issue is the analysis of the bankruptcy systems of different countries. The analysis of the differences between these rules could facilitate research for more efficient bankruptcy rules.

A related area of research is the design of (optimal) bankruptcy rules. This should also enhance our understanding of current rules and the reason why these rules may lead to inefficiencies in economic decisions. Finally, the behavior of the claimants in financial distress situations, and especially the role of banks or informed outsiders, deserves further attention.

Bibliography

Altman, E. I. (1984). A further empirical investigation of the bankruptcy cost question. *Journal of Finance*, 39, 1067–89.

Altman, E. I. (1993). *Corporate Financial Distress and Bankruptcy*, 2nd edn. New York: John Wiley.

Asquith, P., Gertner, R., and Scharfstein, D. (1994). Anatomy of financial distress: An examination of junk-bond issuers. *Quarterly Journal of Economics*, 625–58.

Brown, D. T., James, C. M., and Mooradian, R. M. (1994). Asset sales by financially distressed firms. *Journal of Corporate Finance*, 1, 233–57.

Eberhart, A. C., Moore, W. T., and Roenfeldt, R. L. (1990). Security pricing and deviations from the absolute priority rule in bankruptcy proceedings. *Journal of Finance*, 45, 1457–69.

Franks, J. R., and Torous, W. N. (1989). An empirical investigation of US firms in reorganization. *Journal of Finance*, 44, 747–69.

Franks, J. R., and Torous, W. N. (1994). A comparison of financial recontracting in distressed exchanges and Chapter 11 reorganizations. *Journal of Financial Economics*, **35**, 349–70.

Gilson, S. C., John, K., and Lang, L. H. P. (1990). Troubled debt restructuring: An empirical study of private reorganization of firms in default. *Journal of Financial Economics*, **27**, 315–53.

Haugen, R. A., and Senbet, L. W. (1978). The insignificance of bankruptcy costs to the theory of optimal capital structure. *Journal of Finance*, **33**, 383–93.

Warner, J. B. (1977). Bankruptcy costs: Some evidence. *Journal of Finance*, **32**, 337–47.

Weiss, L. A. (1990). Bankruptcy resolution, direct costs and violation of priority of claims. *Journal of Financial Economics*, **27**, 285–314.

Wruck, K. H. (1990). Financial distress, reorganization, and organizational efficiency. *Journal of Financial Economics*, **27**, 419–44.

foreign exchange management

Vesa Puttonen

The value of a firm can be thought of as the net present value of all expected cash flows. If the firm's future cash flows are largely affected by changes in exchange rates the firm is said to have large foreign exchange exposure. Traditionally, foreign exchange exposure is divided into three elements (Eiteman, Stonehill, and Moffet, 1995):

1   *Transaction exposure:* the effect of possible changes in exchange rates on identifiable obligations of the company. The risk arises from the imbalance of net currency cash flows based on commercial, financial, or any other committed cash flows in a given currency.

2   *Accounting exposure:* arises from consolidation of assets, liabilities, and profits denominated in foreign currency when preparing financial statements (also called translation exposure).

3   *Economic exposure:* extends the exchange exposure beyond the current accounting period. Arises from the fact that changes in future exchange rates may affect the international competitiveness of a firm and therefore the present value of future operating cash flows generated by the firm's activities

(also called operating or competitive exposure).

Increased economic uncertainty translates into higher levels of financial market volatility. This, in turn, subjects any given exposure to a greater degree of risk. This risk is the subject of foreign exchange management whose importance has increased in the turbulent financial environment in recent decades.

Reducing a firm's exposure to exchange rate fluctuations is called hedging. The goal of hedging is to reduce the volatility of a firm's pre-tax cash flows and hence to reduce the volatility of the value of the firm.

The relevance of risk management is an interesting topic itself. Traditional finance theory suggests that, given well diversified portfolios of investors, hedging would not benefit shareholders. The usual reasoning is that investors can diversify their portfolios to manage the exchange risk in a way that matches their preferences. Some argue, however, that managers have better information concerning the current exposure of the firm than investors. Also, hedging reduces the probability that the firm goes bankrupt and reduces agency costs between shareholders and bondholders (Smith, Smithson, and Wilford, 1995).

The findings of Nance, Smith, and Smithson (1993) suggest that firms which hedge have more complex tax schedules, have less coverage of fixed claims (the probability of the firm encountering financial distress increases with lower coverage, the coverage of fixed claims being measured as the earnings before interest and taxes divided by total interest expense), are larger, have more growth options in the investment opportunity set, and employ fewer "substitutes for hedging." Firms with fewer substitutes have fewer liquid assets and higher dividends. The explanation is based on the idea that firms have, in addition to hedging, alternative methods to reduce the conflict of interest between shareholders and bondholders.

Many techniques and instruments have been developed for controlling financial risk. The process that seeks to develop new hedging instruments is called financial engineering. Due to increasingly important international operations of companies and high volatility in exchange rates, financial engineering has become an industry of enormous growth in recent years. However, the basic tools of financial engineering were developed many years ago. The basic hedging tools to control foreign exchange risk are as follows.

1 *Currency forwards* are binding agreements between a buyer and a seller calling for the trade of a certain amount of currency at a fixed rate in a certain date in the future. The buyer benefits if prices increase by the settlement date. Correspondingly, the seller benefits from a price decrease.
2 *Currency futures* are similar to forward contracts with a few exceptions. First, gains and losses are realized each day, not only at the settlement date. The process is called marking to market. Second, futures are traded at organized exchanges, while trading in forwards occurs between banks and firms mainly by telecommunication linkages.
3 *Currency options* are contracts that give the option buyer the right, but not the obligation, to buy (call option) or sell (put option) a certain amount of currency at a fixed price for a prespecified time period.
4 *Currency swaps* are transactions in which two parties agree to exchange an equivalent amount of two different currencies for a specified period of time.

Empirical studies suggest that swaps and forwards are the most frequently used external (or off-balance sheet) hedging instruments. Beside these instruments, firms use internal possibilities for managing exchange risk (i.e., matching, exchange rate clauses, leading and lagging, etc.). There are numerous ways of hedging and financial engineering actively produces new complex instruments for firms' use. Now it becomes extremely important for managers to have clear goals for risk management. Without a clear set of risk management goals, using derivatives can produce problems. Therefore, a firm's risk management strategy must be integrated with its overall corporate strategy (Froot, Scharfstein, and Stein, 1994).

While most hedging instruments are suitable for controlling both the transaction and accounting exposures, their benefit is limited when managing economic exposure. Because economic exposure is rooted in long-term international fundamental forces, it is much more difficult to hedge on a permanent basis. At the same time, its significance as a prerequisite of long-term profitability of a firm has increased in recent decades. Yet many multinational companies have been reluctant to consider economic exposure as an important strategic risk.

Bibliography

Eiteman, D. K., Stonehill, A. I., and Moffet, M. H. (1995). *Multinational Business Finance*, 7th edn. Reading, MA: Addison-Wesley.
Froot, K. A., Scharfstein, D. S., and Stein, J. C. (1994). A framework for risk management. *Harvard Business Review*, **72**, 91–102.
Nance, D., Smith, C. W., Jr., and Smithson, C. (1993). On the determinants of corporate hedging. *Journal of Finance*, **48**, 267–84.
Smith, C. W., Jr., Smithson, C. W., and Wilford, D. S. (1995). *Managing Financial Risk*, 2nd edn. New York: Irwin.

foreign exchange markets

Ismail Ertürk

Foreign exchange markets are the institutional frameworks within which currencies are bought and sold by individuals, corporations, banks, and governments. Trading in currencies no longer occurs in a physical marketplace or in any one country. London, New York, and Tokyo, the major international banking centers in the world, have the largest share of the market, accounting for nearly 60 percent of all transactions. The next four important centers are Singapore, Switzerland, Hong Kong, and Germany. Over half of transactions in the foreign exchange markets are cross-border, that is between parties in different countries. Trading is performed using the telephone network and electronic screens, like Reuters and Telerate. More and more, however, trading is conducted through automated dealing systems which are electronic systems that enable users to quote prices, and to deal and exchange settlement details with other users on screen, rather than by telex machine or telephone. Counterparties in foreign exchange markets do not exchange physical coins and notes, but effectively exchange the ownership of bank deposits denominated in different currencies. In principle, a tourist who makes a physical exchange of local currency for foreign currency is also a participant in the foreign exchange market; indeed, for some currencies, seasonal flows of tourist spending may alter exchange rates, though in most markets rates are driven by institutional trading. Other currencies may not be officially converted except for officially approved purposes and the currency rate is then determined by a parallel market which is more indicative of market trends than officially posted rates by the central bank or by the commercial bankers (Kamin, 1993).

According to the Bank for International Settlement's latest triennial survey of the global foreign exchange market, around US$880 billion worth of currencies are bought and sold daily. This represents a 42 percent growth in size compared to the previous survey of 1989 and makes the foreign exchange market the world's biggest and most liquid market. The time zone positions of major international financial markets make the foreign exchange market a 24-hour global market. Unlike the different stock exchanges and securities markets around the world, the foreign exchange market is virtually continuously active, with the same basic assets being traded in several different locations. Throughout the day, the center of trading rotates from London to New York and then to Tokyo. Less than 10 percent of the daily turnover in foreign exchange transaction is between banks and their customers in response to tangible international payments. The remaining transactions are mostly between financial institutions themselves and are driven by international financial investment and hedging activities that are stimulated by the increasing deregulation of financial markets and the relaxation of exchange controls. Trading activity in foreign exchange markets shows few abnormalities and with the exception of late Friday and weekends, day of the week distortions are minimal. Trading activity in most centers is characterized by a bimodal distribution around the lunch hour. New York, however, has a unimodal distribution of activity, peaking at the lunch hour, which coincides roughly with high activity in London and Frankfurt at the end of the business day in those locations (Foster and Viswanathan, 1990).

CURRENCIES

Although its share is a declining trend, the US dollar remains predominant in foreign exchange turnover. About 83 percent of all foreign exchange transactions involve the US dollar, with main turnover between the US dollar and the Japanese yen, British pound, and the Swiss franc. This small group of currencies accounts for the bulk of interbank trading. Significant amounts of trading occur in other European currencies and in the Canadian dollar, but these can be considered second-tier currencies in that they are not of worldwide interest, mostly because of the limited amount of trade and financial transactions denominated in those currencies. In the third tier would be the currencies of smaller countries whose banks are active in the markets and in which there are significant local markets and some international scale trading. The Hong Kong dollar, the Singapore dollar, the Scandinavian currencies, the Saudi rial, and Kuwait dinar are such currencies. Finally, the fourth tier would consist of what are called the exotic currencies: those for which there are no active international markets and in which transactions are generally arranged on a correspondent-bank basis between banks abroad and local banks in those centers to meet the specific trade requirements of individual clients. This group includes the majority of the Latin American currencies, the African currencies, and the remaining Asian currencies. A currency needs to be fully convertible to be traded in international foreign exchange markets. If there are legal restrictions on dealings in a currency, that currency is said to be inconvertible or not fully convertible and sales or purchases can only be made through the central bank, often at different rates for investment and foreign transactions.

TRANSACTIONS

A spot transaction in the currency market is an agreement between two parties to deliver within two business days a fixed amount of currency in return for payment in another at an agreed upon rate of exchange. In forward transactions the delivery of the currencies, the settlement date, occurs more than two business days after the agreement. In forward contracts short maturities, primarily up to and including seven days, are dominant. There are two types of forward transactions: outright forwards and swaps. Outright forwards involve single sales or purchases of foreign currency for value more than two business days after dealing. Swaps are spot purchases against matching outright forward sales or vice versa. Swap transactions between two forward dates rather than between spot and forward dates are called forward/forwards. Spot transactions have the largest share in total foreign exchange transactions, accounting for just under half of the daily turnover. However, forward transactions have increased in volume faster and now nearly match the share of spot transactions. Activity in currency futures and options, which approximately represents 6 percent of the market, accounts for the rest of the turnover.

Market Efficiency

Market efficiency is of special interest to both academics and market participants with respect to the foreign exchange markets. Modern finance theory implies that prices in the foreign exchange markets should move over time in a manner that leaves no unexploited profit opportunities for the traders. Consequently, no foreign exchange trader should be able to develop trading rules that consistently deliver profits. This assertion seems to be supported by the traders' performance in real life. However, published research results, so far, show evidence of *ex post* unexploited profit opportunities in the currency markets. Dooley and Shafer (1983) also reported that a number of filter rules beat the market even in the *ex ante* sense. Some authors have argued that the filter profits found in exchange markets are explicable in the light of the speculative risk involved in earning them and may perhaps not be excessive or indicative of inefficiency.

A filter rule refers to a trading strategy where a speculator aims to profit from a trend by buying a currency whenever the exchange rate rises by a certain percentage from a trough and selling it whenever it falls by a certain percentage from a peak. If foreign exchange markets were efficient, the forward rate today would be an optimal predictor of future spot rate and by implication would be the best forecaster. The empirical evidence suggests that the forward rate is not an optimal predictor of the future spot rate (i.e., it is a biased predictor). The rejection of forward market efficiency may be attributable to the irrationality of market participants, to the existence of time-varying risk premiums, or to some combination of both these phenomena (Cavaglia, Verschoor, and Wolff, 1994). Crowder (1994) is one of those who argue that once allowance is made for fluctuations in the risk premium, efficiency is preserved. Currently, there is no consensus among researchers on the existence of market inefficiency or on the explanations for the inefficiency.

Participants

The major participants in the foreign exchange markets are banks, central banks, multinational corporations, and foreign exchange brokers. Banks deal with each other either directly or through brokers. Banks are the most prominent institutions in terms of turnover and in the provision of market-maker services. The interbank market accounts for about 70 percent of transactions in the foreign exchange markets. Banks deal in the foreign exchange market for three reasons. First, banks sell and buy foreign currency against customer orders. Second, banks operate in the market in order to meet their own internal requirements for current transactions or for hedging future transactions. Third, banks trade in currencies for profit, engaging in riskless arbitrage as well as speculative transactions. In carrying out these transactions the banks both maintain the informational efficiency of the foreign exchange market and generate the high level of liquidity that helps them to provide effective service to their commercial customers. According to the BIS survey in April 1992 in London, the top 20 banks out of 352, acting as foreign exchange market makers, account for 63 percent of total market turnover. In all international markets there is a continuing trend towards a declining number of market-making banks as a result of both mergers among banks and of the withdrawal of some smaller banks who have inadequate capital to trade at the level needed for profitability in such a highly competitive business.

Non-financial corporations use the foreign exchange market both for trade finance and to cover investment/disinvestment transactions in foreign assets. In both activities the objective of the corporation is to maximize its profits by obtaining the most advantageous price of foreign exchange possible. Although small in scale, the corporations' involvement in foreign exchange markets extends to management of their foreign exchange exposure through derivative products and, in the case of larger corporate entities, to actively seeking profit opportunities that may exist in the market through speculative transactions.

In their role of regulating monetary policies, central banks of sovereign states are often in the position of both buying and selling foreign exchange. The objective of central banks' involvement in the foreign exchange markets is to influence the market-determined rate of their currencies in accordance with their monetary policy. Central banks often enter into agreements, with one central bank lending the other the foreign exchange needed to finance the purchase of a weak currency in the market to maintain the value of their currencies within a mutually agreed narrow band of fluctuations. Stabilization is intended to prevent wild fluctuations and speculations in the foreign exchange market, but central banks are increasingly cautious about signaling a commitment to a fixed intervention rate. Even the Exchange Rate Mechanism (ERM) of the European Union, in which currencies were contained within narrow bands of their central rate, was unable, in spite of the committed support of all European central banks, to prevent a concerted market adjustment. In September 1992 the Bank of England lost many millions of foreign currency reserves in a short and unsuccessful defense of sterling. Both sterling and the Italian lira were on that occasion forced out of the ERM bands.

Risks

Counterparty credit risk, settlement risk, and trading risk are the three major risks that are faced by market participants in the foreign exchange markets. Credit risk relates to the possibility that a counterparty is unable to meet its obligation. Settlement risk arises when the counterparty is able and willing but fails to deliver the currency on settlement day. The settlement of a foreign exchange contract is not simultaneous;

therefore, counterparties are usually not in a position to insure that they have received the countervalue before irreversibly paying away the currency amount. In the foreign exchange markets there are unequal settlement periods across countries. Different time zones may expose the party making the first payment to default by the party making the later payment. In 1974 US banks paid out dollars in the morning to a German bank, Bankhaus Herstatt, but did not receive German marks through the German payment system when German banking authorities closed at 10.30 a.m. New York time. Herstatt received the dollars in the account of its US correspondent but did not pay out the marks. Market risk refers to the risk of adverse movements in the rate of foreign exchange. A market participant in the foreign exchange market risks loss when rates decline and it has a long position (owns the asset) or when rates rise and it has a short position (has promised to supply the asset without currently owning it).

Quotation and Transaction Costs

The exchange rate quoted for a spot transaction is called the spot rate and the rate that applies in a forward transaction is called the forward rate. If a currency is trading at a lower price against another currency on the forward market than on the spot market, it is said to be at a discount. If, however, the currency is more expensive forward than spot, it is said to be at a premium. What determines whether a currency trades at a premium or discount is the interest rate differential in money markets. The currency with higher/lower interest rate will sell at a discount/premium in the forward market against the currency with the lower/higher interest rate. However, some research has shown a small bias in the forward rate explained by a time-varying risk premium.

Traders in the foreign exchange markets always make two-way prices; that is, they quote two figures: the rate at which they are prepared to sell a currency (offer) and the rate at which they are willing to buy a currency (bid). The difference is called the spread and represents the market maker's profit margin. The spread is conventionally very narrow in stable currencies with a high volume of trading. Liquidity is usually extremely good for major currencies and continuous two-way quotations can be obtained. However, in unstable, infrequently traded currencies, it can become a good deal wider. It widens with uncertainty – spreads on internationally traded currencies such as the British pound and US dollar will widen if the international financial markets are in turmoil. The evidence from foreign exchange markets, however, does not support an unequivocal relationship between market liquidity and transaction costs. Bid–ask (offer) spreads are not necessarily lowest when the liquidity is high. More trading by informed risk averse participants brings about higher costs. Bollerslev and Domowitz (1993) report that small traders (banks) in foreign exchange markets tend to increase both the quoted spread and market activity at the beginning and at the end of their regional trading day, because they are more sensitive with respect to their inventory positions at the close than larger banks and have less information based on retail order flow at the beginning than larger banks that operate continuously. Another factor which may effect the transaction cost in foreign exchange markets is unobservable news. News events which change traders' desired inventory positions result in order imbalances, changing the relative demand and supply for the currency, with the potential of changing the spreads (Bollerslev and Domowitz, 1993).

EXCHANGE RATE SYSTEMS

From the end of World War II until 1971 the leading industrialized countries under the hegemony of the US economy committed themselves to a fixed exchange rate system. This period in the international monetary system is known as the Bretton Woods system and aimed to preserve a fixed exchange rate between currencies until fundamental disequilibrium appeared, at which point through devaluation or revaluation a new fixed parity was established. The Bretton Woods system was based on the strength of the US economy, whereby the US government pledged to exchange gold for US dollars on demand at an irrevocably fixed rate (US$35 per ounce of gold). All other participating countries fixed the value of their currencies in terms of gold, but were not required to exchange their currencies into gold. Fixing the price of gold against each currency was similar

to fixing the price of each currency against each other.

With the increasing competitiveness of the continental European economies and the Japanese economy against the US economy, the USA had become unable to meet its obligations under the Bretton Woods system and the fixed exchange rate system gave way to the floating exchange rate system in 1973. Under the floating exchange rate system currencies are allowed to fluctuate in accordance with market forces in the foreign exchange markets. However, even in systems of floating exchange rates where the going rate is determined by supply and demand, the central banks still feel compelled to intervene at particular stages in order to help maintain stable markets. The Group of Seven (G7) council of economic ministers has in the past attempted coordinated interventions in the foreign exchange markets with a view to stabilizing exchange rates. The exchange rate system that exists today for some currencies lies somewhere between fixed and freely floating. It resembles the freely floating system in that exchange rates are allowed to fluctuate on a daily basis and official boundaries do not exist. Yet it is similar to the fixed system in that governments can and sometimes do intervene to prevent their currencies from moving too much in a certain direction. This type of system is known as a managed float. Economists are not in agreement as to which of the exchange rate systems, fixed or floating, can create stability in currency markets and is a better means for adjustments to the balance of payments positions (Friedman, 1953; Dunn, 1983). A fixed exchange rate system is unlikely to work in a world where the participating countries have incompatible macroeconomic policies and the economic burden of adjustments to the exchange rates usually fall on the deficit countries. The floating exchange rate system, on the other hand, has not delivered the benefits that its advocates put forward. The exchange rate volatility during the floating rate period is severe and is not consistent with underlying economic equilibria due to the activities of short-term speculators. The European Union's aim is not to create a fixed exchange rate system, but to create a monetary union where the exchange rate fluctuations are eliminated with adoption of a single currency by the member countries. However, to reach this goal a transitional period where a stability in exchange rates through conversion of member countries' macroeconomic performances to a specified desirable level is necessary. Since the Maastricht Treaty of 1989 the European Union countries have not been successful in achieving these macroeconomic targets, thus raising serious concerns about monetary union.

Bibliography

Bank of England (1992). The foreign exchange market in London. *Bank of England Quarterly Bulletin*, **32**, 408–17.

Bollerslev, T., and Domowitz, I. (1993). Trading patterns and prices in the interbank foreign exchange market. *Journal of Finance*, **48**, 1421–43.

Cavaglia, S. M., Verschoor, W. F., and Wolff, C. C. (1994). On the biasedness of forward foreign exchange rates: Irrationality or risk premia? *Journal of Business*, **67**, 321–43.

Committeri, M., Rossi, S., and Santorelli, A. (1993). Tests of covered interest parity on the Euromarket with high quality data. *Applied Financial Economics*, **3**, 89–93.

Copeland, L. S. (1994). *Exchange Rates and International Finance*, 2nd edn. Wokingham: Addison-Wesley.

Crowder, W. J. (1994). Foreign exchange market efficiency and common stochastic trends. *Journal of International Money and Finance*, **13**, 551–64.

Dooley, M. P., and Shafer, J. R. (1983). Analysis of short run exchange rate behavior: March 1973 to November 1981. In D. Bigman and T. Taya (eds.), *Exchange Rate and Trade Instability*. Cambridge, MA: Ballinger, 187–209.

Dunn, R. M. (1983). *The Many Disappointments of Flexible Exchange Rates*. Princeton Essays in International Finance. Princeton, NJ: University of Princeton Press.

Eichengreen, B., Tobin, J., and Wyplosz, C. (1995). Two cases for sand in the wheels of international finance. *Economic Journal*, **105**, 162–72.

Foster, D., and Viswanathan, S. (1990). A theory of intraday variations in volumes, variances and trading costs. *Review of Financial Studies*, **3**, 593–624.

Friedman, M. (1953). The case for flexible rates. In *Essays in Positive Economics*. Chicago: University of Chicago Press.

Group of Ten Deputies (1993). *International Capital Movements and Foreign Exchange Markets*. Rome: Bank of Italy.

Kamin, S. B. (1993). Devaluation, exchange controls, and black markets for foreign exchange in developing countries. *Journal of Development Economics*, **40**, 151–69.

Krugman, P. (1991). Target zones and exchange rate dynamics. *Quarterly Journal of Economics*, **51**, 669–82.

Tucker, A. L., Madura, J., and Chiang, T. C. (1991). *International Financial Markets*. St Paul, MN: West Publishing.

futures and forwards

John Board and Charles Sutcliffe

A forward or futures contract is one in which completion (in terms of the payment and matching delivery of goods) is deferred, as opposed to spot or cash transactions where the entire transaction takes place immediately. The principal uses of forward and futures contracts are hedging, speculation, arbitrage, and spread trading. Foward and futures contracts are similar in principle, but futures contracts are designed to be traded, whereas forward contracts are usually one-off deals between two parties. This distinction has become less clear-cut in recent years because of the growth of the over the counter markets in forward contracts which have some of the attributes of conventional futures.

For traders to be able to buy and sell futures contracts easily, there must be a well organized marketplace and a product standardized in terms of contract size, quality, delivery date, delivery location, and counterparty (the clearing house) (Houthakker, 1982). This standardization means that futures contracts are very liquid and most positions are closed out before delivery.

A futures market has a centralized marketplace (originally a trading floor but now usually an electronic system) which trades only during specified hours, with widespread public dissemination of the prices, volumes, and open interest. To eliminate counterparty risk, futures markets use a system of marking to the market, together with a requirement for initial margin payments which are managed through a clearing house. Futures markets are also subject to regulation, which may impose, for example, daily price limits, trading halts, and the prohibition of dual trading. There is continued regulatory concern about the possible effect of futures and over the counter trading on the market for the underlying asset.

The price of a forward (or futures) contract is established by "cost of carry" arguments in which the current value of the underlying asset is adjusted for the benefits and costs of the deferred exchange. For an interest rate forward, the no-arbitrage interest rate implicit in the forward price is

$$\left[\frac{(1 + R^L)^{(T+n)/365}}{(1 + R^S)^{T/365}} \right]^{\sqrt{n/365}} - 1$$

where R^L and R^S are the annual interest rates over the period until times $T + n$ and T respectively, T is the delivery date of the forward, and n is the life of the underlying asset.

If interest rates are predictable, Cox, Ingersoll, and Ross (1981) have shown that, in spite of the mark to market rules, forward and futures prices should be the same (in that arbitrage opportunities are available should the prices differ). They noted that this identity of prices does not hold in the presence of stochastic interest rates, and empirical studies suggest that marking to the market can cause small differences between forward and futures prices (Sutcliffe, 1997).

Selling futures or forward contracts does not require ownership of the underlying asset. As a result, the quantity of outstanding futures and forward contracts may exceed the total world supply of the underlying asset, and the volume of trading in forward and futures markets is often much larger than in the underlying spot market, making them among the world's largest markets. The principal types of contracts traded on futures markets are interest rates, currencies, stock indices, agricultural commodities, energy, and metals.

Bibliography

Cox, J. C., Ingersoll, J. E., and Ross, S. A. (1981). The relation between forward prices and futures prices. *Journal of Financial Economics*, **9**, 321–46.

Houthakker, H. S. (1982). The extension of futures trading to the financial sector. *Journal of Banking and Finance*, **6**, 37–47.

Sutcliffe, C. M. S. (1997). *Stock Index Futures: Theories and International Evidence*, 2nd edn. London: International Thomson Business Press.

fuzzy logic

Peter Byrne

In the last 40 years one of the more controversial introductions into the range of decision-making tools have been the ideas of fuzzy logic, fuzzy systems, and fuzzy analysis. Conventional set theory expressed in Aristotelian terms has a binary or Boolean logic: an object (value) is in a set with a truth value of 1 or it is not, with a truth value of 0. Fuzzy logic is, by contrast, multi-valued, and permits degrees of membership of a logical set, with continuous membership values between 0 and 1. The proponents of the methodology argue that classical set theory is simply a special case of fuzzy logic (Zadeh and Kacprzyk, 1992; Watson, Weiss, and Donnell, 1979; Bezdek, 1993; *Economist*, 1994). Opponents argue the reverse, that fuzzy logic, if it exists at all, is merely a subset of traditional logic. Fuzzy logic has its own language and its own mathematics, including crisp sets (Boolean Sets) and degrees of belief, as a means of measuring fuzzy set membership (Kilger and Folger, 1988; Kaufmann and Gupta, 1991).

The main applications of fuzzy logic to date have been in the field of engineering control systems. Controllers have been developed using fuzzy decision rules to provide continuous and variable control for a variety of devices ranging from washing machines to subway trains. It is also important to note that the Japanese have been responsible for most of the development of such systems, reflecting in some people's minds the fundamental difference in thinking which fuzzy logic seems to require, and with which many still argue.

In the context of softer systems such as those used for management, the present position is one of limited progress. It has been argued that fuzzy methods can be used effectively to make decisions that consist of hard (or well understood) elements and soft, uncertain, or vague (fuzzy) factors. In that sense it is claimed to offer an alternative decision analysis paradigm particularly under conditions of uncertainty (Zadeh and Kacprzyk, 1992). It is argued that since the approach calls for an assessment of "possibilities" rather than formal probabilities, it will be more amenable to use by essentially non-quantitative decision-makers, and software systems are available to assist in this.

With the increasing interest among financial analysts in the use of expert systems and neural networks to model financial dealing processes and market performance, it is important to recognize that the other major area where fuzzy methods are gaining popularity is in the ongoing development of hybridized expert and neural network software systems. In fuzzy expert systems, "fuzzified" rules allow a greater variety in the response of the system, dependent upon the degree of belief built into the decision rules. In neural networks, fuzzy logic assists in the necessary learning process when building the network. Assuming, as seems likely, that these systems come to technical maturity and have an impact on the industry, financial analysts may well have to come to understand the terminology of fuzziness.

Bibliography

Bezdek, J. C. (1993). Fuzzy models: What are they, and why? *IEEE Transactions on Fuzzy Systems*, 1, 1–5.

Economist (1994). The logic that dares not speak its name. April 16, 137–9.

Freeling, A. N. S. (1980). Fuzzy sets and decision analysis. *IEEE Transactions on Systems, Man and Cybernetics*, **SMC-10** (7), 341–54.

Kaufmann, A., and Gupta, A. K. (1991). *Introduction to Fuzzy Arithmetic, Theory and Applications*. New York: Van Nostrand Reinhold.

Kilger, G. J., and Folger, T. A. (1988). *Fuzzy Sets, Uncertainty, and Information*. New York: Prentice-Hall.

Kosko, B. (1994). *Fuzzy Thinking: The New Science of Fuzzy Logic*. London: Harper Collins.

Watson, S. R., Weiss, J. J., and Donnell, M. L. (1979). Fuzzy decision analysis. *IEEE Transactions on Systems, Man and Cybernetics*, **SMC-9** (1), 1–9.

Zadeh, L., and Kacprzyk, J. (1992). *Fuzzy Logic for the Management of Uncertainty*. New York: John Wiley.

G

game theory in finance

Suresh Deman

There is a flavor of non-sequential learning games in a well-known saying of Confucius: "Consistency is the virtue of fools and wise people change their minds as they grow wiser." The formulation of common knowledge is not obvious, but commonly believed to be due to Allmann (1976). However, one can also sense the notion of common knowledge in Confucius' dialogue with Ming, which runs as follows: "I know that you know, you know that I know, I know that you know that I know, and so on" (see *Last Emperor of China*).

Economists began to realize the importance of limitation on the information possessed by individuals in understanding economic behavior because such limitation induces agents to change their behavior. The standard assumptions of perfect competition, that individuals are mere price takers, is no longer relevant. Rather, the strategic interactions have potentially profound implications on the behavior of agents in the decision-making process by altering behavior in the rest of the market. Game theory is well suited to modeling takeovers because of the importance of the information and its ability to include a number of sharply delineated sequences of moves and events. Precommitment and information transformation are the two pillars of modern game theory. Thus, the stylized facts and rationality of game theory may be more appropriate for markets in corporate control than for vegetable markets in developing countries.

In the business world, the power of game theory as a management tool rests on reasonably comprehensive assumptions that are embedded in the rules of the game. Players can experiment with different solutions and concepts to problems that are intrinsically insoluble. In other words, there are no unique solutions to the problems. The analysis of the results can be used for greater insights into the real problems the game simulates. In a game involving a large number of players using a wide range of strategies, it is possible to identify strategies that do better than others even if there is no unique correct strategy at all. Allmann (1987) defines game theory as a sort of umbrella or "unified field" theory for the rational side of the social science, where "social" is interpreted broadly to include human as well as non-human players (computers, animals, plants, etc.).

In game theory, the prisoner's dilemma is commonly used to describe certain real-world problems. The central characteristics of a prisoner's dilemma are an array of benefits and detriments associated with alternative courses of action so that the dominant individual strategy is not to cooperate even though, if the parties do not cooperate, pursuit of individual self-interest yields less than optimal results.

There are a wide range of applications of game theory in finance. Typical examples of models are signaling through information transmission in corporate takeovers, capital structure as a commitment, and incentive design for financial intermediation. Game theory has been applied in other literature in finance (e.g., market microstructure, executive compensation, dividends and stock repurchases, external financing, debt signaling, etc.).

APPLICATION 1: THE THEORY OF CORPORATE TAKEOVER BIDS

Grossman and Hart (1980) explain a particular free-rider problem using a game theoretic model with a continuum of players. Suppose that under status quo management, a corporation has value v and if a raider can improve the target's value by x, then its potential value is $v + x$. If the takeover bid is conditional and $v < p < v + x$ (i.e., price p is below the potential value), no shareholders will sell, even though shareholders and management would jointly profit. The shareholders are in the prisoner's dilemma and if the takeover bid is to be successful, then a holdout is better and the shareholders no worse off if it fails. Hence, tendering is not a dominant strategy. So every shareholder holds out and in Nash equilibrium, takeover will never occur. Grossman and Hart strongly argued in favor of exclusionary devices by suggesting that the raider be allowed to dilute the value of the minority shareholder if the raid is successful.

Shleifer and Vishny (1986) point out that if the raider is a large shareholder and, if permitted to profit from secretly purchasing α proportion of shares prior to the tender offer, the free-rider problem can be solved even without dilution. The tender offer can be profitable because the raider can profit on their own shares even if they offer $p > v + x$ and loses on the tendered shares.

Hirshleifer and Titman (1990) relax the assumptions of Shleifer and Vishny and present a model of tender offers in which the bid perfectly reveals the bidder's private information about the size of the value improvement that can be generated by a takeover. They argue that bidders with greater improvements will offer higher premiums to insure that sufficient shares are tendered for majority control. They explain why offers succeed sometimes, but not always. Following Milgrom and Roberts (1982), nature moves first and chooses the raider's "type" to be $x\varepsilon;(0, x \sim)$ and the raider offers a premium of x for each of α proportion of shares. Each of the continuum of shareholders decides whether to sell or not to sell their shares. If over $(0.5-\alpha)$ shareholders accept the tender offer, the payoffs are p for those who accept and $v + x$ for those that refuse. Otherwise, all payoffs are zero.

Bradley and Kim's (1995) analysis of the free-rider problem demonstrated that a necessary condition for a tender offer to be successful is that it should be front-end loaded and this condition should hold regardless of whether the tender offer is a partial or two tier. This is another application of the prisoner's dilemma.

Suppose a corporation is equally owned by two shareholders and its underlying value is US\$80. Let the raider make a tender offer in which 51 percent shares will be purchased at a price of US\$50 and the remaining 49 percent offered a lower price of US\$25 on the condition that 51 percent shareholders tender. If both tender, the share will be purchased *pro rata*. Under these conditions, tendering is a dominant strategy, even though all the shareholders would be better off refusing to sell. It is argued that two-tier tender offers must be outlawed because of their coercive nature. However, Bradley and Kim see no reason to outlaw two-tier offers because it helps reallocate corporate resources to their highest valued use. This allows for greater flexibility in financing takeover activity by reducing the amount of cash that a potential raider must accumulate to pursue an acquisition. They further suggested that the potential for competition among raiders and a dominating intra-firm tender offer can solve the prisoner's dilemma.

Deman (1991, 1994) re-examines Grossman and Hart's (1980) paper and shows under complete and imperfect information that the prisoner's dilemma can be solved. The existence of the mixed strategy symmetric equilibria with or without the dilution shows that we do not really need assumptions of a continuum of players. Deman explores possibilities of two kinds of equilibria: one is "separating equilibria" in mixed strategies in which each type of raider behaves differently and the shareholders randomize their payoffs. The raider of a high type will not offer a low price because such an offer would more than likely not succeed and the raider would lose the potential gain on their initial shares. A less plausible class of equilibria are "pooling equilibria" in which different types of raiders behave in the same way. However, pooling equilibria are ruled out by the reasonable "out-of-equilibrium belief" that price offers will signal the raider's type. In that case, a low-type raider could profitably differentiate themselves from the pooling equilibrium by offering a low price and the shareholder would accept their offer. In fact, a model of finitely many players under potentially confusing signals gives the same results as the continuum-of-players model in which the decision of any individual player does not affect the success of the tender offer. Deman applies a corporate finance–game theoretic model to real-estate takeovers. For example, when considering the problem of the developer negotiating with landowners, a model of finitely many owners appears to be much more realistic. It is well known that takeovers do occur with positive probabilities in models with finitely many players. This result holds independently whether or not these many finitely owners believe that they have an impact on the success of the sale, as pointed out by Shleifer and Vishny (1986), Bagnoli and Lipman (1988), Bebchuk (1989), and Deman (1991).

Kyle and Vila (1991) investigated a model of takeovers in which "noise trading" provides camouflage and makes it possible for a large corporate outsider to purchase enough shares at favorable prices for a takeover to become profitable. Although the model accommodates the possibility of dilution (Grossman and Hart, 1980) and a large incumbent shareholder (Shleifer and Vishny, 1986), neither dilution nor a large incumbent shareholder is necessary for costly takeovers to be profitable. Noise trading tends to encourage costly takeovers that other wise would not occur, and discourage beneficial takeovers that otherwise would occur.

APPLICATION 2: CAPITAL STRUCTURE AS PRECOMMITMENT

Unlike the first example, this is a game under the assumption of symmetric information. The main focus of the game is on commitment rather than on information transmission. In the game, each firm purposely risks bankruptcy to create a conflict of interest between debt and equity that increases its aggressiveness in seeking market shares. The outcome is worse for the firms if they jointly avoid debt, because debt lowers firms' profits while helping the firm that uses it as a commitment tool.

Harris and Raviv (1988) focus on capital structure as an anti-takeover device because common stock carries voting rights while debt does not. The debt–equity decision may effect the outcome of corporate votes and may partly determine the corporate resources. Thus, incumbent management can use short-term financial restructuring as a tactic to influence the form of the takeover attempts and their outcome, assuming that managerial ability to identify good

projects is unknown. In a subgame, perfect reputational equilibrium, managers may choose too much safety compared with the shareholders' optimum. If the firm issues debt, then this incentive aligns the managers' interest with the interests of the shareholders and thus reduces their agency costs of debt. This implies higher optimal leverage when the manager is motivated by his personal reputation than when he is not. This result is different from that of Harris and Raviv.

APPLICATION 3: FINANCIAL INTERMEDIATION – AN INCENTIVE DESIGN

In most models, the players begin with symmetric information, but they know that some players will later acquire an informational advantage over the others. The model that I am going to use here is an example of theory-based institutional economics. The purpose of this is to show that (1) an intermediary is useful only if there are many investors and many entrepreneurs; and (2) incentive contracts have economies of scale compared to monitoring.

Diamond (1984) provides a model of financial intermediaries, so that M risk-neutral investors wish to finance N risk-neutral firms. Each entrepreneur has a project that requires 1 unit in capital and yields Q level of output, where Q is initially unknown to anyone. If $Q < 1$, the entrepreneur genuinely cannot repay the investors, but the problem is that only they, not the investors, will observe Q, so they cannot validate their claim $Q < 1$. The investors must rely on one of two things to insure the truth: namely, monitoring or incentive contract. Under a monitoring scheme, each investor incurs a cost C to observe Q, which makes it a contractible variable, on which payment can be made contingent. The entrepreneur suffers a dissipative punishment $\delta(x)$ under the incentive contract if they repay x. The cost of monitoring is MC, while the expected cost of an incentive contract is $E\delta$. In the absence of an intermediary, if $E\delta < MC$, the incentive contract is preferred. The underlying idea behind the financial intermediary is to eliminate redundancy by replacing M individual monitors with a single monitoring agency. The intermediary itself requires an incentive contract, at cost $E\delta$. To justify its existence, it should spread this cost over many entrepreneurs.

If $N = 1$, the intermediary incurs a cost of C for monitoring and $E\delta$ for its own incentive, whereas a direct investor–entrepreneur contract would cost only $E\delta$. In the above scheme, while information is still symmetric, the institution assumes a particular form to avoid information problems by contracting.

The main driving force behind the existence of financial intermediaries is the asymmetric information which opens doors for a much wider application of game theory. Reputational issues on the part of borrowers become very important and were first analyzed by John and Nachman (1985) in a two-period model. They depicted, in sequential equilibrium, a problem in which agency debt can be decreased when compared with a single-period model. Diamond (1989) uses a somewhat similar model in which borrowers deal with banks over more than one period and have an incentive to build a reputation for repaying loans. This provides a partial improvement of the agency problem in one-shot games in which the borrower prefers riskier investments than the lender would like.

CONCLUSIONS

Game theory has emerged as one of the most powerful techniques of analysis because, in the game, both players are actively trying to promote their own welfare in opposition to that of the opponent. It develops a rational criterion for selecting a strategy in which each player will uncompromisingly attempt to do as well as possible in relation to their opponent by giving the best response. However, game theory is often criticized on the grounds that it is sensitive to minor changes in assumptions and lacks empirical verification. The existence of various equilibria depends on what information is available to players or who moves first. Deman (1987) basically identifies three criteria for a theory to be considered useful: (1) it is consistent with known facts; (2) it provides greater insights and understanding than earlier theories; and (3) it can be used for forecasting future trends, particularly under conditions that differ from the past. The underlying assumption is that both theorists and empiricists have common objectives to describe, explain, relate, anticipate, and evaluate phenomena, events, and relationships crucial to decision-making through theory construction and data collection. Unfortunately, crucial variables are hard to measure, but that does not diminish their importance. As Rasmussen (1989) pointed out, the economist's empirical work has dominated case-by-case verification, replacing the traditional regression running. A theory's sensitivity to assumptions is not a shortcoming. Rather, it is a contribution of the theory, pointing out the important role of what were once thought to be insignificant details of reality in the world. To blame game theory for any failure to predict or for selfishness is like blaming cardiology for heart disease. The failure of macroeconomic forecasts and the growing importance of the microeconomic theory of the firm have brought game theory to the forefront of economic decision-making.

Bibliography

Allmann, R. (1976). Agreeing to disagree. *Annals of Statistics*, **4**, 1236–9.

Allmann, R. (1987). Game theory. In J. Eatwell, M. Milgate, and P. Newman (eds.), *The New Palgrave: A Dictionary of Economics*. New York: Macmillan.

Bagnoli, M., and Lipman, B. (1988). Successful takeovers without exclusion. *Review of Financial Studies*, **1**, 89–110.

Bebchuk, L. (1989). Takeover bids below the expected value of minority shares. *Journal of Financial and Quantitative Analysis*, **24**, 171–84.

Bradley, M., and Kim, E. H. (1995). The tender offer as a takeover device: Its evolution, the free-rider problem, and the prisoner's dilemma. In S. Deman (ed.), *Advances in the Theory of Corporate Takeover Bids: Game-Theoretic Models and Econometric Estimation*. Amsterdam: North-Holland.

Brander, J., and Lewis, T. (1986). Oligopoly and financial structure: The limited-liability effect. *American Economic Review*, **76**, 956–70.

Deman, S. (1987). A review of regional development theories. *International Journal of Development Planning Literature*, **2**, 45–60.

Deman, S. (1991). The theory of takeover bid: A game-theoretic model. *Advances in Econometrics*, **9**, 139–55.

Deman, S. (1994). The theory of corporate takeover bids: A subgame perfect approach. *Managerial and Decision Economics*, **15**, 383–97.

Deman, S., and Wen, K. W. (1994). The theory of real estate takeover: A subgame perfect approach. *Advances in Econometrics*, **10**, 65–182.

Diamond, D. (1984). Financial intermediation and delegated monitoring. *Review of Economic Studies*, **51**, 393–414.

Diamond, D. (1989). Reputation acquisition in debt markets. *Journal of Political Economy*, **97**, 828–62.

Grossman, S., and Hart, O. (1980). Takeover bids, the free-rider problem, and the theory of the corporation. *Bell Journal of Economics*, **11**, 42–64.

Harris, M., and Raviv, A. (1988). Corporate control contests and capital structure. *Journal of Financial Economics*, **20**, 55–86.

Hirshleifer, D., and Titman, S. (1990). Share tendering strategies and the success of hostile takeover bids. *Journal of Political Economy*, **98**, 295–324.

John, K., and Nachman, D. (1985). Risky debt, investment incentives, and reputation in a sequential equilibrium. *Journal of Finance*, **40**, 863–78.

Kreps, D. (1990). *A Course in Microeconomic Theory*. Princeton, NJ: Princeton University Press.

Kyle, A., and Vila, J.-L. (1991). Noise trading and takeovers. *RAND Journal of Economics*, **22**, 54–71.

Milgrom, P. and Roberts, J. (1982). Limit pricing and entry under incomplete information: An equilibrium analysis. *Econometrica*, **50**, 443–59.

Rasmussen, E. (1989). *Games and Information*. Oxford: Blackwell.

Shleifer, A., and Vishny, R. W. (1986). Large shareholders and corporate control. *Journal of Political Economy*, **94**, 461–88.

Von Neumann, J., and Morgenstern, O. (1947). *The Theory of Games and Economic Behaviour*, 2nd edn. New York: Wiley.

growth by acquisition

Nikhil P. Varaiya

Growth is an imperative for corporations. Growth provides corporations with expanding opportunities, enabling them to attract the best executives or motivating workers. Growth is also a means for maintaining or enhancing a firm's relative competitive position. Avoidance of growth in a market where incumbent rivals are relentlessly seeking to increase their market shares can result in a serious loss of market position with the attendant adverse impacts on profitability that can jeopardize long-term survival.

Since growth ultimately must come from markets currently served or new markets to be served, growth by acquisition is the strategy of entry into new product markets by purchasing the common shares or assets of a business or businesses already established in these markets. From the vantage point of the acquiring company, management goals are often stated as rectifying some "problem" or "deficiency" : countering a substantial decline in the company's overall earnings growth; utilizing existing excess capacity; or dealing effectively with a vertical competitive threat.

However, the overriding objective of an acquiring company is taken to be profitable growth by acquisition. That is, an acquisition opportunity will be undertaken only if it is value creating; it must enhance the "market value" of its presently outstanding common shares. Acquisitions are typically associated with the payment of a significant control premium by an acquiring company when it purchases the shares of an acquired company or acquiree. The control premium is the amount by which the offer price per share of the acquiree exceeds its pre-acquisition share price, expressed as a percentage. Over the period 1976–90 premiums in large US industrial acquisitions averaged around 50 percent and ranged up to 185 percent.

THREE CONDITIONS FOR PROFITABLE GROWTH BY ACQUISITION

For an acquisition to create value for an acquirer, three conditions have to be met. First, there must be an improvement in the acquiree's financial performance over time sufficiently large to fully recapture the offer premium. Alberts and Varaiya (1989) develop a model in which required improvements in the acquiree's financial performance are characterized as a combination of required improvements in expected future economic profitability (the difference between expected future return on equity and cost of equity capital) and earnings growth rate to fully recapture the offer premium. Second, there must be a sustainable improvement in the acquiree's operating performance sufficiently large that will in turn generate the improvement in sustainable financial performance necessary to recapture the offer premium and thus make the acquisition profitable. To achieve this improvement in operating performance the acquiree must offer the acquiring company some combination of five significant bargain opportunities (Alberts, 1974):

1   *Position bargain:* management can enhance the acquiree's financial performance by further differentiation of its product or service offering (by enhancing existing attributes and/or adding new ones), further increasing its relative efficiency (by lowering raw material costs by purchasing from acquirer at a lower cost than the acquiree has been paying), or both.

2   *Expansion bargain:* management can profitably extend the sales of the acquiree's products into geographical markets not presently served by it (perhaps because of capital constraints).

3   *Synergy bargain:* management can integrate the acquiree's positioning strategies with those of one or more of the acquiree's other units, and by doing so could bring about further differentiation of the acquiree's offering, a further increase in the acquiree's efficiency, or both.

4   *Leverage bargain:* management can, on determining that the acquiree uses significantly less leverage (the ratio of permanent debt to invested capital) than incumbent rivals, match these rivals' leverage ratios so that the acquiree's economic profitability can be increased, given the other drivers of economic profitability.

5   *Tax bargain:* management can elect to finance the acquisition in a way that allows the acquiree under the current US tax code to allocate some portion of the offer premium to step up the depreciation bases of some of its assets and thereby increase its tax depreciation and decrease its tax liabilities relative to what they would be for the acquiree standing alone.

The third condition for a value-creating acquisition is that management performance in implementing the acquisition will be effective enough to bring about the required improvements in operating performance. At a minimum this requires that the management cadre that will oversee the acquiree have sufficient knowledge to identify the bargain sources of premium recapture. Additionally, the acquiree's organizational structure must be designed to balance its need for autonomy with the imperative of coordinating the acquiree's decisions with those of other business units of the acquiring company (Hill, 1994). Finally, the acquiree's management processes (for example, performance evaluation systems) must be integrated with those of the acquiring company.

EVIDENCE ON ACQUISITION PROFITABILITY

There are four sets of available data to assess the profitability performance of acquisitions: (1) benchmark data which compares the economic profitability and earnings growth improvements necessary for value creation with the levels of such improvements actually observed (Alberts and Varaiya, 1989); (2) company performance data which compares company profitability before and after acquisition (Meeks, 1977; Mueller, 1980; Ravenscraft and Scherer, 1987); (3) case study data (Porter, 1987; Copeland, Koller, and Murrin, 1990); and (4) event study data that compares the short-run and long-run changes in the common stock returns (adjusted for market-wide movements) of acquirers before and after acquisition (Jarrell, Brickley, and Netter, 1988; Agrawal, Jaffee, and Mandelker, 1992; Andrade, Mitchell, and Stafford, 2001). The thrust of these four sets of data is that the acquirer should *not* expect the acquisition to be value creating *if* it pays the magnitude of the offer premium that other companies have paid on average for their acquirees; in fact, the acquirer should expect the acquisition to be significantly value destroying.

However, the historical record on acquisition profitability in conjunction with the three conditions for profitable growth by acquisition does indeed identify for acquiring company management two critical requirements for value-creating growth by acquisition: (1) acquire the right unit in the right market or markets in which entry is sought and effectively implement the acquisition so that the expected financial performance improvements will be realized; and (2) avoid the payment of the typical observed offer premium, but limit it to a fraction of the performance improvement that careful analysis indicates is expected to be generated.

Bibliography

Agrawal, A., Jaffee, J., and Mandelker, G. (1992). The post-merger performance of acquiring firms: A re-examination of an anomaly. *Journal of Finance*, **47**, 1605–22.

Alberts, W. W. (1974). The profitability of growth by merger. In W. W. Alberts and J. E. Segall (eds.), *The Corporate Merger*. Chicago: University of Chicago Press.

Alberts, W. W., and Varaiya, N. P. (1989). Assessing the profitability of growth by acquisition: A premium recapture approach. *International Journal of Industrial Organization*, 7, 133–49.

Andrade, G., Mitchell, M., and Stafford, E. (2001). New evidence and perspectives on mergers. *Journal of Economic Perspectives*, 15, 103–20.

Copeland, T., Koller, T., and Murrin, J. (1990). *Valuation: Measuring and Managing the Value of Companies*. New York: John Wiley.

Hill, C. W. L. (1994). Diversification and economic performance: Bringing strategy and corporate management back into the picture. In R. P. Rumelt, D. Schendel, and D. J. Teece (eds.), *Fundamental Issues in Strategy: A Research Agenda*. Boston, MA: Harvard Business School Press.

Jarrell, G. A., Brickley, J. A., and Netter, J. (1988). The market for corporate control: The empirical evidence since 1980. *Journal of Economic Perspectives*, 2, 49–68.

Meeks, G. (1977). *Disappointing Marriage: A Study of the Gains from Merger*. Occasional Paper 51. Cambridge: Cambridge University Press.

Mueller, D. C. (1980). *The Determinants and Effects of Mergers: An International Comparison*. Cambridge, MA: Oelgeschlager, Gunn, and Hain.

Porter, M. E. (1987). From competitive advantage to corporate strategy. *Harvard Business Review*, 65, 43–59.

Ravenscraft, D. J., and Scherer, F. M. (1987). *Mergers, Sell-Offs, and Economic Efficiency*. Washington, DC: Brookings Institution.

growth and value stocks

Edward Lee

Stocks can be classified into different styles. Two commonly applied equity investment styles are "value" and "growth." Investors pursuing a value style seek to identify stocks that are cheap relative to their fundamentals. Growth style investors look for stocks from companies with higher growth prospects. Valuation ratios such as the earnings–price ratio, the dividend–price ratio, and the book-to-market ratio are commonly used to determine whether a stock belongs to the value or growth category. Value (growth) stocks are from companies with higher (lower) fundamental-to-price ratios. Graham and Dodd (1934) first documented the superior return performance of value stocks in the US. The general consensus in the current empirical literature is that the value style historically outperforms the growth style in the US and several other countries. For instance, Fama and French (1998) show that the annual US $-denominated return spread between value and growth stock portfolios was 6.79 percent, 12.32 percent, 9.85 percent, 9.67 percent, 7.64 percent, and 4.62 percent respectively for the US, Australia, Japan, Singapore, France, and the UK over the period 1975 to 1995.

Explanations of the value premium have been offered from perspectives both for and against the efficient market hypothesis (EMH). Risk compensation explanations justify the value premium in an efficient market where no exploitable stock return regularity should exist. The risk compensation argument suggests that value stocks are associated with certain sources of risk not captured by the capital asset pricing model (CAPM). Brennan, Chordia, and Subrahmanyam (1998) show that the book-to-market ratio, upon which the value premium is commonly based, predicts returns even after adjusting for risk using the Fama and French (1996) three factor model. This implies that the value premium is driven either by unidentified sources of risk beyond the Fama and French (1996) three factor model, or by mispricing. Liew and Vassalou (2000) show the association between the value premium and future changes in GDP and suggest this as evidence that it is related to risk. Daniel and Titman (1997), however, show that the value premium is associated more with company-specific characteristics (based on book-to-market values) than covariance risk.

Behavioral explanations for the value premium relax the assumption of market efficiency. They basically assume that investors make systematic judgmental errors due to behavioral biases. Limits-to-arbitrage prevents the resulting mispricing from being exploited immediately. Lakonishok, Shleifer, and Vishny (1994) suggest that investors incorrectly extrapolate past performance into the future. Thus, they undervalue (overvalue) stocks from companies with improving (declining) fundamentals. Several theories have been advanced to explain such misjudgment. Barberis, Shleifer, and Vishny (1998) suggest that representativeness causes investors to assume that a company's past performance will persist into the future and conservatism makes them adjust to new information slowly. Daniel, Hirshleifer, and Subrahmanyam (1998) suggest that overconfidence and biased self-attribution cause investors to overestimate the precision of their own analyses and neglect public signals.

Whether the value premium is a result of risk compensation or mispricing remains an open question. Whether its economic value persists after accounting for transactions costs and the length of the investment horizon also remains an open question.

Bibliography

Barberis, N., Shleifer, A., and Vishny, R., (1998). A model of investor sentiment. *Journal of Financial Economics*, **49**, 307–43.

Brennan, M. J., Chordia, T. and Subrahmanyam, A. (1998). Alternative factor specifications, security characteristics, and the cross-section of expected stock return. *Journal of Financial Economics*, **49**, 345–74.

Daniel, K., and Titman, S. (1997). Evidence on the characteristics of cross-sectional variation in stock returns. *Journal of Finance*, **52**, 1–34.

Daniel, K., Hirshleifer, D., and Subrahmanyam, A. (1998). A theory of overconfidence, self-attribution, and security market under- and overreaction. *Journal of Finance*, **53**, 1839–85.

Fama, E. F., and French, K. R. (1996). Multifactor explanations of asset pricing anomalies. *Journal of Finance*, **51**, 55–84.

Fama, E. F., and French, K. R. (1998). Value vs growth: The international evidence. *Journal of Finance*, **53**, 1975–99.

Graham and Dodd (1934). *Security Analysis: The Classic 1934 Edition*. New York: McGraw-Hill.

Lakonishok, J., Shleifer, A., and Vishny (1994). Contrarian investment, extrapolation, and risk. *Journal of Finance*, **48**, 1541–78.

Liew and Vassalou, M. (2000). Can book-to-market, size, and momentum be risk factors that predict economic growth? *Journal of Financial Economics*, **57**, 221–46.

H

habit formation

Stuart Hyde

The failure of the traditional time-separable constant relative risk aversion consumption capital asset pricing model to explain the equity premium and risk-free rate puzzles has led to numerous variations of the basic model being proposed. One successful approach which allows for non-separability in utility over time is *habit formation* or *habit persistence*. In habit formation models it is not the absolute level of consumption which is important, but consumption relative to some benchmark level. Essentially, the representative agent's utility depends not only on current consumption but also on consumption in the previous period.

Habit formation models typically define the utility function as taking the form $U(C_t, X_t)$, where C_t is consumption at time t and X_t is the time varying habit or subsistence level which typically depends on previous consumption, $X_t = f(C_{t-1}, C_{t-2}, \ldots)$. The exact form of $U(C_t, X_t)$ varies. Abel (1990) proposes that it should be a power function of the ratio C_t/X_t, while Constantinides (1990), Sundaresan (1989), and Campbell and Cochrane (1999) argue for a power function of the difference $C_t - X_t$. This distinction is important, since ratio models have constant risk aversion while difference models have time varying risk aversion. A further distinction between different types of habit formation model focuses on whether an agent's own decisions affect the level of habit. The habit incorporated in *internal* habit formation models such as those in Constantinides (1990) and Sundaresan (1989) is defined by the representative agent's own previous consumption. In *external* habit formation models such as those in Abel (1990) and Campbell and Cochrane (1999) it is determined in reference to some outside aggregate level of consumption. Finally, the models also allow for differing speeds to which habit adjusts to consumption. Abel (1990) allows the habit to depend on one lag of consumption, while Constantinides (1990), Sundaresan (1989) and Campbell and Cochrane (1999) assume that habit reacts only gradually to changes in consumption.

Abel (1990) names his external habit ratio model "catching up with the Joneses." Here, individuals are concerned with how their own personal consumption relates to everyone else's, and presume that their individual consumption patterns cannot influence aggregate consumption behavior. The utility function for the external ratio model is written as:

$$U_t = E_t \left[\sum_{j=0}^{\infty} \beta^j \frac{(C_{t+j}/X_{t+j})^{1-\gamma} - 1}{1-\gamma} \right] \quad (1)$$

where β is the agent's subjective rate of time preference, γ is equal to the agent's relative risk aversion, the individual's consumption is given by C_t and the habit level, X_t is given by one lag of aggregate consumption,

$$X_t = \overline{C}_{t-1}^{\theta}$$

so utility depends on the ratio between an individual's consumption, C_t, and the habit level X_t which is assumed to be a power function of previous aggregate consumption, $\overline{C}_{t-1}^{\theta}$. θ measures the degree of time non-separability, (i.e., the persistence of previous consumption or habit). As an alternative, we can consider a difference model as proposed by Constantinides (1990), Sundaresan (1989), and Campbell and Cochrane (1999) in which the utility function is:

$$U_t = E_t \left[\sum_{j=0}^{\infty} \beta^j \frac{(C_{t+j} - X_{t+j})^{1-\gamma} - 1}{1 - \gamma} \right] \quad (2)$$

In the internal habit formation models of Constantinides (1990) and Sundaresan (1989) the habit level, X_t, is given by a proportion, θ, of an agent's previous consumption (assuming a one lag dependence):

$$X_t = \theta C_{t-1}$$

where the parameter θ measures the degree of time non-separability, where the higher the value of θ, the greater the habit θC_{t-1}, and therefore the lower the utility derived from current consumption, C_t. In this model relative risk aversion is time varying and is given by

$$\gamma \cdot \frac{C_t}{C_t - X_t}$$

Both the "catching up with the Joneses" and internal habit models fail to adequately explain both the risk-free rate and equity premium puzzles simultaneously. Although they may account for the equity premium they typically also imply high and volatile interest rates. However, a specification which can solve both problems simultaneously is provided by Campbell and Cochrane (1999). They allow the external habit to depend upon a subsistence variable with longer lag structure. Using the difference model utility function, they define the surplus consumption ratio S_t which measures the level of aggregate consumption which is in excess of the habit (i.e., surplus to the subsistence level).

$$S_t = \frac{\overline{C}_t - X_t}{\overline{C}_t}$$

Further, the evolution of S_t is governed by a nonlinear process which insures that the habit level remains below consumption at all times:

$$\ln (S_{t+1}) = (1 - \phi) \ln (\overline{S}) + \phi \ln (S_t)$$
$$+ \lambda [\ln (S_t)] \ln (C_{t+1}) - \ln (C_t) - g$$

$$\lambda \ln (S_t) = \begin{cases} \frac{1}{\overline{S}} \sqrt{1 - 2(\ln (S_t) - \ln (\overline{S}))} - 1 \\ 0 \end{cases}$$

$$\ln (S_t) \le S_{\max}$$
$$\ln (S_t) > S_{\max}$$

$$\overline{S} = \kappa \sqrt{\frac{\sigma}{1 - \phi}}$$

where $\overline{S}$ is the steady state surplus consumption ratio, ϕ dictates its level of persistence, and $\lambda \ln (S_t)$ controls the sensitivity of the ratio. k is the standard deviation of consumption growth and g is the mean of consumption growth. Again, the agent's relative risk aversion is time varying and is given by $\frac{\gamma}{S_t}$. This model is able to generate high risk aversion and account for the equity premium while being consistent with observed consumption growth and interest rates. Excellent discussions of habit formation and consumption asset pricing can be found in Cochrane (2001) and Campbell (2003).

Bibliography

Abel, A. B. (1990). Asset prices under habit formation and catching up with the Joneses. *American Economic Review*, **80**, 38–42.
Campbell, J. Y. (2003). Consumption based asset pricing. In G. Constantinides, M. Harris, and R. Stulz (eds.), *Handbook of the Economics of Finance*, Vol. 1B. Amsterdam: North Holland, 805–87.
Campbell, J. Y. and Cochrane, J. H. (1999). By force of habit: A consumption-based explanation of aggregate stock market behavior. *Journal of Political Economy*, **107**, 205–51.
Cochrane, J. H. (2001). *Asset Pricing*. Princeton, NJ: Princeton University Press.
Constantinides, G. (1990). Habit formation: A resolution of the equity premium puzzle. *Journal of Political Economy*, **98**, 519–43.
Sundaresan, S. M. (1989). Intertemporally dependent preferences and the volatility of consumption and wealth. *Review of Financial Studies*, 2, 73–88.

hedging

Suresh Deman

The concept of hedging has a wide range of applications to real-world problems when there are uncertainties in transactions. Hedging is commonly used by grain dealers, business people, and individuals to protect themselves against uncertainties. It serves mainly two purposes: first, to enter into forward contracts in order to protect the domestic currency value of foreign currency-denominated assets or liabilities; second, managing risk by establishing an offsetting position such that whatever is lost or gained on the original exposure is exactly offset by a corresponding gain or loss on the hedge. A firm can use a variety of techniques for managing transaction exposures. In the literature, a few models use both static and dynamic strategies in discrete and continuous time frameworks. In formulating models for hedging, information plays a very important role. Some of these models will be discussed below under the assumptions of homogeneous and heterogeneous information.

A COMPETITIVE EQUILIBRIUM MODEL

Assume that the agents have homogeneous beliefs and have concave state-dependent utility functions. Let there be a one-period economy with K agents which has one end-of-period consumption good. For simplicity, assume that in period $t = 0$, there is no consumption. Each agent owns a real asset which produces a random amount of the consumption good at the end of the period. There are N possible states of nature, with probabilities $Prob(1), \ldots, Prob(N)$ and agents wish to maximize the expected utility of end-of-period consumption (i.e., $U_i(C_i, \phi)$, where ϕ represents the state of the world.

A financial asset is a claim to a random amount of end-of-period output, which is traded between agents at $t = 0$. A hedging portfolio analysis is simplest if we assume that the hedge portfolio consists of a mixed asset and liability with positive payoffs in some states of the world and negative payoffs in other states. This protects an agent against some particular risky outcome(s) and is balanced so as to give a competitive equilibrium price of zero. Under this formulation, a hedge portfolio is a portfolio which gives positive payoffs in states where the agent would otherwise have a high marginal utility of consumption in "bad" states and negative payoffs in states where they would otherwise have a low marginal utility of consumption in "good" states. An agent is fully hedged if their marginal utility is equalized across the relevant states after purchasing the hedge portfolio. On

the other hand, if the hedge position lowers but does not eliminate the disparity, then they are partially hedged.

The model described above is static. In an intertemporal model, dynamic strategies increase the set of hedging opportunities. Agents can create a rich set of payoff claims by dynamically changing the proportions invested in the individual assets. This process reaches its natural limit because of continuous trading: if an asset price follows Brownian motion, then a continuously adjusted portfolio consisting of only this risky asset and a riskless asset can be constructed which replicates the payoff to any put or call option on the risky asset.

RISK PREMIA AND HEDGING

An economically interesting question is whether agents "pay a premium" to hedge. Assume again that the current price of the hedge portfolio is set to zero by appropriate balancing of the asset and liability sides of the hedge, using a futures contract. If the expected cash flow is negative or positive next period, then the hedge portfolio carries a positive or negative implicit risk premium. If the expected cash flow is zero, then the implicit risk premium is zero.

ROLE OF HEDGER IN A MARKET WITH HETEROGENEOUS INFORMATION

The models discussed above have been formulated under the assumption of homogeneous information across agents. If agents have differential information about the payoffs to assets, then the trading strategies of rational agents cannot have the simple competitive form. Agents must treat trade opportunities as signals of the information of other agents about the value of the trade. The presence of differential information can lead to fewer hedging opportunities and/or raise the expected cost of hedging. Milgrom and Stokey (1982) show that with heterogeneous beliefs rational agents will not trade because their valuation of assets is quite different. In other words, adverse selection can limit trade. If agents have some control over outcomes, then moral hazard problems may also limit hedging opportunities. Some of these external factors may offset mutual benefits from trade of financial assets.

HEDGING IN A MEAN-VARIANCE MODEL

The mean-variance preference model provides a useful framework for empirical analysis of hedging. An investor's optimal position in the hedging instrument can be given by:

$$\omega = E[Y]/(2 * \text{var}[Y]) - \text{cov}[X, Y]/\text{var}[Y]$$

This equation has two parts: the first additive part is called speculative hedge, and the second part is called the pure hedge. It is argued in the literature that uninformed hedgers should set their hedge position equal to the pure hedge. This is equivalent to minimizing variance instead of optimizing over a mean-variance criterion. An OLS can be used to describe the relationship between the payoffs, random endowment, and the hedging instrument. The coefficient β estimates the pure hedge and R^2 estimates the proportion of endowment variance. The latter can be eliminated by setting the hedge position equal to the pure hedge.

The hedging behavior is not simply to smooth consumption over time, but it characterizes formation of a portfolio even in the absence of intermediate consumption. In the discrete time we avoid the need to know the stock's or the option's expected rate of return by using the risk-neutralized probabilities which were completely specified by the stock's price dynamics but did not depend explicitly on the true probabilities determining the expected rate of return. A similar approach can be applied in continuous time framework.

Bibliography

Ingersoll, J. Jr. (1987). *Theory of Financial Decision Making*. Totowa, NJ: Rowman and Littlefield.

Milgrom, R., and Stokey, N. (1982). Information, trade and common knowledge. *Journal of Economic Theory*, **26**, 17–27.

house money effect

Tyler Shumway

The house money effect, proposed to describe the effect of prior outcomes on risky choice, was introduced to finance by Thaler and Johnson (1990). Agents that are subject to the house money effect are inclined to take larger risks when prior outcomes have been positive. The house money effect is an example of mental accounting, in which agents mentally keep quantities of money in artificially separate "accounts." Agents that exhibit the house money effect consider large or unexpected wealth gains to be distinct from the rest of their wealth, and are thus more willing to gamble with such gains than they ordinarily would be. Thaler and Johnson argue that the house money effect is consistent with prospect theory (Kahneman and Tversky, 1979) if agents apply "hedonic editing" to the gambles they face.

Barberis, Huang, and Santos (2001) use the house money effect, along with first order risk aversion, to explain the high volatility of asset prices and the equity premium puzzle.

Bibliography

Barberis, N., Huang, M., and Santos, T. (2001). Prospect theory and asset prices. *Quarterly Journal of Economics*, **116**, 1–53.

Kahneman, D., and Tversky, A. (1979). Prospect theory: An analysis of decision under risk. *Econometrica*, **47**, 263–91.

Thaler, R. H., and Johnson, E. J. (1990). Gambling with the house money and trying to break even: The effects of prior outcomes on risky choice. *Management Science*, **36**, 643–60.

I

initial public offerings (IPOs)

Ivo Welch

In contrast to a seasoned offering, an IPO is the offering of shares of a company that are not publicly traded. The most common are IPOs of fixed-income securities, equity securities, warrants, and a combination of equity shares and warrants ("units"). The term IPO is often used to refer only to equity or unit offerings, and the remainder of this entry concentrates only on equity and unit offerings in the United States.

In "best-effort" IPOs, underwriters act only as the issuer's agent; in "firm-commitment" IPOs, underwriters purchase all shares from the issuer and sell them as principal. In the USA, virtually all IPOs by reputable underwriters are sold as firm commitment. Other special IPO categories are (domestic tranches of) international IPOs, reverse leveraged buyouts (where company shares had been traded in the past), real estate investment trusts (REITs), closed-end funds, and venture-capital backed IPOs, etc. Most IPOs begin trading on Nasdaq.

Most IPOs typically allow a company founder to begin to "cash out" (secondary shares), or begin to raise capital for expansion (primary shares), or both. (Issuers sometimes constrain shares granted to insiders from sale for a significant amount of time after the IPO in order to raise outside demand.) Direct underwriter fees and expenses of the IPO typically range from 7–20 percent (mean of about 15 percent). Auditor fees range from US$0–80,000 (mean of about US$50,000), lawyer fees from US$0–130,000 (mean of about US$75,000). In addition, issuers must consider the cost of warrants typically granted to the underwriter, a three- to six-month duration to prepare for the IPO, the costs and time of management involvement, prospectus printing costs, and subsequent public release requirements. Consequently, many firms avoid IPOs despite the advantages and prestige of a public listing, relying instead on private or venture capital, banks, trade credit, leases, and other funding sources. Even IPO issuers tend to issue only a small fraction of the firm, and return to the market for a seasoned offering relatively quickly.

In the USA, numerous federal, state, and NASD issuing regulations have attempted to curtail fraud and/or unfair treatment of investors. Among the more important rules, in section 11 of the 1993 Securities Act, the Securities and Exchange Commission (SEC) describes necessary disclosure in the IPO prospectus. Issuers are required to disclose all relevant, possibly adverse information. Failure to do so leave not only the issuer, but also the underwriter, auditor, and any other experts listed in the prospectus, liable. SEC rules prohibit marketing or sales of the IPO before the official offering date, although it will allow the underwriter to go on roadshows and disseminate a "preliminary prospectus" (called "red herring"). Further, underwriters must offer an almost fixed number of shares at a fixed price, usually determined the morning of the IPO. (Up to a 15 percent over-allotment ("green shoe") option allows some flexibility in the number of shares.) Once public, the price or number of shares sold must not be raised even when after-market demand turns out better than expected. Interestingly, although US underwriters are not permitted to "manipulate" the market, they are allowed to engage in IPO after-market "stabilization" trading for thirty days.

Some countries (e.g., France) allow different selling mechanisms, such as auctions. Other countries (e.g., Singapore) do not allow the underwriter the discretion to allocate shares to preferred customers, but instead require proportional allocation among all interested bidders.

There are two outstanding empirical regularities in the IPO market that have been documented both in US and a number of foreign markets: on average, IPOs see a dramatic one-day rise from the offer price to the first aftermarket price (a 5–15 percent mean in the USA) and a slow but steady long-term underperformance relative to equivalent firms (a 5–7 percent per annum mean for three to five years after the issue for 1975–84 US IPOs). Prominent explanations for the former regularity, typically referred to as "IPO underpricing," have ranged from the winner's curse (in which investors require average underpricing because they receive a relatively greater allocation of shares when the IPO is overpriced), to cascades (in which issuers underprice to eliminate the possibility of cascading desertions, especially of institutional investors), to signaling (in which issuers underprice to "leave a good taste in investors' mouths" in anticipation of a seasoned equity offering), to insurance against future liability (to reduce the probability of subsequent class action suits if the stock price drops), to preselling (where underpricing is necessary to obtain demand information from potential buyers). The consensus among researchers and practitioners is that each theory describes some aspect of the IPO market. Empirical findings related to IPO underpricing also abound. For example, IPOs of riskier offerings and IPOs by smaller underwriters tend to be more underpriced, and both IPOs and IPO underpricing are known to occur in "waves" (while 1972 and 1983 saw about 500 IPOs, 1975 saw fewer than 10 IPOs; 1991–4 saw

about 500 IPOs per year). Noteworthy is the hot market of 1981, which saw an average underpricing in excess of 200 percent among natural resource offerings.

Explanations for the long-term underperformance have yet to be found. This poor performance is concentrated primarily among very young, smaller IPO firms. (Indeed, IPOs of financial institutions and some other industries have significantly outperformed their non-IPO benchmarks.) Many of the smaller IPO firms are highly illiquid and thus more difficult to short, preventing sophisticated arbitrageurs from eliminating the underperformance. Because once the IPO has passed, shares of IPOs are tradeable, like other securities, the long-run underperformance of IPOs presents first and foremost a challenge to proponents of specific equilibrium pricing models and efficient stock markets.

Other theoretical and empirical work among IPO firms has concentrated on the role of the expert advisors and venture capitalists in the IPO, subsequent dividend payouts, and seasoned equity offerings, institutional ownership, etc. Information on current IPOs is regularly published in the *Wall Street Journal*, the *IPO Reporter, Investment Dealers Digest*, and elsewhere. Securities Data Corp maintains an extensive database of historical IPOs. Institutional and legal details on the IPO procedure can be found in Schneider, Manko, and Kant (1981).

Bibliography

Beatty, R., and Welch, I. (1995). Legal liability and issuer expenses in initial public offerings. *Journal of Law and Economics*.

Benveniste, L. M., and Spindt, P. A. (1989). How investment bankers determine the offer price and allocation of new issues. *Journal of Financial Economics*, **24**, 343–62.

Drake, P. D., and Vetsuypens, M. R. (1993). IPO underpricing and insurance against legal liability. *Financial Management*, **22**, 64–73.

Ibbotson, R., Sindelar, J., and Ritter, J. (1994). The market's problems with the pricing of initial public offerings. *Journal of Applied Corporate Finance*, **7**, 66–74.

Loughran, T., and Ritter, J. R. (1995). The new issues puzzle. *Journal of Finance*, **50**, 23–51.

Loughran T., Ritter J., and Rydqvist, K. (1994). Initial public offerings: International insights. *Pacific-Basin Finance Journal*, **2**, 165–99.

Table 1 Total firm commitments IPOs

	REITs	Closed-end funds	ADRs	Reverse LBO	Other IPOs
1990	0	41	6	13	204
1991	1	37	12	81	405
1992	5	88	35	102	602
1993	44	114	59	68	865
1994	35	39	62	30	638

Ritter, J. R. (1984). The "hot issue" market of 1980. *Journal of Business*, **57**, 215–40.

Ritter, J. R. (1987). The costs of going public. *Journal of Financial Economics*, **19**, 269–82.

Rock, K. (1986). Why new issues are underpriced. *Journal of Financial Economics*, **15**, 187–212.

Schneider, C., Manko, J., and Kant, R. (1981). Going public: Practice, procedure and consequence. *Villanova Law Review*, **27**.

Welch, I. (1989). Seasoned offerings, imitation costs, and the underpricing of initial public offerings. *Journal of Finance*, **44**, 421–50.

Welch, I. (1992). Sequential sales, learning, and cascades. *Journal of Finance*, **47**, 695–732.

insider trading law (US)

Jeffry Netter and Paul Seguin

Federal regulation of insider trading occurs through three main sources: Section 16 of the Securities Exchange Act of 1934, Securities and Exchange Commission (SEC) Rule 10b-5, and SEC Rule 14e-3. The SEC rules are enforced by both SEC and private plaintiffs, while violations of the Securities Exchange Act are crimes that can be prosecuted by the Justice Department. Section 16 of the Securities Exchange Act of 1934 provides the most straightforward regulation of insider trading. This section requires statutorily defined insiders – officers, directors, and shareholders who own 10 percent or more of a firm's equity class – to report their registered equity holdings and transactions to SEC. Under Section 16, insiders must disgorge to the issuer any profit received from the liquidation of shares that have been held less than six months.

The two SEC rules provide more complex regulation of insider trading. Rule 10b-5 states, in part, that "it is unlawful . . . to engage in any act . . . which operates as a fraud or deceit upon any person, in connection with the purchase or sale of any security." However, this rule does not specifically define insider trading. Thus, definitions of insider trading comes from legal and SEC interpretations of Rule 10b-5.

In addressing insider trading cases, the courts have adopted two major theories of liability for illegal insider trading: the classical theory and the misappropriation theory. The classical theory, which has been adopted by the Supreme Court, states that a person violates Rule 10b-5 if they buy or sell securities based on material non-public information while they are an insider in the corporation whose shares they trade, thus breaking a fiduciary duty to shareholders. The classical theory is also called the fiduciary breach theory because it concentrates on those who trade securities of a firm in breach of a duty to the shareholders of that firm. This theory is sometimes referred to as the abstain or disclose theory, because insiders must abstain from trading on material information about their firm until that information has been disclosed.

The classical theory also states that people who trade on material non-public information provided to them by insiders are also in violation of Rule 10b-5. An example of a violation of Rule 10b-5 under the classical theory is the purchase of stock in a firm by its CEO just before the firm announces it is increasing its dividend. Since advance knowledge of a dividend increase is material information and the CEO is an insider, such trading is illegal. The second major theory of insider trading under Rule 10b-5 is the "misappropriation theory," which has not been adopted by the Supreme Court but has been adopted by most lower federal courts. The misappropriation theory was developed by SEC to address insider trading by non-insiders. Although many people consider trading on non-public information undesirable, non-insiders who do so are not liable under the classical theory. However, under the misappropriation theory, Rule 10b-5 is violated when a person misappropriates material non-public information and breaches a duty of trust by using that information in a securities transaction, whether or not they owe a duty to the shareholders whose stock they trade. Thus, those receiving "tips" are liable, even if the provider of the tip is not an insider.

SEC Rule 14e-3 allows for prosecution of insider trading by non-insiders. This rule makes it illegal to trade around a tender offer if the trader possesses material non-public information obtained from either the bidder or the target. Thus, in the case of a tender offer, Rule 14e-3 prohibits insider trading even when no breach of duty occurs.

The penalties for violations of insider trading laws can be severe. Money damages can be up to three times the profit made on the trade, while fines can be up to a million dollars. Further criminal violations of these laws can result in jail time.

insurance

Frank Byrne

Insurance is the process through which individual exposures to a risk of loss can be transferred to a pool in exchange for a premium reflecting the average losses from the given risk to that pool.

The need for insurance arises because the outcome of both business and individual plans are subject to uncertainty and may lead to a variety of outcomes. These range from the acceptable to the disastrous, depending on the out-turn values for a variety of contingencies such as the weather, consumer expenditure levels, or the absence of fires or tornadoes. But risk aversion is general, and this means that certain or near certain outcomes will be preferred to more dispersed and less certain outcomes even if the average or expected chances of gain are equal. As a result, decision-makers are willing to sacrifice some chance of gain in exchange for a reduction in the dispersion of outcomes they face. Insurance therefore comprises the processes of identifying pricing and transferring the financial consequences of exposure to a risk or hazard from principals to counterparties who are better able, by virtue of size, financial resources, or tolerance to risk, to absorb them.

The nature of the risk is relevant to the manner in which risk is transferred. Many risks, particularly financial ones such as exchange rate or interest rate movements, are generally amenable to standardization and insured or hedged by contracts in financial markets. The risks covered by insurance contracts in contrast are generally specific and non-standardized, relate to events such as fire or death which have low probabilities, and hence non-normal distributions, and have negative sum payoffs – in other words, no counterparty gains from the losses resulting from the incidence of an insured event. Risks exhibiting non-normality and negative sum payoffs, where there is a chance of loss

but no chance of gain if an event occurs, are known as "pure" risks; risks such as death or fire affecting individual contracts randomly known as "particular" risks, while risks such as war or flood likely to affect whole sections of the population are described as "fundamental."

In insurance the transfer of risk is implemented through a contract of insurance – an "insurance policy," which sets out the terms and conditions on which a claim may be made and the basis on which the amount of the claim will be determined. This policy is issued in response to a proposal in which the insured or their agent provides full disclosure of facts material to the risks being transferred.

The very nature of the insurance industry, its statistical base and cyclical nature, has led it to develop over a long period as an intensive area for research, supporting the development of actuarial science through the Institute of Actuaries, and devising "probability of ruin" methodologies which are of increasing interest in setting solvency margins to cover the risk exposure of financial institutions. The early academic research was concerned with probability analysis and the estimation of population from sample means and depended on concepts and methodologies familiar in economics and statistics with work on uncertainty, risk theory, and risk pricing (Kloman, 1992; MacMinn, 1987) and the seminal works on insurance by Arrow (1963), Borch (1967), and Pratt (1964). Borch developed the theory of optimal insurance and the determination of risk sharing between the individual and the insurer. Pratt considered the effect of risk averseness on the purchase of insurance together with the degree to which the amount of insurance purchased reflected both the averseness to risk and the "fairness" of the actuarially established premium (i.e., the expected cost of the "risk"). Borch (1967) followed by modifying the classical theories to include "uncertainty." He argued that willingness to transfer risk to insurers is often based on a subjective or perceived view of the impact of an event on the survival of the relevant business or individual rather than the pure probability of the occurrence of the event insured or average likely loss.

Arrow (1963) considered the sharing of risk between risk averse individuals and the less risk averse insurer for a fixed price and identified the nature of the trade-off in insurance between moral hazard, adverse selection, and the transaction costs. Moral hazard effectively defines the boundary of risk transferability and hence of insurability because it arises when the conduct of the insured can materially affect the probability or size of losses under the policy. It may be said that the mere fact of the existence of an insurance contract produces a tendency to reduce the level of care in preventing loss. An individual, insured against theft, may be careless in leaving doors or windows unlocked during a temporary absence, or one with a substantial life or health insurance cover, in spite of the evidence, may continue to smoke to the possible detriment of his or her health. Insurers seek to minimize the effect of moral hazard by *ex ante* action, strict information gathering on the nature of the risk and past claims experience, and by imposing stringent safety conditions during the course of the insurance. As Shavell (1986) pointed out, the effect of each of these actions is to increase costs and, according to degree of overt application by the insurer, to influence the degree of cover sought by the proposer.

Adverse selection reflects the fact that information on the risk factors is asymmetric; that is, the proposer has greater knowledge of his or her risk than the insurer. The result is for the uptake of insurance in any population to be biased towards those most at risk, who have the greatest incentive to insure. Instead of insuring a sample drawn randomly from the population at risk, the actual sample is biased towards above average risk with adverse consequences on claims experience. Over time, rates will increase, further discouraging the better risks from taking out insurance or forcing them to seek partial insurance, while the high risk individual takes full cover (Rothschild and Stiglitz, 1976).

To control for problems of moral hazard and adverse selection the insurance industry relies on certain key principles. "Utmost good faith" is central to all insurance contracts. Purchasers of insurance are effectively "insiders" in terms of their knowledge of their specific risk exposure, while the insurer knows more about the covers and terms of the contract and loss adjustment guidelines. This potentially creates problems of asymmetric information only partly relieved by

the good faith principle that both parties are able to rely on disclosure of material circumstances that might influence the acceptance of the risk, the premiums charged, or the suitability of the policy in relation to cover required.

Applying the full disclosure principle, though, is less than straightforward. In order to avoid adverse selection, insurers have required disclosure even of HIV tests and are currently interested in the possibilities offered by DNA profiling in identifying health and mortality risk. With more and more information insurers can minimize adverse selection by tighter and tighter classification of risk classes, but this raises the concern that the worst risks in the community will no longer be insurable because they are no longer rated in a pool containing lower risk cases. Where moral hazard affects the size of claim, insurers require the insured to carry or "co-insure" part of the risk, so that the insured is still exposed to at least some of the risk.

The problems of adverse selection and moral hazard have stimulated another safeguard for insurers, namely defining the insurable interest. The aim is that insurance provides restitution for tangible loss and is not simply a sophisticated gamble with the underwriter. As an insured is only entitled to receive an indemnity for loss, any rights he or she obtains against another party are transferred to the insurer which pays the claim under the principle of subrogation.

The measure of the claim is related to the amount of the insurable interest. In most circumstances this figure is readily quantifiable – value of property, amount of liability incurred – but where the subject matter of a policy is related to the perceived value of a life or the life of a spouse, then indemnity does not apply and the limiting factor is cost of cover.

PRICING AND THE INSURANCE CYCLE

Factors other than claims and expenses influence insurance pricing, with competition and the availability of investment income on premiums received in advance of claims expenditure the major influences. The result is that the equivalence between premiums and risk may fluctuate widely, swinging the industry from periods of excess capacity and underwriting losses to capacity shortages and high profitability. This volatility in pricing and availability of cover and limits results in the insurance cycle of so called "hard" and "soft" market conditions. Partly, these conditions occur because the "true" probability of and size of losses depends on a long history of claims experience over which the law of large numbers will be reasonably dependable. Rapid change and the current trend to segmentation of the market increase the difficulty of obtaining representative claims experience. In insurance any random period of below average claims experience rapidly builds the reserves required to support expansion through rate reduction, leading to overcapacity and losses when normal claims rates resume. The ultimate cause of the cycle has been the subject of a number of articles suggesting both an industry-wide self-destruct mechanism arising out of a desire to build market share, partly through the presence of favorable extraneous market conditions such as high investment interest rates, or the intrinsic nature of rate setting and accounting time lags involved both in setting future premiums based on past loss records and regulatory and accounting lags (Venezian, 1985; Cummins and Outreville, 1987).

Pricing of standard risk premiums for non-life insurance "classes" are based on historical loss rates and incorporate projected claims rates based on historic data, amount of coverage, degree of risk, both physical and moral, and an assessment of incurred claim incidents which have not currently reported, inflation, investment income, underwriting and claims expense, and selling costs or commissions. Research effected principally to assist regulators has been supplemented, particularly for property and liability insurance, by models incorporating inflation, investment income, outstanding claims, taxation, and an appropriate return on capital employed. D'Arcy and Garven (1990) provide a helpful review of alternative approaches, but in their evaluation of the ability of the alternative pricing approaches to predict underwriting profits, no single approach showed consistent superiority.

Individual policies within each class will be assessed on a number of relevant factors related to the individual's variation from the norm. The importance of standard rating factors equally varies from one class of insurance to another and differences in expectations and claims experience make rates sensitive to market conditions and competition. For the large non-standard risks, particularly in the corporate market, an alternative basis sometimes called "merit" or "experience" rating exists. This arises partly in response to the buying power of multinational clients, but also because the size and complexity of the risks requires syndication across several insurers (including reinsurers). Individual risks and clients are priced on the basis of their variability from the norm in terms of their own claims history. It then becomes common for corporate customers to retain exposure to the "pound swopping" element of cover, where the premium effectively equates to losses plus administration, charging losses as they arise to operating costs but placing catastrophe cover with insurers. Effectively, insurance priced on a "merit" basis is equivalent to a contingent committed line of credit of unknown value with each client paying the value of claims plus a margin over the long run in order to avoid the full costs of the contingent event falling on one financial period.

SELF-INSURANCE AND CAPTIVE INSURANCE

Much of the early research into insurance economics focused upon the search for the degree of optimal insurance and the sharing of the risk between the risk averse individual and the risk neutral insurer (Arrow, 1963, 1971; Raviv, 1979). However, the optimal cover is, in some instances, unavailable in the market. For some risks involving new technology, pollution, and environmental risk the unquantifiable nature of potential liabilities means only limited cover is available. Further, the portfolio effect of a diverse spread of risks within one organization reduces the potential damage to shareholder value of a single loss, which together with their intrinsic financial strength makes risk sharing a more practical use of resources than full insurance coverage. Additionally, the detailed records of loss incidents available within an organization may far outweigh the information held by an insurer.

Partly to overcome lack of market cover, partly to utilize capital more effectively, and partly to avoid the administrative and other non-claims related charges included in premiums, the corporate buyers developed their pooling arrangements and insurance facilities in house through the introduction of "captive" insurance companies. Captive insurance companies are subsidiaries of a single or group of trading companies and were developed solely to insure the risks of their owners. Captives expanded rapidly in the 1970s and 1980s to take advantage of favorable tax regimes in off-shore tax centers at a time when premiums were spiraling and capacity falling in the direct market. Together with other alternative self-funded risk financing such as "risk retention" groups and "pools," they were estimated in 1993 to account for around 25 percent of the US$37 billion spent worldwide on risk financing. Although offering large companies savings on risks such as motor or fire and allowing large risks to be covered by reinsurance, a captive has drawbacks. Tax deductibility of premiums by a parent to a subsidiary may be challenged where premiums are not on an arm's length basis and are designed solely to transfer profits to a low tax regime.

LIFE INSURANCE

Life business differs from general risk insurance because it is generally long term, involves critical assumptions about mortality (the life expectancy of an individual at any given age), and generally results in a claim. The exception here is term assurance, where the contract is option like, expiring without value if the insured survives to the end of cover.

Underwriting in life business requires a calculation of value at policy maturity which involves an estimate of investment returns on accumulated premiums net of deductions to cover risk factors such as age, employment, risky pastimes, and personal and family health history leading to premature claims, the life company's expenses, and a portion of the profit attributable to the shareholders – usually up to a maximum of 10 percent. The remaining profit arising from the life fund is paid to the policy holders by way of a yearly "bonus" declaration, and a maturity bonus on a claim.

The other major form of life contract is by way of an annuity, which requires a series of regular fixed payments for the remaining life of single or joint beneficiaries in exchange for a single front-end payment or usually when com-

bined with a pension plan, regular payments throughout the term. Underwriting of annuities makes some of the same assumptions about mortality and interest rates, though factors such as, say, a poor health risk, are more a matter of the proposer's evaluation than the insurers.

Because annuities ignore individual risk factors it is left to the purchaser to choose single or joint life payments, a minimum payout period, and so on. Pension schemes are constructed by combining a life policy, on an individual or group basis which matures at retirement age and is then converted into an annuity to fund pension payments. Because pension contributions enjoy favorable tax treatment the range of choice in term of payout and annuity options is generally restricted with pension payments from the annuity, which include significant elements of capital repayment treated as earned and hence taxable income whereas annuities purchased outside pension plans would enjoy more favorable treatment.

REINSURANCE

Reinsurance refers to insurance contracts exchanged between insurance companies and may be defined as acceptance by one insurance company of the insurance liabilities contracted by another insurer or reinsurer. The reinsurance contract indemnifies the reinsured for payments they make whether the original contract involved indemnity (recompense for losses), or not, in the case of a life policy. Reinsurance contracts involve the reinsurer in paying an agreed proportion of losses or else losses in excess of an agreed amount, possibly subject to a maximum in either case, in exchange for a premium.

These contract types may be further subdivided into proportional contracts, where only a proportion (e.g., 10 percent) of all risks accepted by the direct insurer is contracted with a reinsurer, surplus lines where the reinsurer accepts the balance of the risk above the amount the direct insurer wishes to cover, and non-proportional or stop loss cover which indemnifies for losses on an account in excess of a specific amount or ratio (e.g., the insurer wishes to limit the level of losses on its theft account to 80 percent). Another variant is excess of loss (risk basis) where the reinsurer pays for any loss on an individual risk above an agreed figure or (occurrence basis) losses above an agreed figure arising from a particular event, such as an earthquake.

The two main methods of arranging reinsurance cover are facultative where the insurer offers a specific risk to the reinsurer, and treaty, where a reinsurer contracts to accept and the insurer agrees to reinsure (cede) all risks in an agreed category.

The reinsurer's role in relation to the insurance market is to provide enlarged capacity both in a class of insurance and also for individual risks. The magnitude of today's major construction risks – Hong Kong Airport, Channel Tunnel, plus hi-tech developments in space – means that the direct market is unable to provide the necessary risk transfer without the use of worldwide reinsurance. Additionally, reinsurers provide security to the direct market by limiting loss potential, stabilizing underwriting margins, spreading the risk across a wide geographical area, and arranging specialist technical and advisory services for the direct insurers. Thus, the reinsurance market provides additional capacity for the direct insurer, allowing a greater spread of risk without the need to provide additional capital. Unfortunately, as argued by Nierhaus (1986), when the prevailing economic conditions are attractive direct insurers use investment income to subsidize underwriting losses and meet market competition on prices, leaving reinsurers, having only the underwriting business premiums, with under-rewarded risk and creating cyclical fluctuations in capacity available and pricing. Indeed, there is the danger that direct underwriters may simply try to control their catastrophe exposures and underwriting losses by reinsurance alone and not by controlling their own gross underwriting procedures.

INSURANCE DERIVATIVES

A new feature of the reinsurance market is the use of banking initiatives to supplement or replace reinsurance contracts. Insurance derivatives are tradable insurance contracts. Introduced by the Chicago Board of Trade (CBOT), they are currently restricted to property catastrophe exposures in the USA. The derivative contract at the CBOT uses statistics related to premiums and losses published by the Insurance Service Office (ISO) to determine the settlement value for insurance futures and options. Whether or not this idea develops to replace or supplement insurance will depend on the volume of transactions and hence the liquidity of the market and the severity of the basis risk faced by insurers using the derivatives market to hedge particular insurance contracts.

INSURANCE COMPANIES AND MARKETS

Insurance in its present form probably started in the eleventh century in Northern Italy in the form of marine cover and was introduced into England by the Lombards in the fourteenth century, with merchants signing their names or underwriting a proportion of the risk of a cargo and the premium on a contract. The Great Fire of London in 1666 prompted the need to provide cover for property and merchants and property owners combined to form the Fire Office, which was amalgamated with the Phoenix in 1705. A variety of new companies, often concentrating on a particular class of business such as life, farming property, glass, or a geographical area, followed. Early companies, especially life offices, were mutual organizations, but to obtain the requisite capital several were formed by Royal Charter and others became joint stock companies.

A special place in insurance history is occupied by Lloyds of London, a unique institution that dominated international insurance from the eighteenth century. Lloyds operates by statutory authorization rather than as a limited liability company. Underwriting capacity in the Lloyds market is provided by syndicates of individuals or "names" who are entitled to write insurance up to 3.3 times the wealth they commit to the market. Names are allocated to syndicates by members' agents and have unlimited liability not just for their share of the syndicate's loss but for the share of any defaulting name. Underwriters acting for syndicates evaluate risks offered to the market by Lloyds brokers, who include the major international insurance brokers. Agents commit their syndicate to a proportion of a risk by signing a "slip" giving details of cover, premium, risk, and commission. Apart from Lloyds of London, the majority of non-life companies operate as joint stock companies, owned by their shareholders; but traditionally a number of large life offices are mutuals, with policy holders effectively the owners of the company. In the USA, for example, although 95 percent of the 2,627 life companies in 1990 were stockholding, the mutuals made up about 46 percent of the total life company assets. With deregulation and rationalization the dependence of mutuals on internally generated retained profits for investment has presented problems and they are being forced to demutualize or merge with commercial or savings banks in order to preserve market share and meet competition from other savings institutions. A further group of companies are state owned.

Life and Non-Life

With the growth of the industry during the nineteenth century, the historic separation of the insurance into life or non-life businesses was partly abandoned by the rise, particularly in the UK, of "composites," transacting both life and non-life business. However, regulations required the separation of life and non-life assets to preclude the settlement of non-life losses from the funds of life policy holders. More recently, with the development of the EC market and standardization across Europe, where composites were either banned or had not been developed, the UK companies have formed their life and non-life businesses into separate companies operating under a holding company.

Long-Term or Life Assurance

Originally providing annuities or cover for death, life assurance developed in the late nineteenth century into a savings product via the endowment policy, which pays either on death or on survival after a fixed term of years. Many of the original life offices, known as "industrial" life offices, collected premiums on a weekly door to door basis, providing money for burials and long-term savings. Those companies, which sold relatively shorter-term cover and annuities and collected premiums yearly, became known as "ordinary" life offices.

Today, life companies provide a wide range of insurance protection, savings, and investment products and pension provision, including annuity plans. Because of the different taxation regulations governing the funds of a life company they may be separated into those which support the protection and savings business and those which are represented by the pensions and annuity business. Life funds made up of premiums and investment income funds are effectively in trust for the policy holders with shareholders, if any, restricted to a maximum 10 percent of the profits allocated to policy holders. Invested funds provide for policy returns on maturity and provide pensions and annuities.

The size and long-term nature of these funds means that life companies play a major role, supplying funds for a wide variety of financial and non-financial organizations as well as for government agencies, both in their home territory and overseas. These policy holders' funds, after expenses such as sales commission and life cover, are invested in domestic and international securities, mainly equities for UK companies but still heavily in bonds for US companies – 35.7 percent in 1991 per Best's Insurance Reports – and most European insurance funds. Indeed, many European countries have imposed upper limits on the investment holdings of shares; for example, a maximum of 20 percent in Germany and 30 percent in Switzerland, or in real estate with a maximum of 25 percent in Germany and 40 percent in France.

Non-Life

Sometimes referred to as "general" business or as "property and casualty," though also including marine and aviation insurance, non-life insurance protects an individual's or company's financial interests in the material benefit arising from property, goods, etc., or from the financial effects of any liabilities they may incur arising, for example, out of the use of property, selling of products, or employment. Originally designed to protect against loss from perils of the sea or from fire, new classes of insurance developed with the industrial revolution. The insurance broker, the principal intermediary in the market, acting as an innovator, developed such classes as consequential loss, with engineering boiler and mechanical failure, third party liability, workmen's compensation, and in the early part of the twentieth century, motor insurance, evolved out of statutory necessity and as a result of industry becoming increasingly international.

The main characteristics of non-life business differ from life assurance in a number of ways.

First, the policies are essentially short term, that is for one year or less, whereas life policies are long-term contracts. Further, the wide variety of risks in general business and the uncertainty of both the number and severity of the claims has an effect on the manner in which the funds are invested. For non-life, there has to be a substantial level of liquidity with a larger proportion of assets being in cash or liquid securities. The risks are illustrated by the conjunction of massive hurricane losses in the UK with the global crash in equity markets in October 1987, the effect of which was to seriously deplete reserves of several insurers and reduce their solvency margins.

Market Developments

The single market in Europe accounts for over 30 percent of worldwide premiums and has several major competitors in world markets. The drive to increase competition in European Community insurance markets started in 1973 with the Freedom of Establishment Directive, followed by Freedom of Services – Life, Non-life, Intermediaries, and Motor Directives have followed, increasing competitive pressures. The result has been a surge of mergers, acquisitions, and alliances both within and across borders, with the development of *Bancassurance/Allfinanz* institutions combining universal banking (including securities business) and insurance in one conglomerate with the aim of cross-selling wider product ranges to existing customers. However, as with life assurance, non-life business for many years has been sold through intermediaries. Indeed, it is only possible to place business at Lloyds of London through an accredited Lloyds broker. In Europe most personal policies are sold through "tied" agents, paid by the company and selling only that company's products.

Because of the complexity and need for professional advice, commercial risks are often handled by insurance brokers, particularly in the Netherlands and UK. Brokers have not the same dominant position elsewhere in Europe, where many companies have their "own agencies." However, with the liberalization of Europe and following the US example, the selling process is changing for large corporations. In the UK risk managers are taking their business out of the market by forming captive subsidiary insurance companies, while the large multinational brokers are breaking into the European market, offering risk management services and competitive placing.

Both life and general insurance companies have experienced increasing rates of customer churn, with a growing portion of life business coming from single premium contracts and general insurers facing lower retention rates. It can be argued that this reflects a better informed market with computer quotation systems and comparative performance statistics more generally available. One successful approach to reducing marketing costs has been direct writing, whereby insurance companies dispense with traditional sales forces and agencies, instead using technology support coupled to telephone and off the page response from the public. Several European companies are experimenting with direct selling, though their heavy reliance on small agencies may well prove an inhibiting factor.

Liberalization in Europe has led to deregulation in many aspects of insurance with greater freedom in designing policy covers and pricing. However, there remains a need to provide consumer protection, and this in turn has produced a range of restrictions on selling methods, thereby replacing one form of regulation with another. In the USA the industry is highly regulated by state agencies. Each state regulatory body monitors the services provided by insurers and regulates the rates charged. Elsewhere industry regulators have wide duties to prevent abuse and to monitor security in the interests of policy holders.

Bibliography

Anderson Consulting (1990). *Insurance in a Changing Europe 1990–1995*. London: Economist Publications.

Arrow, K. J. (1963). Uncertainty and the welfare economics of medical care. *American Economic Review*, **53**, 941–73.

Arrow, K. J. (1971). *Essays in the Theory of Risk Bearing*. Chicago: Markham.

Blazenko, G. (1986). The economics of reinsurance. *Journal of Risk and Insurance*, **53**, 258–77.

Borch, K. H. (1962). Equilibrium in a reinsurance market. *Econometrica*, **30**, 424–44.

Borch, K. H. (1967). The theory of risk. *Journal of the Royal Statistical Society*, **Series B**, 432–67.

Borch, K. H., Aase, K. K., and Sandmo, A. (1990). *Economics of Insurance*. Amsterdam: Elsevier Science.

Brockett, P. L., Cox, S. H., and Witt, R. C. (1986). Insurance versus self-insurance: A risk management perspective. *Journal of Risk and Insurance*, **53**, 242–57.

Carter, R. L. (1983). *Reinsurance*, 2nd edn. London: Kluwer.

Cummins, J. D., and Outreville, J. F. (1987). An international analysis of underwriting cycles in property-liability insurance. *Journal of Risk and Insurance*, **54**, 246–62.

D'Arcy, S. P., and Garven, J. R. (1990). Property-liability insurance pricing models: An empirical evaluation. *Journal of Risk and Insurance*, **57**, 391–430.

Diacon, S. (1990). *A Guide to Insurance Management*. Basingstoke: Macmillan.

Dionne, G., and Harrington, J. R. (eds.) (1992). *Foundations of Insurance Economics*. London: Kluwer.

Ennew, C., Watkins, T., and Wright, M. (1991). *Marketing Financial Services*. Oxford: Butterworth-Heinemann.

Kloman, H. F. (1992). Rethinking risk management. *Geneva Papers on Risk and Insurance*, **64**, 299–313.

MacMinn, R. D. (1987). Insurance and corporate risk management. *Journal of Risk and Insurance*, **54**, 658–77.

Nierhaus, F. (1986). A strategic approach to insurability of risks. *Geneva Papers on Risk and Insurance*, **1**, 83–90.

Pratt, J. W. (1964). Risk aversion in the small and in the large. *Econometrica*, **32**, 122–36.

Raviv, A. (1979). The design of the optimal insurance policy. *American Economic Review*, **69**, 84–96.

Rothschild, M., and Stiglitz, J. E. (1976). Equilibrium in competitive insurance markets: An essay in the economics of imperfect information. *Quarterly Journal of Economics*, **90**, 629–49.

Shavell, S. (1986). The judgment proof problem. *International Review of Law and Economics*, **6**, 45–58.

Venezian, E. C. (1985). Ratemaking methods and profit cycles in property and liability insurance. *Journal of Risk and Insurance*, **52**, 477–500.

Williams, C. A., Jr. and Heins, R. M. (1989). *Risk Management and Insurance*, 6th edn. New York: McGraw-Hill.

international initial public offerings

A. Tourani-Rad

The initial public offering (IPO) of a company's equity is a milestone in its life and it denotes a turning point in the relationship between the company and its owners (*see* INITIAL PUBLIC OFFERINGS (IPOs)). The main reasons for going public are: (1) to raise additional capital for further expansion; (2) to allow the owners to realize partially or wholly their original invest-ments and to rebalance their asset portfolios; (3) to adopt an employee/management compensation share scheme; and (4) to enhance the company's visibility and public prestige. However, a company that wishes its stock to be traded on an organized exchange comes under greater scrutiny by the public and must meet stringent listing requirements.

The decision whether to go public is an intricate one and unique to each company. It involves the selection of the investment banker(s), underwriter(s), the fraction of equity to be sold, and the method and the timing of introduction. Going public is quite expensive. Underwriting fees and other related expenses average 14 percent of the of gross proceeds of stock offerings in the US (Ritter, 1987).

IPOs in European countries are a relatively new development and are of smaller size than in the USA. Until the early 1980s relatively few companies went public in Europe. This pattern, however, has been changing considerably and more IPOs are being issued. Moreover, European IPOs tend to be of well established companies compared to young companies in the USA.

Companies can sell securities to the public at large through several institutional arrangements. The two most extensively used methods are an offer for sale at a fixed price and an offer for sale by tender. The former is a direct, fixed price, fixed quantity offering to investors. In case of oversubscription, the number of shares allocated to each investor will be rationed, though not necessarily on a *pro rata* basis. This method is mandatory in the USA and is widely used in Finland, Germany, Italy, the Netherlands, Sweden, and Switzerland. The offer by tender is essentially a competitive price-and-quantity auction process. Investors are invited to bid over a stated minimum price. Once all bids are in, an offer price is set so that all shares can be allocated to investors. The tender method is used mainly in Belgium, France, and to some extent in the Netherlands. In most European countries there are no regulatory constraints concerning selling mechanisms, whereas in the USA the fixed price method has been the norm.

The key decision in an IPO process concerns setting the price at which the shares are sold to the public. Generally speaking, shares in IPOs are issued at a significant discount relative to their intrinsic value (i.e., IPOs are underpriced). This is a well documented fact and seems to be a recurring phenomenon across various capital markets. The degree of underpricing, however, varies significantly among countries, ranging from 4.2 percent in France to 80.3 percent in Malaysia. Countries with a low level of underpricing are usually those in which most of the firms going public are relatively large and well established, and where the contractual mechanism used has auction-related features. Countries with a high level of underpricing tend to be those with binding regulatory constraints in setting prices, especially in the newly industrialized countries (Loughran, Ritter, and Rydqvist, 1994).

A number of theoretical models, mainly focusing on information asymmetry among the parties involved in an IPO process, attempt to explain why this underpricing occurs. The winner's curse (Rock, 1986) relies on informational asymmetry between two groups of investors: informed and uninformed. The former possess better knowledge about the future prospects of the firm going public than the latter. The informed investors will bid for more shares of the good firms. The uninformed investors cannot distinguish between offers and hence always place the same bid. This process will leave the uninformed investors with a disproportionate amount of the bad issues. Consequently, to persuade the uninformed to participate in the subscription process, firms must underprice so as to compensate them for the bias in the allocation system.

The signaling model (Allen and Faulhaber, 1989; Welch, 1989) is based on asymmetry of information between issuing firms and investors. The good firms can afford to signal their high quality through higher underpricing of their IPOs. Low quality firms cannot signal by underpricing their IPOs because they cannot recapture the cost of the signal. The good firms will sell future offerings at a higher price than would otherwise be the case. The future benefits of IPO underpricing are greater than the present loss. Michaely and Shaw (1994) find support consistent with the winner's curse and not signaling models.

There is strong evidence to suggest that the reputation of the underwriters and the certifying role that they assume is important in explaining the performance of IPOs in both the short and long run. Carter and Manaster (1990) show a significant inverse relationship between the reputation of the underwriter and the level of initial underpricing. Michaely and Shaw (1994) observe that IPOs underwritten by reputable investment bankers perform significantly better over longer periods.

While most models assume that underpricing is a deliberate action, Ruud (1993) suggests that the underpricing is due to underwriter price support actions: stock prices in the immediate aftermarket are allowed to rise, but are prevented from falling below the offer price until the issue is fully sold. Consequently, on average, the first day aftermarket price rises above the true market value of stock and this has been misinterpreted as underpricing. This theory has important implications for some European countries where usually a small number of investment bankers are dominant players and are active in supporting the prices of new issues.

No single theory can provide a definitive answer to the phenomenon of short-term underpricing of IPOs.

A second anomaly associated with IPOs is the existence of cyclical patterns in both the number of issues and the degree of underpricing, which is also referred to as "hot issue" markets (i.e., when the average level of underpricing is distinctly greater in one period than in other period) (Ibbotson, Sindelar, and Ritter, 1994). In addition to the USA, hot issue markets have been documented in several other countries.

A more recent, seemingly anomalous aspect related to IPOs is their long-term underperformance. Several studies in different countries have found the same general pattern in that, when a portfolio of IPO shares is held over a long period, it performs inexplicably poorly compared to a portfolio of shares from similar companies (Loughran, Ritter, and Rydqvist, 1994). In the USA, the long-run underperformance appears to be concentrated among those firms which went public in the heavy-volume years of the early 1980s and among the younger and riskier firms. However, there is, so far, no rigorous explanation and it remains a mystery (Ritter, 1991).

Bibliography

Allen, F., and Faulhaber, G. R. (1989). Signaling by underpricing in the IPO market. *Journal of Financial Economics*, 23, 303–23.

Carter, R. B., and Manaster, S. (1990). Initial public offerings and underwriter reputation. *Journal of Finance*, 45, 1045–67.

Ibbotson, R. G., Sindelar, J. L., and Ritter, J. R. (1994). Initial public offerings. *Journal of Applied Corporate Finance*, 7, 6–14.

Loughran, T., Ritter, J. R., and Rydqvist, K. (1994). Initial public offerings: International insights. *Pacific-Basin Finance Journal*, 2, 165–99.

Michaely, R., and Shaw, W. H. (1994). The pricing of initial public offerings: Tests of adverse selection and signaling theories. *Review of Financial Studies*, 7, 279–319.

Ritter, J. R. (1987). The costs of going public. *Journal of Financial Economics*, 19, 269–81.

Ritter, J. R. (1991). The long-run performance of initial public offerings. *Journal of Finance*, 6, 3–27.

Rock, K. (1986). Why new issues are underpriced. *Journal of Financial Economics*, 15, 187–212.

Ruud, J. S. (1993). Underwriter price support and the IPO underpricing puzzle. *Journal of Financial Economics*, 34, 135–51.

Welch, I. (1989). Seasoned offerings imitation costs and the underpricing of initial public offerings. *Journal of Finance*, 44, 421–50.

intertemporal CAPM

see PORTFOLIO THEORY AND ASSET PRICING

investment banking

Joseph F. Sinkey, Jr.

The earliest known banks, temples, operated as repositories of concentrated wealth. They were among the first places where a need for money and money-changers emerged. The word *bank* traces to the French word *banque* (chest) and the Italian word *banca* (bench). These early meanings capture the two basic functions that banks perform: (1) the safe-keeping or risk-control function (chest); and (2) the transactions function, including intermediation and trading (bench). Taking investment to mean the outlay of money for income or profit, an investment bank functions as a safekeeper, risk manager, trader, and intermediary with respect to the outlay of money for income or profit.

Although modern investment banks (also called securities firms) engage in numerous financial activities, especially in a world characterized by globalization, securitization, and financial engineering, two activities represent the heart of investment banking: bringing new securities issues (debt and equity) to market and making secondary markets for these securities. The first activity captures the underwriting function, while the second reflects the broker/dealer function. As brokers, investment banks bring parties together to trade securities while, as dealers, they trade from their own inventory.

To understand the full range of financial services provided by investment banks, consider the six basic functions performed by a financial system: clearing and settling payments, pooling or subdividing resources, transferring wealth, managing risk, providing price information, and dealing with incentive problems. Since investment banks are a major component of financial systems in developed countries, they play a prominent role in performing most of these functions. In the United States, because of the separation of commercial and investment banking (Glass–Steagall Act of 1933), investment banks perform all of these functions except clearing and settling payments, a task performed mainly by commercial banks in the USA. In contrast, in Germany and Japan where such artificial barriers between investment and commercial banking do not exist, the activities of commercial and investment banks are commingled, and interwoven with the activities of non-financial firms.

In Japan, banks own shares in businesses, which also own shares in the banks. Although cross-holdings tend to be nominal, the practical effect links dissimilar companies together for mutual support and protection. These cross-shareholding groups, called *keiretsu*, provide a unique approach to corporate control based on continuous surveillance and monitoring by the managers of affiliated firms and banks.

The German model links universal banks and industrial companies through the *Hausbank* approach to providing financial services (i.e., reliance on only one principal bank). In addition, incentive compatibilities and monitoring are accomplished by bank ownership of equity shares, bank voting rights over fiduciary (trust) shareholdings, and bank participation on supervisory boards. The *Hausbank* relationship results in companies accessing both capital-market services (e.g., new issues of stocks and bonds) and bank-credit facilities through their "universal bank." By providing all of the financing needed to start a business (e.g., seed capital, initial public offerings of stock, bond underwritings, and working capital), German banks gain *Hausbank* standing. On balance, in the German model, bank–industry linkages involve strong surveillance and monitoring by banks and the potential for a high degree of control in maximizing shareholder value as banks have an equity stake and fiduciary obligations with respect to depository shares.

The investment banking industry in the USA has three tiers: large, full-line firms that cater to both retail and corporate clients; national and international firms that concentrate mainly on corporate finance and trading activities; and the rest of the industry (e.g., specialized and regional securities firms and discount brokers). Examples of key players in the top two tiers are Merrill Lynch in the top tier and Goldman Sachs, Salomon Brothers, and Morgan Stanley in the second tier. In addition, due to the piecemeal dismantling of Glass–Steagall, major US commercial banks such as BankAmerica, Bankers Trust, Chase Manhattan, Chemical, Citicorp, and J. P. Morgan (listed alphabetically) are important global players as investment banks, especially in derivatives activities.

Although the primary regulator of the securities industry in the USA is the Securities and Exchange Commission (SEC, established in 1934), the New York Stock Exchange (NYSE) and National Association of Securities Dealers (NASD) provide self-regulation and monitoring of day-to-day trading practices and activities. Two important SEC rules governing underwriting activities are Rule 415 and Rule 144A. Rule 415 ("shelf registration") permits large issuers to register new issues with the SEC up to two years in advance, and then "pull them off the shelf " (i.e., issue them) when market conditions are most favorable. Rule 144A establishes boundaries between public offerings and private placements of securities. In a public offering, securities are offered to the public at large; in a private placement, securities are "placed" with one or more institutional investors.

Since investment banking can be defined by what investment banks or securities firms do, let us look at the major functions they perform. Investment banks underwrite and distribute new issues of debt and equity. When firms issue securities for the first time, this is called an initial public offering or IPO. How IPOs are priced is an important research question in empirical finance. Securities may be underwritten either on a best-efforts basis, where the investment banker acts as an agent and receives a fee related to the successful placement of the issue, or on a firm-commitment basis, where the investment bank buys the entire issue and resells it, making a profit on the difference between the two prices or the bid–ask spread. A common practice in underwriting public offerings is to form a syndicate to ensure raising enough capital and to share the risk. Trading, market making, funds management (for mutual and pension funds), and providing financial and custodial services, are other functions performed by investment banks.

Financial innovation has been a substantial force in capital markets, and investment banks have played a leading role in this area (e.g., in the development of securitization and in the engineering of risk management products called derivatives). First-mover or innovative investment banks tend to be characterized by lower costs of trading, underwriting, and marketing. Evidence (Tufano, 1989) suggests that compensation for developing new products centers on gaining market share and maintaining reputational capital as opposed to "monopoly pricing" before imitative products appear.

Bibliography

Bloch, E. (1986). *Inside Investment Banking*. Homewood, IL: Dow Jones-Irwin.

Hayes, S. L., III and Hubbard, P. M. (1990). *Investment Banking: A Tale of Three Cities*. Boston, MA: Harvard Business School Press.

Marshall, J. F., and Ellis, M. E. (1994). *Investment Banking and Brokerage: The New Rules of the Game*. Chicago: Probus.

Tufano, P. (1989). Financial innovation and first-mover advantages. *Journal of Financial Economics*, **25**, 213–40.

Iowa Electronic Market

Joyce E. Berg, Robert Forsythe, and Thomas A. Rietz

The Iowa Electronic Market (IEM) is a real-money, computerized futures market operated as a not-for-profit teaching and research tool by the University of Iowa College of Business Administration. As a teaching tool, the IEM provides students with hands-on, real-time experience in a fully functional financial market. As a research tool, the IEM serves as a laboratory, providing a unique source of data for studying financial markets.

MARKET OPERATION

The IEM operates as a continuous electronic double auction with queues. Trading takes place over the Internet and is open to participants worldwide. Registered traders can issue limit orders to buy or sell, or market orders to trade at the best available prices. Outstanding bids and asks are maintained in price- and time-ordered queues, which function as continuous electronic limit order books. Traders invest their own money in the IEM, bearing the risk of loss and profiting from gains.

The futures contracts traded on the IEM have liquidation values tied to the outcomes of future political and economic events such as elections, legislation, economic indicators, corporate earnings announcements, and realized stock price returns. For instance, the 1992 Presidential Election Vote-Share Market traded contracts in "November Clinton" that paid off US$1 times the Clinton share of the two-party vote in the 1992 election. Because these are real futures contracts, the IEM is under the regulatory purview of the Commodity Futures Trading Commission (CFTC). The CFTC has issued a "no-action" letter to the IEM stating that as long as the IEM conforms to certain restrictions (related to limiting risk and conflict of interest), the CFTC will take no action against it. Under this no-action letter, IEM does not file reports that are required by regulation and therefore it is not formally regulated by, nor are its operators registered with, the CFTC.

Contracts are placed in circulation via "unit portfolios." A unit portfolio is a set of contracts with liquidation values that will sum to US$1. The IEM stands ready to buy or sell any unit portfolio at any time for US$1. After purchasing unit portfolios, traders "unbundle" them and trade individual contracts in the market. If held to liquidation, individual contracts receive liquidating payments according to the rules established in the market prospectuses.

THE IEM AS A TEACHING TOOL

The IEM serves as a real-time interactive laboratory in which students learn the language of markets and study the events on which the markets are based. It has been integrated into accounting, economics, finance, and political science classes at more than 30 colleges and universities. The economic stake that students have in the market provides a powerful incentive for learning how markets work and focusing attention on the economic and political events that drive market prices. In this social science laboratory, students learn first hand about the operation of markets, how public information is assimilated in market prices, market efficiency, arbitrage, and the concepts and problems underlying the measurement of economic events. Because students trade based on their own analysis of market factors, they are better able to understand these factors and how market prices impound information about them.

THE IEM AS A RESEARCH TOOL

The IEM combines the features of larger organized futures and securities markets with the experimental control found in laboratory markets. Traders put their own funds at risk and real economic events drive market outcomes. Yet the market structure is simple and controlled, contracts and their payoffs are well specified, and actions are time stamped and identified by trader. Online trader surveys also allow collection of additional individual trader-level data. Since the markets are relatively short lived, a variety of market structure variables can be controlled and manipulated across markets.

The data from these markets have been used to investigate several research issues. The first, and most obvious, is the ability of the IEM to predict a decidedly non-market event such as an election. Like most futures markets, the ability of the IEM to correctly incorporate information about future events can be tested directly, since there is an observable event that ultimately defines the true value of a contract. In contrast to typical futures markets, achieving this informational efficiency is presumably more difficult, since there is no underlying, market-traded asset and, hence, there are no arbitrage conditions that drive the futures and spot prices together. Forsythe et al. (1992) undertook the first of several studies to examine this issue using the data from one market on one election. Using the data from a 1988 US presidential election market designed to predict candidates' vote shares, they examined both the ability of a market to predict an election outcome in an absolute sense as well as relative to public opinion polls. They conclude that the market is efficient in both senses; the IEM's error in predicting Bush's actual winning margin was 0.26 percent, while the average poll error was 2.69 percent.

As additional markets have been conducted, studies have begun to examine cross-market comparisons of the IEM's predictive accuracy. Using the data from 12 vote-share markets from 7 countries, Forsythe, Nelson, and Neumann (1993) looked at IEM's performance relative to election eve public opinion polls, and found that the IEM's forecast outperformed the polls in 9 of the 12 comparisons. Berg, Forsythe, and Rietz (1996) provide a detailed examination of the data from 16 US vote-share election markets to study factors that influence the IEM's predictive ability.

The average absolute prediction errors for these markets range from 0.06 percent to 8.60 percent. Most of the variance in these errors can be explained by market volume, the number of contract types traded, and the level of market imbalance (as measured by absolute differences in election eve weighted bid and ask queues).

A second stream of research examines individual trading behavior. Analyzing the data from the 1988 presidential election market, Forsythe et al. (1992) used trader-level response data to examine how traders' judgments and preferences affect their trading behavior. They found that, on average, traders exhibit systematic trading biases; for instance, at any price the average trader's partisanship leads them to buy more contracts in the candidate they favor than the candidate they do not favor. Nevertheless, the market predicts quite well due to the presence of bias-free marginal traders (traders who regularly submit orders at or near the market). Thus, while an examination of individual trader behavior would lead one to conclude that, on average, traders are biased, market prices do not necessarily reflect these biases. Market dynamics, along with a core of bias-free marginal traders, still lead to unbiased prices.

Oliven and Rietz (1995) provide additional evidence about the behavior of these "bias-free" marginal traders. They compared the "rationality" of price-taking traders (who accept market prices) to that of market-making traders (who set market prices). Using trader-specific data from the 1992 presidential election market to study no-arbitrage restrictions and individual rationality, they found large differences between these two types of traders. Violations of individual rationality are common among price takers (occurring in 38.3 percent of the orders they submit), while rare among market makers (7.8 percent). Since the 1992 market was one of the most efficient to date, this provides further evidence that market prices can be efficient even though individual traders act suboptimally.

Bibliography

Berg, J., Forsythe, R., and Rietz, T. (1996). What makes markets predict well? Evidence from the Iowa Electronic Markets. In W. Guth (ed.), *Understanding Strategic Interaction: Essays in Honor of Reinhard Selten.* Berlin: Springer-Verlag.

Forsythe, R., Nelson, F., and Neumann, G. (1993). The Iowa political markets. Mimeo, University of Iowa.

Forsythe, R., Nelson, F., Neumann, G., and Wright, J. (1992). The anatomy of an experimental political stock market. *American Economic Review*, **82**, 1142–61.

Oliven, K., and Rietz, T. (1995). Suckers are born but markets are made: Individual rationality, arbitrage, and market efficiency on an electronic futures market. Working paper, University of Iowa.

L

leasing

Premal Vora

An agreement between two parties to rent an asset is a leasing arrangement. The owner of the leased asset, the lessor, receives a set of fixed payments for the term of the contract from the lessee. If the lease contains a provision that allows the lessee to cancel at any time or if the lessor is responsible for insurance and maintenance, then it is called an operating lease. Financial leases are long term, carry no cancelation options, and the lessee is responsible for all insurance and maintenance.

It has been pointed out in a number of studies (see Smith and Wakeman, 1985) that leasing would not exist in the absence of capital market imperfections like taxes, transaction costs, and agency costs. The demand for short-term leasing arrangements stems from the need to eliminate the transactions costs of buying and selling an asset (Flath, 1980). In the absence of transaction costs, Myers, Dill, and Bautista (1976) show that lessee and lessor tax rates must differ for a leasing arrangement to be advantageous. A number of other firm and asset characteristics that increase the likelihood of leasing have also been identified (Smith and Wakeman, 1985). Empirical evidence suggests that the market value of both lessee and lessor stock rises upon announcements of new leasing arrangements (Slovin, Sushka, and Poloncheck, 1990; Vora and Ezzell, 1991).

Sale and Leaseback

In a sale and leaseback, an asset is sold and simultaneously leased back by the seller. The rights to ownership are transferred to the buyer/ lessor while the seller/lessee enjoys the rights to services provided by the asset. The financial effects of a sale and leaseback are (1) the lessee gets an immediate inflow of cash equal to the selling price of the asset, while the lessor receives (2) a promise of a stream of fixed lease payments in the future; (3) the salvage value of the asset; and (4) the depreciation tax shields.

Although the sale and leaseback offers the same advantages to the lessee that an ordinary lease arrangement would, it has been suggested that the sale and leaseback can also be used as a device to expropriate wealth from the senior claimholders to the common stockholders of the lessee, since it rearranges the priority of the claims against the lessee in favor of the lessor (Kim, Lewellen, and McConnell, 1978). The empirical evidence suggests that the market value of lessee common stockholders rises when a sale and leaseback is announced (Slovin, Sushka, and Poloncheck, 1990, 1991; Vora and Ezzell, 1991). The source of the gain does not seem to be wealth expropriation, since the value of lessee preferred stock remains unchanged (Vora and Ezzell, 1991). In fact, as suggested in a number of studies (e.g., Myers, Dill, and Bautista, 1976), savings in taxes seems to be the motivating factor behind such sale and leasebacks (Vora and Ezzell, 1991).

Net Advantage to Leasing (NAL)

This is the present value of the benefits that are provided by leasing an asset instead of purchasing it via other financing alternatives. If the NAL of a lease is positive, leasing is preferred over the purchase. In the absence of transaction costs, savings in taxes are considered to be the paramount benefit of leasing. It has been shown that a necessary condition for the NAL to be positive for both lessee and lessor is that their tax brackets must differ (Myers, Dill, and Bautista, 1976; Miller and Upton, 1976; Lewellen,

Long, and McConnell, 1976). The intuition is that an organization that is non-tax paying or even in a low tax bracket would be better off by transferring its depreciation and interest tax shields to a company that pays taxes at a higher tax rate. This can be easily accomplished by entering into a leasing arrangement (either for assets that are newly put into use or for existing assets – by entering into a sale and leaseback). In return for the tax shields, the lessee receives consideration in the form of lower lease payments relative to its outflows under other financing alternatives.

Bibliography

Flath, D. (1980). The economics of short-term leasing. *Economic Inquiry*, **18**, 247–59.

Kim, E. H., Lewellen, W. G., and McConnell, J. J. (1978). Sale-and-leaseback agreements and enterprise valuation. *Journal of Financial and Quantitative Analysis*, **13**, 871–83.

Lewellen, W. G., Long, M. S., and McConnell, J. J. (1976). Asset leasing in competitive capital markets. *Journal of Finance*, **31**, 787–98.

Miller, M. H., and Upton, C. W. (1976). Leasing, buying and the cost of capital services. *Journal of Finance*, **31**, 761–86.

Myers, S. C., Dill, D. A., and Bautista, A. J. (1976). Valuation of financial lease contracts. *Journal of Finance*, **31**, 799–819.

Slovin, M. B., Sushka, M. E., and Polloncheck, J. A. (1990). Corporate sale-and-leasebacks and shareholder wealth. *Journal of Finance*, **45**, 289–99.

Slovin, M. B., Sushka, M. E., and Polloncheck, J. A. (1991). Restructuring transactions by bank holding companies: The valuation effects of sale-and-leasebacks and divestitures. *Journal of Banking and Finance*, **15**, 237–55.

Smith, C. W., Jr. and Wakeman, L. M. (1985). Determinants of corporate leasing policy. *Journal of Finance*, **40**, 895–908.

Vora, P. P., and Ezzell, J. R. (1991). Leasing vs. purchasing: Direct evidence on a corporation's motivations for leasing and consequences of leasing. Working paper, Penn State University.

log exponential option models

Jongchai Kim

Since Black and Scholes (1973) derived the first closed form equilibrium solution for European call options in a continuous time framework, the ability of the BLACK–SCHOLES option pricing model to estimate the market price of publicly traded options has been the topic of a number of studies. Based on the fact that the market value of a call option is a function of five variables – the price of the underlying asset, exercise price of the option, interest rate, time to expiration, and the volatility of the stock return – their model has been examined from different angles.

The Black–Scholes model has two properties that make it useful both theoretically and empirically. First, the popularity of the model is due to the fact that the option price does not explicitly depend on investors' preferences. This is the well-known risk-neutral valuation relationship (RNVR). Under a unique risk-neutral probability density, the value of an option at maturity depends on the value of the underlying asset. Thus, it is possible to calculate the expected value of the option before maturity based on the probability distribution of the terminal value of the underlying asset (i.e., the current value of the call is the discounted value of its expected value at expiration date).

Second, the Black–Scholes model has a form-invariance property. In the Black–Scholes case, both the original and risk-neutral distributions are lognormal. Since the risk-neutral probability density function has the same functional form as the original density, this form-invariance property makes it possible to reduce one of the parameters of the underlying distribution which need to be estimated. In the Black–Scholes model this parameter is the mean associated with a normal probability density function.

When investors' preferences are assumed to be risk neutral such that all securities have the same expected rate of return, we say that the valuation relationship is risk neutral. This implies that while securities with different probability density functions may have different expected rates of returns, when the state-contingent pricing structure is substituted for a security's probability density function, all securities have the same expected rate of return if the valuation relationship is risk neutral. RNVR is used to describe the state-contingent valuation structure from which option pricing formulas are derived. Deriving a RNVR with restrictions on investor preferences in a discrete time framework is similar in spirit to showing that a riskless hedge can be constructed and maintained in a continuous time framework.

Rubinstein (1976) first develops a discrete-time option-pricing formula with bivariate log-normality of terminal-date wealth and asset price and a constant relative risk-averse (CRRA) preference. Surprisingly, the resulting option-pricing formula is identical to the Black–Scholes formula even though only costless discrete-time trading opportunities are available, so that a perfect hedge cannot be constructed. Brennan (1979) shows that the bivariate lognormality with a CRRA utility function and the bivariate normality with a constant absolute risk averse (CARA) utility function are necessary and sufficient to generate a RNVR. Stapleton and Subrahmanyam (1984) obtain similar results for the joint multiplicative binomial process and a CRRA class utility function, and the joint additive binomial process and a CARA class utility function.

Vankudre (1985) shows that Brennan's definition of a RNVR can be relaxed to allow a larger set of RNVRs. He derives simple option-pricing formulas for probability distributions of terminal-date wealth and asset price other than the lognormal or the normal under a relatively weaker condition than the conditions required in earlier papers. Madrigal and Smith (1995) provide necessary and sufficient conditions for the existence and uniqueness of a form invariant RNVR when markets are incomplete. They show that combinations of a CRRA utility function and log exponential distributions or a CARA utility function and linear exponential distributions will generate form-invariant, risk-neutral densities. In these cases option prices will depend on fewer parameters than those which determine the original probability density, since the resulting form-invariant risk-neutral densities do not explicitly contain the parameters of the investors' utility function. This is very important because the utility parameters are not observable. Heston (1993) calls these parameters "invisible parameters" and provides an example with a combination of a CRRA class utility function and log-gamma distribution.

While the issue of which alternative assumptions fit the market data best is largely unre-solved, Kim (1995) empirically tests the impact of underlying distribution assumptions on the option price using three forms of distributions which belong to the log exponential family: inverted gamma, gamma, and lognormal distributions. Interestingly, his findings indicate that the gamma distribution performs better than the other two distributions using standard statistical criteria.

Bibliography

Black, F., and Scholes, M. (1973). The pricing of options and corporate liabilities. *Journal of Political Economy*, 81, 637–54.

Brennan, M. J. (1979). The pricing of contingent claims in discrete time models. *Journal of Finance*, 34, 53–68.

Heston, S. L. (1993). Invisible parameters in option prices. *Journal of Finance*, 48, 933–47.

Kim, J. (1995). The pricing of options for a class of distributions. Working paper, Georgia State University.

Madrigal, V., and Smith, S. D. (1995). Risk-neutral valuation without spanning: The discrete time case. Working paper, Georgia State University and New York University.

Rubinstein, M. (1976). The valuation of uncertain income streams and the pricing of options. *Bell Journal of Economics*, 7, 407–25.

Stapleton, R. C., and Subrahmanyam, M. G. (1984). The valuation of options when asset returns are generated by a binomial process. *Journal of Finance*, 39, 1525–39.

Vankudre, P. P. (1985). The pricing of options in discrete time. PhD dissertation, Wharton School, University of Pennsylvania.

loss aversion

Tyler Shumway

Loss aversion is one of several behaviorally motivated descriptions of choice under uncertainty that together constitute the Prospect Theory proposed by Kahneman and Tversky (1979). In the economic literature, loss aversion is commonly referred to as first order risk aversion. For agents that exhibit loss averse preferences, "losses loom larger than gains," implying that their utility depends both on whether they have won or lost (relative to a pre-specified benchmark) and the magnitude of the gain or loss. If $\pi(t)$ is the quantity that an agent is willing to pay to avoid a gamble of magnitude εt, where ε is an actuarially fair random variable, then standard expected utility theory with conventional risk aversion implies that $\pi'(0) = 0$, or that agents are indifferent to small gambles. By contrast, loss averse preferences are characterized by $\partial \pi / \partial t|_{t=0^+} \neq 0$, or by significant aversion to small gambles (Segal and Spivak, 1990). Loss averse preferences are an example of reference-dependent utility, in which total utility does not depend on the level of wealth or consumption, but on a comparison of wealth or consumption to some time-varying benchmark level.

Loss aversion as proposed by Kahneman and Tversky (1979) was originally combined with risk-seeking in losses, the observation that agents facing a certain loss often prefer to take additional risk in order to potentially avoid the loss. Most subsequent applications of loss aversion have combined it with risk-seeking in losses. Both of these features can be represented by the value function proposed by Tversky and Kahneman (1992):

$$
V^*(x) \begin{array}{ll} = & x^\alpha \qquad\quad x \geq 0 \\ = & -\lambda(-x)^\beta \quad x < 0, \end{array} \qquad (1)
$$

in which x represents wealth net of the benchmark level, both α and β are between zero and one, and λ is positive. Based on experimental evidence, Tversky and Kahneman estimate that both α and β have a value of 0.88 and that λ has a value of 2.25.

While much of the argument for loss aversion is based on experimental evidence, some very compelling facts about expected utility have been pointed out by Rabin (2000). Rabin shows that under standard expected utility preferences, an agent that would reject a gamble with equal probabilities of losing $1,000 and gaining $1,050 would reject a gamble with equal odds of losing $20,000 and gaining *any* quantity of money.

Under loss averse preferences, agents can consistently reject small gambles and accept large gambles with large risk premia.

Loss aversion has been used by a number of researchers to explain financial data. Shefrin and Statman (1985) show that loss averse investors will tend to sell stocks on which they have made a profit before they sell stocks on which they have made a loss. This tendency has come to be known as the disposition effect, and has been documented in a number of different contexts. Benartzi and Thaler (1995) explain the equity premium puzzle with loss aversion. Barberis and Huang (2001) build a model that explains excess volatility and the risk premium observed for value stocks with loss aversion. Coval and Shumway (2004) show that professional traders strongly exhibit loss aversion and that their loss aversion affects prices in the short run but not in the long run.

Bibliography

Benartzi, S., and Thaler, R. H. (1995). Myopic loss aversion and the equity premium puzzle. *Quarterly Journal of Economics*, **110**, 73–92.

Barberis, N., and Huang, M. (2001). Mental accounting, loss aversion, and individual stock returns. *Journal of Finance*, **56**, 1247–92.

Coval, J. D., and Shumway, T. (2004). Do behavioral biases affect prices? *Journal of Finance*, forthcoming.

Kahneman, D., and Tversky, A. (1979). Prospect theory: An analysis of decision under risk. *Econometrica*, **47**, 263–91.

Rabin, M., (2000). Risk aversion and expected-utility theory: A calibration theorem. *Econometrica*, **68**, 1281–92.

Segal, U., and Spivak, A. (1990). "First-order" versus "second-order" risk aversion. *Journal of Economic Theory*, **51**, 111–25.

Shefrin, H., and Statman, M. (1985). The disposition to sell winners too early and ride losers too long: Theory and evidence. *Journal of Finance*, **40**, 777–90.

Tversky, A., and Kahneman, D. (1992). Advances in prospect theory: Cumulative representation of uncertainty. *Journal of Risk and Uncertainty*, **5**, 297–323.

M

market efficiency

Sunil Poshakwale

Market efficiency denotes the relationship between information and share prices in the capital market literature. Although the tests of market efficiency were reported as early as 1900, it was not until 1953 that the idea of market efficiency was put forward by Maurice Kendall. The concept was a byproduct of a chance discovery through his paper on behavior of prices of stocks and commodities. He discovered that security prices follow a random walk that implied that price changes were independent of one another. The formal definition of market efficiency was given by Fama (1970). Fama classified market efficiency into three categories: weak form, semi-strong form, and strong form. According to Fama, a market is efficient in weak form if stock price changes cannot be predicted based on past returns, and semi-strong efficient if stock prices instantaneously reflect any new publicly available information. The strong form of the market efficiency hypothesis states that prices reflect all types of information whether available publicly or privately.

The weak form of the market efficiency hypothesis is that stock returns are serially uncorrelated and have a constant mean. The market is considered weak-form efficient if current prices fully reflect all information contained in historical prices, which implies that no investor can devise a trading rule based on past price patterns to earn abnormal return. A weaker and economically more sensible version of the hypothesis says that prices reflect information to the point where the marginal benefits of acting on the information (profits to be made) do not exceed the marginal costs (Jensen, 1978). This view led to many early tests of weak-form efficiency and

has influenced the interpretations of the various anomalies in stock returns that have been documented so far.

Based on mixed results for and against the efficient market hypothesis, Fama (1991) made changes in all the three categories. In order to cover a more general area of testing weak form of market efficiency, tests for return predictability and forecasting of returns with variables like dividend yields, interest rates, etc. have been included. Also, issues such as cross-sectional predictability for testing asset-pricing models and anomalies like size effect (Banz, 1981), seasonality of returns like the January effect (Keim, 1983; Roll, 1983), and day of the week effect (Cross, 1973; French, 1980) have been included under the theme of return predictability. In the semi-strong form of market efficiency it is assumed that the prices of securities will change immediately and rationally in response to new information and the market neither delays nor overreacts or underreacts in response to the new information. This means that investors cannot earn excess returns by developing trading rules based on publicly available information. When announcement of an event can be dated to the day, daily data allow precise measurement of the speed of the stock price response, which is the central issue for market efficiency. Event studies have become an important part of research in capital markets, since they come closest to allowing a break between market efficiency and equilibrium pricing issues and give direct and mostly supportive evidence on efficiency. Event studies such as those of Ahrony and Swary (1980), Mandelker (1974), and Kaplan (1989) document interesting regularities in response of stock prices to dividend decisions, changes in corporate control, etc.

Strong-form efficiency assumes that prices fully reflect all new information, public or private. The tests of private information help to ascertain whether such information is fully reflected in market prices. Fama (1991) reviews tests for private information and concludes that the profitability of insider trading is now established. Insider trading refers to the use of private information to earn abnormal profits. The evidence that some investment analysts have insider information (Jaffe, 1974; Ippolito, 1989) is balanced by evidence that they do not (Brinson, Hood, and Beebower, 1986; Elton et al., 1993). The concept of an efficient stock market has stimulated both insight and controversy since its introduction to the economics and financial literature. The efficient market hypothesis addresses the consequences of competition in financial markets in determining the equilibrium values of financial assets. Perhaps the most important implication of the hypothesis is that the market price of any security reflects the true, or rational, value of security; thus, in an efficient market, investors are assured that the securities they purchase are fairly priced. A precondition for this strong version of the hypothesis is that information and trading costs, the costs of getting prices to reflect information, are zero.

The fact that in practice the investors have to incur trading costs and that not all behave homogeneously in response to the information has led to a huge amount of research producing evidence for and against the proposition that financial markets are efficient. However, in spite of these controversies, the efficient market hypothesis has contributed to our understanding of how and when economic and industry information is encoded in the prices of securities. The hypothesis has also provided very useful insights on the role of information in determining stock prices.

The early evidence seemed unexpectedly consistent with the theory. The large amount of research in the area of market efficiency tests with the help of common models of market equilibrium like the one factor Sharpe–Lintner–Black (SLB) model, multifactor asset pricing models of Merton (1973) and Ross (1976), and consumption-based intertemporal asset pricing model of Rubinstein (1976), Lucas (1978), and Breeden (1979), provide evidence that the market efficiency is a maintained hypothesis.

However, several papers have uncovered empirical evidence which suggests that stock returns contain predictable components. Keim and Stambaugh (1986) find statistically significant predictability in stock prices using forecasts based on certain predetermined variables. Fama and French (1988) show that long-holding-period returns are significantly negatively serially correlated, implying that 25–40 percent of the variation of longer-horizon returns is predictable from the past returns. Lo and MacKinlay (1988) reject the random walk hypothesis and show that it is inconsistent with the stochastic behavior of weekly returns, especially for smaller capitalization stocks. Empirical evidence of anomalous return behavior in the form of variables like P/E ratio, market/book value ratio (Fama and French, 1992) has defied rational economic explanation and appears to have caused many researchers to strongly qualify their views on market efficiency.

The efficient market hypothesis is frequently misinterpreted to imply perfect forecasting abilities. In fact, it implies only that prices reflect all available information. When we talk of efficient markets, we mean that the market is functioning well and prices are fair. Thus, in assessing the efficiency of the market on the basis of observed behavior of stock returns, and observed predictability of returns in particular, one must judge whether the observed behavior is rational. Given the subjectivity of judgment of rational behavior, it is not surprising that the question of whether markets are efficient is hotly debated.

Bibliography

Ahrony, J., and Swary, I. (1980). Quarterly dividend and earning announcements and stock holders' returns: An empirical analysis. *Journal of Finance*, **35**, 1–12.

Bachelier, L. (1900). *Théorie de la spéculation*. Paris: Gauthiers-Villars.

Banz, R. W. (1981). The relationship between return and market value of common stocks. *Journal of Financial Economics*, **9**, 3–18.

Black, F. (1972). Capital market equilibrium with restricted borrowings. *Journal of Business*, **45**, 444–65.

Breeden, D. T. (1979). An intertemporal asset pricing model with stochastic consumption and investment opportunities. *Journal of Financial Economics*, **7**, 265–96.

Brinson, G. P., Hood, L. R., and Beebower, G. L. (1986). Determinants of portfolio performance. *Financial Analysts Journal*, **42**, 39–44.

Cross, F. (1973). Price movements on Fridays and Mondays. *Financial Analysts Journal*, **29**, 67–79.

Elton, E. J., Gruber, M. J., Das, S., and Hlavka, M. (1993). Efficiency with costly information: A reinterpretation of evidence from managed portfolios. *Review of Financial Studies*, 6, 1–22.

Fama, E. F. (1970). Efficient capital markets: A review of theory and empirical work. *Journal of Finance*, 25, 383–417.

Fama, E. F. (1991). Efficient capital markets II. *Journal of Finance*, 46, 1575–618.

Fama, E. F., and French, K. R. (1988). Permanent and temporary components of stock returns. *Journal of Political Economy*, 96, 246–73.

Fama, E. F., and French, K. R. (1992). The cross-section of expected stock returns. *Journal of Finance*, 47, 427–66.

French, K. R. (1980). Stock returns and the weekend effect. *Journal of Financial Economics*, 8, 55–69.

Ippolito, R. A. (1989). Efficiency with costly information: A study of mutual fund performance 1965–84. *Quarterly Journal of Economics*, 104, 1–23.

Jaffe, J. (1974). Special information and insider trading. *Journal of Business*, 47, 410–28.

Jensen, M. C. (1978). Some anomalous evidence regarding market efficiency. *Journal of Financial Economics*, 6, 95–101.

Kaplan, S. (1989). The effect of management buyouts on operating performance and value. *Journal of Financial Economics*, 24, 217–54.

Keim, D. B. (1983). Size-related anomalies and stock return seasonality. *Journal of Financial Economics*, 12, 13–32.

Keim, D. B., and Stambaugh, R. F. (1986). Predicting returns in stock and bond markets. *Journal of Financial Economics*, 17, 357–90.

Kendall, M. G. (1953). The analysis of economic time series. Part I: Prices. *Journal of the Royal Statistical Society*, 96, 11–25.

Lintner, J. (1965). The valuation of risk assets and the selection of risky investments in stock portfolios and capital budgets. *Review of Economics and Statistics*, 47, 13–37.

Lo, A. W., and MacKinlay, A. C. (1988). Stock market prices do not follow random walks: Evidence from a simple specification test. *Review of Financial Studies*, 1, 41–66.

Lucas, R. E. (1978). Asset prices in an exchange economy. *Econometrica*, 46, 1429–45.

Mandelker, G. (1974). Risk and return: The case of merging firms. *Journal of Financial Economics*, 1, 303–36.

Merton, R. C. (1973). An intertemporal capital asset pricing model. *Econometrica*, 41, 867–87.

Roll, R. (1983). Vas ist das? The turn of the year effect and the return premia of small firms. *Journal of Portfolio Management*, 9, 18–28.

Ross, S. A. (1976). The arbitrage theory of capital pricing. *Journal of Economic Theory*, 13, 341–60.

Rubinstein, M. (1976). The valuation of uncertain income streams and the pricing options. *Bell Journal of Economics*, 7, 407–25.

Sharpe, W. F. (1964). Capital asset prices: A theory of market equilibrium under conditions of risk. *Journal of Finance*, 19, 425–42.

Markov switching models in finance

Allan Timmermann

Since their introduction into economics by Hamilton (1989), Markov switching models have become very popular in both applied and theoretical work in finance. They are now routinely used to model the dynamics of financial time series such as exchange or interest rates, stock returns, and dividend growth.

Markov switching models allow the probability distribution of a time-series process to shift discretely between a finite set of "states" or "regimes." To illustrate this idea, consider an $n \times 1$ vector of asset returns $\mathbf{y}_t = (y_{1t}, \ldots, y_{nt})'$ whose mean, covariance, and autocorrelations are driven by a discrete state variable, S_t, that varies from 1 through k, k being the number of states:

$$\mathbf{y}_t = \mu_{s_t} + \sum_{j=1}^{p} A_{j,s_t} \mathbf{y}_{t-j} + \varepsilon_t. \quad (1)$$

Here $\mu_{s_t} = (\mu_{1s_t}, \ldots, \mu_{ns_t})'$ is an $n \times 1$ vector of intercepts in state s_t, A_{j,s_t} is the $n \times n$ matrix of autoregressive coefficients associated with lag j in state s_t, and $\varepsilon_t = (\varepsilon_{1t}, \ldots, \varepsilon_{nt})' \sim N(0, \Omega_{s_t})$ follows a multivariate normal distribution with zero mean and covariance matrix Ω_{s_t}.

Unless current and future values of the state variable are observed, a probability law must be assumed for S_t. Markov switching models commonly assume that only the past state, S_{t-1}, affects the probability of the current state, so that S_t follows a first-order Markov process:

$$\Pr(S_t = j | S_{t-1} = i) = p_{ij}, \ i, j = 1, \ldots, k. \quad (2)$$

Various authors (e.g., Gray, 1996) have refined this specification by allowing the state transitions from S_{t-1} to S_t to be a logit or probit function of a vector of observable variables (including a constant), z_{t-1}:

$$\Pr(S_t = j | S_{t-1} = i, z_{t-1}) = \Phi(\beta'_{ij} z_{t-1}),$$
$$i,j = 1, \ldots, k, \tag{3}$$

where $\Phi(.)$ is the probit function. Another possibility is to let state transitions reflect duration dependence so that the probability of remaining in a given state depends on the length of time already spent in that state.

To complete the model specification, a distribution for ε_t is required. Most studies have assumed that ε_t is normally distributed so that return distributions under Markov switching are probability-weighted mixtures of normals as opposed to simple (deterministic) sum of normals. This allows regime switching models to flexibly approximate a wide class of distributions with features similar to those often found in financial time-series such as fat tails (*see* FAT TAILS IN FINANCE), skew, and volatility clustering.

These points are best illustrated in the simple univariate two-state model ($n = 1$, $k = 2$) with no autoregressive terms, constant transition probability, and normally distributed increments, ε. Suppose that returns are normally distributed in state 1, $N(\mu_1, \sigma_1^2)$ while in state 2 they are, $N(\mu_2, \sigma_2^2)$ and the matrix of transition probabilities takes the form

$$P = \begin{pmatrix} p_{11} & 1 - p_{11} \\ 1 - p_{22} & p_{22} \end{pmatrix}.$$

As a special case, when $p_{11} = 1 - p_{22}$, the previous state does not matter to the current state probability and S_t follows a simple Bernoulli process.

Let the probability of state 1 be π_1 so the state-2 probability is $(1 - \pi_1)$. The first four moments of the return distribution in this simple model are

$$E[y_t] = \pi_1 \mu_1 + (1 - \pi_1)\mu_2$$
$$Var(y_t) = \pi_1 \sigma_1^2 + (1 - \pi_1)\sigma_2^2$$
$$+ \pi_1(1 - \pi_1)(\mu_1 - \mu_2)^2$$
$$E[(y_t - \bar{\mu})^3] = \pi_1(1 - \pi_1)(\mu_1 - \mu_2)(3(\sigma_1^2 - \sigma_2^2)$$
$$+ (1 - 2\pi_1)(\mu_1 - \mu_2)^2)$$
$$E[(y_t - \bar{\mu})^4] = \pi_1(1 - \pi_1)(\mu_1 - \mu_2)^2$$
$$((\mu_1 - \mu_2)^2(1 - 3\pi_1(1 - \pi_1))$$
$$+ 6(1 - \pi_1)\sigma_1^2 + 6\pi_1\sigma_2^2)$$
$$+ 3(\pi_1\sigma_1^4 + (1 - \pi_1)\sigma_2^4).$$

These expressions show that the difference between the mean parameters ($\mu_1 - \mu_2$) is a key determinant of the properties of the probability distribution under Markov switching. If $\mu_1 = \mu_2$ then the model cannot capture skews or bimodalities in the return distribution, although it can generate fat tails, as can be seen from the expression for the fourth moment. Provided that $\mu_1 \neq \mu_2$, regimes will generally give rise to skews and the difference between the means will also affect the variance and the tail thickness (fourth moment) of the return distribution.

It can also be shown that returns as well as squared returns will generally be serially correlated under Markov switching, meaning that the model can generate mean-reversion and autoregressive conditional heteroskedasticity effects (cf. Timmermann, 2000).

Estimation of the parameters of regime switching models is typically done by maximizing the likelihood function of the data. The likelihood function is fully captured through the equations specifying which variables are affected by regime switching, distributional assumptions for the innovation term, ε_t, and the state transitions, p_{ij}. In practice, computations make use of the EM algorithm or by reparameterizing the likelihood function and using a recursive optimization algorithm. More recently, Bayesian approaches have also been proposed. For an introduction to some of these methods, see Kim and Nelson (1999).

Testing for the presence of multiple states ($k > 1$) is difficult, since the state transition parameters are unidentified under the null hypothesis of a single state ($k = 1$), introducing a so-called unidentified nuisance parameter problem. This means that some statistical tests do not follow standard distributions. If the null of a single state can be rejected, the next question that arises is how many states to include. Here there are fewer guidelines available, but one can use a range of specification tests on the residuals from the model (e.g., testing if these follow the assumed parametric distribution) or alternatively choose the number of states through an information criterion.

Most often, the underlying state variable, S_t, is unobserved and state probabilities have to be filtered from the time-series of data. These state probabilities are often of separate interest and regime switching models are increasingly used to model shifts in investors' expectations concerning market fundamentals (e.g., dividend growth or risk-premia) and asset prices.

As one would expect, state probabilities tend to vary significantly over time in many empirical studies. This can give rise to interesting time variations in the risk–return trade-off as measured, for example, by the conditional Sharpe ratio (cf. Perez-Quiros and Timmermann, 2000). Because the risk–return trade-off can vary significantly across states, the asset allocation implications of regimes can be important. Suppose a regime switching model identifies a bull and a bear state in stock returns, the first characterized by large positive mean returns and relatively low return volatility, while the second state has high volatility but small mean returns. Also suppose that the two states are persistent so that the probability of being in the bull state next period is higher if the starting point is the bull state than if the starting point was the bear state. Then the optimal allocation to stocks will be greater the higher the probability that the current state is a bull state. Furthermore, as the investment horizon grows, a buy-and-hold investor's allocation to the risky asset will tend to decline if starting from the bull state (since the probability of switching to a bear state grows, the longer the horizon), while the opposite pattern follows if the initial state was the bear state.

A question that naturally arises is what generates the regime switching that is modeled through the unobserved discrete variable, S_t. One possibility is factors such as policy shifts or major technology or price shocks (e.g., the oil price shocks in the 1970s). It is perhaps more difficult to imagine that identical regimes literally repeat over time. A regime switching model with a relatively small set of states can instead be viewed as an approximation, since the conditional probability distribution implied by such a model will be a convex combination of the individual probability distributions within each state.

Bibliography

Gray, S. (1996). Modeling the conditional distribution of interest rates as regime-switching process. *Journal of Financial Economics*, **42**, 27–62.

Hamilton J. (1989). A new approach to the economic analysis of nonstationary time series and the business cycle. *Econometrica*, **57**, 357–84.

Kim, C.-J., and Nelson, C. R. (1999). *State-space models with regime switching*. Cambridge, MA: MIT Press.

Perez-Quiros, G., and Timmermann, A. (2000). Firm size and cyclical variations in stock returns. *Journal of Finance*, 1229–62.

Timmermann, A. (2000). Moments of Markov switching models. *Journal of Econometrics*, **96**, 75–111.

mergers and acquisitions

Nick Collett

DEFINITIONS AND NATURE OF ACTIVITY

Mergers or acquisitions occur when the assets and activities of two independently controlled corporations are combined under the control of a single corporation. A merger is negotiated directly between the management of an acquiring company and the management of a target company, and the proposals are approved by the separate boards of directors before shareholders vote on them. If recommendation for a merger is not forthcoming from target company directors, an acquirer can then make a public tender offer to target company shareholders (for all or part of the equity), and a hostile takeover bid is launched, which if accepted by the target company shareholders, results in an acquisition. However, acquisition is commonly used even where no hostile bid occurs – for example, where a company acquires an unquoted company or a subsidiary with the agreement of the previous owners.

Demergers are also possible. A demerger takes place when part of a company's assets or operations are divested in a flotation, management buyout (MBO), or leveraged buyout (LBO). The ICI pharmaceuticals subsidiary is a good example of a large demerger, involving the flotation of Zeneca as a separate company.

Merger activity, in terms of both number and value, is closely connected with stock market buoyancy in both the USA (Nelson, 1966) and the UK (Golbe and White, 1988). Peak volumes of activity occurred in the 1920s, 1960s, and 1980s during long bull markets. Bishop and

Kay (1993) suggest that this interrelationship is counter-intuitive, since one would expect companies to buy physical assets when the price of companies is high, and to prefer companies to new investment when the price of companies is low. One theory which explains this relationship is that the incidence of corporate misvaluation is greater in bull markets than in bear markets, and thus highly valued companies are able to issue shares at prices that allow them to acquire enterprises whose valuations have not increased so dramatically. Another explanation suggests that mergers occur during periods of strong economic performance because confidence is high and the inevitable risk of major expansion is acceptable during bull markets. Behind both these theories lies the role of corporate management, who need to consider not only extending their control to other companies, but also safeguarding their control of existing assets by performing well enough to deter takeover. Mergers are seen as a major element in the market for corporate control and a major avenue through which shareholders can deal with the agency problems presented by the shareholder–manager relationship (Jensen and Ruback, 1983).

MERGERS AND THEORETICAL VIEWS ON THE MARKET FOR CORPORATE CONTROL

Many economists have seen takeovers as the mechanism by which shareholders (principals) can exercise control over managers (agents) and that only firms which maximize stock market value will survive (Friedman, 1953). With separation of the ownership and control of production, shareholders can still exercise control through their ability to sanction a takeover. Early neoclassical economists saw the threat of takeover as enough to insure the efficient use of resources by managers. Jensen and Meckling (1976) linked takeovers to the whole range of principal–agent issues in corporate governance. These include the costs of structuring a set of contracts with managers, the costs of monitoring and controlling managerial behavior, and the costs of shareholders acting against any breach of contract by managers. Takeovers as a market selection device can then be seen as a means of insuring that firms with incentive contracts which optimize shareholder interests will survive, while those that do not are taken over. Alternatively, because optimal incentive contracts are infeasible, the takeover mechanism in practice helps to reduce agency costs by targeting those firms with the highest agency costs for takeover (Jensen, 1988).

The above theories rest on an efficient and effective markets view of mergers. Many economists have challenged this. Shleifer and Vishny (1988) pointed out that acquirers may themselves be dominated by empire-building, rather than value-maximizing, managers. This is consistent with the theory of the firm articulated by Marris (1964), which proposed that managers were motivated by superior compensation in large firms and that growth by acquisition fulfills this desire as effectively as economic growth (Mueller, 1969). Peacock and Bannock (1991) identified the high transaction costs involved in takeovers as a major weakness of the effective market view, with managers as insiders having better information than potential acquirers. Stein (1988, 1989) shows that asymmetric information allows managers to defend a takeover threat by inflating current earnings. This gives shareholders inaccurate information, and undermines takeovers as a function of control over managers. Thus, information asymmetry penalizes acquirers at the expense of acquirees (Helm, 1989), and Singh (1971) pointed out that it was much easier for large firms to take over small firms than vice versa, suggesting that takeovers are a less than perfect managerial control device. Grossman and Hart (1980) argue that shareholders in practice may be an obstacle to the optimum level of takeovers because the "free-rider" problem reduces the chances of takeover bids succeeding. The optimal strategy for shareholders (in particular, small shareholders) is always to refuse any offer, in the hope of an improved offer. If all shareholders adopted this strategy then no disciplinary bids would occur. Others have gone further by suggesting that the market for corporate control may actually be perverse, rather than just inefficient.

Shleifer and Summers (1988) suggest that efficiency gains measured by stockholder gains are outweighed by losses incurred by managers and workers. Under this hypothesis, they suggest takeovers are on balance harmful to economic efficiency.

EMPIRICAL EVIDENCE ON THE MARKET FOR CORPORATE CONTROL

There is an enormous empirical literature on mergers profiling acquirers and targets, and measuring the economic consequences of mergers in terms of profits and shareholder returns. The theoretical contributions on principal–agency issues, and perverse selection, have, however, received less attention. In this section we look at the kind of firms which are taken over, or remain independent, in the market for corporate control.

Early studies in the USA looked at profitability, size, growth, and earnings multiples of acquired companies (Hayes and Taussig, 1967). The assumption behind these studies is that companies which underperform their peers do so because of poor management, and that in an efficient market for corporate control, those companies will fall prey to takeover. The studies showed that in the 1950s and 1960s acquired firms tended to be relatively unprofitable, had low growth, and were cash rich. Schwartz (1982) and Harris et al. (1982) were able to forecast underperforming companies which were likely to be taken over, using probit analysis. However, Palepu (1986), who conducted the most exhaustive of all US studies, found that the financial variables were not useful in predicting targets, a finding that challenges the corporate control explanation for mergers.

Singh (1971, 1975), looked at the size, profitability, short-term change in profitability, and growth characteristics of acquiring and acquired firms in the UK between 1955–60 and 1967–70. In the first period, significantly more than 50 percent of acquired firms were below the median for size, profitability, and growth. Between 1967 and 1970 targets were again below the median for profitability and profit growth, but size and growth were not significant. Kumar (1984) confirms both the size and growth for 1967–74, and Cosh et al. (1989) confirm the result for size and growth for 1981–3 and 1986; however, they find that the profitability of acquired firms is indistinguishable from industry averages during the 1980s, suggesting that the 1980s' merger wave was different from early periods.

Acquiring companies in the UK are generally larger than non-acquirers, and grow faster (organically), but are not (with the exception of those merging most intensively or involved in diversifying mergers) unduly profitable (Cosh, Hughes, and Singh, 1980).

Compared with acquired companies, acquirers present a picture of superior profits, growth, and size for the acquiring companies during the period 1955–60. In the 1967–70 period they again dominate on size and growth, but not on profitability. In the 1980s, acquiring company profitability is greater than that of acquired companies, but the result is statistically insignificant.

The implication of these findings for both the USA and the UK is that the market for corporate control does not conform neatly to the profit maximization assumption of neoclassical theory, since efficiency (profit or market value) has not been demonstrated as the only (indeed, perhaps not the preeminent) criterion determining acquisition activity. Indeed, size matters as much if not more because evidence suggests that a relatively inefficient large company has a better chance of survival than a relatively much more efficient smaller company. The threat of takeover is more likely to encourage firms to increase their size rather than their profitability. It is hard to see takeovers as a mechanism for principals to exercise control over managers, when unsuccessful managers can defend themselves by enlarging their company through acquisition.

MEASURING THE ECONOMIC BENEFITS OF MERGERS

Despite recent signs of European activity, mergers remain largely an Anglo-Saxon phenomenon. Any unexciting economic performance by the UK and USA raises the inevitable question of whether takeovers are economically beneficial. Furthermore, the takeover battles of the 1980s have shown that financial advisors play a leading part in precipitating mergers and benefiting from them, and shareholders are naturally concerned to see whether on aggregate an undue proportion of any benefit is realized by advisors and managers.

Assessing the economic consequences of merger activity leads to difficult methodological problems. One approach has been to contrast the combined pre-merger profits of the two companies with the post-merger performance. The comparison typically adjusts for economic changes across time by using a sector relative measure so that positive benefits from merger are only deduced if the merged entity improves its position in the sector. Bias is still evident in most of the studies, since no account is taken of the dispersion of profits across firms.

In the USA studies have found that mergers do not generally increase profits. Markham (1955) and Reid (1968) looked at mergers over long periods that straddled World War II, and concluded that profits of the business combination did not exceed the profits of the premerged companies. Mueller (1980) found that after-tax profits increased, but before-tax profits showed a relative decline, suggesting a decline in efficiency, partly paid for by the taxpayer. Piper and Weiss (1974) and Ravenscraft and Scherer (1987), using different control procedures and time periods, both found declines in profitability.

For the UK, Singh (1971) and Kumar (1984) both reported small declines in post-tax return on net assets after merger, after allowing for accounting adjustments. Cosh, Hughes, and Singh (1980), who did not allow for the downward accounting bias, found that more than half their sample of merged firms improved their profitability relative to the control groups, and that the improvement is particularly pronounced for non-horizontal mergers. If the downward accounting bias is adjusted upwards then the result is even more favorable to mergers. The major study to cover the 1980s merger boom (Cosh et al., 1989) shows that profitability was if anything lower after merger than before, and that the mergers which were successful in terms of post-merger profit enhancement were cases where both parties had been relative underperformers before merger.

Because of the likelihood of mean reversion (outperforming companies are likely to become average performers even without any merger activity), problems with accounting differences, and with matched samples, many studies look at shareholder returns as well as, or instead of, profits (see, for example, Cosh, Hughes, and Singh, 1980; Cosh et al., 1989; Franks and Harris, 1989).

A recent survey of 19 US merger studies shows consistent positive returns for acquired company shareholders with a median gain of 19.7 percent (Mueller, 1992). Acquiring company shareholders, on the other hand, have cumulative returns substantially below the market portfolio in the six months post-merger in 12 out of 15 studies, with a median return of −7.2 percent. These losses continue for several years after the mergers (Agrawal, Jaffe, and Mandelker, 1992; Mueller, 1992). Prior to merger announcements, acquiring firms registered positive cumulative returns in all ten studies which looked at stock performance for at least twelve months before announcement. The median cumulative abnormal gain over this period was +13.2 percent. So, in the USA, the evidence tends to support the view that firms generally undertake acquisitions when they have outperformed the market (Halpern, 1983; Mueller, 1992). The large gain to acquired company shareholders overshadows the negative returns to acquirer shareholders and this is normally construed as a net social benefit (Council of Economic Advisors, 1985).

In the UK, Cosh, Hughes, and Singh (1980) found that acquiring firms had better shareholder returns in the first year after merger, but after that the acquirers deteriorated relative to the control group. Cosh, Hughes, and Singh (1989) found that for 1981–3, acquiring firms performed worse in the three years post-merger than the three years pre-merger. Using event study methodology, Franks and Harris (1989) found that acquirers gain slightly in the post-merger period, but when the measurement period is extended to 24 or 36 months, negative residuals occur. Overall, therefore, these studies suggest an opportunistic motive with acquirers launching their bids when their prices are relatively high, and that either acquisitions do not provide medium term benefits or that the acquirer return performance then falls towards the market return.

The overall shareholder returns are positive, however, because of the significant premiums which target companies command. Franks and Harris (1989) report premiums between 25–30 percent in the period of four months before and one month after the first bid date. The premiums are substantially above this average when the bid is in cash, suggesting that companies need to offer a higher premium when they are taking all the benefits of acquisition for their own shareholders.

TYPES OF MERGER

Most mergers do not fit neatly into one category, and definitions are not uniformly applied, with an obvious difference between the economics and strategy literature. In the economics literature it is common to see mergers defined as horizontal mergers, between competitors; vertical mergers, involving acquisitions of suppliers or customers; and conglomerate mergers, of companies with no complementary markets or production processes.

One motive for horizontal mergers is to achieve market share even if the firm is not dominant enough to exert monopoly or oligopoly power. Merging firms might be expected to increase prices to achieve higher profits, but Salant, Switzer, and Reynolds (1983) found that horizontal mergers were unprofitable. However, the disappearance of a firm may lead remaining competitors to expand production and depress prices. Deneckere and Davidson (1985) show that only if rival firms respond to the takeover by raising prices does the merging firm benefit. Further evidence of this can be found in specific industries, such as the airline industry (Kim and Singal, 1993).

The other important horizontal motive is cost reduction. Scale economies may result at the plant level (Pratten, 1971) or from operating several plants within one firm (Scherer et al., 1975). Most studies have failed to find significant cost improvements (Mueller, 1980).

Thus, it is difficult to substantiate the argument that market power justifies merger activity, not least because a dominant position would generally conflict with competition policy and invite regulatory intervention (Weir, 1993).

Motives for vertical integration include eliminating price distortions in factor inputs when suppliers have market power, reducing bargaining costs between vertically linked firms in the presence of asymmetric information, and reducing contracting cost between vertically linked companies (Williamson, 1989). Lubatkin (1987) investigated the post-merger performance of vertical acquisitions over various periods up to five years. He found a positive abnormal return over the short term, but a negative abnormal return over the three to five year period. Seth (1990), however, confirmed the earlier result of Rumelt (1974) that companies making vertical acquisitions do not perform as well as those making horizontal, or unrelated, acquisitions.

With conglomerate mergers the motives are diversification to reduce a company's dependence on existing activities, and perhaps achieve uncorrelated, or negatively correlated profitability, which would lower the holding company's cost of capital; and the transference of managerial competence across dissimilar business activities. In a well functioning capital market, diversification should not provide a worthwhile motive, since shareholders can achieve required allocations in their own portfolios (Porter, 1987). The managerial competence motive is often allied to the free cash flow hypothesis for mergers (Jensen, 1986), which sees leveraged deals as an effective way of shareholders replacing poor management with good management and keeping management effective because of the high debt burden.

INTERNATIONAL COMPARISONS OF MERGER ACTIVITY

Domestic mergers in the USA still account for a large proportion of worldwide acquisition activity. In 1985, 85 percent of all deals were in the USA. By 1989 this had fallen to 50 percent. Europe (in particular, the UK) account for most of the other transactions. After the recessionary years of 1990–2, in which the number of European mergers fell considerably, recent evidence suggests that activity is rising again, and that both continental European firms and American cross-border deals are growing in importance.

Historically, and through the 1980s, most European mergers were ones in which British firms took over other British firms (Bishop and Kay, 1993). The explanations for this lie in the relatively undeveloped capital markets in continental countries, and the different attitudes to corporate governance, particularly in Germany. There are three reasons to believe that this may change during the next few years. First, many European companies feel they are uncompetitive against their American counterparts and may use mergers as a means of rationalizing. Second, privatization programs and EU competition policy may lead to merger induced restructuring, particularly in sectors such as airlines and telecommunications. Third, larger international shareholdings in European firms are starting to foster takeovers, and the German banks are already selling stakes in German corporations for their own reasons and as a result of political pressure.

Thus, there is good evidence to support a prediction that European corporate activity will embrace mergers at a time when Anglo-Saxon academics are skeptical about the overall economic benefits, and the question of whether mergers primarily serve shareholder, manager, or advisor interests is unresolved.

Bibliography

Agrawal, A., Jaffe, J. F., and Mandelker, G. N. (1992). The post-merger performance of acquiring firms: A re-examination of an anomaly. *Journal of Finance*, **47**, 1605–21.

Auerbach, A. J. (ed.) (1988). *Corporate Takeovers: Causes and Consequences*. Chicago: National Bureau of Economic Research, University of Chicago Press.

Bishop, M., and Kay, J. (1993). *European Mergers and Merger Policy*. Oxford: Oxford University Press.

Cosh, A. D., Hughes, A., Lee, K., and Singh, A. (1989). Institutional investment: Mergers and the market for corporate control. *International Journal of Industrial Organization*, 73–100.

Cosh, A. D., Hughes A., and Singh, A. (1980). The causes and effects of takeovers in the UK: An empirical investigation for the late 1960s at the micro-economic level. In D. C. Mueller (ed.), *The Determinants and Effects of Mergers*. Cambridge, MA: Oelgeschlager, Gunn, and Hain.

Council of Economic Advisors (1985). *Annual Report*. Washington, DC: US Government Printing Office.

Deneckere, R., and Davidson, C. (1985). Incentives to form coalitions with Bertrand competition. *Rand Journal of Economics*, **16**, 473–86.

Franks, J. R., and Harris, R. S. (1989). Shareholder wealth effects of corporate takeovers: The UK experience 1955–85. *Journal of Financial Economics*, **23**, 225–50.

Friedman, M. (1953). *Essays in Positive Economics*. Chicago: University of Chicago Press.

Golbe, D. L., and White, L. J. (1988). A time series analysis of merger acquisitions in the UK economy. In A. J. Auerbach (ed.), *Corporate Takeovers: Causes and Consequences*. Chicago: University of Chicago Press.

Grossman, S. J., and Hart, O. D. (1980). Takeover bids: The free-rider problem and the theory of the corporation. *Bell Journal of Economics*, **11**, 42–64.

Halpern, P. (1983). Corporate acquisitions: A theory of special cases? A review of event studies applied to acquisitions. *Journal of Finance*, **38**, 297–317.

Harris, R. S., Stewart, J. F., Guilkey, D. K., and Carleton, W. T. (1982). Characteristics of acquired firms: Fixed and random coefficients probit analysis. *Southern Economic Journal*, **49**, 164–84.

Hayes, S., and Taussig, R. (1967). Tactics of cash takeover bids. *Harvard Business Review*, **45**, 135–48.

Helm, D. (1989). Mergers, takeovers, and the enforcement of profit maximization. In J. Fairburn and J. A. Kay (eds.), *Merger and Merger Policy*. Oxford: Oxford University Press.

Hindley, B. (1970). Separation of ownership and control in the modern corporation. *Journal of Law and Economics*, **13**.

Hogarty, T. F. (1970). Profits from mergers: The evidence of fifty years. *St John's Law Review*, **44**, 378–91.

Jensen, M. C. (1986). Agency costs of free cash flow, corporate finance and takeovers. *American Economic Review*, **76**, 323–9.

Jensen, M. C. (1988). Takeovers: Their causes and consequences. *Journal of Economic Perspectives*, **2**, 21–48.

Jensen, M. C., and Meckling, W. H. (1976). Theory of the firm: Managerial behavior, agency costs and ownership structure. *Journal of Financial Economics*, **3**, 305–60.

Jensen, M. C., and Ruback, R. (1983). The market for corporate control: The scientific evidence. *Journal of Financial Economics*, **11**, 5–50.

Kim, E. H., and Singal, V. (1993). Mergers and market power: Evidence from the airline industry. *American Economic Review*, **83**, 549–69.

Kumar, M. S. (1984). *Growth, Acquisition and Investment*. Cambridge: Cambridge University Press.

Lubatkin, M. (1987). Merger strategies and stakeholder value. *Strategic Management Journal*, **8**, 39–53.

Markham, J. W. (1955). Survey of the evidence and findings on mergers. In *Business Concentration and Price Policy*. New York: National Bureau of Economic Research.

Marris, R. L. (1964). *The Economic Theory of "Managerial" Capitalism*. London: Macmillan.

Mueller, D. C. (1969). A theory of conglomerate mergers. *Quarterly Journal of Economics*, **83**, 643–59.

Mueller, D. C. (1980). *The Determinants and Effects of Mergers: An International Comparison*. Cambridge, MA: Oelgeschlager, Gunn, and Hain.

Mueller, D. C. (1992). Mergers. In *The New Palgrave Dictionary of Money and Finance*. London: Macmillan, 700–7.

Nelson, R. L. (1966). Business cycle factors in the choice between internal and external growth. In W. Alberts and J. Segall (eds.), *The Corporate Merger*. Chicago: University of Chicago Press.

NIESR (1994). *National Institute of Economic and Social Research Study into Executive Pay*. London: NIESR.

Palepu, K. G. (1986). Predicting takeover targets: A methodological and empirical analysis. *Journal of Accounting and Economics*, 8, 3–36.

Peacock, A., and Bannock, G. (1991). *Corporate Takeovers and the Public Interest*. Aberdeen: Aberdeen University Press for the David Hume Institute.

Piper, T. F., and Weiss, S. J. (1974). The profitability of multibank holding company acquisitions. *Journal of Finance*, 29, 163–74.

Porter, M. E. (1987). From competitive advantage to corporate strategy. *Harvard Business Review*, 45, 43–59.

Pratten, C. F. (1971). *Economies of Scale in Manufacturing Industry*. Cambridge: Cambridge University Press.

Ravenscraft, D. J., and Scherer, F. M. (1987). *Mergers, Sell-Offs and Economic Efficiency*. Washington, DC: Brookings Institution.

Reid, S. R. (1968). *Mergers, Managers and the Economy*. New York: McGraw-Hill.

Rumelt, R. P. (1974). *Strategy, Structure and Economic Performance*. Cambridge, MA: Harvard University Press.

Salant, S. W., Switzer, S., and Reynolds, R. J. (1983). Losses from horizontal merger: The effects of an exogenous change in industry structure in Cournot-Nash equilibrium. *Quarterly Journal of Economics*, 98, 185–99.

Scherer, F. M., Beckensten, A., Kaufer, E., and Murphy, R. D. (1975). *The Economics of Multi-Plant Operation: An International Comparisons Study*. Cambridge, MA: Harvard University Press.

Schwartz, S. (1982). Factors affecting the probability of being acquired: Evidence for the United States. *Economic Journal*, 92, 391–8.

Seth, A. (1990). Value creation in acquisitions: A re-examination of performance issues. *Strategic Management Journal*, 11, 99–115.

Shleifer, A., and Summers, L. H. (1988). Breach of trust in hostile takeovers. In A. J. Auerbach (ed.), *Corporate Takeovers: Cause and Consequences*. Chicago: University of Chicago Press.

Shleifer, A., and Vishny, R. W. (1988). Value maximization and the acquisition process. *Journal of Economic Perspectives*, 2, 7–20.

Singh, A. (1971). *Takeovers: Their Relevance to the Stock Market and the Theory of the Firm*. Cambridge: Cambridge University Press.

Singh, A. (1975). Takeovers, economic "natural selection," and the theory of the firm: Evidence from the post-war UK experience. *Economic Journal*, 85, 497–515.

Stein, J. C. (1988). Takeover threats and managerial myopia. *Journal of Political Economy*, 96, 61–80.

Stein, J. C. (1989). Efficient stock markets, inefficient firms: A model of myopic corporate behavior. *Quarterly Journal of Economics*, 104, 655–69.

Utton, M. A. (1974). On measuring the effects of industrial mergers. *Scottish Journal of Political Economy*, 21, 13–28.

Weir, C. (1993). Merger policy and competition: An analysis of the Monopolies and Mergers Commission's decisions. *Applied Economics*, 25, 57–66.

Williamson, O. E. (1989). Transaction cost economics. In R. Schmalensee and R. Willig (eds.), *Handbook of Industrial Organization*. Amsterdam: North-Holland.

mutual funds

Paul Seguin

Mutual funds are equity claims against prespecified assets held by investment companies (firms that professionally manage pools of assets). Thus, a share of a mutual fund is an equity claim, typically held by an individual, against a professionally managed pool of assets.

Mutual funds provide four benefits to individual investors. First, since most mutual funds are well diversified, these funds allow individuals with limited capital to hold diversified portfolios. Second, since mutual funds are professionally managed, an individual investor can obtain the benefits of professional asset management at a fraction of the cost of privately retaining a professional manager. Third, mutual funds can provide superior liquidity both during the holding period of the fund and at liquidation. Since transaction costs are not typically proportional to order dollar values, mutual funds can rebalance portfolios at a lower proportional cost than an individual investment can. Furthermore, to liquidate a portfolio, mutual funds require the sale of only a single security (the fund). Finally, mutual funds reduce book-keeping and clerical costs by automatically reinvesting dividends or coupons and by providing quarterly performance reports and annual consolidated statements for investors' tax purposes.

Mutual funds carry several costs for investors. Management fees, charged daily against the net asset value of the fund, are summarized, aggregated, and reported quarterly. Load funds charge a one-time fee to the investor whenever shares are purchased (a "front-end" load) and/or sold (a "back-end load"). Some back-end load fees are contingent on the holding period. For

example, a back-end load fee of (5–1 percent ×
years held) means that an investor can escape the
back-end load fee if the shares are held for five
years or more. Such contingent back-end fees
are often called "contingent deferred sales
loads." Finally, investment companies may
charge mutual fund holders "12b-1 fees" to
reimburse the investment company for
marketing, advertising, reporting, and maintaining investor relations.

The most important dichotomy in the analysis
of mutual funds is the distinction between open
end and closed end funds. In an open end fund,
purchases and sales of shares in the fund can be
made through the investment company at any
time. Thus, the number of shares outstanding
and the amount of capital under management
vary constantly. Further, such transactions
occur at the stated net asset value (NAV). The
NAV, which is calculated at least daily, is the
current market value of the fund's assets divided
by shares outstanding.

In contrast, shares of a closed end fund are
issued by the investment company only once and
are fixed thereafter. As a result, individuals
wishing to buy or sell shares of an established
closed end fund must identify a counterparty
willing to take the other side of the transaction.
This is why closed end funds, but not open end
funds, are listed on stock exchanges. Often, secondary market transactions of a closed end fund
occur at prices that differ from the fund's NAV.
Funds with market prices above their NAV
trade at a premium; funds with market prices
below their NAV trade at a discount. Closed end
funds do not charge an explicit front-end load
fee. Instead, this fee is charged implicitly,
through the difference between the higher purchase price and the NAV of the fund.

A second important distinction between
mutual funds is their investment "style." Some
funds are "passively" managed; that is, holdings
of the mutual fund are rarely altered and the fund
mimics a benchmark index such as the Standard
and Poor's 500 Index. However, the vast majority of mutual funds are "actively" managed, with
portfolio holdings frequently altered according
to management discretion. One example of an
actively managed style is "market timing,"
where a manager dynamically alters a fund's
weights in stocks, bonds, and short-term debt
in anticipation of future moves.

Actively managed funds are classified by the
type of assets they hold. For example, some
funds invest only in tax-exempt municipal
bonds, while others invest only in mortgage-
backed debt obligations. Equity funds are normally classified as growth funds (containing
speculative stocks with low dividend yields),
income funds (containing less volatile, higher
yield stocks, and sometimes bonds), or balanced
funds (containing elements of both growth and
income funds).

Furthermore, some equity funds consider
only foreign issues, while others, called "country
funds," invest only in equities in one particular
foreign country. Since many countries restrict
foreign investment, a closed-end fund may be
the only viable avenue for investing in a particular country. Thus, a foreign country closed end
fund is likely to trade at a premium.

In the USA, mutual funds, and the investment companies that manage them, are regulated under the Investment Company Act of
1940. Under this Act, the Securities and Exchange Commission (SEC) is granted authority
to regulate mutual funds. Investment companies, like the equity market, are regulated by
disclosure, rather than merit, regulation. Consequently, mutual fund regulation focuses on mandatory disclosure of information, including the
filing of a prospectus at the time of issue as well
as quarterly and annual reports. To prevent potential conflicts of interest, regulation limits the
holdings of brokers and underwriters in a mutual
fund.

noise trader

Richard W. Sias

Black (1986) defines noise trading as trading on noise as if it were information. In addition, he notes the importance of noise trading in capital markets: "Noise makes financial markets possible but also makes them imperfect." That is, in a world without noise traders, all trading is motivated by informational advantages. Recognizing they will be trading against another informed investor, traders will be reluctant to transact. Noise traders provide the necessary liquidity to financial markets. In providing liquidity, however, they also provide noise.

WHY DO NOISE TRADERS TRADE?

Noise trading may arise for various reasons. Some investors may simply enjoy trading or erroneously believe they have unique information or insights. In addition, some traders may trade on "sentiment." Shiller (1984), for example, argues that evidence from social psychology, sociology, and marketing suggests that individual investors' decisions are likely to be influenced by fads or fashion. Alternatively, Friedman (1984) suggests that institutional investors may be more inclined to trade on sentiment, due to the close-knit nature of the investment community, the importance of performance relative to other institutional investors, and the asymmetry of incentives. Similarly, Froot, Scharfstein, and Stein (1992) develop a model in which rational short-horizon investors may trade on the same signal, but the signal need not be related to fundamental value (e.g., technical analysis). Trueman (1988) suggests that institutional investors may engage in noise trading because it provides an imperfect signal to clients that the manager is informed. In sum, noise trading may result from perceived information advantages, sentiment, trading appearing in the utility function, or agency problems.

THE IMPACT OF NOISE TRADING ON PRICES

Noise trading can explain excess volatility in security prices (i.e., price will be more volatile than value), temporal patterns in stock prices (e.g., momentum and/or mean-reversion), and the use of technical analysis and positive feedback trading (Shleifer and Summers, 1990). The magnitude of noise traders' impact on security prices will depend on both the degree of noise trading in the market and the systematic nature of noise trading. The greater the degree of noise trading, the greater the deviation between price and value. As the deviation between price and value increases, rational arbitrageurs should work to push prices toward fundamental value. In real markets, however, arbitrage is costly (e.g., short sale proceeds are not available for investment). Moreover, in a world with noise traders and finite horizons, arbitrage can be risky. For example, rational arbitrageurs with limited horizons may be forced to unwind their positions in a period when noise traders have pushed prices even further away from fundamental values (DeLong et al., 1990).

If noise trading is cross-sectionally independent, then the impact of noise traders on a security's price is likely to be small relative to a world in which noise trading is cross-sectionally correlated. That is, if orders from noise traders are equally likely to be buy or sell initiated at a point in time, then many noise traders' orders will cancel out and the impact on price should be relatively small. Alternatively, if the noise traders' orders generally come from the same direction (i.e., primarily buy initiated or primarily sell initiated), their impact on a security's price is likely to be large. A similar argument holds for the expected impact of noise traders on the market. If noise traders' orders are cross-sectionally correlated across securities, then they are likely to impact market averages. That is, if noise traders systematically enter (or exit) financial markets, market averages may be affected. Empirical evidence regarding the impact of noise traders on security prices is mixed. Lee, Shleifer, and Thaler (1991) argue that the systematic noise trading of individual investors influences both closed-end fund share discounts (since individual investors play a more important role in closed-end fund shares than in the market for the underlying assets of the funds) and the prices of small capitalization securities (that are also dominated by individual investors). Although there is evidence that there is some correlation between closed-end discounts and the returns of small capitalization securities, there is considerable debate regarding the statistical and economic significance of the correlation (Chen, Kan, and Miller, 1993).

Alternatively, recent investigations into the behavior of institutional investors suggests that noise trading by institutional investors may impact security prices. Wermers (1994) documents results consistent with the hypothesis that some mutual funds engage in positive feedback trading and that such trading moves prices. Assuming that previous returns do not indicate future fundamental values, this suggests that some institutional investors engage in systematic noise trading.

CAN NOISE TRADERS SURVIVE?

Historically, the impact of noise trades has been assumed to be minimal, since noise traders should lose wealth (and therefore eventually become unimportant) when trading against rational "smart money" arbitrageurs. Shiller (1984), however, argues that there is little reason to suspect that rational smart money speculators dominate financial markets. DeLong et al. (1990, 1991) develop formal models that allow for the survival of noise traders. In DeLong et al. (1991), noise traders systematically underestimate variances of risky assets and therefore invest a greater fraction of their wealth in the risky asset than would an otherwise equally risk averse rational investor. Their excessive risk taking may not only allow noise traders to survive, but they may also come to dominate the market. Alternatively, in DeLong et al. (1990), the actions of noise traders are cross-sectionally correlated (systematic) and influence asset prices. Like any other systematic risk, the risk impounded by the random sentiments of noise traders should be priced. Thus, noise traders may be compensated for a risk that they create. Moreover, even though the model predicts that noise traders will lose (on average) when trading against rational arbitrageurs, noise traders may garner higher rates of returns than sophisticated investors if they concentrate their holdings in assets that have a greater sensitivity to innovations in noise trader sentiment.

Sias, Starks, and Tinic (1995) examine the issue of whether investors are compensated for bearing noise trader risk. Specifically, DeLong et al. (1990) suggest that assets with greater sensitivity to noise trader risk will tend to sell below fundamental values (reflecting the pricing of noise trader risk). They suggest that such a scenario can explain the fact that most closed-end funds sell at a discount to their underlying assets (assuming individual investors are noise traders). Specifically, the discount from fundamental values reflects the additional risk from the ownership structure: closed-end fund shares are held primarily by noise traders (individual investors), but noise traders play a less important role in the underlying assets of the funds. Thus, under these conditions, passive closed-end fund shareholders should garner larger returns than passive investors of the underlying assets as compensation for bearing noise trader risk. Sias, Starks, and Tinic (1995) demonstrate that, despite selling at discounts, (passive) closed-end fund shareholders do not garner larger returns than the holders of the underlying assets. In fact, discounts are just large enough to cover the expenses incurred by the funds. In addition, Sias, Starks, and Tinic (1995) demonstrate that, holding capitalization constant, NYSE stocks with greater exposure to individual investors (and presumably greater exposure to noise trader risk) earn lower returns than stocks with greater exposure to institutional investors.

UNRESOLVED ISSUES

Our understanding of noise traders is small relative to their likely importance in the market. Thus, noise traders represent a substantial and promising area for future research. Some of the key questions to be answered include: Who are the noise traders? Why do they trade? Is their trading independent or systematic? What is their impact on security prices? What is the relationship between informed traders and noise traders? Finally, how can noise traders survive?

Bibliography

Black, F. (1986). Noise. *Journal of Finance*, 41, 529–43.

Chen, N., Kan, R., and Miller, M. (1993). Are the discounts on closed-end funds a sentiment index? *Journal of Finance*, 48, 795–800.

DeLong, B., Shleifer, A., Summers, L., and Waldmann, R. (1990). Noise trader risk in financial markets. *Journal of Political Economy*, 98, 703–38.

DeLong, B., Shleifer, A., Summers, L., and Waldmann, R. (1991). The survival of noise traders in financial markets. *Journal of Business*, 64, 1–19.

Friedman, B. (1984). Comment on Shiller's stock prices and social dynamics. *Brookings Papers on Economic Activity*, 2, 504–8.

Froot, K., Scharfstein, D., and Stein, J. C. (1992). Herd on the street: Informational inefficiencies in a market with short-term speculation. *Journal of Finance*, 47, 1461–84.

Lee, C., Shleifer, A., and Thaler, R. (1991). Investor sentiment and the closed-end fund puzzle. *Journal of Finance*, 46, 75–109.

Shiller, R. (1984). Stock prices and social dynamics. *Brookings Papers on Economic Activity*, 2, 457–98.

Shleifer, A., and Summers, L. (1990). The noise trader approach to finance. *Journal of Economic Perspectives*, 4, 19–33.

Sias, R., Starks, L., and Tinic, S. (1995). Is noise trader risk priced? Working paper, Washington State University, University of Texas, and Koc University.

Trueman, B. (1988). A theory of noise trading in securities markets. *Journal of Finance*, 43, 83–95.

Wermers, R. (1994). Herding, trade reversals, and cascading by institutional investors. Working paper, University of Colorado.

note issuance facilities

Arie L. Melnik and Steven E. Plaut

A note issuance facility (NIF) is a medium-term commitment under which a borrower can issue short-term paper in its own name. The NIF commitment is typically made for a few years, while the paper is issued on a revolving basis, most frequently for maturities of three or six months. A broader range of maturities, however, is available, ranging from seven days up to one year. Most euronotes are denominated in US dollars and are issued in large denominations. They may or may not involve underwriting services. When they do, they are sometimes referred to as RUFs (revolving underwriting facilities). When they do not, they are often called euro-commercial paper programs (ECPs). When underwriting services are included in the contract, the underwriting banks are committed either to purchase any notes the borrower is unable to sell, or to provide standby credit.

NIFs have some features of the US commercial paper market and some features of commercial lines of credit or loan commitments by banks. Like commercial paper, notes issued under NIFs are short-term, non-secured debt of large corporations with high credit ratings. Like loan commitment contracts, NIFs generally include multiple pricing components for various contract features, including a market-based interest rate and fees known as participation, facility, and underwriting fees. The interest on notes issued is generally a floating rate based on LIBOR, the London Interbank Offered Rate, but occasionally other bases are used. The contract often includes a series of clauses or covenants that allow the NIF provider to revoke the arrangements under certain circumstances. These may have to do with deteriorations in the borrower's creditworthiness or external changes that affect the costs to the NIF providers.

The provider of NIFs agrees to accept notes issued by the borrower throughout the term of the contract and to distribute them either at a fixed margin or on a "best efforts" basis to investors. The notes are distributed under prearranged terms. Underwriting services in the NIF means that the borrower is assured a given interest rate and rapid access to funds. Like underwriting arrangements in other markets (Baron, 1982; Bloch, 1989; Courtadon, 1985; Freeman and Jachym, 1988), NIFs are provided by a lead manager who puts together a tender panel of banks. These then purchase the notes for distribution and occasionally for themselves. The shares of each panel member are determined in the underwriting agreement. The panel members usually agree to take up notes that cannot be placed or to extend automatically short-term loans to the issuer in place of such notes.

There are several variations on the basic product. Twenty years ago banks introduced NIFs with an issuer-set margin, where the issuer determines the margin (spread over LIBOR) at which notes will be offered. Notes not taken up (at the issuer set margin) are allocated to the underwriters at a pre-set cap rate. During the same period the multiple component facility (MCF) was introduced as another major development in the market for euronotes. This type of facility allows the borrower to draw funds in several currencies or in several forms, including short-term advances, swingline credits, etc. The borrower gains greater flexibility, choosing the maturity, loan form, and interest rate base of his or her credit utilization.

A growing proportion of new facilities have included extra borrowing options. The most popular option has been short-term advances, enabling borrowers to draw in any of several forms of instruments. Options for such alternatives were included in around 50 percent (by value) of the underwritten facilities arranged since 1986. One of the most popular has been swinglines, which enable borrowers to draw at short notice (generally same-day funds) to cover any delay in issuing notes.

While in the early 1980s most NIFs did include some form of underwriting service, more recently a growing number of NIFs have been arranged partly or entirely without underwriting commitments. Non-underwritten NIFs expanded from about 33 percent in 1985 to 70 percent in 1992. Most of these facilities, known today as euro-commercial paper (ECP), are similar to underwritten NIFs except that they do not include underwriting guarantees or standby credit in case notes cannot be sold. The borrowers under such facilities have been of the highest credit rating. They are presumably confident in their ability to sell notes without underwriting services. As a result they are able to save the cost of underwriting.

As noted by Melnik and Plaut (1991), the main borrowers in the euronote market were banks and OECD governments. After 1983, note issuing techniques rapidly gained popularity, mainly as a low-cost substitute for syndicated credits. High quality corporate borrowers entered the market and became the largest borrowers. Corporate borrowers rose from an average of 40 percent of the market in 1983 to over 70 percent in 1990. On the lending side, the underwriting function of NIFs has been largely performed by international commercial banks, but these banks hold only limited amounts of the paper. According to various estimates, non-bank investors purchased about 30 percent of notes issued in 1985. By 1992 non-bank firms held 60–75 percent. The principal non-bank investors are money-market funds, corporations, insurance companies, and wealthy individuals. For these investors, euronotes offer an alternative to bank certificates of deposit.

Three fees are payable on NIFs: participation or front-end management fees (a single payment whose frequent value is 10 basis points); underwriting fees between 5 and 15 basis points, paid annually; and facility fees, also paid annually. Facility fees range from 5 to 10 basis points, and sometimes rise over the life of the facility. Comparisons of the cost of note issuance facilities and syndicated credits have shown that NIFs are on average between 10 and 40 basis points cheaper than syndicated credits (see Bankson and Lee, 1985; Goodman, 1980; Howcroft and Solomon, 1985). The savings are positive because the lower interest spread usually more than offsets the other fees.

Bibliography

Bankson, L., and Lee, M. (1985). *Euronotes*. London: Euromoney Publications.

Baron, D. P. (1982). A model of the demand for investment banking advising and distribution services for new issues. *Journal of Finance*, 37, 955–76.

Bloch, E. (1989). *Inside Investment Banking*, 2nd edn. Homewood, IL: Dow-Jones Irwin.

Courtadon, C. L. (1985). *The Competitive Structure of the Eurobond Underwriting Industry*. Salamon Center Monograph. New York: New York University Press.

Freeman, J. L., and Jachym, P. C. (1988). Syndication. In J. P. Williamson (ed.), *The Investment Banking Handbook*. New York: John Wiley.

Goodman, L. S. (1980). The pricing of syndicated euro-currency credits. *Federal Reserve Bank of New York Quarterly Review*, 5, 1020–8.

Howcroft, J. B., and Solomon, C. (1985). *Syndicated Lending by Banks*. Bangor: University of Wales Press.

Melnik, A. L., and Plaut, S. E. (1991). *The Short-Term Eurocredit Market*. Salomon Center Monograph Series in Finance and Economics. New York: New York University Press.

persistence of performance

Debra A. Glassman

Performance persistence refers to a portfolio manager's ability to consistently deliver investment returns above (or below) a benchmark return. Persistence means that a manager with a good performance in the past is likely to have superior performance in the future, or that a manager who performs poorly is likely to continue to perform poorly.

The question of whether there is persistence in the performance of professional portfolio managers has long been important, both for academic research and for practical decision-making. Investors put a lot of time and money into the process of evaluating managers. Pension fund sponsors pay consultants to identify superior managers, and individual investors seek out funds that are ranked highly by the various fund evaluation services. The empirical evidence of persistence remains controversial. Academics view evidence of persistent abnormal profits as inconsistent with the efficient markets hypothesis. Furthermore, biases present in standard data on manager returns can make it appear that good performance persists, even when it does not.

METHODOLOGY FOR EMPIRICAL TESTING OF PERFORMANCE PERSISTENCE

Empirical tests for the persistence of performance involve two steps. The first is the calculation of a performance measure, usually denoted alpha. The second step is the assessment of how well alpha predicts future performance.

MODELS FOR PERFORMANCE EVALUATION

Traditionally, performance is measured by the average portfolio returns, net of a fixed benchmark return, over some historical period. Such an approach uses unconditional expected returns as the performance baseline. It assumes that no information about the state of the economy is used to form expectations.

The unconditional alpha can be calculated in a number of ways. A widely used unconditional alpha is the intercept from a regression of the manager's portfolio return on a benchmark return. A simplified version of this alpha is the average value of portfolio returns in excess of the benchmark. Unconditional alphas have been estimated using various benchmark returns. The capital asset pricing model implies that the market portfolio should proxy for the benchmark. The existence of differences in manager investment styles suggests the use of a benchmark specific to each manager's style (e.g., a small capitalization stock index for "small cap" managers). Unconditional alphas can also be estimated using multiple benchmark models.

Unconditional measures of performance are known to be biased when managers adjust their risk exposures in response to market conditions. If biases in alpha persist over time, they can distort inferences about the persistence of performance.

Models of "conditional performance evaluation" make expected returns and risks a function of a set of predetermined, publicly available information variables, such as dividend yields and interest rates. Such models can be estimated by regressing portfolio returns on benchmark returns and on the cross-products between benchmark returns and the information variables (Ferson and Schadt, 1996). The intercept in such a regression is a conditional alpha. Variants of the conditional model include multiple benchmark models and models in which alpha varies over time as a function of the information variables.

METHODOLOGY FOR ASSESSING PERSISTENCE

One way to assess persistence is to rank managers by their performance and to compare the rankings across time periods. Performance persistence can also be examined by testing for serial correlation in the residuals from a market model regression. Another approach is to estimate a set of cross-sectional regressions in which future performance for a manager is regressed on a measure of past performance. The choice of the variable representing future performance raises important issues. Some researchers compare future alpha to past alpha. The advantage of this is that alpha is a risk-adjusted measure. The disadvantage is that likely sources of bias in alphas may be correlated over time, creating spurious evidence of persistence in performance. An alternative approach is to relate future returns to past alpha. Future returns are the variable of most practical interest, but they are not risk adjusted.

When cross-sectional regressions are used, regression errors may be correlated, since the returns of the managers are likely to be correlated at a given date. The estimator must take account of this cross-sectional correlation. When the future return horizon is longer than the sampling interval, the time series of slope estimates will be autocorrelated due to overlapping data. The estimates of standard errors must be adjusted for this autocorrelation.

EVIDENCE

The literature on the persistence of mutual fund performance is large and dates back to work by Jensen (1969) and Carlson (1970). The evidence has been mixed from the start: Jensen finds significant correlation between alphas in successive decades, while Carlson reports insignificant rank correlations across decades. More recently, Hendricks, Patel, and Zeckhauser (1993) find persistence only up to one year, but Goetzmann and Ibbotson (1994) find persistence at one month, one year, and two year horizons, and Grinblatt and Titman (1994) report persistence over five years. Brown and Goetzmann (1994) report persistence of both superior and inferior performance. However, Shukla and Trzcinka (1994) and Carhart (1995) find that persistence is concentrated in the poorly performing funds, a result also suggested by Jensen (1969).

Only a few studies have examined the persistence of performance for pension fund managers. Christopherson and Turner (1991) find no evidence of persistence in alpha for horizons of one year and five years. Lakonishok, Shleifer, and Vishny (1992) find some persistence in rankings for two to three year investment horizons, but no evidence of persistence at shorter horizons. Using conditional performance evaluation models, Christopherson, Ferson, and Glassman (1996) find evidence of persistence at longer (two to three year) horizons, and it is concentrated among poorly performing managers. They report that conditional models provide more power to detect persistence than unconditional measures.

ISSUES OUTSTANDING

Overall, the evidence on mutual funds and pension funds suggests that there is more persistence at longer horizons than shorter ones and that persistence is concentrated among inferior managers. However, the evidence is not yet conclusive, and a number of issues remain to be resolved.

A key issue is the degree of survivorship bias in manager return data. If investors seek out superior managers and drop inferior ones, then databases of managers are biased towards including the surviving superior managers. This tends to create a bias towards finding persistence of superior performance. In fact, the process by which managers enter and leave databases (and, more generally, the process by which managers are hired and fired) is complicated and merits further investigation.

Another issue is whether managers deliver returns that are larger than portfolio management fees. The determination of fees is particularly difficult when examining the management of pension fund monies, since posted fees are likely to exceed actual fees, at least for some pension fund sponsors.

The finding of persistence among poorly performing managers raises the question of why inferior managers are retained. Is this irrationality on the part of investors? Lakonishok, Shleifer, and Vishny (1992) suggest that poor managers may provide services, such as research, that investors value and that compensate for poor returns.

The differences in performance persistence between mutual funds and pension funds provide another area for future research. For example, Christopherson, Ferson, and Glassman (1996) observe that conditional measures can detect persistence in pension fund performance, whereas unconditional measures are sufficient to detect persistence for mutual fund returns. This could indicate that pension fund managers are evaluated in a more sophisticated manner, with the implication that the market for pension fund monies is more informationally efficient.

Bibliography

Brown, S. J., and Goetzmann, W. N. (1994). Attrition and mutual fund performance. Working paper, New York University.

Carhart, M. (1995). On persistence in mutual fund performance. Working paper, University of Southern California.

Carlson, R. S. (1970). Aggregate performance of mutual funds, 1948–1967. *Journal of Financial and Quantitative Analysis*, **5**, 1–32.

Christopherson, J. A., and Turner, A. L. (1991). Volatility and predictability of manager alpha: Learning the lessons of history. *Journal of Portfolio Management*, **18**, 5–12.

Christopherson, J. A., Ferson, W. E., and Glassman, D. A. (1996). Conditioning manager alphas on economic information: Another look at the persistence of performance. Working paper, University of Washington.

Ferson, W. A., and Schadt, R. (1996). Measuring fund strategy and performance in changing economic conditions. *Journal of Finance*, **51**, 425–62.

Goetzmann, W. N., and Ibbotson, R. G. (1994). Do winners repeat? *Journal of Portfolio Management*, **20**, 9–18.

Grinblatt, M., and Titman, S. (1994). The persistence of mutual fund performance. *Journal of Finance*, **47**, 1977–84.

Hendricks, D., Patel, J., and Zeckhauser, R. (1993). Hot hands in mutual funds: Short-run persistence of relative performance, 1974–1988. *Journal of Finance*, **48**, 93–130.

Jensen, M. (1969). Risk, the pricing of capital assets, and the evaluation of investment portfolios. *Journal of Business*, **42**, 167–247.

Lakonishok, J., Shleifer, A., and Vishny, R. (1992). The structure and performance of the money management industry. *Brookings Papers on Economic Activity*, 339–91.

Shukla, R., and Trzcinka, C. (1994). Persistent performance in the mutual fund market: Tests with funds and investment advisors. *Review of Quantitative Finance and Accounting*, **4**, 115–36.

portfolio management

Douglas Wood

Portfolio management is concerned with distributing investible liquidity across a range of available assets and liabilities with the objective of providing risks and returns that achieve performance objectives. Portfolio management therefore comprises objective setting (establishing the relative importance of delivering capital and income growth and providing stability of principal and income to actual or prospective investors), asset allocation (where the available funds are distributed across geographic markets and security categories to exploit broad market and currency movements), and security selection (the choice of particular securities in each category that offer the best value in terms of portfolio objectives).

So far as objective setting is concerned, this is conducted in either a direct or indirect mode. Direct objectives emerge from detailed customer financial reviews conducted in approved form by financial intermediaries licensed by a regulatory authority. Alternatively, pension or insurance fund trustees might set portfolio managers income and growth objectives relative to a specific benchmark such as the *Financial Times/Actuaries All Share Index*. Indirect objective setting arises where portfolios in the form of mutual funds (unit trusts and investment trusts in the UK) are offered to the public, in which case the basic strategy in terms of exposure to equities or bonds or to UK, European, or Far Eastern markets will be outlined in a prospectus. Arising from this strategy, a benchmark in terms of the growth, income, and capital stability characteristics of a particular index (e.g., European equity, North American bond) will be defined and the security reported in that category by the financial press.

Historically, the distinction between portfolio management and investment management arises from new ideas about risk diversification introduced in the 1950s by Harry Markowitz (1952) with the observation that the variability of returns for a collection of assets depended on the correlation of asset returns with each other and not just on the weighted average of the individual assets. Diversifying investments across a range of substantially uncorrelated securities, whether within one country or increasingly internationally (Levy and Sarnat, 1970), provides portfolio managers with lower variability for the same return or a higher return for the same variability than any single one of the underlying national or international securities.

The theory of diversification was developed by Sharpe (1963) and Lintner (1965) to show that where large numbers of securities are used to create a fully diversified portfolio the effect is to eliminate the specific risks relating to each particular asset, leaving only the systematic risk, the common risks to which all securities are exposed. This systematic risk or market risk is effectively equivalent to the riskiness of the market portfolio and provides the reference benchmark for risk pricing used in the capital asset pricing model or CAPM.

Depending on diversification strategy, portfolio management may be active or passive. Passive portfolio management aims to replicate the performance, say, of a particular stock index by neutral weighting, whereby asset distribution in the portfolio matches the proportions of each asset or asset class in the index to be proxied. In contrast, under active portfolio management elements in the portfolio are either overweight (overrepresented) or underweight (underrepresented) relative to the target index. The intention is to produce outperformance relative to the target index by overrepresentation of assets or asset classes expected to outperform the relevant index. Active management therefore involves frequent rebalancing of both the asset allocation and the individual underlying security holdings to reflect changes in the expected risks and returns.

This rebalancing will aim to exploit timing effects. The relative returns for different countries and for the different types of security such as equities bonds and money market balances within a country vary with economic conditions

of growth, inflation, etc. By overweighting the portfolio with the asset most likely to outperform under the anticipated economic climate the portfolio manager aims to outperform a portfolio that maintains unchanged weightings throughout the economic cycle.

If the choice of assets is simplified to comprise simply high risk (equity) investments that generally outperform under economic recovery and low risk (bonds and cash) that outperform in conditions of economic slowdown and recession, timing effectiveness can be measured relative to a benchmark portfolio with fixed equity and bond/cash proportions. In principle the benchmark portfolio could be fully invested in equities with the bond/cash proportion zero, but a fund manager wishing to increase equity exposure relative to the benchmark could borrow cash to invest more than 100 percent of portfolio value in equities. Significant leverage (using debt to purchase equities in excess of the total value of the fund) is encountered both in closed end funds and in the speculative hedge funds, but open-ended mutual funds are prohibited from borrowing and in practice most portfolios contain liquidity either to meet imminent liabilities (pension payouts, insurance claims, fund withdrawals) or from uninvested new contributions. To reflect this, the benchmark portfolio might have 20 percent cash/bonds and 80 percent equity. If the equity index yields 7 percent and money market rates are 5 percent, an active fund with a 30 percent/70 percent allocation will earn 0.3×5 percent $+0.7 \times 7$ percent or 6.4 percent, an underperformance relative to the benchmark return (0.2×5 percent $+0.8 \times 7$ percent or 6.6 percent) of 0.2 percent.

The timing stances of a variety of funds in respect of cash, bonds, and equities are illustrated in a sample of portfolio recommendations published regularly by *The Economist* (table 1).

Table 1 Sample portfolio recommendations (%)

	Merrill Lynch	Lehman Brothers	Nikko Securities	Daiwa Europe	Credit Agricole	Credit Suisse
Equities	45	50	65	55	65	30
Bonds	40	40	30	40	35	48
Cash	15	10	5	5	0	22

Source: *Economist*, January 7, 1995, p. 72.

Strictly, performance comparison between portfolios should specifically adjust for the *ex ante* risks taken by the portfolios, otherwise portfolio managers would simply increase risk levels to improve returns. The CAPM model provides a framework for risk adjustment by using beta or the correlation of returns of a security or portfolio with the returns of the market portfolio as a proxy for riskiness with the market portfolio definitionally having a beta of one. The beta is then multiplied by the risk premium or historical outperformance of equities relative to government bonds to provide a risk adjusted benchmark return. Thus, if the risk premium is 7 percent, then a portfolio with a beta of 1.5 has to achieve returns 7 percent higher than a portfolio with a beta of 0.5 before outperformance is demonstrated. Unfortunately, in recent years the risk premium has been rather volatile (see table 2).

As an alternative, Merton (1981) argued that as returns of an all-equity portfolio are more variable (risky) than an all-bond portfolio, risk differences due to composition should be proxied by using option performance. Perfect timing is equivalent to holding cash plus call options on the entire equity portfolio with benchmark adjustments using reduced options to reflect any equity proportion.

The two best-known portfolio performance yardsticks are the Sharpe measure and the Treynor measure. Sharpe (1966) measures return differences from average relative to the standard deviation of returns, while Treynor (1965) measures return differences from average relative to beta, or systematic risk.

Within the overall asset allocation, active portfolio management involves security analysis aimed at picking the best value way of investing allocated funds in asset categories such as bonds, deposits, real estate, equities, and commodities. Portfolios, though, mainly emphasize bonds and equities for the simple reason that they have high liquidity (reasonable quantities can be bought or sold at market price) and low transaction costs. In analyzing securities, portfolio managers utilize either fundamental analysis or technical analysis. Fundamental analysis utilizes financial and non-financial data to locate undervalued securities which, relative to the market, offer growth at a discount, assets at a discount, or yield at a discount. Although brokerage houses, among others, invest heavily in such analysis, if successful it would contradict the efficient market hypothesis (EMH), which argues that the market prices of securities already incorporate all information in the market and that therefore it is impossible in the long term to outperform the market. Nevertheless, relatively simple transformations such as Gordon's (1963) growth model relating share prices to dividends and dividend growth are widely used in security selection. There is an extensive literature, including Fama (1969), on signaling, where factors such as dividend changes or investment announcements are used to explain security price changes.

The arbitrage pricing theory (APT) developed by Ross (1976) provides a more general formal framework for analyzing return differences based on the basis of multiple factors such as industry, size, market to book ratio, and other economic and financial variables.

Not surprisingly, the possibility of beating the passive or buy and hold strategies indicated by the EMH has attracted considerable attention, with Banz (1981) among the first to detect an anomaly in the risk-adjusted outperformance of small firms followed by Keim's (1983) analysis of a January effect. End of month, holiday, and weekend effects together with price/book anomalies have also been reported, but with an overall effect small relative to transaction costs. Despite this limited success, market practitioners con-

Table 2   Real returns on investment in US dollar terms, 1984–93 annual average

	Equities	Bonds	Cash
France	18	14.5	9.5
Holland	17.5	11.5	8
Britain	15	8.5	7.5
Germany	14	9	7.5
Switzerland	13.5	8	6.5
Italy	13	14	9.5
Japan	13	13.5	10
USA	12	11	3
Australia	10.5	11	6
Canada	3.5	11	5.5

Source: *Economist*, May 14, 1994.

tinue to offer simple guidelines that they have used to produce exceptional returns. Jim Slater (1994) reports favorable results for a stock picking exercise that uses principles developed by the legendary Warren Buffett and more recently by O'Higgins and Downes (1992), who report in *Beating the Dow* that picking the ten highest yielding shares from the 30 Dow Jones Industrial Index and then investing in the five cheapest (in dollar price) of these shares produced a gain of 2,800 percent against a 560 percent gain on the Dow over 18 years. It is unclear, though, what these authors have to gain by disclosing such valuable procedures.

Technical analysis or chartism is an alternative and widely used technique in portfolio management. In direct contradiction to the weak-form version of the EMH, which states that all information contained in past securities prices is incorporated in the present market price, technical analysts use past patterns to project trends. These patterns may be simply shapes, described for example as "head and shoulders," "double tops," "flags," and so on, or more elaborate short-term or long-term trend lines, all of which are used to generate buy or sell signals. Evaluations of technical analysis have generally run into problems because of subjectivity in classifying signals, but work in neural networks (Baestans, Van den Berg, and Wood, 1994) has provided objective evidence of information in the trend lines used by technical analysts, much of it in non-linear components neglected in some econometric analysis.

The relatively recent development of large, liquid derivative markets – security and index options and futures – has revolutionized the asset allocation process because it allows portfolio managers to proxy the exposure of one asset allocation despite holding a portfolio consisting of a completely different set of assets. A bond or money market portfolio together with equity index futures contracts effectively proxies an equity portfolio. An equity portfolio together with the purchase of put options and sale of call options is similarly equivalent to a fixed interest portfolio. Portfolio managers are able to use derivatives to segment risks asymmetrically. An equity portfolio or index future hedged by put options gives the downside stability of a bond portfolio and the upward opportunities of an equity portfolio. This allows the portfolio manager to create funds with partial or full performance guarantees where investors are offered half any upward movement in the equity market, plus the return of their original investment.

Index-based derivatives are particularly popular with portfolio managers because they provide market diversification with very low transaction costs and none of the trading and monitoring activity involved in maintaining a portfolio of securities that mimicked the index. A portfolio manager wishing to hold a long-term position in equities but at the same time wanting a flexible asset allocation will typically use an index transaction to adjust exposure. A sale of an index future on 20 percent of the portfolio is equivalent to a 20/80 bond equity portfolio.

The possibility of altering positions in this way without transactions on the spot market has generated a number of new techniques. Program trading, for example, involves buying or selling bundles of shares. A portfolio manager with a bundle of shares that provide an adequate proxy for the market index may use program trading to arbitrage between the spot market and index futures, with the transaction itself being computer initiated. In other words, if index futures rise in value it may be profitable to buy a bundle of shares that proxy the index in the spot market. Alternatively, the index future price may fall and a portfolio manager who has bought in the forward market may then program sell in the spot market, depressing the spot market which then transmits a further downward signal to the futures market, arguably increasing the risk of a major price melt down (Roll, 1988).

The second major development is dynamic hedging. Because of the low cost and flexibility of futures markets a portfolio manager can optimize the portfolio on a continuous rather than one off basis. Dynamic hedging incorporates the possibility of new information and the dynamic hedge ratio, for a portfolio reflects the quantity of an option that must be traded to eliminate a unit of risk exposure in a portfolio position. This depends on the delta, which measures the sensitivity of the value of an option to a unit change in the price of the underlying asset, and/or the ratio of the dollar value of the portfolio to the dollar value of the futures index contract multiplied by the beta or systematic risk of the portfolio.

Bibliography

Baestans, D., Van den Berg, W. M., and Wood, D. (1994). *Neural Solutions for Trading in Financial Markets.* London: F. T. Pitman.

Banz, R. (1981). The relationship between return and market value of common stocks. *Journal of Financial Economics*, **9**, 3–18.

Fama, E. (1969). The adjustment of stock prices to new information. *International Economic Review*, **9**, 7–21.

Gordon, M. J. (1963). Optimal investment and financing policy. *Journal of Finance*, **18**, 264–72.

Keim, D. (1983). Size related anomalies and stock return seasonality: Further empirical evidence. *Journal of Financial Economics*, **12**, 12–32.

Levy, H., and Sarnat, M. (1970). International diversification of investment portfolios. *American Economic Review*, **60**, 668–75.

Lintner, J. (1965). The valuation of risk assets and the selection of risky investments in stock portfolios and capital budgets. *Review of Economics and Statistics*, **47**, 13–37.

Markowitz, H. (1952). Portfolio selection. *Journal of Finance*, **7**, 77–91.

Merton, R. C. (1981). On market timing and investment performance, I: An equilibrium theory of value for market forecasts. *Journal of Business*, **54**, 363–406.

O'Higgins, M., and Downes, J. (1992). *Beating the Dow: High Return, Low Risk Method for Investing in the Dow-Jones Industrial Stocks with as Little as $5,000.* New York: Harper Collins.

Roll, R. (1988). The international crash of October 1987. *Financial Analysts Journal*, **45**, 20–9.

Ross, S. (1976). The arbitrage theory of capital asset pricing. *Journal of Economic Theory*, **13**, 341–60.

Sharpe, W. F. (1963). A simplified model for portfolio analysis. *Management Science*, **9**, 227–93.

Sharpe, W. F. (1966). Mutual fund performance. *Journal of Business*, **39**, 119–38.

Slater, J. (1994). *The Zulu Principle Revisited.* London: Orion.

Strong, R. A. (1993). *Portfolio Construction, Management and Protection.* St Paul, MN: West Publishing.

Treynor, J. (1965). How to rate management of investment funds. *Harvard Business Review*, **43**, 63–75.

portfolio performance measurement

David Blake

The principal activities of a portfolio (or fund) manager are portfolio structuring and adjustment on behalf of a client. The manager uses the client's funds to purchase a portfolio of (generally) risky assets, based on the client's specified objectives and the fund manager's assessment of asset risks and returns, with the aim of beating an agreed target or benchmark of performance. At the end of an agreed period (usually a year), the fund manager's performance will be measured.

THE COMPONENTS OF PORTFOLIO
PERFORMANCE MEASUREMENT

The questions that are important for assessing how well a fund manager performs are how to measure the *ex post* returns on the portfolio, how to measure the risk-adjusted returns on the portfolio, and how to assess these risk-adjusted returns. To answer these questions, we need to examine returns, risks, and benchmarks of comparison.

EX POST RETURNS

There are two ways in which *ex post* returns on the fund can be measured: time-weighted rates of return (or geometric mean) and money-weighted (or value-weighted) rates of return (or internal rate of return). The simplest method is the money-weighted rate of return, but the preferred method is the time-weighted rate of return, since this method controls for cash inflows and outflows that are beyond the control of the fund manager. However, the time-weighted rate of return has the disadvantage of requiring that the fund be valued every time there is a cash flow.

Consider table 1 on the value (V) of and cash flow (CF) from a fund over the course of a year.

The money-weighted rate of return is the solution to (assuming compound interest)

$$V_2 = V_0(1 + r) + CF(1 + r)^{1/2} \qquad (1)$$

or to (assuming simple interest)

$$V_2 = V_0(1 + r) + CF\left(1 + \frac{1}{2}r\right) \qquad (2)$$

In the latter case, this implies that

$$= \frac{V_2 - (V_0 + CF)}{V_0 + \frac{1}{2}CF} \qquad (3)$$

Table 1 Fund value and cash flow

	0	6 months	1 year
Value of fund	V_0	V_1	V_2
Cash flow		CF	

The time-weighted rate of return is defined as

$$= \frac{V_1}{V_0} \frac{V_2}{V_1 + CF} - 1 \qquad (4)$$

If the semi-annual rate of return on the portfolio equals r_1 for the first six months and r_2 for the second six months, then we have

$$V_1 = V_0(1 + r_1) \qquad (5)$$

and

$$\begin{aligned} V_2 &= (V_1 + CF)(1 + r_2) \\ &= [V_0(1 + r_1) + CF](1 + r_2) \end{aligned} \qquad (6)$$

Substituting (5) and (6) into (4) gives

$$\begin{aligned} &= \frac{V_0(1 + r_1)}{V_0} \left[\frac{[V_0(1 + r_1) + CF](1 + r_2)}{V_0(1 + r_1) + CF} \right] - 1 \\ &= (1 + r_1)(1 + r_2) - 1 \end{aligned}$$
$$(7)$$

which is a chain-linking of returns between cash flows.

It is clear that the time-weighted rate of return reflects accurately the rate of return realized on the portfolio. This is because both cash inflows and outflows are beyond the control of the fund manager, and their effects should be excluded from influencing the performance of the fund. This is the case for the time-weighted rate of return, but not the money-weighted rate of return.

Adjusting for risk The *ex post* return has to be adjusted for the fund's exposure to risk. The appropriate measure of risk depends on whether the beneficiary of the fund's investments has other well-diversified investments or whether this is his only set of investments. In the first case, the market risk (beta) of the fund is the best

measure of risk. In the second case, the total risk or volatility (standard deviation) of the fund is best.

Benchmarks of comparison In order to assess how well a fund manager is performing, we need a benchmark of comparison. Once we have determined an appropriate benchmark, we can then compare whether the fund manager outperformed, matched, or underperformed the benchmark on a risk-adjusted basis.

The appropriate benchmark is one that is consistent with the preferences of the client and the fund's tax status. For example, a different benchmark is appropriate if the fund is a gross fund (and does not pay income or capital gains tax, such as a pension fund) than if it is a net fund (and so does pay income or capital gains tax, such as the fund of a general insurance company). Similarly, the general market index will not be appropriate as a benchmark if the client has a preference for high-income securities and an aversion to shares in rival companies or, for moral reasons, the shares in tobacco companies, say. Yet again, a domestic stock index would not be an appropriate benchmark if half the securities were held abroad. There will therefore be different benchmarks for different funds and different fund managers. For example, consistent with the asset allocation decision, there will be a share benchmark for the share portfolio manager and a bond benchmark for the bond portfolio manager.

MEASURES OF PORTFOLIO PERFORMANCE

There are two performance measures based on risk-adjusted excess returns, each distinguished by the risk measure used. The first is the excess return to volatility measure, also known as the Sharpe measure (Sharpe, 1966). This uses the total risk measure or standard deviation:

$$\text{Excess return to volatility (Sharpe)} = \frac{r_p - r_f}{\sigma_p}$$
$$(8)$$

where r_p is the average return on the portfolio (usually geometric mean) over an interval, σ_p is the standard deviation of the return on the portfolio, and r_f is the average risk-free return (usually geometric mean) over the same interval.

The second performance measure is the excess return to beta measure, also known as the Treynor measure (Treynor, 1965). This uses the systematic risk measure or beta,

$$\text{Excess return to beta (Treynor)} = \frac{r_p - r_f}{\beta_p} \quad (9)$$

where β_p is the beta of the portfolio.

The Sharpe measure is suitable for an individual with a portfolio that is not well diversified. The Treynor measure is suitable for an individual with a well-diversified portfolio.

The Treynor measure, for example, is shown in figure 1: funds A and B beat the selected benchmark (BM) on a risk-adjusted basis, whereas funds C and D did not.

Performance measures based on alpha values   As an alternative to ranking portfolios according to their risk-adjusted returns in excess of the riskless rate, it is possible to rank them according to their alpha values. Again, two different performance measures are available depending on the risk measure used.

If the risk measure is total risk, the appropriate alpha value is defined with respect to the capital market line:

$$\bar{r}_p = r_f + \left(\frac{\bar{r}_m - r_f}{\sigma_m}\right)\sigma_p \quad (10)$$

where $\bar{r}_p$ is the expected return on the portfolio, $\bar{r}_m$ is the expected return on the market, and σ_m is the standard deviation of the return on the market.

The corresponding alpha value is

$$\alpha_\sigma = r_p - \bar{r}_p \quad (11)$$

If the risk measure is systematic risk, the relevant alpha value is defined with respect to the security market line:

$$\bar{r}_p = r_f + (\bar{r}_m - r_f)\beta_p \quad (12)$$

The corresponding alpha value is

$$\alpha_\beta = r_p - \bar{r}_p \quad (13)$$

This is also known as the Jensen differential performance index (Jensen, 1969). Funds with superior investment performance will be those with large positive alpha values.

The decomposition of total return   Having discussed various measures of the performance of

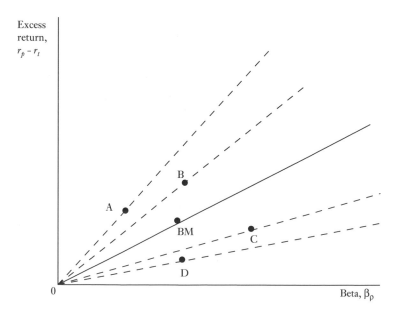

Figure 1   Excess return to beta

a fund, the next task is to identify the sources of that performance. This involves breaking down the total return into various components. One way of doing this is known as the Fama decomposition of total return (after Fama, 1972): see figure 2. Suppose that fund P generates a return r_p and has a beta of β_p. The fund has performed well over the period being considered. Using the Jensen performance measure, it has a positive alpha value, equal to $(r_p - \bar{r}_p)$. The total return r_p can be broken down into four components:

return on the portfolio = riskless rate + return from client's risk + return from market timing + return from security selection (14)

The first component of the return on the portfolio is the riskless rate, r_f; all fund managers expect to earn the riskless rate. The second component of portfolio return is the return from the client's risk. The fund manager will have assessed the client's degree of risk tolerance to be consistent with a beta measure of β_c, say. The client is therefore expecting a return on the portfolio of at least r_c. The return from the client's risk is therefore $(r_c - r_f)$.

The third component is the return from market timing. This is also known as the return from the fund manager's risk. This is because the manager has chosen (or at least ended up with) a portfolio with a beta of β_p which differs from that expected by the client. Suppose the fund manager has implicitly taken a more bullish view of the market than the client by selecting a portfolio with a larger proportion invested in the market portfolio and a smaller proportion invested in the riskless asset than the client would have selected. In other words, the fund manager has engaged in market timing. With a portfolio beta of β_p, the expected return is r_p, so that the return to market timing is $(\bar{r}_p - r_c)$.

An alternative test for successful market timing is due to Treynor and Mazuy (1966). A successful market timer increases the beta of his portfolio prior to market rises and lowers the beta of his portfolio prior to market falls. Over time, a successful market timer will therefore have portfolio excess returns that plot along a curved line. To test this, a quadratic curve is fitted using historical data on excess returns on the portfolio and on the market:

$$(r_{pt} - r_{ft}) = a + b(r_{mt} - r_{ft}) + c(r_{mt} - r_{ft})^2 \quad (15)$$

where both b and c are positive for a successful market timer: see figure 3.

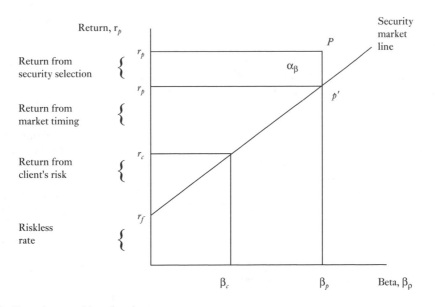

Figure 2 Fama decomposition of total return

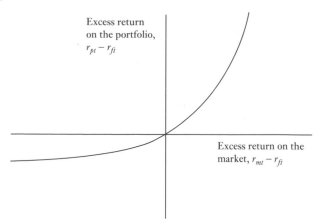

Figure 3   Successful market timing

The fourth component is the return to selectivity (i.e., the return to security selection), which is equal to $(r_p - \bar{r}_p)$.

The decomposition of total return can be used to identify the different skills involved in active fund management. For example, one fund manager might be good at market timing but poor at stock selection. The evidence for this would be that their $(r_p - r_c)$ was positive but their $(r_p - \bar{r}_p)$ was negative; they should therefore be recommended to invest in an index fund but be allowed to select their own combination of the index fund and the riskless asset. Another manager might be good at stock selection but poor at market timing; they should be allowed to choose their own securities, but someone else should choose the combination of the resulting portfolio of risky securities and the riskless asset.

THE EVIDENCE ON PORTFOLIO
PERFORMANCE

A number of studies have tried to measure the performance of fund managers; most of them have involved an examination of the performance of US institutional fund managers. They have examined the managers' abilities in security selection, market timing, and persistence of performance over time.

Studies to determine the ability of fund managers to pick stocks calculate the Jensen alpha values of the funds. Shukla and Trzcinka (1992), using data from 1979 to 1989 on 257 mutual funds, found that the average *ex post* alpha

value was negative (-0.74 percent per annum) and that only 115 funds (45 percent) had positive alphas. Similar results were found for US pension funds by Lakonishok, Schleifer, and Vishny (1992). These results suggest that a typical fund manager has not been able to select shares that on average subsequently outperform the market.

However, these results have to be modified when shares are separated into two types: value shares (which have low market-to-book ratios) and growth shares (which have high market-to-book ratios). Fama and French (1992) found a strong negative relationship between performance and market-to-book ratios. Firms with the 1/12th lowest ratios had higher average returns than firms with the 1/12th highest ratios (1.83 percent per month, compared with 0.30 percent per month over the period 1963–90), suggesting that value strategies outperform growth strategies.

The market timing skills of fund managers have been examined in papers by Treynor and Mazuy (1966) and Shukla and Trzcinka (1992). Treynor and Mazuy examined 57 mutual funds between 1953 and 1962 and found that only one had any significant timing ability. The later study of 257 funds by Shukla and Trzcinka found that the average fund had negative timing ability, indicating that the average fund manager would have done better by executing the opposite set of trades.

Hendricks, Patel, and Zeckhauser (1993) examined 165 mutual funds between 1974 and

1988 for persistence of performance over time (i.e., whether good (or bad) performance in one period was associated with good (or bad) performance in subsequent periods). They found that the 1/8th of funds with the best performance over a two-year period subsequently had an average 8.8 percent per annum superior return over the subsequent two year period compared with the 1/8th of funds with the worst performance over the same two year period. But this was the average superior performance, and the performance of individual funds can differ significantly from the average. This is shown clearly in a study by Bogle (1992), who examined the subsequent performance of the top 20 funds every year between 1982 and 1992. He found that the average position of the top 20 funds in the following year was only 284th out of 681, just above the median fund.

All these results indicate that fund managers (at least in the USA) are, on average, not especially successful at active portfolio management, either in the form of security selection or in market timing. However, there does appear to be some evidence of consistency of performance, at least over short periods. But as the saying goes: past performance is not necessarily a good indicator of future performance.

Bibliography

Bogle, J. (1992). Selecting equity mutual funds. *Journal of Portfolio Management*, **18**, 94–100.
Fama, E., (1972). Components of investment performance. *Journal of Finance*, **27**, 551–67.
Fama, E., and French, K. (1992). The cross-section of expected returns. *Journal of Finance*, **47**, 427–65.
Hendricks, D., Patel, J., and Zeckhauser, R. (1993). Hot hands in mutual funds: Short-run persistence of relative performance, 1974–1988. *Journal of Finance*, **48**, 93–130.
Jensen, M. (1969). Risk, the pricing of capital assets and the evaluation of investment portfolios. *Journal of Business*, **42**, 167–247.
Lakonishok, J., Schleifer, A., and Vishny, R. (1992). The structure and performance of the money management industry. *Brookings Papers on Economic Activity: Microeconomics*, 339–79.
Sharpe, W. F. (1966). Mutual fund performance. *Journal of Business*, **39**, 119–38.
Shukla, R., and Trzcinka, C. (1992). Performance measurement of managed portfolios. *Financial Markets, Institutions and Instruments*, **1**.
Treynor, J. (1965). How to rate management of investment funds. *Harvard Business Review*, **43**, 63–75.
Treynor, J., and Mazuy, K. (1966). Can mutual funds outguess the market? *Harvard Business Review*, **44**, 131–6.

portfolio theory and asset pricing

Ian Garrett

The modern theory of asset pricing has its foundations in modern portfolio theory, developed by Markowitz (1952, 1959). Under the assumption that rational, risk-averse investors with homogeneous expectations base their decisions to maximize the expected utility of wealth on the mean and variance of returns Markowitz shows that diversification gives investors the possibility of lowering the risk of their portfolio for a given level of expected return. The insight is that diversification across assets allows investors to substantially reduce idiosyncratic (company-specific) risk and that it may be possible to do this without altering the expected return on the portfolio. To illustrate, suppose there are two risky assets, A and B, with expected returns and variances given by $E(R_A)$ and σ_A^2, and $E(R_B)$ and σ_B^2 respectively. The correlation between the returns on the assets is ρ_{AB}. Suppose an investor invests the fraction ω of their wealth in asset A and the remainder in asset B. Algebraically, the expected return on the portfolio of the two assets is

$$E(R_P) = \omega E(R_A) + (1 - \omega)E(R_B) \qquad (1)$$

while the variance of the return on the portfolio is

$$\sigma_P^2 = \omega^2 \sigma_A^2 + (1 - \omega)^2 \sigma_B^2 + 2\omega(1 - \omega)\rho_{AB}\sigma_A\sigma_B \qquad (2)$$

As long as $\rho AB < 1$, the investor can gain in terms of reducing risk without decreasing the expected return by combining the two assets into a portfolio rather than holding only one asset. Figure 1 shows the expected return and variance of portfolios combining assets A and B in different proportions. *ZB* is the mean-variance efficient frontier. It represents the

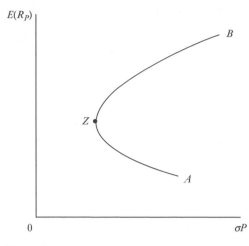

Figure 1

minimum variance opportunity set, since at any point on the efficient frontier it is not possible to decrease the variance of the portfolio while maintaining the same level of expected return. Portfolios that locate on the efficient frontier are efficient portfolios. This result generalizes to the case of n assets. It is also possible to construct any mean-variance efficient portfolio from a weighted average of any two other efficient portfolios. This is known as two fund separation. The particular efficient portfolio an investor chooses to hold will be determined by their preference for risk.

Consider now the introduction of a risk-free asset and denote the return on this asset by R_f. As can be seen from figure 2, the efficient frontier is now a straight line that is tangential to the efficient frontier in the absence of a risk-free

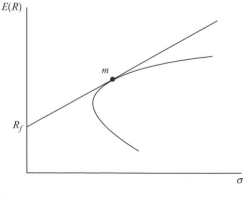

Figure 2

asset at point m. Irrespective of their preferences, investors will only consider combining the risk-free asset with one risky portfolio: the market portfolio, m. The portfolio m only contains systematic risk. This result provides the foundation for the capital asset pricing model (CAPM) developed by Sharpe (1964), Lintner (1965), and Mossin (1966).

THE CAPITAL ASSET PRICING MODEL (CAPM) AND THE INTERTEMPORAL CAPM (ICAPM)

The premise that underlies the (unconditional) CAPM is that investors should only be rewarded for bearing systematic risk since unsystematic (idiosyncratic) risk can be eliminated through diversification. The CAPM states that the expected return on a risky asset will equal the return on a risk-free asset plus a risk premium that reflects the systematic risk of the asset. For an asset, i, the CAPM is

$$E(R_i) = R_f + \beta_i E(R_m - R_f) \qquad (3)$$

where $E(R_i)$ is the expected return on asset i, R_f is the return on the risk-free asset, $E(R_m)$ is the return on the market portfolio, and $\beta_i = \frac{\sigma_{im}}{\sigma_m^2}$, which measures the covariance of the asset's return with the market return, scaled by the variance of the return on the market. The risk premium for asset i is $\beta_i E(R_m - R_f)$. Black (1972) derived the CAPM for an economy without a riskless asset (the zero-beta CAPM).

The CAPM has several interesting empirical implications. In particular, (3) implies that in the time-t cross-sectional regression

$$\bar{r}_i = \alpha_i + \lambda_m \beta_i + \varepsilon_i \qquad (4)$$

where $\bar{r}_i$ denotes the average excess return on asset i and ε_i is an error term, the intercept term α should equal zero and β should be the only factor that is significant in explaining average excess returns. λ is the price of risk and should equal the average excess return on the market portfolio.

The unconditional CAPM has been tested extensively, but neither the early nor more recent evidence is encouraging, with studies typically finding that β alone cannot explain the cross-section of returns. In a comprehensive examination of cross-sectional returns in the US, Fama and French (1992) find that there is little relation between average stock returns and β after controlling for the effects of size (measured by the market value of equity) and the ratio of book value of equity to market value of equity. For the UK, Strong and Xu (1997) find that the only variables that are consistently significant in explaining the cross-section of UK stock returns are book-to-market equity and leverage. Results from these and other studies suggest that models with more than one factor are needed to explain average stock returns. It is worth noting, however, that Roll (1977), in his famous critique of tests of the CAPM, argues that it is not possible to test the CAPM. This is because a test of the CAPM requires that the market portfolio be observable. However, the market portfolio, which is a value-weighted portfolio of all assets, including non-traded assets, is not observable. Any test of the CAPM is therefore only a test of whether the *ex post* proxy chosen for the market portfolio (usually a broad-based equity index) is mean-variance efficient. Failure to accept that the proxy is mean-variance efficient does not mean that the CAPM has been rejected. However, results from empirical tests do not seem to be sensitive to the use of broader proxies for the market portfolio, such as portfolios that contain equity and bonds.

Merton (1973) examines the Sharpe-Lintner CAPM in a continuous time setting and extends the model to the case where the investment opportunity set is stochastic. If the investment opportunity set does not change over time, Merton shows that a continuous-time version of the CAPM holds. However, if the investment opportunity set is stochastic, Merton shows that a multi-beta CAPM results:

$$E(R_i - R_f) = \beta_{im}E(R_m - R_f) + \beta_{is}E(R_s - R_f) \tag{5}$$

where the last term is the excess return on a portfolio that hedges shifts in the investment opportunity set. There is still a problem here, however, as it is difficult to identify the hedge portfolio.

THE ARBITRAGE PRICING THEORY (APT)

The unconditional CAPM and ICAPM are equilibrium models derived from making as-

sumptions about investor preferences. The arbitrage pricing theory (APT) derived by Ross (1976) uses no-arbitrage arguments to arrive at an expression for expected returns. The no-arbitrage argument has found widespread usage in finance (in pricing options and examining the impact of capital structure on the value of the firm, to name but two) and is intuitively straightforward. In general, assets with the same systematic risk should offer the same return. If they do not, sell the overvalued assets short and use the proceeds to invest in the undervalued assets. This strategy, uses none of the investors' wealth and the profit from the strategy is risk-free. It does insure, however, that the prices of the assets will be driven back to their equilibrium values.

Ross (1976) assumes that returns are generated by the following k-factor model:

$$R_{it} = E(R_i) + \sum_{j=1}^{k} b_{ij}F_{jt} + \varepsilon_{it} \tag{6}$$

where R_{it} are the returns on asset i at time t, the F_j are the systematic risk factors, b_{ij} is the sensitivity of the returns on asset i to factor j and ε_{it} is the idiosyncratic return. Just as returns can be separated into systematic and idiosyncratic components, so the variance of returns can be split into that relating to the factors (systematic risk) and that which is idiosyncratic. Since idiosyncratic risk can be diversified away, the expected return is only influenced by systematic risk and is given by

$$E(R_i) \approx \lambda_0 + \sum_{j=1}^{k} b_{ij}\lambda_j \tag{7}$$

where λ_0 is the return on the risk-free asset and λ_j is the price of risk for the jth systematic risk factor and is the same for all assets. The risk premium for asset i is given by $\sum_{j=1}^{k} b_{ij}\lambda_j$. (7) will only hold as an equality if there is an infinite number of assets, for only then will idiosyncratic risk be completely diversified away. This is one reason why Shanken (1982, 1985) questions whether the APT is actually testable (but see also Dybvig and Ross, 1985). Connor (1984) shows that it is possible to derive a version of the APT using equilibrium arguments.

There has been a substantial amount of empirical work on the APT (for a review, see Connor and Korajczyk, 1995). One of the problems faced in testing the APT is that the model is silent on the number of factors, k, that are priced and what these k factors actually are. One way to test the APT is to use factor analysis (Roll and Ross, 1980) or asymptotic principal components (Connor and Korajczyk, 1988) to extract the factors. One of the problems with this approach is that since factor analytic methods are purely statistical it is difficult to put an economic interpretation on the factors. Chen, Roll and Ross (1986) overcome this problem by explicitly specifying macroeconomic variables such as expected and unexpected inflation, unexpected growth in industrial production, the spread between long-term and short-term interest rates and the like, as the systematic risk factors. This latter approach is not without its problems, however, since there is little in the way of theory to guide the choice of macroeconomic variables that may be systematic risk factors. It is perhaps not surprising, therefore, to find that different studies find different macroeconomic factors to be significant in explaining returns (compare the factors found to be significant for the UK in Clare and Thomas, 1994, and Antoniou, Garrett, and Priestley, 1998, for example.)

The Fama–French Three Factor Model

Another multi-factor model that has been proposed in the literature is the Fama–French three factor model (Fama and French, 1993, 1996). The three factor model is motivated by the empirical finding that size and the ratio of book-to-market equity have consistent and significant explanatory power for US stock returns at the very least (Fama and French, 1992, 1993). The Fama–French three factor model is

$$E(R_i) = R_f + \beta[E(R_m) - R_f] + s_i SMB + h_i HML \tag{8}$$

where SMB and HML capture the size and book-to-market effects, respectively. SMB and HML are factor-mimicking hedge portfolios constructed from stock returns. Details on how these factors are constructed can be found in Fama and French (1993). This model performs very well empirically and is capable of explaining many of the anomalies that the CAPM is not capable of explaining, such as the overreaction effect (see Fama and French, 1996). One possible objection to the model is that it is an empirically driven one designed to capture anomalies such as the size effect that the CAPM is incapable of explaining. Fama and French (1995), however, argue that the premia associated with SMB and HML are consistent with a multi-factor version of Merton's ICAPM. Brennan, Wang, and Xia (2004: 1744) argue that to interpret significant risk factors in the light of the ICAPM, the factors must not just be correlated with returns but should be innovations in the state variables that *predict future returns innovations*. The evidence in Liew and Vassalou (2000) that size and book-to-market predict economic growth (GDP) suggests that SMB and HML might indeed be proxies for the hedge portfolio in Merton's ICAPM.

The Conditional CAPM

The asset pricing models considered so far are unconditional in that they are models of the cross-section of average asset returns at a point in time. Implicit in these models is the assumption that expected returns and βs are constant. However, it does not seem unreasonable to suppose that expected returns and risk change over time as the economy moves through phases of the business cycle, for example. The conditional CAPM (Harvey, 1989) allows for this by conditioning expected returns at time t on the information available at time $t - 1$ when the expectation is formed. This allows expected returns and risk to change from period to period as new information arrives. The conditional CAPM is given by

$$E(R_{it} - R_{ft}|\mathbf{Z}_{t-1}) = \frac{(\sigma_{im,t}|\mathbf{Z}_{t-1})}{(\sigma_{m,t}^2|\mathbf{Z}_{t-1})} E(R_{mt} - R_{ft}|\mathbf{Z}_{t-1}) \tag{9}$$

where R_{jt} is the return on asset j at time, σ_{im} is the covariance t, and $\mathbf{Z}_{t-1}$ is the information set available when the expectation about excess returns in time period t are formed. $\mathbf{Z}$ contains variables such as the aggregate dividend yield, measures of the term structure, the differential between the return on three-month treasury bills, and the return on one-month treasury bills, and other variables that may capture movements in the business cycle or predict excess stock returns.

THE CONSUMPTION CAPM (CCAPM)

The CCAPM (Lucas, 1978; Breeden, 1979) considers the intertemporal portfolio and consumption choices of a single "representative agent" investor. Investors choose consumption and investment to maximize the expected present value of the utility of consumption (Hansen and Singleton, 1982):

$$E_t\left[\sum_{j=0}^{\infty} \delta^j U(C_{t+j})\right] \qquad (10)$$

subject to

$$C_t + \sum_{j=1}^{N} P_{jt}Q_{jt} \le \sum_{j=1}^{N} (P_{jt} + D_{jt})Q_{jt-i} + W_t \qquad (11)$$

where c_t is consumption in time period; $0 \le \delta \le 1$ is the discount factor; $U(\cdot)$ is a strictly concave utility function with $\frac{\partial U(C_t)}{\partial C_t} > 0$ and $\frac{\partial^2 U(C_t)}{\partial C_t^2} < 0$; P_{jt} is the price of security j at time t; Q_{jt} is the quantity of security j held at time t; D_{jt} is the dividend paid on security j at time t, and W_t is exogenously given labor income at time t. The first order condition is

$$P_{jt}U'(C_t) = \delta E_t[(P_{jt+1} + D_{jt+1})U'(C_{t+1})] \quad (12)$$

where $U'(C_t)$ is the first derivative of U with respect to consumption. Rewriting (12) as

$$E_t\left[\delta \frac{U'(C_{t+1})}{U'(C_t)} R_{jt+1}\right] = 1 \qquad (13)$$

gives us a general form of the CCAPM. Assumptions about the form of the utility function and distributional assumptions about asset returns and consumption then lead to an estimable model. For example, assuming that investors have time-separable preferences and constant

relative risk aversion, then a utility function of the form $U(C_t) = \frac{C_t^{1-\gamma}-1}{1-\gamma}$ where γ is the coefficient of relative risk aversion gives

$$E_t\left[\delta\left(\frac{C_{t+1}}{C_t}\right)^{-\gamma} R_{jt+1}\right] = 1 \qquad (14)$$

and assuming that asset returns and consumption are conditionally lognormally distributed gives

$$\begin{aligned} &E_t(r_{i,t+1}) + \ln\delta - \gamma E_t(\Delta c_{t+1})+ \\ &0.5(\sigma_{r_i}^2 - \gamma^2 \sigma_{\Delta c}^2 - 2\gamma\sigma_{r_i,\Delta c}) = 0 \end{aligned} \qquad (15)$$

where $r_{i,t+1} = \ln(1 + R_{i,t+1})$, $\Delta c_{t+1} = \ln(C_{t+1}/C_t)$, and $\sigma_{i,j}$ is the covariance between i and j. If the CCAPM holds for all assets, it must hold for risk-free as well as risky assets. In terms of returns on a risky asset in excess of the risk free rate, we therefore have

$$E_t(r_{it+1} - r_{ft+1}) + \frac{\sigma_i^2}{2} = \gamma\sigma_{ic}$$

or

$$\ln E_t\left(\frac{1 + R_{it+1}}{1 + R_{ft+1}}\right) = \gamma\sigma_{ic}$$

which states that excess returns are a function of the covariance between asset returns and consumption growth rather than returns on the market portfolio. Unfortunately, the empirical evidence does not lend support to the CCAPM. See chapter 8 in Campbell, Lo, and MacKinlay (1997) for further details on the CCAPM, while Cochrane (2001) offers a more advanced but very readable treatment of asset pricing models.

Bibliography

Antoniou, A., Garrett, I., and Priestley, R. (1998). Macroeconomic variables as common pervasive risk factors and the empirical content of the Arbitrage Pricing Theory. *Journal of Empirical Finance*, 5, 221–40.

Black, F. (1972). Capital market equilibrium with restricted borrowing. *Journal of Business*, 45, 444–55.

Breeden, D. (1979). An intertemporal asset pricing model with stochastic consumption and investment opportunities. *Journal of Financial Economics*, 7, 265–96.

Brennan, M. J., Wang, A. W., and Xia, Y. (2004). Estimation and test of a simple model of intertemporal capital asset pricing. *Journal of Finance*, **59**, 1743–75.

Campbell, J. Y., Lo, A., and MacKinlay, A. C. (1997). *The Econometrics of Financial Markets* Princeton, NJ: Princeton University Press.

Chen, N.-F., Roll, R., and Ross, S. (1986). Economic forces and the stock market. *Journal of Business*, **59**, 383–403.

Clare, A., and Thomas, S. (1994). Macroeconomic factors, the APT and the UK stock market. *Journal of Business Finance and Accounting*, **21**, 309–30.

Cochrane, J. H. (2001). *Asset Pricing*. Princeton, NJ: Princeton University Press.

Connor, G. (1984). A unified beta pricing theory. *Journal of Economic Theory*, **34**, 13–31.

Connor, G., and Korajczyk, R. (1988). Risk and return in an equilibrium APT. *Journal of Financial Economics*, **21**, 255–89.

Connor, G., and Korajczyk, R. (1995). The Arbitrage Pricing Theory and multifactor models of asset returns. In R. Jarrow, V. Maksimovic, and W. Ziemba (eds.), *Handbooks in Operations Research and Management Science, Vol. 9: Finance*. Amsterdam: Elsevier Science.

Dybvig, P., and Ross, S. (1985). Yes, the APT is testable. *Journal of Finance*, **40**, 1173–88.

Fama, E. F., and French, K. R. (1992). The cross-section of expected stock returns. *Journal of Finance*, **47**, 427–65.

Fama, E. F., and French, K. R. (1993). Common risk factors in the returns on stocks and bonds. *Journal of Financial Economics*, **33**, 3–56.

Fama, E. F., and French, K. R. (1995). Size and book-to-market factors in earnings and returns. *Journal of Finance*, **50**, 131–56.

Fama, E. F., and French, K. R. (1996). Multifactor explanations of asset pricing anomalies. *Journal of Finance*, **51**, 55–84.

Hansen, L. P., and Singleton, K. (1982). Generalized instrumental variables estimation of nonlinear rational expectations models. *Econometrica*, **50**, 1269–85.

Harvey, C. R. (1989). Time-varying conditional covariances in tests of asset pricing models. *Journal of Financial Economics*, **24**, 289–318.

Liew, J., and Vassalou, M. (2000). Can book-to-market, size and momentum be risk factors that predict economic growth? *Journal of Financial Economics*, **44**, 169–203.

Lintner, J. (1965). The valuation of risky assets and the selection of risky investments in stock portfolios and capital budgets. *Review of Economics and Statistics*, **47**, 13–37.

Lucas, R. (1978). Asset prices in an exchange economy. *Econometrica*, **46**, 1426–45.

Markowitz, H. (1952). Portfolio selection. *Journal of Finance*, **7**, 77–91.

Markowitz, H. (1959). *Portfolio Selection: Efficient Diversification of Investments*. New York: John Wiley.

Merton, R. C. (1973). The theory of rational option pricing. *Bell Journal of Economics and Management Science*, **4**, 141–83.

Mossin, J. (1966). Equilibrium in a capital asset market. *Econometrica*, **35**, 768–83.

Roll, R. (1977). A critique of the Asset Pricing Theory's tests: Part I. *Journal of Financial Economics*, **4**, 129–76.

Roll, R. and Ross, S. (1980). An empirical examination of the Arbitrage Pricing Theory. *Journal of Finance*, **35**, 1073–103.

Ross, S. (1976). The arbitrate theory of capital asset pricing. *Journal of Economic Theory*, **13**, 341–60.

Shanken, J. (1982). The Arbitrage Pricing Theory: Is it testable? *Journal of Finance*, **37**, 1129–40.

Shanken, J. (1985). Multi-beta CAPM or equilibrium-APT? A reply. *Journal of Finance*, **40**, 1189–96.

Sharpe, W. F. (1964). Capital asset prices: A theory of market equilibrium under conditions of risk. *Journal of Finance*, **19**, 442–445.

Strong, N., and Xu, X. (1997). Explaining the cross-section of UK expected stock returns. *British Accounting Review*, **29**, 1–23.

price/earnings ratio

Michelle A. Romero

The price/earnings (P/E) ratio is a valuation tool calculated as current stock price divided by annual earnings per share. The earnings statements from the previous 12 months are typically used, although P/E forecasts are calculated with 12 month earnings estimates. P/E can be used to value individual stocks or the market as a whole.

CORPORATE P/E

The P/E ratio is used as a fundamental benchmark to relate a stock's price to corporate performance. The company's management may influence the ratio through accounting practices, the management of growth and market expansion, and the capital structure. The price, however, is driven by the investment community's confidence in the predictability of stable or optimistic earnings. This sentiment reflects projections about earnings, profitability, and cost of capital, as well as intangible factors such as confidence in the quality of management and the prospects of the industry.

Graham and Dodd (1934) cite the multiplier of ten as the historically accepted valuation standard before the 1927–9 bull market. Given the volatility of the elements affecting P/E, it is impossible to adhere to firm parameters of "acceptable" rates of valuation. High P/E ratios, which may be 25/1 or more, are to be expected for growth stocks with a promising outlook. P/E ratios in the range of 20/1 may be expected for moderate-growth companies with stable earnings.

It is difficult to compare P/E values for companies from one country to another. Differing accounting conventions and methods to state earnings and value assets contribute to distortions which may be hard to control for. Cultural biases towards understating or inflating earnings also affect the validity of comparison.

In the research of stock performance, the P/E ratio has been examined theoretically as it is correlated to other factors such as risk, firm size, and industry effects. The efficient market hypothesis states that security prices reflect all current and unbiased information and that securities with higher risk should bring higher rates of return. Basu (1977) examined the investment performance of stocks and determined that low P/E portfolios earned higher risk-adjusted rates of return than high P/E securities, thus indicating market inefficiency. Banz (1981) examined the "size effect" and determined that small firms have higher risk-adjusted returns than large firms, and that P/E may be a proxy for the size effect. Peavy and Goodman (1983) showed that stocks with low P/E multiples outperform high P/E stocks after controlling for the "industry effect" which occurs when characteristically low or high P/E industries skew the results in an analysis of an undifferentiated group.

MARKET P/E

The P/E ratio of the S&P 500, FT-A 500, or other market indices may be examined as a predictor of future market profitability as a whole. Bleiberg (1989), however, could conclude only generally that based on historic P/E ratios of the S&P 500 and the distribution of subsequent returns, stock returns will be higher (lower) in the periods following low (high) P/E multiples, and that the market will do better as the P/E ratio falls. He illustrated that from 1959 to 1965 the S&P produced an annualized rate of return

of 11.1 percent, despite the fact that the P/E ratio never fell below 16 and quite often hovered at highs between 18 and 22.

The P/E ratio serves best as an indicator of the present sentiments of the investment community, either with respect to one stock or the market as a whole. It can swing with volatility up or down based on the intangible values and estimates used to judge the premium of an issue or the health of the general investing climate. Although general inferences can be made about the patterns which emerge from the trends of the P/E ratio movement, there is no clear evidence that it can be reliably used to profitably time the market.

Bibliography

Banz, R. W. (1981). The relationship between return and market value of common stocks. *Journal of Financial Economics*, 9, 3–18.

Basu, S. (1977). Investment performance of common stocks in relation to their price-earnings ratios: A test of the efficient market hypothesis. *Journal of Finance*, 32, 663–81.

Bleiberg, S. (1989). How little we know...about P/Es, but perhaps more than we think. *Journal of Portfolio Management*, 15, 26–31.

Graham, B., and Dodd, D. L. (1934). *Security Analysis*. New York: Whittlesey House, McGraw-Hill.

Peavy, J. W., III and Goodman, D. A. (1983). The significance of P/Es for portfolio returns. *Journal of Portfolio Management*, 9 (2), 43–7.

price momentum and overreaction

Weimin Liu

One of the most intriguing properties of stock market behavior is that stock returns measured over intervals of less than a year (3 to 12 months) exhibit positive serial correlation, or price momentum. That is, stocks tend to repeat their performance in the past 3 to 12 months over the next 3 to 12 months. To exploit this phenomenon, investors should buy past intermediate-term (3 to 12 months) winning stocks and sell past intermediate-term losing stocks.

The most influential paper examining the momentum investing strategy is Jegadeesh and Titman (1993). They examine 16 momentum strategies based on the US stock market over the period 1965 to 1989 and find that each strategy can generate significant abnormal returns. For instance, a 6 × 6 momentum strategy, which buys an equally weighted portfolio of stocks in the highest decile of price performance over the previous six months and sells an equally weighted portfolio of stocks in the lowest decile of price performance over the prior six months and holds these positions for the subsequent six months, realizes a significant profit of about 1 percent per month on average. Fama and French (1996) find that the price momentum effect is robust to controlling for risk using their three factor model.

The price momentum effect is also found in major markets throughout the world. Rouwenhorst (1998) finds that return continuation is present in 12 European countries, and an internationally diversified price momentum strategy earns returns of around 1 percent per month, which is very close to the return that Jegadeesh and Titman (1993) report for the US. Liu, Strong, and Xu (1999) show that significant price momentum profits are available and robust to various risk controls in the UK over the period 1977 to 1998.

The striking presence of the price momentum effect across different markets worldwide represents strong evidence against the efficient markets hypothesis—a cornerstone of modern finance—at the most basic level. Consequently, numerous empirical studies have explored the sources of these apparent momentum profits. These explorations generally fall into three categories. The first tries to offer rational explanations for apparent momentum profits. Studies in this category explain apparent momentum profits as arising from such factors as compensation for growth rate risk (Johnson, 2002) and as a manifestation of time-varying expected returns (Chordia and Shivakumar, 2002). The second eschews rationality in favor of behaviural explanations. Examples here include Daniel, Hirshleifer, and Subrahmanyam (1998) and Hong and Stein (1999). The third category examines the extent to which price momentum is a manifestation of other effects. Examples of other effects include earnings momentum (Chan, Jegadeesh, and Lakonishok, 1996) and industry momentum (Moskowitz and Grinblatt, 1999).

It is apparent that if the momentum profits are due to the last two sources, the momentum strategy should be exploitable. On the other hand, the momentum effect can be regarded as an illusion if it is due to the first source, since the significant momentum profits reflect compensation for bearing higher risk.

While researchers have not reached a consensus on what generates momentum profits, recent studies have shown that liquidity risk (ignored in the CAPM and Fama–French three factor model) is important in explaining the cross-section of asset returns. Pastor and Stambaugh (2003) find that momentum profits are less attractive after accounting for four factors: the Fama–French three factors plus a liquidity factor. Liu (2004) shows that both winning and losing stocks tend to be less liquid. Liu (2004) concludes that the momentum strategy is unlikely to be profitable or implementable because of the practical difficulty of short-selling illiquid losing stocks.

An alternative to the momentum strategy is the contrarian strategy. Researchers have shown that the contrarian strategy of buying past losing stocks and selling past winning stocks is profitable over short-term (less than a month) or long-term (three to five years) horizons. The classic papers examining the contrarian investment strategy are DeBondt and Thaler (1985) for the long-term overreaction hypothesis, and Lo and MacKinlay (1990) (among others) for the short-term return reversals. However, contrarian profits either over the short-term or the long-term have been largely explained by subsequent studies. Jegadeesh and Titman (1995) provide evidence that the short-term return reversal is related to the bid–ask spread. Fama and French (1996) claim that their three factor model captures the reversal of long-term returns documented by DeBondt and Thaler (1985).

Bibliography

Chan, L. K. C., Jegadeesh, N., and Lakonishok, J. (1996). Momentum strategies. *Journal of Finance*, **51**, 1681–1713.

Chordia, T., and Shivakumar, L. (2002). Momentum, business cycle, and time-varying expected returns. *Journal of Finance*, **57**, 985–1019.

Conrad, J., and Kaul, G. (1998). An anatomy of trading strategies. *Review of Financial Studies*, **11**, 489–519.

Daniel, K., Hirshleifer, D., and Subrahmanyam, A. (1998). Investor psychology and security market under- and overreactions. *Journal of Finance*, **53**, 1839–85.

DeBondt, W. F. M., and Thaler, R. H. (1985). Does the stock market overreact? *Journal of Finance*, **40**, 793–805.

Fama, E. F., and French, K. R. (1996). Multifactor explanations of asset pricing anomalies. *Journal of Finance*, **51**, 55–84.

Hong, H., and Stein, J. C. (1999). A unified theory of underreaction, momentum trading, and overreaction in asset markets. *Journal of Finance*, **54**, 2143–84.

Jegadeesh, N., and Titman, S. (1993). Returns to buying winners and selling losers: Implications for stock market efficiency. *Journal of Finance*, **48**, 69–91.

Jegadeesh, N., and Titman, S. (1995). Short-horizon return reversals and the bid–ask spread. *Journal of Financial Intermediation*, **4**, 116–32.

Johnson, T. C. (2002). Rational momentum effects. *Journal of Finance*, **57**, 585–608.

Liu, W. (2004). Liquidity premium and a two-factor model. Working paper, University of Manchester.

Liu, W., Strong, N. C., and Xu, X. (1999). The profitability of momentum investing. *Journal of Business Finance and Accounting*, **26**, 1043–91.

Lo, A., and MacKinlay, A. C., (1990). When are contrarian profits due to stock market overreaction? *Review of Financial Studies*, **3**, 175–205.

Moskowitz, T. J., and Grinblatt, M. (1999). Do industries explain momentum? *Journal of Finance*, **54**, 1249–90.

Pastor, L., and Stambaugh, R. F. (2003). Liquidity risk and expect stock returns. *Journal of Political Economy*, **111**, 642–85.

Rouwenhorst, K. G. (1998). International momentum strategies. *Journal of Finance*, **53**, 267–84.

privatization options

Vihang R. Errunza, Sumon C. Mazumdar, and Amadou N. R. Sy

Over the last decades, the sales of state owned enterprises (SOEs) have reached dramatic levels on a worldwide scale. However, there is no consensus over the optimal means and financial strategies that are necessary for a successful privatization. Moreover, the empirical evidence regarding the "success" of privatizations in achieving their stated objectives has been mixed. Studies such as those conducted by Kay and Thompson (1986) argue that privatizations did not promote economic efficiency. However, empirical analyses such as Megginson, Nash, and Van Randenborgh (1994) suggest otherwise.

ALTERNATIVE METHODS OF PRIVATIZATION

At the theoretical level, there is no model that explains the diversity of the methods of sale. It is generally accepted that there is no single "best" method and that each case should be examined on its own merit (Baldwin and Bhattacharyya, 1991).

Public offerings of shares   This option involves the partial or complete sale to the public of an SOE's shares. It frequently dominates alternate modes of privatization and has often been of record breaking proportions. The offer can be on a fixed price basis, in which case the issuer determines the offer price before the sale. Perotti and Serhat (1993) find evidence from 12 countries that such sales tend to be made at highly discounted fixed price offerings. Alternatively, the offer can be made on a tender basis, where the investors indicate the price they are willing to pay.

Private sales of shares   In a private sale of shares, the government sells the shares to a single entity or a group. The sale can be a direct acquisition by another corporate entity or a private placement targeting institutional investors. Megginson, Nash, and Van Randenborgh (1994) point out that France and Mexico systematically used this method to transfer ownership to a few large "core" shareholders.

Pricing strategies involve a negotiation or a competitive bidding process. The disclosure policy can be an auction.

Cornelli and Li (1995) warn that the investor with the highest bid may not necessarily be the one who will run the privatized firm in the most efficient way. They give examples of Fiat, Mercedes-Benz, and Volkswagen, which acquired majority stakes of several Eastern European car makers. These companies may not necessarily believe that the acquired factories *per se* have great potential value. They may have been motivated to acquire them mainly to gain a foothold in local markets.

Private sale of SOEs' assets   The transaction basically consists of the sale of specific assets rather than the sale of the company's shares.

Fragmentation This method consists of the re-organization of the SOE into several entities that will be subsequently privatized separately (e.g., the break up of a monopoly).

New private investment in an SOE This operation takes place when the government adds more capital by selling shares to private investors, usually for rehabilitation and expansion purposes. This method dilutes the government's equity position.

Management and employee buyout This transaction refers to the new acquisition of a controlling interest in a company by a small group of managers. Employees can also acquire a controlling equity stake with or without management. The assets of the acquired company are usually used as collateral to obtain the financing necessary for the buyout.

Leases and management contracts These options involve a transfer of control, rather than ownership, to the private sector. In a lease, the lessee operates the SOE's assets and facilities and bears some burden of maintenance and repair in exchange for a predetermined compensation. The lessee has to make the payment regardless of the profitability of the firm.

The management contractor, on the contrary, assumes no financial responsibility for the running of the enterprise. A World Bank report (1995) found that although management contracts have not been widely used, they were generally successful when attempted. Using a worldwide search, they found only 150 management contracts, mainly in areas where output is easily measurable and improvements tangible.

For a review of the techniques discussed above, see Vuylsteke (1988).

Mass privatization Mass privatization is very popular in Eastern Europe and other former centrally planned economies in Central Asia. It involves a rapid give away of a large fraction of previously state owned assets to the general public. Boycko, Shleifer, and Vishny (1994) cite numerous examples of mass privatization, such as free grants of shares to workers and managers in the enterprises employing them; distribution of vouchers to the whole population, with the subsequent exchange of those vouchers for shares in SOEs; and free grants of shares of mutual funds, specially created to manage a portfolio of shares of SOEs, to the whole population.

PRE- AND POST-PRIVATIZATION OPTIONS

If the chosen method is through a public equity offering, the government and the new management have several pre- and post-privatization options concerning the strategy to maximize the revenues from such a privatization. Errunza and Mazumdar (1995) assume that a SOE's debt may be perceived as a junior secured debt contract. Thus, the risk premium on a SOE's debt is less than that of a comparable private firm. This difference in risk premium is the value of the government's loan guarantee. When a SOE is privatized, this guarantee may be potentially removed, leading to a wealth transfer from debt holders to equity holders. Other factors such as production efficiencies, monopoly power, government debt guarantees, tax shields, and bankruptcy costs affect the value of this loan guarantee and hence the potential gains from privatization. Errunza and Mazumdar (1995) believe there are various optimal government financial strategies that would maximize the gains from privatization:

1 The value gains from privatization are likely to be relatively smaller when implemented by governments with overall riskier public sector operations. Further, the government should prioritize its privatization program by selling off its most heavily subsidized firms.

2 The government should prioritize its privatization program by selling off firms from minor sectors first, and under certain conditions, the government could improve the valuation gains to equity holders by undertaking riskier investment strategies prior to privatization. Similarly, value gains from a privatization are higher for firms with the highest levels of debt.

3 A more active role by the government in the management of the company even after privatization may not necessarily be detrimental to the firm's shareholders, since it may enhance tax shields and wealth transfers from debt holders. Moreover, to maintain SOE ownership in domestic private hands, appro-

priate tax subsidies and restrictions should be considered.

4 SOEs that were well managed prior to privatization, or have fully exploited any monopoly power in the product market, or may be handicapped with bureaucratic malaise or trade union pressures after privatization, would be less attractive to investors, *ceteris paribus*. Indeed, the prospects for the new management, of capitalizing on unrealized gains would be smaller under these scenarios.

5 If post-privatization bankruptcy costs are significant, then the firm may be forced to reduce its debt level as well as opt for safer investments. The first hypothesis is empirically validated by Megginson, Nash, and Van Randenborgh (1994).

Bibliography

Baldwin, C., and Bhattacharyya, S. (1991). Choosing the method of sale: A clinical study of Conrail. *Journal of Financial Economics*, 30, 69–98.

Boycko, M., Shleifer, A., and Vishny, R. W. (1994). Voucher privatization. *Journal of Financial Economics*, 35, 249–66.

Cornelli, F., and Li, D. D. (1995). Large shareholders, private benefits of control, and optimal schemes of privatization. Working paper, London Business School.

Errunza, V. R., and Mazumdar, S. C. (1995). Privatization: A theoretical framework. Working paper, McGill University.

Kay, J., and Thompson, D. (1986). Privatization: A policy in search of a rationale. *Economic Journal*, 96, 18–38.

Megginson, W., Nash, R., and Van Randenborgh, M. (1994). The financial and operating performance of newly privatized firms: An international empirical analysis. *Journal of Finance*, 49, 1231–52.

Perotti, E., and Serhat, G. (1993). Successful privatization plans. *Financial Management*, 22, 84–98.

Vuylsteke, C. (1988). *Techniques of Privatization of State-Owned Enterprises, Vol. I: Methods and Implementation*. Technical paper 88. Washington, DC: World Bank.

World Bank (1995). *Bureaucrats in Business: The Economics and Politics of Government Ownership*. Policy research report. New York: Oxford University Press.

program trading

John Board and Charles Sutcliffe

The New York Stock Exchange defines a program trade as the simultaneous trading of at least 15 stocks with a total value of over US$1 million and, since May 1988, has required the reporting of program trades, classified under 17 categories. These categories include index arbitrage, which accounted for half of NYSE program trading in 1989 (Quinn, Sofianos, and Tschirhart, 1990), index substitution, portfolio insurance, tactical asset allocation, and portfolio realignment. During June 1989, the average program trade on the NYSE was valued at US$9 million and involved shares in 177 different companies (Harris, Sofianos, and Shapiro, 1990). Program trading is neither defined nor recorded by the London Stock Exchange.

The 1987 stock market crash was initially blamed on program trading in general, and portfolio insurance in particular (Brady, 1988). This blame was based on the possible market impact of these very large trades, and on the feature of some portfolio strategies which require selling (buying) a basket of shares in an already falling (rising) market, so amplifying the initial price movement. However, the general conclusion from a large number of subsequent studies (Miller, 1988; Furbush, 1989) is that there is little theoretical or empirical evidence to support this view. Subsequent NYSE regulations limit the scope and nature of program trading (e.g., by limiting the use of the Super DOT system) during unusual market conditions.

Program trading involves the simultaneous trading of a basket of shares, and this may or may not involve computers. Although index arbitrageurs use computers both to monitor the relationship between actual and no-arbitrage prices in real time, and to deliver the program trading instructions to the floor of the NYSE (via Super DOT), many non-program traders also rely on computers to provide information on trading opportunities and to submit orders to trade.

One effect of program trading may be to increase the measured volatility of a market index based on trade prices. Usually, roughly equal numbers of shares in the index will have been bought and sold so that the bid–ask spread tends to cancel out. However, just after a program trade to buy (sell) many shares, most of the prices used in the index calculation will be ask (bid) prices and movements in the index will be exaggerated by about half the bid–ask spread. A different effect is that a program trade temporarily insures that most of the last trade prices are recent, so removing the "stale" price effect (which biases measured volatility downwards). While both of these effects will increase measured volatility, neither of them implies any economically adverse consequences of program trading.

Modest increases in measured US stock market volatility associated with program trading have been found by Duffee, Dupiec, and White (1992) and Thosar and Trigeorgis (1990), while Grossman (1988) found no such increase. A modest increase is consistent with the bid–ask and stale price effects (Harris, Sofianos, and Shapiro, 1990).

Bibliography

Brady, N. F. (Chairman) (1988). *Report on the Presidential Task Force on Market Mechanisms.* Washington, DC: US Government Printing Office.

Duffee, G., Dupiec, P., and White, A. P. (1992). A primer on program trading and stock price volatility: A survey of the issues and the evidence. In G. G. Kaufman (ed.), *Research in Financial Services: Private and Public Policy*, Vol. 4. Greenwich, CT: Jai Press, 21–49.

Furbush, D. (1989). Program trading and price movement: Evidence from the October market crash. *Financial Management*, 18, 68–83.

Grossman, S. J. (1988). Program trading and market volatility: A report on interday relationships. *Financial Analysts Journal*, 44, 18–28.

Harris, L., Sofianos, G., and Shapiro, J. E. (1990). Program trading and intraday volatility. NYSE Working Paper No. 90-03.

Miller, M. H. (Chairman) (1988). *Final Report of the Committee of Enquiry Appointed by the CME to Examine the Events Surrounding 19 October 1987.* Chicago: Chicago Mercantile Exchange.

Quinn, J., Sofianos, G., and Tschirhart, W. E. (1990). Program trading and index arbitrage. Appendix F in *Market Volatility and Investor Confidence*. Report to the Board of Directors of the NYSE. New York: NYSE

Thosar, S., and Trigeorgis, L. (1990). Stock volatility and program trading: Theory and evidence. *Journal of Applied Corporate Finance*, 2, 91–6.

project financing

Reena Aggarwal and Ricardo Leal

During the next decade it is estimated that much more than US$1 trillion will be needed to finance power projects, transport facilities, and other infrastructure around the world. Privatization continues to create a large demand for capital. International consortiums are being formed to finance these large projects. The project finance industry, while it has matured considerably, still faces tremendous risk. Commercial banks were the traditional source of funding for project finance until 1990, when investment bankers started taking large deals to capital markets. Besides traditional project financiers, companies and developers are also turning to pension funds and limited partnerships for capital.

In a general loan, the issuance of securities or simply borrowing the money and the payment of the loan are not specifically associated with the cash flows generated by a given project or economic unit. Generally, loan collateral does not have to be generating income to pay for the loan. In contrast, cash flow from the operation of the project is the sole source of return to lenders and equity investors in project financing. The project may be supported through guarantees, output contracts, raw material supply contracts, and other contractual arrangements.

In project financing, securities are issued or loans are contracted that are directly linked to the assets and the income generating ability of these assets in the future. In other words, project financing means that securities are issued or loans are contracted that are based on the expected income generation of a given project or economic unit. By the same token, the collateral, if any, are the assets related to the project or belonging to the economic unit. A project is financed on its own merits and not on the general borrowing ability of the economic unit that is sponsoring it.

Project financing may be called off-balance sheet financing because it may not affect the sponsor's income or balance sheet. It has no effect on the sponsor's credit rating as well because the financing is not provided based on the income generation ability of the sponsor and does not use the sponsor's assets as collateral.

The sponsor of the project to be financed has to show its commitment and possibly give guarantees to the lenders on the repayment of the loans. It is obvious that the lenders will agree to project financing only if they have some sort of commitment from the sponsor, which is the economic unit with assets in place and borrowing power, to back up the project financing and to carry out the projects execution properly. So project financing does not mean that the project is totally independent from the sponsors, who have to show commitment to the project to satisfy the lender's assessment of the project's credit risk.

Sometimes a project cannot be financed off the balance sheet if it has not yet commenced. Lenders use standard credit analysis tools to verify the project's attractiveness. They do not see the project as equity or as venture capital. Therefore, the sponsor may have to commit resources at the initial stages of the project to get it off the ground and later seek off-balance sheet financing.

There are many reasons for the sponsor to look for project financing. In general, a sponsor would prefer not to have the project reported on its balance sheet, so that it does not affect its financial ratios or credit standing. The sponsor desires that its credit risk and that of the project be judged independently. There could be many reasons why the sponsor would seek project financing, including advantages available only to the project. Some sources of subsidized or favorable financing may only be available for the project itself. The project may be able to meet legal and other restrictions while the sponsor may not. This type of situation often arises when the project is being carried out in a foreign country or in areas of business with special needs.

Project financing is made up of the securities or loans that are contracted by the project, the sponsors, and other institutions that may be involved. The securities can be any type of debt securities, from the usual short-term and long-term securities such as commercial paper or bonds to other securities particularly designed to tap a specific source or to capture a specific advantage provided by the project. The entities involved may also make a difference. Sometimes it may be better that one of the sponsor's subsidiaries or associated joint ventures will carry out or provide guarantees to the project.

Designing project financing involves executing the appropriate credit analysis of the project with conservative estimates, assessing all the legal, tax, and any other relevant restrictions and advantages stemming from the nature of the project, selecting institutions or entities that should participate in the project in its different stages, and determining the securities and types of loans that will be issued. Project financing is a type of financial engineering and participants must carefully analyze several issues, including the economics of the transaction, sponsorship, construction, technology, and environmental needs.

Several changes have occurred related to the sources and access to economic development for project financing. Capital constraints are increasing the cost of doing business, and lenders are requiring additional recourse and guarantees. Equity capital is tight and bank credit criteria have been tightened. Many commercial lending institutions are constrained by regulatory or reserve requirements or internal policies in lending to projects in developing nations as a result of country, political, currency, and other risks associated with such lending. Successful financing of projects in developing nations will often require support from the host nation.

Bibliography

Bemis, J. R. (1992). Access to and availability of project financing. *Economic Development Review*, **10**, 17–19.

Forsyth, G. J., and Rod, J. R. (1994). Project finance and public debt markets. *International Financial Law Review, Capital Markets Yearbook*, 5–10.

Nevitt, P. K. (1988). *Project Financing*, 2nd edn. London: Euromoney Publications.

Siddique, S. (1995). Financing private power in Latin America and the Caribbean. *Finance and Development*, **32**, 18–21.

real options

Dean A. Paxson

Real options are opportunities (or commitments) to acquire or develop or dispose of real assets at a price determined (or estimated) in the present but settled, or delivered, in the future. Like financial options, there is conceptually an underlying asset, or liability, that determines the option value at termination, but unlike financial options, real options are not commonly traded, are often difficult to identify, and may involve more complex methods for valuation.

Real option theory has been applied to a wide variety of characteristic aspects of projects, including deferring investment commitments, choices in selection, sequential alternative actions, follow-on investment opportunities, and flexibility in projects (including maintenance and/or abandonment).

There are several extensive surveys of real option valuation and applications (e.g., Sick, 1989; Trigeorgis, 1993; Dixit and Pindyck, 1994). This introduction will only cover some critical articles in the development of real option theory, showing some generic analytical solutions and some common applications.

Jevons (1871) was arguably the first to identify real (environmental) options in the prospective utility of a commons which "might be allowed to perish at any moment, without harm, if we could have it recreated with equal ease at a future moment, when need of it arises." Although Merton (1973) believed options are "relatively unimportant financial securities," he also believed that a theory of contingent claims pricing could lead to a unified theory of (speculative) markets and the term and risk structure of interest rates. Myers (1977) showed that option analysis is an appropriate valuation technique for a

firm's growth opportunities; Banz and Miller (1978) applied the theory for state contingent claims to practical capital budgeting; Mason and Merton (1985) argued that the flexibility of a project is "nothing more (or less) than a description of the options made available to management." McDonald and Siegel (1986) studied the optimal timing of investment in an irreversible project; Majd and Pindyck (1987) modeled sequential investment decisions and outlays; and Ingersoll and Ross (1992) argued that almost every project competes with itself postponed, with uncertainty in interest rates.

The valuation of real options is dependent on assumptions regarding the life, variable stability, and payouts on the underlying inputs. This is a short menu of some analytical solutions for real options of increasing complexity.

Almost all contingent–claim pricing models commence with some basic assumptions regarding the diffusion process for the underlying asset of the contingent claim. In line with the conventional approaches, assume that the present value (P) of future cash flows for a project follows a diffusion process such that:

$$dP = \mu(P)dt + \sigma(P)dz_p \qquad (1)$$

where μ = the drift rate of the underlying asset, σ = the annualized standard deviation of P and dz_p = a Wiener process with zero drift and unit variance.

Many authors have provided solutions for the value of any contingent $W(P)$ claim on such a (more valuable) asset as:

$$0.5\sigma^2 W_{pp} + (rP - D)W_p - rW + W_t + \hat{D} = 0 \quad (2)$$

where the subscripts denote partial derivatives, r is the riskless rate, D is the net payout to the holder of the underlying asset, and D^a is any payout on any asset converted into the more valuable asset.

If the real option is a finite-life European option, and the underlying asset value is lognormally distributed with a geometric diffusion process (that is $\mu(P) = \mu$ and $\sigma = \sigma^*(P)$) and D is proportional to the price, Merton (1973) showed an analytical solution as:

$$W(P) = e^{-\delta T} P N(d_1)$$
$$- e^{-rT} K N(d_2) + \frac{\hat{D}}{r}(1 - e^{-rT}) \tag{3}$$

where $N()$ is the cumulative density formula for a normally distributed variable with zero mean and unit variance, and

$$d_1 = \frac{\ln(e^{-\delta T} P/K) + (r + 0.5\sigma^2)T}{\sigma\sqrt{T}} \tag{4}$$

and

$$d_2 = d_1 - \sigma\sqrt{T} \tag{5}$$

where $K =$ the "exercise" price of the option, $T =$ the time to expiration, and $\delta =$ the dividend expressed as a continuous return.

If the real option is a perpetual American option, which might be exercised at any time and the project value follows a lognormal process, a solution provided by various authors, including Sick (1989), is:

$$W(P) = \frac{\hat{D}}{r} + \frac{P^*}{\gamma}\left(\frac{P}{P^*}\right)^\gamma \tag{6}$$

where

$$P^* = \frac{\gamma}{\gamma - 1}\left(K + \frac{\hat{D}}{r}\right) \tag{7}$$

and

$$\gamma = 0.5 + \frac{\delta - r}{\sigma^2} + \sqrt{\left(0.5 + \frac{\delta - r}{\sigma^2}\right)^2 + \frac{2r}{\sigma^2}} \tag{8}$$

For a similar perpetual real option, with normally distributed prices, Sick (1989) provides an easy solution as:

$$W(P) = \frac{\hat{D}}{r} + \frac{1}{\gamma}e^{\gamma\,(P-P^*)} \tag{9}$$

where

$$P^* = \frac{\hat{D}}{r} + K + \frac{1}{\gamma} \tag{10}$$

and

$$\gamma = \frac{\lambda B - \mu + \sqrt{(\lambda B - \mu)^2 + 2r\sigma^2}}{\sigma^2} \tag{11}$$

B is the value beta of the underlying asset, $B = \sigma(P)\rho(dz_p \text{ and } dz_{\text{market}})$, and λ is the risk aversion coefficient.

The case where there is a required investment, rather than an exercise price for the real option, and both the investment cost and the present value of the project are risky, is described by various authors, including Quigg (1993). Suppose the investment cost (X) follows a stochastic process:

$$\frac{dX}{X} = \alpha_x dt + \sigma_x dz_x \tag{12}$$

and the value of the project P follows a similar process:

$$\frac{dP}{P} = (\alpha_P - x_2)dt + \sigma_P dz_P \tag{13}$$

where x_2 are the payouts on the project, and ρdt is the constant correlation between dz_X and dz_P. Also assume that the drift rates of X and P can be represented as v_X and v_P, that is expected future cash flows under risk adjusted probabilities, discounted at the risk free rate, and the risk aversion coefficients for X and P are constant parameters, λ_X and λ_P.

The value of such a real option $V(P, X)$ is

$$\frac{1}{2}\sigma_X^2 X^2 V_{XX} + \sigma_{XP} XP V_{XP} + \frac{1}{2}\sigma_P^2 P^2 V_{PP}$$
$$+ v_X X V_X + v_P P V_P - rV + \beta P = 0 \tag{14}$$

where β is any annual investment expense (such as alternative or opportunity costs).

For simplification, let $z = P/X$ and $W(z) = V(X,P)/X$, the relative value of the project option to the investment costs, and

$$\omega^2 = \sigma_X^2 - 2\rho\sigma_X\sigma_P + \sigma_P^2 \qquad (15)$$

Then equation (15) is simplified as:

$$\frac{1}{2}\omega^2 z^2 W'' + (v_p - v_x)zW' \\ + (v_x - r)W + \beta_z = 0 \qquad (16)$$

In solving this differential equation, assume there is a ratio of project value to the investment costs z^*, at which it is optimal to commence production, and that there are certain other boundary conditions. The solution is:

$$V(P,X) = X(Az^j + k) \qquad (17)$$

where

$$A = (z^* - 1 - k)(z^*)^{-j} \qquad (18)$$

$$z^* = \frac{j(1+k)}{(j-1)} \qquad (19)$$

$$k = \frac{\beta z}{(r - v_x)} \qquad (20)$$

$$j = \omega^{-2}(0.5\omega^2 + v_x - v_p \\ + [\omega^2(0.25\omega^2 - v_p - v_x + 2r) \qquad (21) \\ + (v_x - v_p)^2]^{0.5})$$

Quigg (1993) applied this model to value development land; Capozza and Sick (1991) used a real option approach to explain part of the discount between leased and "fee-simple" (freehold) land; and Williams (1995) extended real option theory to price real assets with costly search.

Several authors have built on Jevons's real option valuation of natural resources. Brennan and Schwartz (1985) determined not only the value but also the optimal development, management, and abandonment decisions regarding mining projects; Paddock, Siegel, and Smith (1988) valued offshore petroleum leases; and Bjerksund and Ekern (1990) valued several sequences of petroleum development projects.

Finally, research and development, where there is substantial uncertainty regarding both the research budget and the discovery value, is modeled in Newton, Paxson, and Pearson

(1996). Other areas of production and equipment flexibility are modeled by many authors, such as Triantis and Hodder (1990). Real options are explicit or implicit in many areas of finance, as well as ordinary life, so future research will no doubt cover complex and exotic applications.

Bibliography

Banz, R. W., and Miller, M. H. (1978). Prices for state contingent claims: Some estimates and application. *Journal of Business*, 51, 653–72.

Bjerksund, P., and Ekern, S. (1990). Managing investment opportunities under price uncertainty: From "last chance" to "wait and see" strategies. *Financial Management*, 19, 65–83.

Brennan, M. J., and Schwartz, E. S. (1985). Evaluating natural resource investments. *Journal of Business*, 58, 135–57.

Capozza, D. R., and Sick, G. A. (1991). Valuing long-term leases: The option to redevelop. *Journal of Real Estate Finance and Economics*, 4, 209–24.

Dixit, A., and Pindyck, R. (1994). *Investments Under Uncertainty*. Princeton, NJ: Princeton University Press.

Ingersoll, J. E., Jr. and Ross, S. A. (1992). Waiting to invest: Investment and uncertainty. *Journal of Business*, 65, 1–29.

Jevons, W. S. (1871) [1965]. *The Theory of Political Economy*. New York: Augustus M. Kelley.

McDonald, R., and Siegel, D. R. (1986). The value of waiting to invest. *Quarterly Journal of Economics*, 101, 707–27.

Majd, S., and Pindyck, R. S. (1987). Time to build, option value and investment decisions. *Journal of Financial Economics*, 18, 7–28.

Mason, S. P., and Merton, R. C. (1985). The role of contingent claims analysis in corporate finance. In E. Altman and M. Subrahmanyam (eds.), *Recent Advances in Corporate Finance*. Homewood, IL: Irwin, 7–54.

Merton, R. C. (1973). The theory of rational option pricing. *Bell Journal of Economics and Management Science*, 4, 141–83.

Myers, S. C. (1977). Determinants of corporate borrowing. *Journal of Financial Economics*, 5, 147–75.

Newton, D. P., Paxson, D. A., and Pearson, A. W. (1996). Real R&D options. In A. Belcher, J. Hassard, and S. Proctor (eds.), *R&D Decisions*. London: Routledge, 273–82.

Paddock, J. L., Siegel, D. R., and Smith, J. S. (1988). Option valuation of claims on real assets: The case of offshore petroleum leases. *Quarterly Journal of Economics*, 103, 479–508.

Quigg, L. (1993). Empirical testing of real option-pricing models. *Journal of Finance*, 48, 621–40.

Sick, G. (1989). *Capital Budgeting with Real Options.* Salomon Brothers Center for the Study of Financial Institutions. Monograph Series in Finance and Economics. New York: New York University Press.

Triantis, A. J., and Hodder, J. E. (1990). Valuing flexibility as a complex option. *Journal of Finance*, **45**, 549–66.

Trigeorgis, L. (1993). Real options and interactions with financial flexibility. *Financial Management*, **22**, 202–24.

Williams, J. T. (1995). Pricing real assets with costly search. *Review of Financial Studies*, 8, 55–90.

regulation of US equity markets

Paul Seguin

The basic concept underpinning much of US federal securities regulation is disclosure regulation. An alternative form of regulation, ignored by Congress but used by some states, is based on the concept of merit regulation, where government judges the quality of an investment. Thus, federal securities laws are unlike, say, drug regulation by the FDA, where a government agency approves new drugs.

Equity market disclosure is regulated mainly through the Securities Act of 1933 (1933 Act) and the Securities Exchange Act of 1934 (1934 Act). The 1933 Act concentrates on the regulation of distribution of securities in the primary market, while the 1934 Act concentrates on security distribution in the secondary market.

The 1933 Act requires significant disclosures at the time a firm plans to issue new publicly traded securities in an effort to prevent fraud in the sale of new securities. Under the 1933 Act, a firm issuing securities to the public must follow a prescribed registration process. The issuing firm (aided by investment banks) prepares registration documents that require approval by the Securities and Exchange Commission (SEC) before the securities can be sold. A prospectus, the major component of this set of registration documents, must be disseminated to all potential investors. The prospectus details the issuer's businesses and properties, significant provisions of the securities offered, and the management of the issuer, as well as providing financial statements that have been certified by independent public auditors. In addition, due diligence requires anyone who signs a registration statement

to investigate the accuracy of the information within the document. The SEC examines completed registration documents for compliance with disclosure requirements. Once the documents are approved by the SEC, the offering can be made to the investing public.

Federal securities laws also regulate underwriter behavior during the selling period, specifically the act of price stabilization. "Stabilization" covers numerous practices, but the commonly accepted definition, outlined in a 1940 SEC release, is "the buying of a security for the limited purpose of preventing or retarding a decline in its open market price in order to facilitate its distribution to the public." Although the SEC recognized that stabilization was a form of manipulation, under Section 9(a)(6) of the Securities Exchange Act of 1934, the SEC deemed stabilization activities as necessary to offset a temporary market glut of securities. Rule 10b-7 of the 1934 Act regulates the stabilization activities of participants in an offering at the time of distribution. First, the intent to stabilize must be disclosed in the prospectus. Second, a valid stabilizing bid must not exceed either the bid of the highest independent bidder or the offer price. Third, stabilization must cease once the offer is "distributed," that is, when all offered securities are in the hands of the investing public.

The 1933 Act applies to all securities offered to the public in the USA and outlines penalties for deficient registration statements. However, there are exemptions to the provisions of the 1933 Act, including offerings to limited numbers of sophisticated investors ("private placements"), intrastate offerings which are instead regulated by the individual states, certain government issued securities, and certain small offerings. Securities offered under one of these exemptions are unregistered and so cannot generally be resold. This inherent lack of secondary market liquidity adversely affects the primary market value of these securities. To mitigate this problem, the SEC adopted Rule 144A, which allows for some secondary trading of securities issued under an exemption, but only among qualified institutional buyers. Rule 144A offers are subjected to significant disclosure and SEC scrutiny.

One intention of the provisions in Rule 144A is to aid foreign issuers of securities. These firms face severe restrictions when issuing securities in the USA, most notably in complying with US registration requirements and accounting standards. Although US exchanges such as the NYSE and Nasdaq would prefer exemptions from some restrictions for foreign issuers, the SEC has resisted most exemptions.

The second major security Act is the 1934 Act, which is primarily concerned with the secondary market. Though the 1934 Act has been amended often in response to changing conditions, the theme behind the 1934 Act is, as with the 1933 Act, disclosure. The 1934 Act requires periodic reporting, including 10K filings, by firms with publicly traded securities. Though most regulation of corporate governance is at the state level, the 1934 Act provides for some federal regulation of corporate governance with regulations on proxy solicitations and tender offers. Proxy rules govern (1) what must be contained in a proxy solicitation and (2) what contact between a firm and shareholders or between shareholders is considered a proxy solicitation (and is thus subject to regulation). Tender offer regulations, formulated in 1968 with the Williams Act, extend disclosure requirements to anyone making a tender offer for a firm and to investors who hold over 5 percent of the shares of a firm.

Furthermore, the 1934 Act regulates insider trading, short selling, fraudulent, or manipulative acts, and margin requirements. The 1934 Act, as amended by several SEC rules, defines both financial fraud and insider trading. Under the 1934 Act, margin accounts and margin eligibility are regulated by both the SEC and the Federal Reserve Board. The current initial and maintenance margin rates are 50 percent and 67 percent, respectively. That is, a qualified investor may borrow up to 50 percent of the value of a portfolio of margin eligible securities, but is subject to a margin call if the value of this portfolio falls to or below 67 percent of its original value. Margin eligible securities are securities listed on the NYSE, Amex, or Nasdaq's National Market, as well as other securities deemed eligible by the Federal Reserve Board. In addition, the 1934 Act regulates exchanges and broker-dealers. Under this act, exchanges and broker-dealers must register with the SEC, which also monitors exchange rules.

Finally, the 1934 Act provided for the establishment of the SEC, with powers to monitor disclosure and enforce the securities acts and other security laws. Securities regulations can be enforced through three channels. First, the SEC can seek injunctions and monetary penalties for violations of the securities acts. Second, in many cases, violations of the securities acts can lead to civil suits by private party plaintiffs. Third, the Justice Department can pursue criminal penalties for certain violations of the securities acts.

restructuring and turnaround

Nick Collett

Corporate restructuring and turnaround occurs where there is a major rearrangement of stakeholder claims, possibly including a change of control. The reason for restructuring is underperformance, either relative to industry norms, leading to acquisition, or threatened survival, in which case debtholders gain control and force changes to protect their interests.

In the USA and UK the 1960s saw a merger wave in which conglomerate mergers were a prominent feature. By 1980 industrialists and academics were questioning the performance of large diversified groups, and the decade saw considerable restructuring through divestments and sell-offs, leveraged buyouts, management buyouts, and takeovers. The restructuring is typically asset restructuring or financial (liability) restructuring, although a common theme of all restructuring places greater onus on management to improve the company's performance to avoid takeover and the consequent loss of their own control over assets.

Asset restructuring may involve the sale of property or operating assets, and can be accompanied by leaseback or simple outsourcing of work which was formerly done using the assets which have been sold. For example, the car industry has outsourced increasing numbers of components and design work, so that some manufacturers are now primarily coordinators of design, assembly, and marketing, relying on suppliers for the majority of inputs. Asset restructuring also occurs when companies demerge their activities, and distribute free shares in subsidiaries to original shareholders to eliminate a conglomerate discount. This is a common way of disposing of non-core activities, In the UK, ICI did this with Zeneca, and both Williams Holdings and Albert Fisher demerged car dealerships, one by distributing free shares to existing shareholders, and the other by selling 100 percent of the shares in the dealership to institutions.

Financial restructuring changes the liability side of the balance sheet and can generally take two forms. First, debt can be swapped for equity so that a company with a negative net worth balance sheet is recapitalized. This reduces the interest burden of the company and restores the company to solvency, with the expectation that at some point in the future dividends will be paid again; but debt equity swaps dilute the interests of original shareholders, possibly to the point where control is lost. Alternatively, and typically in management buyouts (MBOs) and leveraged buyouts (LBOs), new capital structures are created with a small proportion of equity and substantial debt, some with security over designated assets and some unsecured. These restructurings are often "going private" transactions in which the company (or part of it) is bought out by management or by new owners. The company continues in private ownership until performance and general stock market conditions allow a flotation at a price which gives investors (and managers in MBOs) a suitably high return (often 40 percent + per annum in the first half of the 1980s). Celebrated examples of new ownership restructurings which fall into the LBO category because of the very high gearing associated with the buyout are the Kohlberg, Kravis, Roberts and Co. buyout of R. J. R. Nabisco and the Isosceles buyout of Gateway. Many MBOs are also LBOs because of the level of gearing (50 percent or more of total capital).

Almost all studies show that financial restructuring proposals benefit shareholders. DeAngelo, DeAngelo, and Rice (1984) find that reprivatizing quoted companies gives shareholders gains averaging more than 40 percent. Kaplan (1989a) and Lehn and Poulsen (1989) report similar results. Research into announcements of divestitures, spin-offs, or liquidations by Hite, Owers, and Rogers (1987), and Bagwell and Shoven (1989) also show large premiums for shareholders.

A number of explanations have been advanced (and tested) for this market reaction. Tax savings might occur if the restructured entity uses large amounts of debt and achieves large tax deductions on interest payments, at the same time as lenders are not generating taxable profits (Gilson, Scholes, and Wolfson, 1987). Overpayment by investors may explain part of the premium in post-1985 buyouts (Kaplan and Stein, 1991), but does not provide an explanation for buyouts analyzed before then. Transfers of wealth from bondholders may occur, especially in refinancings involving increased leverage. Asquith and Wizman (1990) report that bonds in such events lose an average of 2.8 percent of their value, but that this accounts for at most 6.8 percent of the increase in equity value. The employee wealth transfer hypothesis (Shleifer and Summers, 1988) argues that the market anticipates enhanced profits and cash flows as employment levels are reduced and/or employee remuneration is cut. Kaplan (1989b), Smith (1990), and Lichtenberg and Siegel (1990) fail to find any significant reduction in employment levels, and Lichtenberg and Siegel do not find any wage reductions. Lowenstein (1985) proposes that manager–external investor information asymmetries are important because managers have information about the company and knowledge of potential operating improvements that other investors would not have. Kaplan (1989a), Smith (1990), and Muscarella and Vetsuypens (1990) all present results which fail to support this explanation. Jensen (1986, 1989) argues that leveraged refinancings reduce agency costs and provide new incentives by persuading managers to increase operating cash flows to pay down loans and benefit shareholders, and also by giving the manager a larger stake in the residual profit of the company. Baker and Wruck (1989) and Palepu (1990) offer support to these explanations.

The employee–wealth transfer hypothesis, manager–external investor information asymmetries, and reduced agency costs and new incentive explanations all require operational changes post restructuring, and in many cases this means corporate turnaround and revitalization. Kaplan (1989b) found that companies involved in large MBOs between 1979 and 1985 increased their operating income (before depreciation), reduced their capital expenditures, and increased their net cash flow, relative to industry control samples. The operating income improvements expressed as a percentage of both sales and assets were approximately 20 percent, and the net cash flow to sales and assets approximately 50 percent better than the control groups. The big difference in the levels of improvement from operating income to net cash flow suggest that managers in restructured companies are able to make big savings in working capital and capital expenditure and that this is beneficial at least in the short term to shareholders. These results are corroborated by Smith (1990) and Lichtenberg and Siegel (1990).

So, in conclusion, the corporate restructuring of the 1980s produced gains to shareholders and owner/managers. These were marginally at the expense of bondholders, but not at the expense of employees. Inevitably, these results to a large extent reflect the buoyant economic conditions of most of the decade. The generally depressed state of both the buyout and mergers and acquisitions market suggests that these results may not be generalizable to the more depressed economic conditions experienced on either side of the Atlantic in the first half of the 1990s.

Bibliography

Asquith, P., and Wizman, T. (1990). Event risk, covenants and bondholders' returns in leveraged buyouts. *Journal of Financial Economics*, **27**, 195–214.

Bagwell, L. S., and Shoven, J. B. (1989). Cash distributions to shareholders. *Journal of Economic Perspectives*, **3**, 129–40.

Baker, G., and Wruck, K. (1989). Organizational changes and value creation in leveraged buyouts: The case of O. M. Scott and Sons Company. *Journal of Financial Economics*, **25**, 163–90.

DeAngelo, H., DeAngelo, L., and Rice, E. (1984). Going private: Minority freezeouts and stockholder wealth. *Journal of Law and Economics*, **27**, 367–401.

Gilson, R. M., Scholes, M., and Wolfson, M. (1987). Taxation and the dynamics of corporate control: The uncertain case for tax motivated acquisitions. In J. Coffee, L. Lowenstein, and S. Rose-Ackerman (eds.), *Takeovers and Contests for Corporate Control*. New York: Oxford University Press.

Hite, G., Owers, J., and Rogers, R. C. (1987). The market for interfirm asset sales: Partial sell-offs and total liquidations. *Journal of Financial Economics*, **18**, 229–52.

Jensen, M. (1986). Agency costs of free cash flow, corporate finance and takeovers. *American Economic Review*, **76**, 323–9.

Jensen, M. (1989). The eclipse of the public corporation. *Harvard Business Review*, **67**, 61–74.

Kaplan, S. (1989a). Management buyouts: Evidence on taxes as a source of value. *Journal of Finance*, **44**, 611–32.

Kaplan, S. (1989b). The effects of management buyouts on operations and value. *Journal of Financial Economics*, **24**, 217–54.

Kaplan, S., and Stein, J. (1991). The evolution of buyout pricing and financial structure in the 1980s. Working paper, University of Chicago.

Lehn, K., and Poulsen, A. (1989). Free cash flow and stockholder gains in going private transactions. *Journal of Finance*, **44**, 771–88.

Lichtenberg, F., and Siegel, D. (1990). The effects of leveraged buyouts on productivity and related aspects of firm behavior. *Journal of Financial Economics*, **27**, 165–94.

Lowenstein, L. (1985). Management buyouts. *Columbia Law Review*, **85**, 730–84.

Muscarella, C., and Vetsuypens, M. (1990). Efficiency and organizational structure: A study of reverse LBOs. *Journal of Finance*, **45**, 1389–414.

Palepu, K. (1990). Consequences of leveraged buyouts. *Journal of Financial Economics*, **27**, 247–62.

Shleifer, A., and Summers, L. (1988). Breach of trust in hostile takeovers. In A. C. Auerbach (ed.), *Corporate Takeovers: Causes and Consequences*. Chicago: University of Chicago Press.

Smith, A. (1990). Corporate ownership structure and performance: The case of management buyouts. *Journal of Financial Economics*, **27**, 143–64.

retail banking

Derek F. Channon

Historically, retail banking was a relatively simple business. Commercial banks, operating essentially via a branch network, took in consumer deposits which were then usually used to provide loans, in most countries on overdraft, to the corporate sector. In return for deposits held in current accounts the banks provided free transaction services largely by the use of checks in most developed economies. Personal loans to consumers were also available but did not constitute a significant proportion of a bank's loan portfolio. There was little or no segmentation of the consumer market.

As late as the end of the 1960s electronic personal products were in their infancy, automated teller machine (ATM) networks undeveloped, and credit finance, while accepted as a necessity by commercial banks, was treated as a peripheral and somewhat unsavoury product.

The role of the branch was to provide a complete service range to all forms of clients. The branch manager was expected to both operate as administrator and credit assessor (within narrow limits) and to have knowledge of the domestic services provided by the bank. International services were usually provided by specialist international branches. The system tended to be paper based, negative in customer attitude and focus, slow, expensive, and seriously lacking in marketing and selling efforts (Channon, 1988).

The structure of the industry in the UK had been stable for over fifty years until 1968, when the first major merger occurred between banks with the creation of the National Westminster. In West Germany the major banks were not really interested in retail banking, leaving this to the Landesbank, while in France retail custom was approached in a similar manner to the UK. In the USA retail banking was largely provided by small local institutions due to legal constraints at state level on geographic coverage. An exception to this was the state of California, where state-wide branching was permitted. This led to the development of large multi-branch institutions such as the Bank of America, while elsewhere retail banking tended to be the province of local community banks. In Japan, the leading city banks were also much more concerned with corporate clients than with personal customers.

By the mid-1970s around the world retail banking could be considered to be a Cinderella business with personal customers tolerated rather than sought after and many poorer customers predominantly serviced by savings banks, mortgage institutions, and the like, which tended to be denied access to the bank-dominated clearing systems, usually with the tacit support of central banks. Interest rates were usually fixed in conjunction with the central banks and competition was minimal.

The Impact of Deregulation

In the mid-1970s Citibank, operators of a branch network in New York, questioned the viability of its retail banking operation. At this time it operated some 260 branches and employed 7,000 people. The bank concluded that retail banking could be viable but only if costs were strictly controlled. Customers were carefully segmented to only service profitable accounts and technology was used to substitute for premises and people.

In addition, led by savings and loans banks, it became normal to offer interest on current accounts and to unbundle interest and transaction costs. Moreover, US regulations provided opportunities to non-banks to offer some retail financial services to selected customer groups which were superior to those offered by the banks themselves and at the same time cost less. The most notable of these was the development of the cash management account (CMA), a product developed by Merrill Lynch for retail customers with over US$20,000 in cash or securities. This new account was to revolutionize retail banking (Kolari and Zardkoohi, 1987).

In 1978, US regulations restricted interest rates paid to 5.25 percent while domestic inflation was high and money market rates were running at some 18 percent. In return for a small annual fee the CMA allowed investors to withdraw bank deposits and place them into the account which aggregated the funds into a mutual fund. Money was invested in the capital markets at the going market rate. At the same time investors were provided with a check book and a Visa card. To avoid being classified as a bank and thus being subject to the banking regulations, the two services were operated by Bank One of Columbus, Ohio, one of a new breed of emerging, high technology banks.

Investors also received a comprehensive monthly statement of all transactions conducted using the CMA. The statement showed to investors assets held in money market funds, stocks and bonds, dividends and interest received, securities trading, check and credit card transactions, margin loans taken and paid off, and interest charged.

Funds placed in the CMA could be in the form of cash, stocks, and bonds. All cash was placed in one of a series of money market funds which paid interest at market rates. All dividends and interest received were automatically swept into the money market funds unless required to cover transactions incurred. If transactions exceeded available cash then this would automatically trigger sales of assets held in money market funds and if these, too, were inadequate an automatic margin loan could be generated against an account holder's stocks or bonds.

By the mid-1990s the repercussion of the CMA and its derivatives had had a major impact on retail banking around the world. Despite its dramatic success, however, even today few banks have sufficiently developed their information technology capabilities to be able to provide a similar product on a fully integrated basis (Snirreff, 1994).

The success of the money market funds forced regulators to relax control on interest rate ceilings. In addition, the use of technology allowed banks, and in particular Citibank, to transform the cost structure of the industry and turn retail banking into an increasingly attractive proposition. By the mid-1980s Citibank had reduced its branch network in New York to 220 and its staff to 5,000, yet service quality was improved by the introduction of over 500 ATMs. Market share of assets doubled and profitability increased dramatically. This success was soon mirrored elsewhere, as commercial banks began to rediscover the potential of retail banking and turned away from the blind pursuit of the large corporate market.

Retail Market Diversification

By the mid-1990s commercial banks had rapidly increased the range of retail banking products on offer. This had been stimulated by new moves into the market by other non-banks such as retailers, insurance companies, consumer appliance manufacturers, and the like. Uninhibited by regulatory constraint which applied to banks, these institutions often enjoyed a significant cost advantage over the banks, as well as in many cases being more innovative and marketing oriented.

Up until the early 1970s most institutions could be classified as operating in distinct sectors with readily definable boundaries. By the mid-1990s there had been a dramatic convergence of all these specialist institutions, such that each

tended to operate in the others' traditional marketplace.

Thus, banks have become heavily involved in mortgage finance, while housing specialists have transformed themselves into full retail banks. Retailers offered credit cards, loans, investment products, insurance, and the like. Capital goods manufacturers and automobile producers provided house finance, leasing, trade finance, and credit cards, with a company such as General Electric Capital Services being a market leader in some 26 financial service industry segments, including being the largest operator of store credit cards in the world. Increasingly, it had become more difficult to precisely define a bank except that such institutions were classified by being subject to bank regulatory authorities, while most non-bank retail financial service providers took great pains to avoid being formally classified as banks.

By 1994, British banks were all involved in investment management products, both debit and credit cards, were introducing telephone banking, personal financial advice, consumer loans, a wide variety of deposit products, interest-bearing transaction accounts, an increasingly diverse range of mortgage products, and retail share shops. Overall in Europe, where deregulation had proceeded further, banks had strongly entered the market for insurance products, notably for life products. Mortgage protection and household insurance were significant areas in non-life. Keen to increase the throughput of their expensive branch networks, the banks had been relatively successful in developing their insurance business. *Bancassurance* or *Allfinanz* was a key element in the developing strategies of many major European banking and insurance groups.

Delivery System Transformation

The traditional vehicle for the delivery of retail banking, the branch network, has come under increasing pressure in recent times. This can be attributed to a number of causes. First, the increased diversification of banks has led to specialization, and in particular the separation of corporate and retail banking. As a result, corporate accounts tended to be serviced via specialist corporate branches, and serviced by relationship officers, who are trained to perform a very different task to that of the traditional branch manager. Second, it had become recognized that retail customers did not require a full service range from every branch, but rather within a location area simple transaction branches or ATMs could fulfil customer requirements at sharply reduced levels of costs (Prendergast and Marr, 1994). The micromarket concept substitutes low cost, limited service delivery systems within a defined geographic area for full service branches, except where considered essential (Aractingi, 1994).

Third, the role of the branch manager needed to be modified or eliminated by the use of centralized technology. Fourth, further labor savings could be achieved by the use of smart ATMs or in branch machinery and electronic data capture, so sharply reducing the number of in-branch personnel needed. Fifth, branches had come under serious pressure from alternative delivery systems with dramatically lower costs while also offering customers the opportunity to determine the time and place when they conducted their banking transactions.

These pressures in the mid-1990s were leading an increasing number of banks to rationalize their networks and their employees with little or no loss in customer service or satisfaction. New branch configurations and delivery system combinations are therefore developing rapidly, such as the hub and spoke concept (Channon, 1988). At the same time there had been a rapid move to open plan branch configurations, specialist branches such as mortgage shops, fully automated branches, and limited service operations. Despite these efforts, however, the cost of operating branch networks remained high. In the UK the average cost–income ratio for operating a retail branch network was around 55 percent. This compared very unfavorably with a telephone banking operation where nearly all banking services, except cash dispensing, 24 hours per day and year round, could be provided with a cost–income ratio as low as 20 percent.

OTHER DELIVERY SYSTEM ALTERNATIVES

In addition to telephone banking, which by 1995 in the USA already accounted for some 25 percent of transactions, other new delivery systems included smartcards (which can be used as a substitute for cash), smart ATMs, home banking, and virtual reality systems, either in branches or via home computer systems. Substantial experimentation was underway around the world in each of these alternative service delivery mechanisms and it is expected that the further cost pressure will result in additional sharp rationalization and re-engineering of traditional branch-based banking.

FUTURE PROSPECTS

Retail banking has evolved rapidly since its Cinderella position at the beginning of the 1970s. Technology has resulted in many new nontraditional entrants able to gain competitive advantage, a massive increase in consumer product choice and mode of service delivery, strategic convergence between historically separated financial service providers, separation of corporate from retail banking, a move to electronic versus paper based systems, and the adoption of a marketing orientation.

For the future, traditional branch-based retail banking can expect to continue to decline, integrated databases will permit even more refined customer segmentation and product design, staff numbers will continue to fall as paper-based systems are converted to electronic systems and the customer determines the time, the place, the institution, and the product to be used in retail banking operations.

Bibliography

Aractingi, E. (1994). The next great downsizing initiative. *Journal of Retail Banking*, 16, 19–22.

Channon, D. F. (1988). *Global Banking Strategy*. New York: John Wiley.

Kolari, A., and Zardkoohi, A. (1987). *Bank Costs, Structure and Performance*. Lexington, MA: D. C. Heath.

Prendergast, G., and Marr, N. (1994). Towards a branchless banking society. *International Journal of Retail and Distribution Management*, 22, 18–26.

Snirreff, D. (1994). The metamorphosis of finance. *Euromoney*, 25, 36–42.

risk analysis

Thomas F. Siems

Risk can be simply defined as exposure to change. It is the probability that some future event, or set of events, will occur. Hence, risk analysis involves the identification of potential adverse changes and the expected impact on the organization or portfolio as a result. There are many types of risk to which organizations can be exposed, some that are more easily identified and quantified and others that seem beyond control. A few of the more common risks that require analyses and management include price (or market) risks, credit (or default) risks, legal and regulatory risks, and operational risks.

When evaluating risks, a deviation in an outcome from that which is expected is not necessarily for the worse. In fact, with unbiased expectations, propitious deviations are just as likely as unfavorable ones. Nevertheless, downside risks, or the possibilities of unwanted outcomes, are typically of greatest interest to analysts. For example, in the first half of 1986, world oil prices plummeted, falling by more than 50 percent. While this was a boon to the economy as a whole, it was disastrous to oil producers and companies that supply machinery and equipment to energy industry producers. How could companies that are sensitive to changes in oil prices manage the risks associated with a downward plunge in the price of oil?

Generally speaking, there are three different ways to manage financial risks: purchase insurance, proactively manage the firm's assets and liabilities, and hedging. These approaches are not mutually exclusive; they can be used alone or in conjunction with one or both of the other two approaches.

The first approach, buying insurance, is only viable for certain types of financial risk: predictable risks whose probabilities can be assessed with a fairly high degree of certainty. Insurable risks typically include the risk of loss from fire, theft, or other disaster. Insured organizations pay an insurance premium for the removal of the risk. In effect, the insured risks of many individual firms are transferred to the insurer, but, because the individual risks are not highly correlated (that is, they are unsystematic), the insurer's per firm risk is quite small. In other words, since the risks are independent of one another, the premiums received from all the firms tend to offset the payments to the firms that suffer a loss. This is a simple application of portfolio theory.

The second approach to managing financial risks involves the careful balancing of a firm's assets and liabilities so as to meet the firm's objectives and minimize its risk exposure. The key to using this approach is holding the right combination of on-balance sheet assets and liabilities. Ideally, asset/liability management should strive to match the timing and the amount of cash inflows from assets with the timing and the amount of cash outflows from liabilities. However, precisely matching cash flows can be extremely difficult and expensive. Therefore, firms should concentrate instead on making the value difference between assets and liabilities as insensitive to exogenous shocks as possible. This is commonly referred to as portfolio immunization.

The final approach, hedging, involves the taking of offsetting risk positions. This is similar to asset/liability management except that hedging usually involves off-balance sheet positions. A hedge is a position that is taken as a temporary substitute for a later position in another asset (liability) or to protect the value of an existing position in an asset (liability) until the position can be liquidated. The financial tools most often used for hedging are forwards, futures, options, and swaps. Collectively, these tools are commonly referred to as derivative instruments, or derivative contracts.

The appropriate approach to managing financial risks depends on the complexity of the risks and the sophistication of the risk manager. Risks that are insurable and more easily priced can be managed by purchasing insurance. However, most financial risks are not insurable. Thus, risk managers often employ either asset/liability management techniques or hedging strategies. While these two approaches to risk management are similar, the former usually involves on-balance sheet positions and the latter off-balance sheet activities. However, hedging strategies are often superior to asset/liability management activities because they can be implemented quicker and often do not require the sacrifice of better, more profitable, opportunities.

Bibliography

Fabozzi, F. J., and Zarb, F. G. (1986). *Handbook of Financial Markets: Securities, Options and Futures.* Homewood, IL: Dow Jones-Irwin.

Knight, F. H. (1921). *Risk, Uncertainty and Profit*. New York: Houghton-Mifflin.

Smith, C. W., Jr. (1995). Corporate risk management: Theory and practice. *Journal of Derivatives*, 3, 21–30.

rollover risk

Anthony Neuberger

Traders will often maintain a long-term position in a futures market by holding a contract until near to its maturity, closing out the position and establishing a new position of similar size in a contract with a longer maturity. This is known as rolling a position forward. In following such a strategy the trader faces certain risks which would not arise if they had maintained a position in a single long-dated futures contract.

In particular the strategy is affected by the difference between the price at which the old contract is terminated and the new contract is entered into. The price difference between futures contracts on the same underlying asset but with different maturities is known as a calendar spread. The spread is predictable if the futures contracts are trading at their theoretical fair value. However, futures contracts often trade at a premium or discount to fair value, and this gives rise to rollover risk.

Suppose, for example, that the trader wants to be long on a futures contract. If the futures contract which they hold is trading at a discount to fair value and the contract which they want to roll into is trading at a premium then the trader will make a loss on rolling over. They are selling cheap and buying dear. Clearly, the position could well be the other way round, in which case the trader would make a rollover gain.

In principle, the trader could avoid rollover risk by entering into a futures contract whose maturity extends at least as far as the horizon over which the trader wants to maintain the position. In practice, there are a number of reasons why the trader may not wish to do this. First, there may not exist any traded futures contracts with a sufficiently long maturity. Second, the longer-dated contracts which are traded may be illiquid. In most futures markets much of the liquidity is in the contracts closest to maturity. The bid–ask spread tends to be narrower, and it is generally possible to deal in larger size in short-dated contracts. Third, rollover risk represents an opportunity as well as a danger. If the trader can forecast the behavior of the calendar spread, the strategy of rolling from contract to contract may have a lower expected cost than a strategy of maintaining a position in a single long-dated contract.

ROLLOVER RISK IN THE COMMODITIES MARKET

The issue of rollover risk has come into particular prominence since the substantial losses incurred by the German company Metallgesellschaft and its US oil refining and marketing subsidiary MGRM. In brief, MGRM sold oil forward on long-term fixed price contracts and hedged itself by buying short-dated oil futures, and similar over the counter products, which it rolled forward. As the oil price fell it was required to fund its futures position; eventually, the position was closed out in 1994 with MGRM incurring substantial losses (Culp and Miller, 1995).

The nature of the risks taken by MGRM can be understood by considering a very simple world with zero interest rates where an agent at time 0 writes a forward contract to deliver one barrel of oil in T months' time at a price of US$$K$/barrel. The agent hedges by buying one-month futures and holding them to maturity, rolling forward monthly. At time T they buy the oil on the spot market and deliver it to the client. Assume that each month the futures contract final settlement price is equal to the spot price; the agent's profit on the whole strategy is:

$$K - S(0) + \sum_{t=0}^{T-1} [S(t) - F(t)]$$

where $S(t)$ is the spot price of oil at time t and $F(t)$ is the futures price at time t for a futures contract with one month to maturity.

This equation shows that the profit can be decomposed into two parts. The first is the difference between the contract price and the spot price, both of which are fixed at the outset. The second is related to the difference between the spot price and the contemporaneous futures price over the life of the contract.

Historically, the oil market has tended to be in backwardation. The near-term future has tended to trade above the longer maturity future. So the second term in the equation has generally been positive. There has been much discussion about why this has occurred and whether it can be expected to persist (Litzenberger and Rabinowitz, 1995).

Spot and futures prices are tied together by arbitrage trades. The cash and carry relation means that the future price should equal the spot price less the yield from holding the asset (the convenience yield less any storage costs), plus the cost of financing. If the spot is high relative to the futures, agents who have surplus oil will earn high returns by selling the oil spot and buying it forward. Conversely, if the spot is low the arbitrage trade involves buying the spot, storing it, and selling it forward.

The relationship is not very tight. The costs of performing the transaction may be quite substantial. Furthermore, neither the convenience yield nor the cost of storage is constant; they will tend to vary substantially with the level of inventory. If there are large inventories the marginal storage cost will be high, the marginal convenience yield will be low, and the future may trade at a premium (contango) without permitting arbitrage. When inventories are low, the converse may hold, and the future will trade at a discount (backwardation).

The significance of rollover risk in a long-term hedging strategy depends on the stability of the term structure of oil futures prices. Culp and Miller (1995) and Mello and Parsons (1995) offer conflicting views of this in the specific context of the Metallgesellschaft case.

ROLLOVER RISK IN THE FINANCIAL MARKETS

Rollover risk tends to be smaller with financial futures than with commodity futures. Storage costs for the underlying asset (a bond, or a portfolio of shares) are much lower and more predictable than for commodities. The yield from owning the underlying asset is the coupon or dividend on the financial asset, which can normally be predicted rather precisely, at least in the short term.

Nevertheless, the arbitrage between the future and the spot asset is neither costless nor riskless. This means that financial futures do not trade exactly at their theoretical value. To the extent that the difference between the two is hard to predict, rollover risk is a problem for the trader who is rolling over financial futures contracts just as it is for commodity futures.

Bibliography

Culp, M., and Miller, M. (1995). Metallgesellschaft and the economics of synthetic storage. *Journal of Applied Corporate Finance*, **7**, 62–76.

Hotelling, H. (1931). The economics of exhaustible resources. *Journal of Political Economy*, **39**, 137–75.

Litzenberger, R. H., and Rabinowitz, N. (1995). Backwardation in oil futures markets: Theory and empirical evidence. *Journal of Finance*, **50**, 1517–45.

Mello, A., and Parsons, J. E. (1995). Maturity structure of a hedge matters: Lessons from the Metallgesellschaft debacle. *Journal of Applied Corporate Finance*, **8**, 106–18.

S

scrip dividend

M. Ameziane Lasfer

Scrip dividend is the practice of offering share-holders the option to receive shares in lieu of cash when companies make a distribution. In the UK, the popularity of this option has grown significantly in recent years. While other forms of dividend distributions, such as cash dividends and share repurchases, are mandatory and involve cash outflows, scrip dividend payment does not affect the firm's cash position and it is offered as an option whereby share-holders are able to choose between receiving dividends in cash or their equivalent in the form of shares.

The method of paying scrip dividends in the United Kingdom is different from the way stock dividends and/or dividend reinvestment plans are offered in other countries. For example, unlike stock dividends offered in the USA, where the recipient shareholder is not taxed and does not generally have an opportunity to opt for cash (McNichols and Dravid, 1990), scrip dividends entitle the shareholder to choose between the offered share (the scrip) and the cash and both these alternatives are taxed at the personal income tax rate. Moreover, the scrip dividend option is different from dividend re-investment plans adopted by many companies in Australia, where the newly issued shares are normally at a discount of 5–10 percent (Chan, McColough, and Skully, 1993). With scrip divi-dends companies are capitalizing part of their distributable profits in order to issue new shares without any discount offered.

Scrip dividends are a cheaper means of ac-quiring shares because shareholders are not charged brokerage fees, commission, or any other costs for the allotment of shares. They also provide issuing firms with an ideal oppor-tunity to retain cash without altering their divi-dend payout policies to meet fixed charges, in particular in the period of severe recession. Moreover, given that scrip dividends allow a firm to retain cash, they reduce the cash shortage problem (Eisemann and Moses, 1978).

Under the classical system of corporation tax, where the taxation of dividends at the firm level and in the hands of shareholders is not linked, scrip dividends, like stock dividends in the USA, are a cosmetic financial manipulation with no effect on the firm and its shareholders (Lako-nishok and Lev, 1987). On the other hand, in an imputation system such as the one in operation in the UK, scrip dividends allow firms to save in taxes because, unlike cash dividends, scrip divi-dends are not subject to the advanced corpor-ation tax. Firms can thus retain cash and avoid potential tax loss. However, the firms' tax savings are not likely to be shared by all share-holders because the tax credit on scrip dividends can only be claimed by tax-paying investors. Tax-exempt investors forgo the tax credit when they opt for scrip dividends and, as a result, their after-tax return from scrip dividends is likely to be lower than that on cash dividends. Therefore, tax-exempt investors will prefer cash rather than scrip dividends and shareholders whose cash dividend income is taxed at a higher rate than capital gains will prefer scrip dividends for which the firm will issue additional shares. Given that tax-exempt investors are the largest group in the London Stock Exchange, the take-up rate of the scrip in the UK amounts to an average of 4 percent. To increase the take-up rate, a number of companies offered enhanced scrip dividends where the notional dividend used to compute the number of shares offered is higher than cash dividend by up to 50 percent.

Empirically, Lasfer (1995) showed that firm's decision to issue scrip dividend is not motivated by taxes, cash shortage, or signaling. Instead, managers appear to retain cash through scrip dividends to maximize their own utility.

Bibliography

Chan, K. K. W., McColough, D. M., and Skully, M. T. (1993). Australian tax changes and dividend reinvestment announcement effects: A pre- and post-imputation study. *Australian Journal of Management*, 18, 41–62.

Eisemann, P. C., and Moses, E. A. (1978). Stock dividends: Management's view. *Financial Analysts Journal*, 34, 77–80.

Lakonishok, J., and Lev, B. (1987). Stock splits and stock dividends: Why, who and when. *Journal of Finance*, 42, 913–32.

Lasfer, M. A. (1995). Firms' characteristics and the payment of scrip dividends. Working paper 95/3, Centre for Empirical Research in Finance and Accounting, City University Business School.

McNichols, M., and Dravid, A. (1990). Stock dividends, stock splits and signaling. *Journal of Finance*, 45, 857–79.

share repurchases

M. Ameziane Lasfer

The purchase by a company of its own shares is an alternative to cash dividend distribution. This practice involves using surplus cash and/or debt to buy back in the marketplace a proportion of the issued share capital. In the UK the ability of a company to repurchase its own shares was introduced in the Companies Act 1981. Share repurchases are now an accepted tool of corporate financial management in most major developed markets (Barclay and Smith, 1988; Bagwell and Shoven, 1989; Rees and Walmsley, 1994).

The accounting treatment of share repurchases differs across countries. In the United Sates, shares acquired by the issuing company can either be retired or continue to be held as treasury stock in the published balance sheet for future resale. These shares are issued but not outstanding; they cannot be voted, they pay or accrue no dividends, and they are not included in any of the ratios measuring value per common

share. In contrast, in the UK, shares repurchased by a company must be cancelled so that they cease to exist.

Firms can either use the open market or the tender offer method to repurchase their own shares. Under the open market repurchase method, a firm can simply enter the market and repurchase shares without revealing its identity unless the disclosure is required by law. The tender offer method involves the declaration of intention and the purchase of substantial proportions of equity at a significant premium.

There are a number of motives for share repurchases. Given that they are a substitute for cash dividends, share repurchases can be used by firms to reduce their shareholders' tax liability. They are also used to provide for the exercise of stock options and warrants and the conversion of convertible securities. A company subject to a takeover bid can use share repurchases to counter the tender offer (Bagnoli, Gordon, and Lipman, 1989; Sinha, 1991). Share repurchases allow firms to alter their debt to equity ratio, in particular when debt is issued to finance the acquisition of shares.

In the academic literature, the signaling motive has emerged as one of the most important explanations for share repurchases (Dann, 1981; Vermaelen, 1986; Ikenberry, Lakonishok, and Vermaelen, 1995). The signaling approach is motivated by asymmetric information between the market and a firm's managers. When the firm is undervalued, mangers can choose to buy back, in the expectation that share prices will adjust immediately after this signal to the less informed market participants. Ikenberry, Lakonishok, and Vermaelen (1995) show that the first signal through the announcement of a repurchase program is ignored by the market, but that after the repurchase, the share price continues to rise significantly, implying that the managers buy shares at a bargain price.

Bibliography

Bagnoli, M., Gordon, R., and Lipman, B. L. (1989). Stock repurchases as a takeover defense. *Review of Financial Studies*, 2, 423–43.

Bagwell, L. S., and Shoven, J. B. (1989). Cash distribution to shareholders. *Journal of Economic Perspectives*, 3, 129–40.

Barclay, M. J., and Smith, C. W. (1988). Corporate pay-out policy: Cash dividend versus open-market repur-chases. *Journal of Financial Economics*, **22**, 61–82.

Dann, L. (1981). Common stock repurchases: An analysis of bondholders and stockholders. *Journal of Financial Economics*, **9**, 115–38.

Ikenberry, D., Lakonishok, J., and Vermaelen, T. (1995). Market under-reaction to open market share repur-chases. *Journal of Financial Economics*, **39**, 181–208.

Rees, B., and Walmsley, T. (1994). The impact of open market equity repurchases on UK equity prices. Working paper, University of Strathclyde.

Sinha, S. (1991). Share repurchase as a takeover defense. *Journal of Financial and Quantitative Analysis*, **26**, 233–44.

Vermaelen, T. (1986). Common stock repurchase and market signaling: An empirical study. *Journal of Financial Economics*, **13**, 137–51.

short-termism

Istemi S. Demirag

In principle, any investment decision requires a willingness to sacrifice present cash flows in return for improved cash flows in future. The time horizons of the decision taker may therefore affect willingness to invest. An economically rational organization applies an infinite time horizon to all its investment decisions, simply discounting future revenues according to its cost of capital. Short-term pressures (S-TP), then, could be defined as factors acting upon (or within) an organization which cause decision-makers (explicitly or implicitly) either to use a discount rate higher than its cost of capital, and/or to choose some time horizon beyond which future revenues are ignored altogether. Com-panies subject to such pressures will tend to behave in a short-termist way; that is, they will reduce the rate of investment below the "eco-nomically rational" level, and/or bias it towards "short-term" projects. In other words, they will act as economically irrational.

However, this does not mean that where there are no S-TP, we would find economic rational-ity. Therefore, a more robust definition would be "factors tending to raise the discount rate applied (explicitly or implicitly) and/or to fore-shorten the time horizon." Again, the effect would be to reduce the rate of investment and increase the bias towards projects with short

payback periods. This latter definition (but not the former) allows S-TP to include factors like high interest rates and low profitability, which increase the opportunity cost of capital.

There is evidence that British industry ex-perienced during the 1980s a definite intensifi-cation of short-term pressures which continued throughout the 1990s. High real interest rates throughout the decade, and severe recession and overvaluation at the beginning, were external factors obviously making for short-term pres-sures; there also appears to have been an increase in the takeover threat and other manifestations of shareholder impatience with poor financial performance. Privatization, deregulation, and the liberalization of procurement in the defense and telecommunications industries presumably pushed in the same direction.

Muellbauer (1986) and others show the re-markably rapid growth of productivity in British manufacturing since 1980. The rate of product innovation, on the other hand, is not at all impressive: this can be inferred, for example, from Pavitt and Patel's (1988) Anglo-German comparisons of patenting rates for the late 1960s and the early 1980s, and from the alarming deterioration in the UK balance of trade on manufacturing.

It is widely argued that the extent of short-termism differs considerably among countries, and is particularly prevalent in Britain and the United States, with damaging effects on the technological progress and long-term economic prospects of those countries (Pavitt and Patel, 1988). Equally, however, there are clearly pro-nounced differences in "technological progres-siveness" between industries in Britain and the United States, which may well be linked to dif-ferences in short-term pressures (Patel and Pavitt, 1987a, 1987b, 1988).

Several financial, managerial, organizational, and behavioral sources of short-termism have been suggested and in examining these perhaps it is useful to distinguish between external and internal sources of short-term pressures (Demirag, 1996).

DETERMINANTS OF EXTERNAL PRESSURES

The cost of capital   The opportunity cost of cap-ital is determined by the availability, acceptabil-ity, cost, and period of external funds and also by the extent to which external funds are required. The higher the (opportunity) cost of capital, the more pressures will be put on firms for short-termist behavior.

The quality of information available to shareholders (and lenders) and the pressures upon them   Given perfect information, and a willingness to take account of it, shareholder pressure would be for economic rationality, which is the maximization of the present value of the firm's profits to eternity. To the extent that shareholders lack information relevant to the medium-term and long-term outlook, such as on technological progress "in the pipeline," they will tend to respond excessively to current profit, cash flow, and dividend figures, and similar data easily available.

The sensitivity of the firm to the views of shareholders and lenders   Shareholders' views of the firm's performance and prospects are reflected by the share price. Management will be sensitive to the share price to the extent that it fears a hostile takeover and/or it wishes to issue new equity in order to raise funds for new investments or to pay for a possible takeover. Under a hostile takeover threat it will be more sensitive to S-TP, if it expects possible "predators" to be better informed than the market.

The accounting standards for intangible assets   To the extent that it is possible to capitalize "intangible" assets in published accounts, the firm will be able to reduce the impact of research and development spending on current declared profits. (But note that this will only be relevant if very strong and adverse assumptions are made about market efficiency. Firms can always publish R&D expenditures and leave the more competent readers of their accounts to make their own allowances.)

The "tangibility" of desired investment   To the extent that the firm's desired investment (i.e., any deterioration in current cash flow intended to lead to an improvement in future cash flow) is in assets which can be capitalized, such as "hardware" (plant and machinery), there is again no need for current profits to be reduced.

It must be noted, however, that the capitalization of expenditures is not a long-term solution. First, the capital base is immediately increased, which tends to reduce the measured return on

capital next year. Second, increased depreciation will reduce profits.

The predictability of the return on assets   If at some point in the future it becomes clear that the money spent has been wasted, it will be necessary, or at least proper, to write it off at once. Thus, if R&D on such a project has been capitalized, as with the Rolls Royce RB211, profits over a period will have been maintained, only to lurch suddenly downwards. This will make the firm more vulnerable to a takeover bid than if the annual expenditure on R&D had been written off contemporaneously.

DETERMINANTS OF INTERNAL PRESSURES

The level of technology of the firm and industry   The importance of intangible investment will be greater, and the predictability of return (on all investment) lower, in a high technology industry; that is, one in which technology is sophisticated and quickly changing. This will tend to increase short-term pressures. The quality of information available to shareholders and lenders will also tend to be lower, relative to what is required for an accurate assessment of the firm's prospects. (On the other hand, any shareholders in, or lenders to, a high technology industry, may recognize that the prospects of firms in it depend heavily on their technological performance and that they should not invest in it unless they are willing and able to assess this.)

MANAGEMENT PERCEPTIONS OF EXTERNAL FINANCIAL MARKETS

It is conceivable that managers may perceive short-term pressures from capital markets even where they do not exist. Where this is the case these perceptions will contribute to short-term behavior in their organizations. However, if company managers perceive short-termism and act accordingly, but the market is interested in long-term prospects, in a negative feedback system, share prices will fall until managers learn that their perceptions were wrong.

Nevertheless, this argument has certain limitations. Changes in share price are not unambiguous: prices reflect many issues and management's commitment to long-term perspectives is just one of the many factors which influence share prices. Investors may well have long-term financial objectives, but these object-ives can only be realized to the extent that they can obtain the information relevant to the long-term prospects of firms from the managers themselves (Pike, Meerjanssen, and Chadwick, 1993). But if managers think investors are short-termist, then it is unlikely that they will disclose this information to the investors: thus manage-ment's view of the markets will be self-fulfilling (Demirag, 1996).

MANAGEMENT REMUNERATION

If top management's main stakes in the firm are salaries (and they expect to retire before long), profit related bonuses, and stock options which they will soon be able to exercise, then personal self-interest may be little affected by the long-term performance of the firm. This distortion of goals may well induce a distortion of percep-tions: managers may not wish to know that their actions are not for the best in the longer term. On the other hand, managers may well be responsible for deciding on their own system of remuneration, and we may then treat their cul-ture as the prime mover (it may of course have been overt or tacit shareholder pressure which determined the remuneration system). Until re-cently, the pay of top managers in Britain was much less tied to firms' financial results or share price than in the United States (Vancil, 1979; Cosh and Hughes, 1987). However, the trend has been to copy the USA in this respect.

ORGANIZATIONAL STRUCTURE AND MANAGEMENT CONTROL STYLE

In large and diversified firms, how far middle managers share top management's goals and ob-jectives for the firm will depend, again, on cul-ture and structure. In multidivisional firms, financial control seems to be the dominant style of control. Goold and Campbell (1987) describe financially controlled firms where the headquar-ters is slim, supported only by a strong finance function, but prime profit responsibility is pushed right down to the lowest level.

GOAL CONGRUENCE

It is important to note that the "financial control style" does not only generate or transmit short-term pressures, that is pressures which fore-shorten the time horizons of decision takers. It also generates pressures which narrow the spatial field of vision of decision takers. That is, those managing a given profit center tend to concern themselves with whatever will improve their results: cooperation with other parts of the firm will be given a low priority. Any form of techno-logical progress which requires, or is facilitated by, such cooperation will therefore be inhibited.

In summary, short-termism is probably the single most important concept in the manage-ment of technology and in other investment decisions. In practice it is often not easy to iden-tify its impact on investment decisions, as there is more than one source which gives rise to short-term pressures. The possible sources of short-termism include financial, managerial, organizational, and behavioral factors, which often interact. How these pressures may result in short-termism in some companies and indus-tries and how they may be resisted in other cases will continue to be debated. More case-study based research is needed to better understand the sources of short-term pressures and their impact on the management of technology and in other investment decisions.

Bibliography

Cosh, A. D., and Hughes, A. (1987). The anatomy of corporate control: Directors, shareholders and execu-tive remuneration in giant US and UK corporations. *Cambridge Journal of Economics*, 11, 401–22.

Demirag, I. S. (1995). Short-term performance pressures: Is there a consensus view? *European Journal of Finance*, 1, 41–56.

Demirag, I. S. (1996). The impact of managers' short-term perceptions on technology management and R&D in UK companies. *Technology Analysis and Strategic Management*, 8, 21–32.

Demirag, I. S. (1998). *Corporate Governance, Accountabil-ity and Pressures to Perform: An International Study*. Stamford, CT: JAI Press; reprinted 2001, Elsevier Science.

Goold, M., and Campbell, A. (1987). Managing diversity: Strategy and control in diversified British companies. *Long Range Planning*, 20, 42–52.

Muellbauer, J. (1986). The assessment: Productivity and competitiveness in British manufacturing. *Oxford Review of Economic Policy*, 2, 1–25.

Patel, P., and Pavitt, K. (1987a). The elements of British technological competitiveness. *National Institute Eco-nomic Review*, 122, 72–83.

Patel, P., and Pavitt, K. (1987b). Is Western Europe losing the technological race? *Research Policy*, 16, 59–85.

Patel, P., and Pavitt, K. (1988). Technological activities in FR Germany and the UK: Differences and determinants. Working paper, SPRU.

Pavitt, K., and Patel, P. (1988). The international distribution and determinants of technological activities. *Oxford Review of Economic Policy*, 4, 35–55.

Pike, R., Meerjanssen, J., and Chadwick, L. (1993). The appraisal of ordinary shares by investment analysts in the UK and Germany. *Accounting and Business Research*, 23, 489–99.

Vancil, R. F. (1979). *Decentralization: Managerial Ambiguity by Design*. Homeward, IL: Dow Jones-Irwin.

sovereign risk

Philip Chang

Strictly speaking, sovereign risk arises when a sovereign government fails to honor its foreign debt obligations. Sovereign risk is unique because, unlike a private loan where there are well established legal proceedings to handle default and bankruptcy, there is no international court with the jurisdiction to deal with the defaults of sovereign governments.

However, when a government cannot or will not service its foreign debt for financial reasons (e.g., it does not possess sufficient foreign exchange reserves), it will in all likelihood forbid its private sector borrowers to remit foreign exchange to their international lenders as well. Therefore, both sectors will fail to honor the debt, even if the private borrower is creditworthy in terms of its current assets in domestic currency. In practice, therefore, sovereign risk has a broader meaning and is not limited to a sovereign loan. It is the risk that the actions of a government may affect the ability of that government, or government affiliated corporations, or private borrowers residing in the country, to honor foreign debt obligations.

It is for this reason that the terms "sovereign risk" and "country risk" are often used interchangeably. It is this broader definition of sovereign risk which is implied in the following discussion.

Before World War II, most foreign debts were in the form of bonds held by numerous bondholders all over the world. When a country encountered difficulties in servicing foreign debts, a common practice was repudiation (i.e., a simple cancelation of all its debt obligations).

After World War II, most of the international loans are from a smaller number of banks, and the most common form of sovereign risk is rescheduling (i.e., announcing a delay in payment and renegotiating the terms of the loan) (Saunders, 1994). The most notable event that taught the international banking community an unforgettable lesson about the importance of sovereign risk is the debt moratorium declared by the Mexican government in 1982, and which triggered the subsequent international debt crisis.

Analysis of Sovereign Risk

When making an international loan, a lender must assess two types of risk. The first is the creditworthiness of the borrower itself. This analysis is the same as a credit analysis of any domestic borrower. The second risk to assess is the sovereign risk of the country. In principle, a lender should not extend credit to a foreign borrower if the sovereign risk is unacceptable, notwithstanding that the borrower may have good credit quality. This second type of risk, or sovereign risk, should be the predominant consideration in international lending decisions.

The analysis of sovereign risk involves both economic and political analysis. Economic analysis should be primarily concerned with the capability of an economy to generate foreign exchange reserves. The foreign exchange reserves are the common pool of resources that both the private sector and the government rely upon when servicing foreign debt. These reserves are the cumulative international balance of payments of a country which, in turn, depends upon its current account balance, or its foreign trade performance measured by exports minus imports. Macroeconomic theory reveals that a trade deficit (surplus) is the result of aggregate demand (aggregate consumption plus investments plus government spending), being greater (smaller) than aggregate production of a country. Therefore, all factors that influence the aggregate demand and aggregate production of an economy should be analyzed in order to understand the economics of sovereign risk.

In terms of political analysis, the focus is on the political decision-making process through which debt repudiation and rescheduling decisions are made. Also of importance is the capability of the political system to support the economic system and to maintain the credit quality of the country. By undertaking a dual analysis of both the economic and political systems of a country, an analyst can come to a comprehensive understanding of the sovereign risk.

Comparable international financial data can be found in the publications of supranational organizations such as the World Bank and the International Monetary Fund. It might also be helpful for analysts to take advantage of the cross-country credit ranking provided by such credit rating agencies as Moody's and Standard and Poor's, and financial publishers such as Euromoney and Institutional Investor.

FORECASTING SOVEREIGN RISK

In addition to a complete macroeconomic analysis, analysts can also study a number of financial ratios indicative of the financial soundness of a country. Examples of these ratios and their relationship with sovereign risk exposure include debt ratio (foreign currency debt/GDP; foreign currency debt/exports), positive; import ratio (imports/foreign exchange reserves), positive; trade surplus ratio (trade surplus/GDP), negative; budget balance ratio (government budget deficit/GDP), positive; investment ratio (aggregate investment/GDP), negative; and inflation rate, positive. Based on selected ratios and the history of sovereign risk events across countries, a discriminant analysis model can be built to predict sovereign risks.

An alternative way to forecast sovereign risk is to utilize information in the secondary market for developing country debt, a market developed by major banks in the mid-1980s. The prices of these loans reflect the market's collective assessment about the sovereign risk of the indebted countries. Regression analysis can be performed to determine what variables (similar to those discussed above) are significantly associated with the prices of these loans and to estimate the extent of the association. Based on the projected values of the variables, this model can then be used to predict loan prices. Changes in loan prices are indicative of possible changes of sovereign risk (Boehmer and Megginson, 1990).

POLITICAL RISK

Political risk arises when actions of a government or other groups in the political process adversely interfere with the operation of business. These actions may include expropriation, confiscation, foreign exchange control, kidnapping, civil unrest, *coups d'état*, and war. While both economics and politics should be considered in the analysis of sovereign as well as political risks, the emphasis of sovereign risk is on economics and the focus of political risk is on the political process. Since sovereign risk events are the result of governmental actions, it can be viewed as part of political risk. Organizations such as the Economist Intelligence Unit and Business International conduct extensive political risk analysis. Their publications are useful resources for international business executives.

Bibliography

Boehmer, E., and Megginson, W. L. (1990). Determinants of secondary market prices for developing country syndicated loans. *Journal of Finance*, **45**, 1517–40.

Saunders, A. (1986). *The International Debt Problem: Studies in Banking and Finance*. Amsterdam: North-Holland.

Saunders, A. (1994). Sovereign risk. In *Financial Institutions Management: A Modern Perspective*. Boston, MA: Irwin, 261–92.

Shapiro, H. D. (1994). Country credit: Accentuate the positive. *Institutional Investor*, **94**, 93–9.

Van Duyn, A. (1994). Country risk: Where in the world is Japan? *Euromoney*, 177–80.

speculation

David Brookfield

Speculation is often seen in pejorative terms, although it is widely recognized in trading and academic circles as providing a useful economic function. In the commodity markets, for example, which are often characterized by output uncertainty and (hence) price volatility, an optimal market equilibrium is achieved when participants can exchange risk through the process of speculation (Courchane and Nickerson, 1986). In this sense, speculators are often seen as the counter-parties to hedge traders who wish to offload an exposure to risk. Marshall's view was that speculation was only marginally distinguishable from gambling. However, in a more refined distinction, Floersch (Vice Chairman, Chicago Board Options Exchange, in Strong,

1994) sees gamblers as creating risk where none exists, and speculators as accepting an existing risk. In this sense, hedgers offer a market for risk which speculators accept at a price. The speculators' unique skill is in their ability to judge whether the risk is worth taking at a particular price and, in so doing, they will try to ascertain and learn from information that others do not have (Froot, Scharftstein, and Stein, 1992).

Speculation is not restricted to financial markets. Agricultural products, gold, and other precious metals are the subject of speculative trading. In this sphere, gold is often seen as fundamentally a speculative venture since traders mostly do not take delivery but can trade in gold certificates, gold futures, and futures options. However, the important risk hedging function is still evident, since gold is often a safe refuge in times of political or economic uncertainty.

Many of the controversies surrounding speculation relate to the association of speculators with destabilized markets and huge financial losses, particularly in recent times with respect to currency markets and also in the use of derivative securities. While financial losses can be a natural consequence of taking a position in a security, the question of a destabilized market is a subject of debate. Traditionally, speculation is seen as an activity that assists in moving prices to equilibrium (Friedman, 1953) and, as such, cannot be the cause of market destabilization. Critics of speculation would argue that the use of derivative securities, for which there might be a huge open interest relative to the supply of the deliverable commodity, is indicative of how such assets might be destabilizing by giving rise to price runs unrelated to the scarcity of the underlying commodity. Moreover, the ease at which a substantial position can be created through the use of leverage can give rise to a resulting price dynamic against which the market, itself, cannot fight. While the desired role of speculation is not disputed, the pertinent question – which will help determine its impact – is whether speculation results from a rational/fundamentals-based realignment or is a response to noise trading whereby apparently random events can give rise to destabilizing trading responses. The often observed coexistence of speculation and instability has led to considerable theoretical

work in an attempt to identify and quantify possible linkages between the two and a number of different markets have been investigated.

Speculative activity in foreign exchange is often a two-edged sword. On the one hand, speculation within the context of an underlying stable economic policy can create a framework within which long-term fundamentals prevail as the principal driving forces in currency movements. Speculators then look to longer-term horizons and this has been seen as a mechanism by which currency volatility can be reduced. On the other hand, Krugman and Miller (1992) argue that stop–loss orders made by speculators can undermine the stability of a currency if a currency target zone, such as the ERM, is not seen as effective. Badly misjudged target zones can create speculative runs on the expectation that a currency will be forced to leave a target zone (as in the departure of sterling from the ERM in 1992).

In principle, trading in derivatives markets (on currencies, bonds, stocks, and stock indices) cannot be destabilizing because – if the pricing of these securities is correct – options and futures of all types only serve to make easier the taking of positions which enable the exchange of risk. In general, derivative assets can only present a picture of a situation that already exists, but in an easier-to-trade manner. In particular, futures trading, for example, is largely perceived to perform the role of price discovery and thereby enable the process of risk transfer. However, speculators in futures are often criticized for not trading on the basis of fundamentals (Maddala and Yoo, 1991), thereby creating excessive volatility and raising the risk premiums faced by hedgers when it is their economic role to reduce premiums, thereby allowing the easier transacting of risk. The issue is an empirical one. In measuring average levels of speculation with average volatility, Edwards and Ma (1992) report no correlation, whereas some degree of association should be present for there to be a relationship.

On a global scale, the crash of 1987 revealed a situation in which an extremely destabilized market was associated with hedging/speculation and derivatives trading. Program trading and portfolio insurance have been accused of destabilizing the market and these subjects are covered elsewhere.

Bibliography

Courchane, M., and Nickerson, D. (1986). Optimal buffer stock and futures market policies for commodity price stabilization. Duke Working Paper in Economics, No. 43,12.

Edwards, F. R., and Ma, C. (1992). *Futures and Options*. New York: McGraw-Hill.

Friedman, M. (1953). *Essays in Positive Economics*. Chicago: University of Chicago Press.

Froot, K. A., Scharftstein, D. S., and Stein, J. C. (1992). Herd on the street: Informational inefficiencies in a market with short-term speculation. *Journal of Finance*, 47, 1461–84.

Krugman, P. R., and Miller, M. (1992). Why have a target zone? *Carnegie Rochester Conference Series on Public Policy*, 38, 279–314.

Maddala, G. S., and Yoo, J. (1991). Risk premia and price volatility in futures markets. *Journal of Futures Markets*, 11, 165–78.

Strong, R. A. (1994). *Speculative Markets*. New York: Harper Collins.

stability of returns

David M. Power

Over the last decades a large number of researchers have investigated the temporal stability of various dimensions of equity returns. The extensive academic interest in this area is hardly surprising given the importance of stability (or at least predictability) in returns to professional investors attempting to construct optimal portfolios on the basis of historic information; if returns are not stable, or if the instability is unpredictable, then such attempts are futile. Early investigations in this area concentrated on developed stock markets such as the UK and the USA, while more recent studies have typically focused on both emerging and developed stock markets. In addition, the majority of the research has examined the stability of relationships between the returns earned by equity indices of different national markets by analyzing correlation or covariance matrices rather than focusing on the stability of other aspects of the return distribution for individual equities. However, a growing number of investigations have begun to examine whether the mean return and the variance of returns are also stable over time.

The time periods covered, the countries examined, the statistical tests employed, and the interpretation of the results have all varied across the different studies undertaken in the substantive literature. For example, Makridakis and Wheelwright (1974) used principal component analysis to investigate the intertemporal stability of the correlation matrix of daily returns (in US dollars) of 14 developed stock markets over the period 1968–70. They found that the correlation coefficients were both unstable and unpredictable. Their early finding was confirmed in two later investigations: a study by Hilliard (1979) that analyzed daily returns for ten developed stock market indices over the period July 1973 to April 1974 (a period which included the OPEC oil embargo) using spectral analysis which suggested that no stable relationship existed between intercontinental returns; and a study by Maldonado and Saunders (1981) which reported that correlations of monthly index returns for five countries followed a random walk. However, Phillipatos, Christofi, and Christofi (1983) employed principal component analysis and found that the correlation matrix for returns of 14 developed stock markets was stable over two ten-year periods (1959–68 and 1969–78), but not over shorter horizons. This finding of stability over long horizons contradicted the earlier study of Panton, Lessig, and Joy (1976). They analyzed their data using cluster analysis – a technique which aggregates indices together into groups, or clusters, according to their degree of similarity – and found considerable stability in the relationship between the returns of their sample for one year and three year periods, but weaker stability in the correlations of returns for five year periods.

A special virtue of more recent investigations has been the multiplicity of advanced statistical techniques employed and the greater range of markets investigated. For example, Cheung and Ho (1991) use five different tests to examine the intertemporal stability of the relationships between the weekly domestic-currency returns of seven emerging stock markets and four developed stock markets in the Asian-Pacific region over the period 1977–88. In general, their findings suggested that relationships between returns were unstable, although evidence of instability decreased for longer-horizon returns according to their principal component analysis. Sinclair, Power, and Lonie (1996) used four tests to investigate the intertemporal stability of returns for a larger, more diverse group of emerging markets drawn from Europe, Latin America, and Africa, as well as the Asian-Pacific region, over a longer time period, 1977–92. Although they report that these relationships are unstable, they found that this instability may be sufficiently predictable to permit a portfolio strategy based on historic variance/covariance matrices to outperform the UK market by a substantial margin in the following period.

Sinclair et al. (1997) investigated the intertemporal stability of the mean and the variance of quarterly returns as well as the correlations among returns for a sample of 16 Western European markets over the period 1989–94. They found a great deal of variability in the mean returns and in the volatility of returns over the time period covered by their analysis and suggest that the international fund manager not blessed with perfect foresight would have had great difficulty in achieving the theoretical gains available from international diversification on an *ex ante* basis. This finding – that the volatility of returns varies over time – is not new. Ever since the pioneering work of Engle (1982), a class of models termed autoregressive conditionally heteroscedastic (ARCH) has been developed which allows the variance of the series analyzed to alter through time. The results from fitting these models to return data for both developed and emerging stock markets suggest that volatility does vary over time, although not in a totally random fashion. For example, Fraser and Power (1995) report that in eight of the nine emerging markets analyzed there was a tendency for volatility shocks to persist over several months. They attribute this time-varying volatility to the non-linear flow of information to the stock market. Lamoureaux and Lastrapes (1990) provide empirical evidence to support this contention that a clustering in the share volatility data is associated with "the process generating information flow to the market." Specifically, for their sample of the 20 most actively traded shares in the S&P 500 index, the proportion with significant ARCH effects declined from 75 percent to 20 percent when an information variable was included in the analysis.

The question of whether returns are stable or not has moved on from the narrow focus on the relationships between equity returns for developed markets to consider different dimensions of returns for shares traded across a broader range of markets. The evidence seems to suggest that returns may not be stable, although this instability may not be random.

Bibliography

Cheung, Y. L., and Ho, Y. K. (1991). The intertemporal stability of the relationships between the Asian emerging equity markets and the developed equity markets. *Journal of Business Finance and Accounting*, 18, 235–54.

Engle, R. F. (1982). Autoregressive conditional heteroscedasticity with estimates of the variance of UK inflation. *Econometrica*, 50, 987–1008.

Fraser, P., and Power, D. M. (1995). Conditional heteroscedasticity in the equity returns from emerging markets. *Advances in Pacific Basin Financial Markets*, 2, 331–47.

Hilliard, J. (1979). The relationship between equity indices on world exchanges. *Journal of Finance*, 34, 103–14.

Lamoureaux, C. G., and Lastrapes, W. D. (1990). Heteroscedasticity in stock return data: Volume versus GARCH effects. *Journal of Finance*, 45, 221–30.

Makridakis, S., and Wheelwright, S. (1974). An analysis of the interrelationships among the major world stock exchanges. *Journal of Business Finance and Accounting*, 1, 195–215.

Maldonado, R., and Saunders, A. (1981). International portfolio diversification and the intertemporal stability of international stock market relationships. *Financial Management*, 10, 54–63.

Panton, D., Lessig, P., and Joy, M. (1976). Comovement of international equity markets: A taxonomic approach. *Journal of Financial and Quantitative Analysis*, 11, 415–31.

Phillipatos, G. C., Christofi, A., and Christofi, P. (1983). The intertemporal stability of international stock market relationships: Another view. *Financial Management*, 12, 63–9.

Sinclair, C. D., Power, D. M., and Lonie, A. A. (1996). An investigation of the stability of relationships between returns from emerging stock markets. *Applied Financial Economics*.

Sinclair, C. D., Power, D. M., Lonie A. A., and Helliar, C. V. (1997). An investigation of the stability of returns in Western European markets, 1989–1994. *European Journal of Finance*.

state-contingent bank regulation

S. Nagarajan and C. W. Sealey

It is well known that government sponsored deposit insurance creates incentives for bank shareholders to shift risk to the insurer (moral hazard), and/or may attract only high risk banks to the system (adverse selection). Current legislation in many countries attempts to solve the incentive problems encountered in bank regulation by mandating policies such as risk adjusted deposit insurance premiums, strict capital requirements, and prompt closure policies, etc. Results from recent literature, however, suggest that such regulatory policies are neither necessary nor sufficient, *per se*, to solve the incentive problems: for instance, risk adjusted deposit insurance premiums do not mitigate risk shifting by banks (John, John, and Senbet, 1991). Prompt (or even early) closure of insolvent banks is also unlikely to solve the moral hazard problem and, moreover, even fixed rate deposit insurance, if accompanied by a rational policy of forbearance, can be incentive compatible (Nagarajan and Sealey, 1995). In fact, fairly priced deposit insurance premiums may actually be inconsistent with incentive compatibility in the absence of *ex post* deposit insurance subsidies (Chan, Greenbaum, and Thakor, 1992).

A common theme in the above works is that they all involve some type of *ex post* contracting in order to achieve incentive compatibility. In particular, if the regulator sets up appropriate *ex post* rewards and/or punishments that are triggered by *ex post* outcomes, then bank shareholders are induced to weigh the potential returns from *ex ante* risk shifting against any *ex post* cost associated with such behavior. Under certain conditions, banks choose higher asset quality *ex ante* than would otherwise be the case, although they may not necessarily choose first best.

State-contingent bank regulation, first proposed by Nagarajan and Sealey (1996), extends existing notions of *ex post* pricing to a new concept of bank regulation. Its key distinguishing feature is the design of policy mechanisms that are contingent on the performance of banks, not in absolute terms, but relative to that of the market. State-contingent regulation works as follows. First, a bank's total risk is decomposed into its market (systematic) and idiosyncratic components, and the regulator prices the deposit insurance based on the bank's performance relative to the market. Such a mechanism is more informationally refined than a corresponding mechanism based on absolute performance. The reason is that the regulator can filter out that part of performance that is attributable to factors beyond the bank's control, and thus make a more informed (although still imperfect) evaluation of the bank's choice of unobservable asset quality and/or risk class.

Nagarajan and Sealey (1996) have shown that moral hazard and adverse selection problems in bank regulation can be completely alleviated by a wide range of simple relative-performance mechanisms that involve (1) *ex post* rewards to banks in some states of nature and penalties in others, and (2) a minimum capital requirement. Specifically, banks may be rewarded if a modest performance in a particular period was achieved despite poor market conditions, and penalized if it was helped by good market performance. Two families of optimal regulatory mechanisms, one for moral hazard and another for adverse selection, are derived, which have the following properties distinguishing them from much of the literature on incentive compatible bank regulation:

1 First-best outcomes are achieved under both moral hazard and adverse selection.
2 No deposit insurance subsidy is required to achieve incentive compatibility, even when loan markets are competitive.
3 Since deposit insurance is priced fairly, these mechanisms do not create economy-wide distortions in resource allocation.

There are two issues of concern to the regulator: the informational task of identifying and filtering out systematic risks; and implementing the state-contingent mechanism itself. Regarding the first issue, banks' systematic risk exposures can be estimated using current examination procedures, and hence the mechanisms are not very informationally demanding. In fact, the assessment of systematic or factor risks in regulating banks is also shared by the current Bank for International Settlements' guidelines on risk adjusted capital requirements, which weight various categories of bank loans differently, thus implicitly assigning higher weights to higher systematic risks. Note that this weighting scheme reflects the systematic risks of a loan portfolio, and has nothing to do with unique risks, as the latter get diversified away in any sizeable loan portfolio.

With regard to implementation, the optimal capital requirement might be coordinated with the state-contingent, *ex post* premiums, in order to insure that the bank has enough capital to pay the penalty in the relevant states. Penalty collection is also made easier by the fact that the bank's payoff in penalty states need not be low, and can even be higher than in reward states. Finally, *ex post* refunds of deposit insurance premiums are quite feasible, and have in fact occurred in some countries (e.g., the USA), although they have not been based on relative performance in the past.

Bibliography

Chan, Y., Greenbaum, S. I., and Thakor, A. V. (1992). Is fairly priced deposit insurance possible? *Journal of Finance*, **47**, 227–45.

John, K., John, T. A., and Senbet, L. (1991). Risk-shifting incentives of depository institutions: A new perspective on federal deposit insurance reform. *Journal of Banking and Finance*, **15**, 895–915.

Nagarajan, S. and Sealey, C. W. (1995). Forbearance, deposit insurance pricing, and incentive compatible bank regulation. *Journal of Banking and Finance*, **19**, 1109–30.

Nagarajan, S. and Sealey, C. W. (1996). State-contingent bank regulation. Working paper, McGill University.

stochastic processes

Giovanni Barone-Adesi

A stochastic process is a collection of random variables $X(t)$ indexed by a parameter t, which usually represents discrete or continuous time. If we fix a time t, $X(t)$ is a random variable; if we fix a point in the joint probability space describing the process for all values of t, $X(t)$ is a path of the process through time.

Stochastic processes are said to be stationary if the joint distribution of $X(t_1 + h)$, $X(t_2 + h) \ldots$ does not depend on h. This property states that the law of the process is invariant with respect to time. Stochastic processes are said to be Markovian if their history provides no information about their future evolution beyond the information provided by the knowledge of their current state. The evolution of a stochastic process for $t \to \infty$ may approach a steady point or a stationary distribution or grow without bounds. A mixture of these outcomes is possible. The conditional distribution of $X(t+h)$ given $X(t)$ is known as the transition probability. If transition probabilities do not depend on t and the increments of the process through time are independent of each other, the process is called a random walk.

Important examples of random walk processes in management applications are the Poisson process and the standard Brownian motion. The Poisson process is often used to represent the random independent arrivals of customers to a service center. Its value at time t, given $X(0) = 0$, is described by the Poisson distribution:

$$P\{X(t) = i | X(0) = 0\} = \frac{(\lambda t)^i \exp{(-\lambda t)}}{i!}$$

where $i = 0, 1, 2, \ldots$ The interval before the arrival time of next customer is distributed according to a negative exponential function and it is often used to model equipment malfunction rates.

The Brownian motion process is used to represent the evolution of stock prices and other quantities subject to frequent small shocks. The increments of the Brownian motion over time are described by the equation:

$$dX(t) = \mu dt + \sigma dz(t) \qquad (2)$$

where μ and σ can be functions of $X(t)$ and t and $dz(t)$ represents the random shock to the process, the limit of the product

$$\Delta z(t) = \sqrt{\Delta t}.x \qquad (3)$$

for $\Delta t \to 0$, where x is drawn from a standard normal distribution. The process $z(t)$ is known as a Wiener process. Often, the logarithm of the stock price is assumed to follow a Brownian motion in order to maintain constant returns to scale. The Brownian motion travels an infinite distance in any discrete time interval, but it has zero velocity because it changes its course infinitely many times. Brownian motions with independent increments are unsuitable for many applications to interest rates and bond prices, for which the Ornstein–Uhlenbeck mean reverting model is preferred. The increments of this process are described by the equation

$$dX(t) = K(c - X(t))dt + \sigma dz(t) \qquad (4)$$

where c is a centrality parameter towards which the process is attracted at a speed proportional through a factor K to its current distance from c. The above processes are Markovian, but the Ornstein–Uhlenbeck process is not a random walk because its increments are not independent through time.

The Brownian motion process is continuous, but almost surely not differentiable with respect to time. Increments of functions of Brownian motions, and time $y(t)$, can be related to increments in the underlying Brownian motion, $X(t)$, by Ito's lemma:

$$dy(t) = \frac{\partial y(t)}{\partial X(t)} dX(t) + \frac{\partial y(t)}{\partial t} dt$$
$$+ \frac{1}{2} \frac{\partial^2 y(t)}{\partial X(t)^2} \sigma^2 dt \qquad (5)$$

Ito's lemma takes the place of the chain rule of ordinary calculus in the study of stochastic processes. Ito's stochastic integrals represent functions $f(X(t),t)$ in terms of the underlying Wiener processes.

Functions $F_n(X_1, X_2 \ldots X_n)$ of a stochastic process $(X_1, X_2 \ldots X_n)$ are said to be martingales if the expected value of F_{n+1} equals F_n, supermartingales if the value of the function at time $n + 1$ is expected to be lower than its value at time n, submartingales if it is expected to be greater. The concept of martingale reflects the notion of fair game and it has many useful applications in financial markets. Future security prices discounted at the risk free rate follow a martingale under the assumption of investors being indifferent to risk. More general functions of stochastic processes may be reduced to martingales by changing the probability measures associated with the random variables $X(t)$. This result is known as Girsanov's theorem and it is widely used in the valuation of derivative securities. It allows for the valuation of securities to be independent of their expected rate of return, which can be taken to be the risk free rate for ease of computation.

A stopping time τ is a rule to stop sampling a stochastic process. If a reward function is associated with the outcomes of the stochastic process up to time τ, the optimal stopping time, τ^*, maximizes the expected value of the reward function. More general interventions on stochastic processes are objects of stochastic control theory, where a variable influencing the process is modulated in order to maximize a given function of the process.

stock market indices

Christian Helmenstein and Christian Haefke

Stock market indices measure the value of a portfolio of stocks relative to the value of a base portfolio as a weighted average of stock prices. Stock market indices as aggregate measures are an instrument to meet the information requirements of investors by characterizing the development of global markets and specific market segments (descriptive function). In their function as a basis of derivative instruments, stock market indices facilitate the application of certain portfolio strategies such as hedging and arbitrage (operative function).

In order to perform these functions, a stock market index should fulfill statistical as well as economic requirements. The statistical requirements for indices in general were summarized by Fisher (1922), Eichhorn (1976), and Diewert (1986). Crucial for stock market indices are (1) invariance to changes in scale; (2) symmetric treatment of components; (3) time reversal, that is, the index between any two dates will not be changed if the base period of the index is changed from one date to another; and (4) indifference to the incorporation of new stocks, that is, *ceteris paribus*, the inclusion or removal of a stock will not change the index compared to its previous value. As a representative stock market index only contains a selection of stocks, index construction involves a sampling problem.

The commonly used stock indices belong to one of the following three categories: averages, capitalization weighted indices, and performance indices. The most prominent representative of the class of averages is the Dow Jones Industrial Average (DJIA). The DJIA is a price weighted average of 30 blue chip stocks traded at the New York Stock Exchange (NYSE). The DJIA, comprising 12 stocks, first appeared in 1896 with a value of 40.94. In its present form with 30 common stocks the DJIA was first published in 1928. For the purpose of futures trading, the Chicago Board of Trade formed the Major Market Index, which comprises 20 shares of which 16 are also included in the DJIA. Since 1975 the Nikkei 225 Stock Average has been calculated on the basis of stocks traded in the first section of the Tokyo Stock Exchange. In the case of all these indices, reductions of stock prices due to stock splits, as opposed to dividend payments, are accounted for in order to leave the average unaffected. The main disadvantage associated with the calculation method of these averages is the fact that a given percentage price change of a high priced stock induces a larger change of the average than an identical percentage change of a low priced stock.

The majority of stock indices belong to the category of capitalization weighted indices using the Laspeyres, Paasche, or Fisher formula. The most prominent indices are the Standard and Poor's 500 (NYSE/AMEX/OTC market), the TOPIX (Tokyo Stock Exchange, first section), the FT-SE 100 (London Stock Exchange), the CAC 40 (Paris Stock Exchange), the SMI (24 Swiss stocks), and the FAZ-Index (100 German stocks). Due to its breadth, the S&P 500 is widely used by portfolio managers as a benchmark for the performance of their portfolios (Berlin, 1990). Empirical studies show that the average pre-tax return of the S&P 500 portfolio between 1925 and 1986 reached 12.1 percent per annum, while a portfolio of government bonds yielded 4.7 percent per annum on average. Since 1982 the S&P 500 has served as the basis for cash-settled stock index futures contracts. Some of the above indices contain an additional adjustment factor to allow for the case when the outstanding capital significantly exceeds the free floating capital.

The increasing use of stock market indices as a basis for derivative products called for provisions to allow a balanced reflection of the descriptive and the operative function. In response to this requirement the DAX (30 shares listed at the Frankfurt Stock Exchange), introduced in 1988, was constructed as performance index (Janssen and Rudolph, 1992). The Swiss Performance Index and the FAZ Performance Index followed afterwards. These indices measure the total return of a portfolio under the following assumption: dividend payments and the hypothetical money value of share warrants from rights offers are immediately reinvested in the respective stock to obtain the change of the overall value of a particular portfolio compared to the value at a given base period.

For specific purposes, a variety of other indices has been developed. In order to provide a benchmark needed for international asset allocation, Morgan Stanley Capital International developed the MSCI World Index, which is based on 1,609 securities listed on the stock exchanges of 22 countries. In contrast to all indices mentioned above, the value line arithmetic index assigns the same weight to each stock. It represents approximately 95 percent of the market values of all US securities. On the basis of portfolios which comprise stocks from a specific industry, a large variety of branch indices such as the Dow Jones Transportation Average, the AMEX Oil Index, or the NYSE Utility Index have been constructed. In order to study the performance of initial public offerings, for each major European stock exchange the Institute for Advanced Studies established an initial public offerings index (IPOX), which is isomorphic to the respective stock market index (Haefke and Helmenstein, 1995). When IPOX futures become available, investors will have an instrument at hand to fully participate in promising initial public offerings without being rationed. Due to the increasing interest in derivatives, Trinkaus and Burkhardt designed the TUBOS as real-time index to measure the performance of German warrants vis-à-vis the DAX.

Bibliography

Berlin, H. M. (1990). *The Handbook of Financial Market Indexes, Averages, and Indicators.* Homewood, IL: Dow Jones-Irwin.

Diewert, W. E. (1986). Microeconomic approaches to the theory of international comparisons. Technical working paper No. 53. Cambridge, MA: NBER.

Eichhorn, W. (1976). Fisher's tests revisited. *Econometrica*, **44**, 247–56.

Fisher, I. (1922). The making of index numbers: A study of their varieties, tests, and reliability. Publications of the Pollak Foundation for Economic Research, No. 1. New York: Houghton-Mifflin.

Haefke, C., and Helmenstein, C. (1995). Neural networks in the capital markets: An application to index forecasting. In M. Gilli (ed.), *Computational Methods in Economics and Finance*. Dordrecht: Kluwer Academic Publishers.

Janssen, B., and Rudolph, B. (1992). *Der Deutsche Aktienindex DAGS*. Frankfurt: Knapp.

syndicated euroloans

Arie L. Melnik and Steven E. Plaut

Syndicated euroloans consist primarily of medium-term, unsecured, and secured credits provided by syndicates of international banks. Maturities range from one to twelve years, with average maturity of about five years. Technically, euroloans are usually renewable six month loans, rolled over or extended through the designated maturity. The interest rate floats, usually with relation to LIBOR. As such, euroloans in many ways resemble medium-term note issuance facilities.

The euroloans are granted by syndicates of banks formed for that purpose on a loan-by-loan basis. The managing bank, or a few banks jointly, assemble the syndicate and draw up loan agreements, receiving management fees. These are then shared with lead banks in the form of participation fees. The lead banks provide funding for the loan according to a formula agreed upon in the syndicate agreement.

There are several forms of syndicated euro-lending:

1 *Traditional syndicated bank loans:* this type usually has a floating interest rate and fixed maturity, drawn once and repaid according to an agreed schedule. Normally one, two, or even three banks negotiate the loan, and they, in turn, draw other banks into the syndicate. A single bank acting as agent

(one of the lead banks) administers the loan after execution, gathering the funds from the lenders for the borrower to withdraw during a fixed time (the commitment period), distributing repayments from the borrower to the lenders, and representing the lenders if any problems arise with the borrower.

2 *Revolving credit:* has the same attributes as a syndicated bank loan but allows the borrower repeatedly to draw the loan, or a portion thereof, and to repay what it has drawn at its discretion or according to a set formula during the life of the loan. This resembles revolving credit arrangements such as overdraft accounts or credit lines in the domestic market.

3 *Standby facility:* borrowers are not restricted to a commitment period during which they must draw down the funds. They may, instead, pay a contingency fee until they choose to draw the loan, at which time the contractual interest rate begins to run.

The lead manager that serves as the agent bank is usually responsible for negotiating the conditions of the loan with the borrower, circulating an information memorandum, marketing the loan to other banks, and preparing the loan documentation. As noted by Melnik and Plaut (1991), if the loan is particularly large or complicated, a number of managers may share these duties. Potential lenders who have indicated an interest in the loan get the information memorandum, which covers the following main points: (1) outlines of the terms of the loan agreement (maturity, repayment fees, and interest rates, etc); (2) summary of the agreements signed or to be signed; (3) details of the project or purpose of the loans; (4) financial analysis of the proposal/project; and (5) where relevant, a consultant's report.

The lead manager offers prospective syndicate members a chance to participate in the loan. The choice depends on several factors (Berlin and Loeys, 1986; Melnik and Plaut, 1995). The size of the loan is important; more banks will be invited to join in a very large loan. The riskiness of the loan is also a factor that is positively correlated with the number of participants. The borrower may have preferences regarding inclusion (or exclusion) of certain banks. This could be based on its relationship with a bank or group of banks or because it operates in (or hopes to expand into) a certain part of the world.

Of those banks approached, there will inevitably be some that are unable or unwilling to join in for a number of reasons. They may already have reached their lending ceiling for the borrower's country. There may be legal restrictions on lending to the borrower's country or to companies engaged in certain types of businesses. Finally, they may find the terms of the loan insufficiently attractive or the underlying project too risky to justify the advance.

The interest rate on euroloans is expressed directly as a spread over the banks' marginal cost of funds, usually LIBOR. The participating banks normally raise funds on the short-term eurocurrency markets for successive three, six, or twelve month periods throughout the life of the loan. A formula in the loan agreement fixes these periods, known as the loan rollover dates. These are the same as repricing dates. It is therefore the bank's funding of the loan, rather than the loan itself, that is rolled over. The banks merely pass on the prevailing interest rate at each rollover period, adding to it an agreed percentage margin, or spread, that represents their profit, based on their assessment of risks and their overhead costs.

Management fees are paid to the lead managers for negotiating the loan agreement and marketing the loan. They are generally expressed as a percentage of the total amount of the loan and negotiated with the borrower, bearing in mind various factors, such as size and complexity of the loan, market competition, the borrower's relationship with the manager, etc. These fees are paid at the time the loan agreement is signed. The fees usually contain three components: (1) agent's fees to cover administrative expenses; (2) underwriting fees paid to the banks underwriting the loan; and (3) participation fees to the participant banks in proportion to the amount of their participation.

The level of spreads and the size of fees are determined by the creditworthiness of the borrower, the size and terms of the loan, the state of the market, and the degree of competition for the loan. Just as in the domestic market, the cost of loans varies across borrowers in the euromarkets, but there are even more factors to consider. Besides the questions regarding the borrowers and their business there are considerations of politics, economics, and geography.

Bibliography

Berlin, M., and Loeys, J. (1986). Bond covenants and delegated monitoring. *Journal of Finance*, **43**, 397–412.

Melnik, A., and Plaut, S. E. (1991). *The Short-Term Eurocredit Market*. Salomon Center Monograph Series. New York: New York University Press.

Melnik, A., and Plaut, S. E. (1995). Industrial structure in the eurocredit underwriting market. Presented at the European Financial Management Association, London.

tactical asset allocation

Ed Vos

Sharpe (1992) defines asset allocation as "the allocation of an investor's portfolio across a number of 'major' asset classes." Asset allocation generally refers to the division of investment capital among the various available investment categories such as stocks, bonds, money market instruments, derivative funds, real estate, and other asset classes. Usually, both domestic and international markets are considered in the allocation process.

Performance measurement of mutual fund managers by researchers such as Sharpe (1966) and Jensen (1968) compared the returns of a fund to those of an index after adjusting for systematic risk as measured by beta. These studies found that mutual funds underperformed risk adjusted index portfolios. In the 1980s several studies found that systematic risk adjusted mutual fund performance was not significantly different from the index. Grinblatt and Titman (1989) found that the results of such studies was highly dependent upon the index used for benchmarking mutual fund performance. They showed that by changing benchmarks, it is possible to show that some classes of mutual funds provided superior performance.

Debates on the appropriateness of the index used for benchmarking, on the suitability of the capital asset pricing model derived beta as a risk measurement, and on the dual hypothesis problem between the efficient market hypothesis and any asset pricing model, all contributed to a need for a more acceptable way to judge the performance of mutual fund managers.

Brinson, Hood, and Beebower (1986) took a different approach by measuring the contribution that "active" management had over a passive benchmark. They defined the investment process in four steps. First, decide on which asset classes to include and which to exclude from the portfolio. Second, decide on the normal or long-term policy weights for each of the asset classes allowed in the portfolio. Third, alter the investment mix weights away from the policy weights in an attempt to capture excess returns from short-term fluctuations in asset prices. Fourth, select individual securities within an asset class to achieve superior returns relative to that asset class. The first two steps have become known as strategic asset allocation (SAA), while the third step is known as tactical asset allocation (TAA).

By breaking returns down into the active (tactical) and passive (strategic) portions, it becomes possible to make judgments on performance without arguments on indices, betas, and dual hypothesis problems. Subsequently, TAA continues to be widely used by fund managers.

It is important to distinguish between TAA and more active forms of investment such as dynamic asset allocation or market timing. Unlike the latter two, TAA is a disciplined approach to shifting away from SAA benchmarks and sticking to those weightings. Dynamic asset allocation and market timing, on the other hand, are attempts to pick market peaks and troughs. Because SAA and TAA are more disciplined approaches, they are seen as contrarian by nature. This is because in order to rebalance a portfolio back to benchmarks, it is necessary to sell assets in the asset class which has performed well in order to buy assets in the class which has performed badly.

The value of TAA, however, seems minimal when compared to SAA. Many studies (Brinson, Hood, and Beebower, 1986; Droms, 1989; Brinson, Singer, and Beebower, 1991) show that

SAA contributes more than 80 percent of the returns and most often between 92 percent and 98.6 percent of the returns. TAA, therefore, is an attempt to add additional returns to the SAA benchmark. Some studies claim that TAA actually reduces returns. In order to obtain positive TAA performance, fund managers are increasingly turning to sophisticated computer models to help predict future returns. There are claims that, in good years, some TAA computer programs have delivered up to 15 percent above the SAA benchmark. Others claim that since TAA adds so little to the returns, serious questions must be asked about the costs of TAA in terms of increased (or decreased) risk and increased (or decreased) costs of management.

Bibliography

Brinson, G. P., Hood, R., and Beebower, G. L. (1986). Determinants of portfolio performance. *Financial Analysts Journal*, **42**, 39–44.

Brinson, G. P., Singer, B. D., and Beebower, G. L. (1991). Determinants of portfolio performance II: An update. *Financial Analysts Journal*, **47**, 40–8.

Droms, W. G. (1989). Market timing as an investment policy. *Financial Analysts Journal*, **45**, 73–7.

Grinblatt, M., and Titman, S. (1989). Portfolio performance evaluation: Old issues and new insights. *Review of Financial Studies*, **2**, 393–422.

Jensen, M. C. (1968). The performance of mutual funds in the period 1945–1964. *Journal of Finance*, **23**, 389–416.

Sharpe, W. F. (1966). Mutual fund performance. *Journal of Business*, **39**, 119–38.

Sharpe, W. F. (1992). Asset allocation: Management style and performance. *Journal of Portfolio Management*, **18**, 7–19.

term structure models

Klaus Sandmann

Measured by the number of discussion papers and published articles, the theory of the term structure of interest rates is one of the most active fields of research in the literature on finance. This is partly due to the theoretically demanding questions these models create and partly to the direct practical significance of these models for the financial management of interest rate risks. The first step in modeling

the term structure is the dynamic specification of bond prices for different maturities, as well as the forward rate processes relative to each other under the requirement of no arbitrage. All models of the term structure of interest rates are relative pricing models in the sense that the dynamics of the bond price process are derived relative to the initially observed prices at time $t = 0$. Given a term structure model, the second step is the pricing of interest rate dependent contingent claims relative to the assumed model of the term structure. The different modeling approaches are characterized by the time framework, which may be discrete or continuous. Depending on which of the stochastic processes are exogenous to the model we furthermore distinguish between the direct (i.e., the bond price–based approach) and the indirect (i.e., the forward rate–based approach). Mainly due to the work of El Karoui et al. (1991) these two approaches are now understood within a unified framework.

The first term structure model in a narrow sense was proposed by Ho and Lee (1986). It was developed within a finite discrete time binomial lattice framework as a model for the entire term structure. Denote by $B_{j,i}(1 + l)$ in the lattice vertex j the price of a zero coupon bond with face value 1 at time $t_i \varepsilon \{0 = t_0 < \ldots < t_n = T\}$ and time to maturity of $1 + l$ periods. Assume an exogenous transition probability p as given, constant in time and state. For all $j = 0, \ldots, N - 1; i = 0, \ldots, j; l = 0, \ldots, N - j$ the entire term structure is described by

$$B_{j,1}(1 + l) \begin{cases} B_{j+1,i+1}(l) = \frac{B_{j,i}(1+l)}{B_{j,i}(1)} \cdot h(l) & \text{with probability } p \\ B_{j+1,i}(l) = \frac{B_{j,i}(1+l)}{B_{j,i}(1)} \cdot h^*(l) & \text{with probability } 1-p \end{cases}$$

where the perturbation functions $h(.)$ and $h^*(.)$ are independent of time and state, depending only on the remaining time to maturity l. The path independence and the no arbitrage condition yield

$$h(l) = \frac{1}{p + (1 - p)\delta^l} \text{ and } h^*(l) = h(l) \cdot \delta^l$$

where δ is an additional parameter of the model. By induction the price process of a zero coupon bond with one period to maturity is determined by

$$B_{j,i}(1) = \frac{B_0(j+1)}{B_0(j)} \cdot h^*(j) \cdot \delta^{-i}$$

$$\forall j = 0, \ldots, n-1; \quad \forall i = 0, \ldots, j$$

This implies that the logarithmic return per period $r_{i,j}$ takes the form

$$r_{j,i} := -\frac{1}{\Delta t} \ln B_{j,i}(1)$$

$$= \frac{1}{\Delta t} \left(\ln \frac{B_0(j)}{B_0(j+1)} \right.$$

$$\left. + \ln \left(\delta^{-j} \cdot p + (1+p) \right) + i \cdot \ln(\delta) \right)$$

The continuous time limit of the Ho–Lee model is a special case of the Heath, Jarrow, and Morton (1992) term structure approach. Instead of zero coupon bond prices continuously compounded, forward rate processes are modeled as stochastic processes. Let (Ω, F, P) be a probability space and denote for all $t < u$ by

$$f(t, u) = -\frac{\partial \ln B(t, u)}{\partial u}$$

the continuously compounded forward rate on a riskless bond $B(t,u)$ at time t with maturity u. For fixed T these forward rate processes are assumed to satisfy the following stochastic differential equation:

$$df(t, u) = \mu(t, u, \omega)dt$$
$$+ \sigma(t, u, \omega)dW(t) \ \forall 0 \leq u \leq T$$

where $f(0,.)$ is the given, non-random initial forward rate curve, $W(t)$ an n-dimensional standard Brownian motion. The instantaneous drift $\mu(.,.,.)$ and the n-dimensional instantaneous volatility vector $\sigma(.,.,.)$ are assumed to be adapted to the filtration induced by $W(t)$. Starting from the initial curve $\{f(0,u): u \in [0, T]\}$ the Brownian motion $W(t)$ determines the fluctuation of the entire forward rate curve. The Heath–Jarrow–Morton model is the general framework for forward rate based term structure models assuming necessary regularity conditions on the functions $\mu(.,.,.)$ and $\sigma(.,.,.)$.

For one-factor models the dynamics of the term structure are completely determined by the continuously compounded short rate process $\{r(t): = f^{(t,t)}\}_{t \in [0,T]}$. In specifying the volatility functions $\sigma(.,.,.)$ such that the continuously compounded short rate is Markov, these models are special cases of the Heath–Jarrow–Morton model. The majority of these models are of the form

$$dr(t) = (\theta(t) - a \cdot r(t))dt + \sigma(t) \cdot r(t)^\beta dW(t)$$

For $a = 0$ and $\beta = 0$ one obtains the continuous time Ho–Lee model, for $\beta = 0$ the generalized Vasicek (1977) model, for $\beta = 1$ the class of lognormal models, and for $\beta = 0.5$ the generalized Cox–Ingersoll–Ross (1985) model. In the case of $\beta = 0$ the short and forward rate becomes negative with positive probability. Models with $\beta = 1$ (e.g., Brennan–Schwartz, 1977; Dothan, 1978; Black Karasinski, 1991; Hull–White, 1990a) guarantee positive rates. However, lognormal models have another serious drawback: expected rollover returns are infinite, even if the rollover period is arbitrarily short (Hogan and Weintraub, 1993). The choice of $\beta = 0.5$ can be viewed as a plausible compromise between the two extremes. However, for American interest rate data from June 1964 to December 1989, Chan et al. (1992) showed that short rate movements are best explained by choosing $\beta = 1.5$. Sandmann and Sondermann (1994) point out that the problem with $\beta = 1$ disappears if one follows the way interest rates are quoted in practice and models the effective annual or nominal rate instead of the continuous rate. The assumption that the nominal short rate follows a lognormal model implies that the dynamics of the continuously compounded short rate are

$$dr(t) = (1 - e^{-r(t)})$$
$$\left[\left(\theta(t) - \frac{1}{2}(1 - e^{-r(t)})\sigma^2 \right) dt + \sigma dW(t) \right]$$

Along this line, Sandmann, Sondermann, and Miltersen (1995), Brace aqnd Musiela (1995), and Goldys, Musiela, and Sondermann (1994) consider models where the stochastic process of nominal rates for finite compounding periods are lognormally distributed.

Instead of the forward rate processes, the direct approach to term structure modeling starts with the dynamics of zero bond prices. This approach is originally concentrated on two specific zero coupon bond price processes, ignoring the rest of the initial term structure (e.g., Ball and Torous, 1983; Schaefer and Schwartz, 1987; Bühler, 1988; Kemna, de Munnik, and Vorst, 1989; Jamshidian, 1989; Briys, Crouhy, and Schöbel, 1991; Käsler, 1991). In our exposition we follow El Karoui et al. (1991), who provided a unified framework and extended this approach to fit the entire term structure.

Let (Ω, F, P) be a probability space. For all maturities $u \leq T$ the dynamics of the stochastic processes for default free zero coupon bonds with face value 1 are assumed to fulfil the stochastic differential equation

$$dB(t, u) = \alpha(t, u)B(t, u)dt$$
$$+ B(t, u)\tau(t, u)dW(t) \; \forall t \leq u$$

where $B(0,u)_{w \leq T}$ is the non-random initial curve of the zero coupon bonds and $B(u,u) = 1$ with probability one. The instantaneous drift α (.,.) and the volatility function τ (.,.) with $\tau(t, t) = 0$ have to satisfy some regularity conditions and $W(t)$ is an n-dimensional Brownian motion under the probability measure P. If τ (.,.) is non-stochastic the above specification is known as the Gaussian term structure model, because it implies normally distributed continuously compounded rates.

Let $\{F_t\}_{t \leq T}$ be the natural filtration given by $W(t)$. For simplicity, assume that $W(t)$ is a one-dimensional Brownian motion. Consider a predictable portfolio strategy $\{\phi_1(t), \phi_2(t)\}_t$ consisting of two zero coupon bonds with different maturities $u_1 < u_2$ such that the portfolio yields a riskless return. Under the assumption of no arbitrage the riskless return must be equal to the instantaneous spot rate, i.e.,

$$\Phi_1(t)dB(t, u_1) + \Phi_2(t)dB(t, u_2) = r(t)dt$$

This classical duplication argument implies by no arbitrage that the excess return per unit risk of a zero coupon bond under the probability

measure P is independent of the maturity, i.e., there exists a function $\lambda(t,r)$ such that

$$\forall u \leq T \colon \lambda(t, r)$$
$$= \frac{E_p[dB(t, u)|B(t, u)] - B(t, u)r(t)dt}{\sqrt{V_p[dB(t, u)]}}$$

Given sufficient regularity conditions on the function $\lambda(.,.)$ the economy with risk premium can be transformed into an economy without risk premium. Define

$$\frac{dP^*(t)}{dP(t)} :=$$
$$\exp\left\{ -\int_0^t \lambda(s, r(s))dW - \frac{1}{2}\int_0^t \lambda^2(s, r(s))dt \right\}$$

where by $P(t)$ resp. $P^*(t)$ the restriction on the σ-algebra J_t is denoted and using Girsanov's Theorem, the process

$$dW^*(t) := \lambda(t, r(t))dt + dW(t)$$

is a standard Brownian motion under the probability measure P^*. The change of probability measure has no influence on the volatility coefficients in the differential equations, whereas the instantaneous drifts are replaced by $r(t)$. In this artificial economy, the expected rate of return over the next time interval of length dt will for any asset be equal to $r(t)$:

$$dB(t, u) = r(t)B(t, u)dt + B(t, u)\tau(t, u)dW(t)$$
$$\forall t \leq u$$

P^* is called the equivalent martingale measure since the discounted price processes of any security in this market is a martingale under P^*. The solution of the risk neutral differential equation for a zero coupon bond is given by

$$B(t, u) = B(0, u) \cdot \exp\left\{ \int_0^t (\tau(s) - \frac{1}{2}\tau^2(s, u))ds \right.$$
$$\left. + \int_0^t \tau(s, u)dW(s) \right\}$$
$$= \frac{B(0, u)}{B(0, t)} \cdot \exp\left\{ -\frac{1}{2}\int_0^t (\tau^2(s, u) - \tau^2(s, t))ds \right\}$$
$$\cdot \exp\left\{ \int_0^t (\tau(s, u) - \tau(s, t))dW(s) \right\}$$

The relationship between the direct approach and the indirect approach is determined by the volatility function $\tau(.,.)$. For $\tau(t,u) = \sigma(u-t)$ we obtain the continuous time Ho–Lee model; for the specification

$$\tau(t, u) = \frac{\sigma}{a}(1 - \exp\{-a \cdot (u - t)\})$$

corresponds to the generalized Vasicek model and the Cox–Ingersoll–Ross (1985) square root model can be obtained by

$$\tau(t, u) = \frac{-2(1 - \exp\{-\gamma \cdot (u - t)\})}{2\gamma + (a - \gamma)(1 - \exp\{-\gamma(u - t)\})}$$

with

$$\gamma = \sqrt{a^2 + 2\sigma^2}$$

Using the bank account as a numeraire, discounted asset prices are martingales under P^*; thus, the price of an interest rate contingent claim is determined by the expected discounted value of the payoff stream. In many cases the payoff of the contingent claim depends only on the value of the underlying security (bond) at the exercise date. In such a situation El Karoui and Rochet (1989) and Jamshidian (1991) introduced a second measure transformation known as the time T_0 forward risk adjusted measure. This basically corresponds to a change of numeraire from the bank account to the zero coupon bond with maturity T_0. This can be interpreted as a transformation from the spot market to the forward market with delivery at time T_0. The time T_0 forward risk adjusted measure is defined by

$$\frac{dP^{T_0}}{dP^*} := \frac{\exp\left\{-\int_0^{T_0} r(s)ds\right\}}{B(0, T_0)}$$

which in the framework of Gaussian term structure models is equal to

$$\frac{dP^{T_0}}{dP^*} :=$$
$$\exp\left\{-\frac{1}{2}\int_0^{T_0}\tau^2(s, T_0)ds + \int_0^{T_0}\tau(s, T_0)dW(s)\right\}$$

By Girsanov's Theorem, the process

$$dW^{T_0}(t) := dW^*(t) - \tau(t, T_0)dt$$

is a standard Brownian motion under P^* and the time T_0 forward price process of the zero coupon bond is equal to:

$$d\frac{B(t, u)}{B(t, T_0)} = \frac{B(t, u)}{B(t, T_0)} \cdot (\tau(t, u) - \tau(t, T_0))dW^{T_0}$$

The time T_0 forward risk adjusted measure is of practical importance for the pricing of those interest rate contingent claims with a final payoff only depending on the realization of the underlying security at time T_0. Within the Gaussian term structure framework the $t_0 = 0$ arbitrage price of a European call option on a zero coupon bond with maturity $T > T_0$, exercise price K, and exercise date T_0 is determined by

$$
\begin{aligned}
\text{Call}[B(t, T), K, T_0] &= B(0, T_0)E_{P_{T_0}}[\max\{B\\
&\quad (T_0, T) - K, 0\}]\\
&= B(0, T)N(d)\\
&\quad - K \cdot B(0, T_0)N(d - v(T_0))
\end{aligned}
$$

where N(.) denotes the standard normal distribution, and

$$d := \frac{\frac{B(0, T)}{K \cdot B(0, T_0)} + \frac{1}{2}v^2(T_0)}{v(T_0)}$$

$$v^2(T_0) := \int_0^{T_0}(\tau(s, T) - \tau(s, T_0))^2 ds$$

The advantage of the Gaussian term structure model is that for a large class of interest rate contingent claims the arbitrage price is determined by analytical closed form solutions similar to the one given above. However, in order to overcome the drawback of negative spot and forward rates, one has to assume state dependent volatilities for forward rate and/or bond price processes, leading to a loss of analytical tractability. As a consequence, numerical methods such as those presented by Hull and White (1990b) and Schmidt (1994) become more and more important. Theoretical elegance aside, practical applicability requires derivative prices to be available within seconds to keep up with the volatile market.

Bibliography

Ball, C. A., and Torous, W. N. (1983). Bond price dynamics and options. *Journal of Financial and Quantitative Analysis*, **18**, 517–31.

Black, F., and Karasinski, P. (1991). Bond and options pricing when short rates are lognormal. *Financial Analysts Journal*, **47**, 52–9.

Black, F., Derman, E., and Toy, W. N. (1990). A one-factor model of interest rates and its application to treasury bond options. *Financial Analysts Journal*, **46**, 33–9.

Brace, A., and Musiela, M. (1994). A multifactor Gauss–Markov implementation of Heath, Jarrow and Morton. *Mathematical Finance*, **2**, 259–83.

Brace, A., and Musiela, M. (1995). The market model of interest rate dynamics. Working paper, University of New South Wales.

Brennan, M. J., and Schwartz, E. S. (1977). Savings bonds, retractable bonds and callable bonds. *Journal of Financial Economics*, **5**, 67–88.

Briys, E., Crouhy, M., and Schöbel, R. (1991). The pricing of default-free interest rate cap, floor and collar agreements. *Journal of Finance*, **46**, 1879–92.

Bühler, W. (1988). Rationale bewertung von optionsrechten auf anleihen. *Zeitschrift für betriebswirtschaftliche Forschung*, **10**, 851–83.

Chan, K. C., Karolyi, G. A., Longstaff, F. A., and Sanders, A. B. (1992). An empirical comparison of alternative models of the short-term interest rate. *Journal of Finance*, **47**, 1209–27.

Courtadon, G. R., and Weintraub, K. (1989). *An Arbitrage Free Debt Option Model Based On Lognormally Distributed Forward Rates*. New York: Citicorp. North American Investment Bank.

Cox, J. C., Ingersoll, J. E., Jr., and Ross, S. A. (1985). A theory of the term structure of interest rates. *Econometrica*, **53**, 385–407.

Dothan, L. U. (1978). On the term structure of interest rates. *Journal of Financial Economics*, **6**, 59–69.

El Karoui, N., and Rochet, J.-C. (1989). A Pricing formula for options on coupon bonds. Working paper 72, SEEDS.

El Karoui, N., Lepage, C., Myneme, R., Roseau, N., and Viswanathan, R. (1991). The valuation and hedging of contingent claims with Markovian interest rates. Working paper, Université de Paris 6.

Goldys, J. D., Musiela, M., and Sondermann, D. (1994). Lognormality of rates and term structure models. Working paper, University of New South Wales.

Heath, D., Jarrow, R., and Morton, A. (1992). Bond pricing and the term structure of interest rates: A new methodology for contingent claims valuation. *Econometrica*, **60**, 77–105.

Ho, T., and Lee, S.-B. (1986). Term structure movements and the pricing of interest rate contingent claims. *Journal of Finance*, **41**, 1011–30.

Hogan, M., and Weintraub, K. (1993). The lognormal interest rate model and eurodollar futures. Discussion paper. New York: Citibank.

Hull, J., and White, A. (1990a). Pricing interest rate derivative securities. *Review of Financial Studies*, **3**, 573–92.

Hull, J., and White, A. (1990b). Valuing derivative securities using the explicit finite difference method. *Journal of Financial and Quantitative Analysis*, **25**, 87–100.

Hull, J., and White, A. (1993). One factor interest rate models and the valuation of interest rate derivative securities. *Journal of Financial and Quantitative Analysis*, **28**, 235–54.

Jamshidian, F. (1989). An exact bond option formula. *Journal of Finance*, **44**, 205–9.

Jamshidian, F. (1990). The preference-free determination of bond and option prices from the spot interest rate. *Advances in Futures and Options Research*, **4**, 51–67.

Jamshidian, F. (1991). Forward induction and construction of yield curve diffusion models. *Journal of Fixed Income*, **1**, 62–74.

Käsler, J. (1991). Optionen auf anleihen. PhD thesis, University of Dortmund.

Kemna, A. G. Z., de Munnik, J. F. J., and Vorst, A. C. F. (1989). On bond price models with a time-varying drift term. Discussion paper, Erasmus University, Rotterdam.

Longstaff, F. A., and Schwartz. E. S. (1992). Interest rate volatility and the term structure: A two-factor general equilibrium model. *Journal of Finance*, **47**, 1259–82.

Miltersen, K. R. (1994). An arbitrage theory of the term structure of interest rates. *Annals of Applied Probability*, **4**, 953–67.

Rady, S., and Sandmann, K. (1994). The direct approach to debt option pricing. *Review of Futures Markets*, **13**, 461–514.

Sandmann, K., and Sondermann, D. (1994). On the stability of lognormal interest rate models and the pricing of eurodollar futures. Discussion paper No. B-263, Department of Statistics, University of Bonn.

Sandmann, K., Sondermann, D., and Miltersen, K. R. (1995). Closed form term structure derivatives in a Heath–Jarrow–Morton model with lognormal annually compounded interest rates. *Research Symposium Proceedings (CBOT)*, 145–64.

Schaefer, S. M., and Schwartz, E. S. (1987). Time-dependent variance and the pricing of bond options. *Journal of Finance*, **42**, 1113–28.

Schmidt, W. M. (1994). *On a General Class of One-Factor Models for the Term Structure of Interest Rates*, Frankfurt: Deutsche Bank Research.

Vasicek, O. A. (1977). An equilibrium characterization of the term structure. *Journal of Financial Economics*, **5**, 177–88.

threshold models

Ruey S. Tsay

Threshold models are piecewise linear models with non-linearity driven by a threshold variable. Proposed by Tong (1978) to describe various non-linear characteristics commonly observed in time-series data, such as asymmetric limit cycles, the models have been widely used in economic modeling and forecasting. They have also become popular in finance, especially in volatility modeling and the study of index arbitrage and price co-movements.

Like Markov switching models, threshold models also use the concept of regimes. However, instead of using the latent state variable to define regimes, a threshold model employs an observable variable to determine the regimes and their switching. Let $y_t = (y_{1t}, \ldots, y_{nt})'$ be an n-dimensional financial time series, z_t be a scalar stationary, continuous variable whose value is known at time t, and Ψ_t be the public information available at time t. The process $\mathbf{y}_t$ follows a k-regime threshold model if

$$y_t = \phi_j(\Psi_{t-1}) + \sum_j \varepsilon_t, \text{ if } \delta_{j-1} < z_t \le \delta_j \quad (1)$$

where $\phi_j(\Psi_{t-1})$ is an n-dimensional linear function associated with regime j, $\sum_j$ is the $n \times n$ square-root matrix of the positive definite matrix $\sum_j \sum_j'$, $\varepsilon_t = (\varepsilon_{1t}, \ldots, \varepsilon_{nt})'$ is a sequence of independent and identically distributed random vectors with mean 0 and covariance matrix I_n, the $n \times n$ identity matrix, and the real numbers $\{\delta_j\}$ satisfy $\delta_0 = -\infty < \delta_1 < \delta_2 < \cdots < \delta_k = \infty$. The variable z_t is referred to as the threshold variable and $\{\delta_j\}$ are the thresholds. From the definition, the model partitions the space of the threshold variable z_t into k regimes and employs different linear models for different regimes.

To illustrate, consider the simple case of $n = 1$ and $k = 2$. Suppose r_t is the daily log return of an asset such that $r_t = \sigma_t \varepsilon_t$ with $\sigma_t^2 = (r_t|\Psi_{t-1})$ being the conditional variance of r_t. Denote $y_t = \ln(\sigma_t^2)$. A simple two-regime threshold stochastic volatility model is

$$y_t = \begin{cases} \phi_0 + \phi_1 y_{t-1} + \sigma_1 \varepsilon_t & \text{if } r_{t-1} \le 0 \\ \beta_0 + \beta_1 y_{t-1} + \sigma_2 \varepsilon_t & \text{if } r_{t-1} > 0. \end{cases} \quad (2)$$

Here, the threshold variable is the past return r_{t-1} and zero is the threshold. This model can capture the asymmetric responses in volatility caused by past positive and negative returns. One would expect that $\phi_0/(1 - \phi_1) > \beta_0/(1 - \beta_1)$ because negative returns tend to be associated with larger volatility.

The model is an *open-loop* threshold model. If z_t is a measurable function of past values of y_t (e.g., $z_t = y_{i,t-d}$ with $d \ge 1$), then the model becomes a self-exciting threshold autoregressive (SETAR) model with delay d. Properties of SETAR models differ markedly from those of linear models. For instance, Chen and Tsay (1991) show that if y_{t-d} is the threshold variable and $\phi_0 = \beta_0 = 0$, then the series y_t is geometrically ergodic if

$$\phi_1 < 1, \beta_1 < 1, \phi_1\beta_1 < 1, \phi_1^{s(d)}\beta_1^{t(d)} < 1,$$
$$\phi_1^{t(d)}\beta_1^{s(d)} < 1,$$

where $s(d)$ and $t(d)$ are non-negative integers depending on d, and $s(d)$ and $t(d)$ are odd and even numbers, respectively. In particular, if $d = 1$, then $s(d) = 1$ and $t(d) = 0$. The ergodicity condition becomes $\phi_1 < 1$, $\beta_1 < 1$, and $\phi_1\beta_1 < 1$. This is rather different from the condition $-1 < \phi_1 < 1$ of the AR(1) model $y_t = \phi_1 y_{t-1} + \varepsilon_t$. For example, the y_t process below is ergodic

$$y_t = \begin{cases} -1.1y_{t-1} + \varepsilon_t & \text{if } y_{t-1} \le 0 \\ 0.9y_{t-1} + \varepsilon_t & \text{if } y_{t-1} > 0. \end{cases}$$

To investigate index arbitrage in finance, let f_t be the logarithm of futures price of the shares underlying a futures contract at time t that expires at time $t + \tau$ and p_t be the logarithm of price at t on the cash market for the same shares. It is well known that both f_t and p_t are unit-root non-stationary (e.g., Dwyer, Locke, and Yu, 1996). A simple cost-of-carry model says that

$$f_t - (r - w)\tau = p_t$$

where r is the risk-free interest rate and w denotes the dividend rate. If the transaction cost is approximately constant, then the condition for arbitrage with a long position in the cash index and a short position in the futures contract is

$$f_t - p_t - (r - w)\tau > c,$$

where c is a constant. The corresponding condition for being long in futures and short in cash is

$$f_t - p_t - (r - w)\tau < -c.$$

In other words, when the magnitude of $f_t - p_t - (r - w)\tau$ exceeds the transaction cost, then the series $\{f_t\}$ and $\{p_t\}$ are subjected to the impact of arbitrage, forcing f_{t+j} and p_{t+j} to move closer to each other for $j \geq 1$. For other values of $f_t - p_t - (r - w)\tau$, the two processes are not subjected to the influence of arbitrage. Putting all of the concepts together, one has a plausible error-correction model with threshold co-integration for f_t and p_t. See Balke and Fomby (1997) for further information on threshold co-integration.

Let $y_{1t} = f_t - f_{t-1}$ and $y_{2t} = p_t - p_{t-1}$. Suppose the impact of arbitrage appears with a delay of d time units, and we define $z_{t-d} = f_{t-d} - p_{t-d} -(r - w)d$. Then, the model for y_t becomes

$$
y_t =
\begin{cases}
\beta_1 z_{t-1} + \sum_{i=1}^{p}\phi_{i,1}y_{t-i} + \sum_1 \varepsilon_t \\
\qquad \text{if } z_{t-d} > c \\
\beta_2 z_{t-1} + \sum_{i=1}^{p}\phi_{i,2}y_{t-i} + \sum_2 \varepsilon_t \\
\qquad \text{if } -c \leq z_{t-d} \leq c \\
\beta_3 z_{t-1} + \sum_{i=1}^{p}\phi_{i,3}y_{t-i} + \sum_3 \varepsilon_t \\
\qquad \text{if } z_{t-d} < -c,
\end{cases}
\tag{3}
$$

where β_j are 2×1 vectors, and $\phi_{i,j}$ are 2×2 matrices associated with regime j. Here we use the cost-of-carry model to define the co-integrating series. The threshold co-integration implies that β_2 should be zero, but both β_1 and β_3 are non-zero. Empirical experience based on 1-minute log returns of Standard and Poor 500 index futures suggests that $d = 1$ and supports threshold co-integration (Dwyer, Locke, and Yu, 1996, Tsay, 1998).

Model specification and estimation of the threshold model can be found in Tsay (1998). Under some regularity condition, the threshold c is a discontinuity point of the model so that it has a faster convergence rate and can be estimated by

minimizing the residual sum of squares. The order p and delay d can be chosen by the model selection criteria under the assumption that they are finite. Conditioned on p, d, and c, other parameters can easily be obtained by the least squares method.

Because z_{t-d} is known at time t, the regime of the observation y_t for $t > d$ is known. This dramatically simplifies the estimation of threshold models. Specifically, conditioned on the first max $\{p, d\}$ observations, the likelihood function of the data does not involve any latent variable and can easily be evaluated. The uncertainty in regime reappears in forecasting when the forecast horizon is greater than the delay d, however.

Dwyer, Locke, and Yu (1996) employ a reduced model

$$
z_t =
\begin{cases}
\phi_{0,1} + \sum_{i=1}^{p}\phi_{i,1}z_{t-i} + \sum_{i=1}^{p}\theta_{i,1}y_{2,t-i} \\
\qquad +\sigma_1\varepsilon_t \text{ if } z_{t-d} > c \\
\phi_{0,1} + \sum_{i=1}^{p}\phi_{i,2}z_{t-i} + \sum_{i=1}^{p}\theta_{i,2}y_{2,t-i} \\
\qquad +\sigma_2\varepsilon_t \text{ if } -c \leq z_{t-d} \leq c \\
\phi_{0,3} + \sum_{i=1}^{p}\phi_{i,3}z_{t-i} + \sum_{i=1}^{p}\theta_{i,3}y_{2,t-i} \\
\qquad +\sigma_3\varepsilon_t \text{if } z_{t-d} < -c,
\end{cases}
\tag{4}
$$

where $y_{2t} = p_t - p_{t-1}$, to investigate index arbitrage. This provides an approximation of the threshold error-correction model and can be treated as a univariate SETAR model plus the exogenous variable y_{2t}. Procedures for building such models, including testing for threshold non-linearity, have been investigated in the literature (e.g., Tsay, 1989). Limiting properties of least squares estimates for the model have also been established (e.g., Chan, 1993; Chan and Tsay, 1998). Generally speaking, the least squares estimates of thresholds are obtained by searching over empirical quantiles of the threshold variable. If the thresholds are discontinuity points of the model, then the estimate of the threshold follows a compound Poisson distribution. If the threshold model is continuous at the threshold, then the usual normal asymptotics continue to apply. Similar to Markov switching models, the problem of unidentified nuisance parameters exists under the null hypothesis of a linear model because the latter contains no thresholds.

Finally, a three-regime threshold model can be thought of as an approximation to the underlying non-linear model. The two outer regimes take care of the two extremes in the threshold space, whereas the middle regime represents the majority of the data.

Bibliography

Balke, N. S., and Fomby, T. B. (1997). Threshold co-integration. *International Economic Review*, 8, 627–45.

Chan, K. S. (1993). Consistency and limiting distribution of the least squares estimator of a threshold autoregressive model. *Annals of Statistics*, 21, 520–33.

Chan, K. S., and Tsay, R. S. (1998). Limiting properties of least squares estimator of a continuous threshold autoregressive model. *Biometrika*, 85, 413–26.

Chen, R. and Tsay, R. S. (1991). On the ergodicity of TAR(1) processes. *Annals of Applied Probability*, 1, 613–34.

Dwyer, G. P., Jr., Locke, P., and Yu, W. (1996). Index arbitrage and non-linear dynamics between the S&P 500 futures and cash. *Review of Financial Studies*, 9, 301–32.

Tong, H. (1978). On the threshold model. In C. H. Chen (ed.), *Pattern Recognition and Signal Processing*. Amsterdan: Sijhoff and Noordhoff, 101–41.

Tsay, R. S. (1989). Testing and modeling threshold autoregressive processes. *Journal of the American Statistical Association*, 84, 231–40.

Tsay, R. S. (1998). Testing and modeling multivariate threshold models. *Journal of the American Statistical Association*, 93, 1188–1202.

time series analysis

Stephen J. Taylor

A series of measurements made in chronological order is a time series. Finance research has concentrated on series of prices and returns to investors, although there has also been interest in series of earnings and dividends. Time series analysis is a collection of statistical methods that is used to understand the dynamic behavior of the measured quantity, and to make forecasts about future values.

The earliest important insights into financial time series may be attributed to Holbrook Working and Maurice Kendall. The first detailed analysis of investment returns using time series methods is Fama (1965). Fama studied long time series of returns from US stocks and made three observations that have been corroborated in numerous subsequent studies. First, the sample correlation between the return during some period and the return during any subsequent period is close to zero. Prices follow a random walk when the theoretical correlations are zero for any pair of returns during different periods and expected returns are constant. Second, large positive and large negative returns are more likely than other returns to be followed by large returns. This phenomenon, known as volatility clustering or conditional heteroskedasticity, can be detected by measuring correlations between squared returns. Third, the distribution of returns is fat tailed compared with the normal distribution because extreme returns are far more frequent than predicted by normal theory.

Methods for testing the random walk hypothesis usually rely on some alternative description of price behavior to motivate the tests. Trends in prices are one alternative, differences between fundamental values and market prices are another, and both alternatives motivate the variance-ratio test of Lo and MacKinlay (1988). An alternative is the idea that prices are chaotic. Empirical studies show that the random walk hypothesis is at least a good approximation. There is little evidence to support the ideas of chaotic dynamics. There is some evidence for trends in exchange rates and the prices of some firms, particularly small firms, but the evidence remains controversial. Trading rules based upon price forecasts obtained from time series models are of little value after transactions costs and do not contradict the idea of market efficiency, except for forex markets where time series rules obtain profits similar to those provided by some forms of technical analysis.

Time series models for price volatility have attracted enormous interest in recent years because they can be used to forecast volatility and hence value derivatives. Engle (1982) developed the ARCH (autoregressive conditional heteroskedasticity) class of models that provide successful descriptions of future volatility conditioned on a set of recent observations. These models are very flexible and many new specifications have been developed. The GARCH model of Bollerslev, Chou, and Kroner (1992) has become a popular choice.

Bibliography

Bollerslev, T., Chou, R. Y., and Kroner, K. F. (1992). ARCH modeling in finance: A review of the theory and empirical evidence. *Journal of Econometrics*, **52**, 5–59.

Engle, R. F. (1982). Autoregressive conditional heteroscedasticity with estimates of the variance of United Kingdom inflation. *Econometrica*, **50**, 987–1007.

Fama, E. F. (1965). The behavior of stock market prices. *Journal of Business*, **38**, 34–105.

Lo, A. W., and MacKinlay, A. C. (1988). Stock market prices do not follow random walks: Evidence from a simple specification test. *Review of Financial Studies*, **1**, 41–66.

Taylor, S. J. (2004). *Asset Price Dynamics and Prediction*. Princeton, NJ: Princeton University Press.

trading mechanisms

Anne Vila Fremault

Financial securities such as bonds, stocks, currency, or derivatives can be traded in a wide variety of trading mechanisms or institutional arrangements. Traditionally, securities are traded in an organized market setting: buyers and sellers, or their respective agents, meet each other on a centralized trading floor. To insure that trades can be matched with minimal delays, most exchanges employ market makers, whose task it is to match trades and take positions out of their own inventory if no matching party can be found without causing large price changes. As a compensation for the risk they incur in doing so, market makers charge a higher price when selling (the ask price) than when buying (the bid price). This results in the bid–ask spread, a transaction cost borne by the public. In some markets (e.g., the NYSE), market makers have an explicit obligation to provide these liquidity services, whereas in others (e.g., futures markets such as LIFFE), market makers are driven by a profit maximizing motive only. Furthermore, market makers can have a quasi-monopoly (there actually is competition in the form of public limit orders, e.g., the NYSE), or face a large number of competing market makers (e.g., LIFFE).

Developments in communications and information technology have enabled financial markets to develop electronic or screen-based trading. In these systems, the centralized floor is replaced by a centralized computer system. Market participants do not meet each other, but enter orders directly into the system. These orders will be automatically matched according to explicit priority rules (e.g., time and price priority). Limit orders that cannot be matched will be entered into the central limit order book, to be executed, if possible, against future incoming orders.

The relative merits of the two systems is being debated by academics and practitioners alike (Kofman and Moser, 1995; Fremault Vila and Sandman, 1995). Proponents of the traditional floor mechanisms argue that market makers on the floor are critical in providing liquidity, especially when large order imbalances develop and prices move very fast. Furthermore, they suggest that the open environment of the floor is an important source of information for all participants in the trading process. By contrast, screen-based systems offer potentially faster execution and reporting, thereby reducing so called immediacy risk (the possibility that the executed price differs from the price at which an order was entered). But theoretical and empirical studies fail to determine whether the absence of market makers in the screen-based system hampers liquidity. Likewise, it is unclear whether the computerized system is more transparent (the central limit order book is usually visible to all market participants) or less transparent (traders do not face each other).

A very different trading environment is the over the counter market. This trading system ceases to be centralized. Instead, it is a dispersed network of dealers, linked by telephones and computers. At any point in time, multiple dealers provide quotes at which they are willing to trade with the public. Most of the world's bond markets and currency markets, as well as some stock markets (e.g., Nasdaq and LSE), are organized this way. It is usually argued, yet not proven – witness the controversy around Nasdaq quotes (Christie and Huang, 1994) – that the competition between dealers results in lower transaction costs (i.e., bid–ask spreads) than in the centralized trading systems. It is further suggested that the over the counter trading system can play a useful role in markets with relatively low liquidity (Chan and Lakonishok, 1995) and/or very heterogeneous products (e.g., complex derivatives).

Several alternative trading systems, such as electronic clearing systems like INSTINET and Tradepoint, challenge the role of the traditional market systems, by offering longer trading hours, and by promising improved execution and reduced transaction costs.

Bibliography

Chan, L., and Lakonishok, J. (1995). A cross-market comparison of institutional equity trading costs. Working paper, University of Illinois.

Christie, W., and Huang, R. (1994). Why do Nasdaq market makers avoid odd-eight quotes? *Journal of Finance*, **49**, 1813–40.

Fremault Vila, A., and Sandman, G. (1995). Floor trading versus electronic screen trading: An empirical analysis of market liquidity and information transmission in the Nikkei Stock Index futures markets. Working paper, London School of Economics.

Kofman, P., and Moser, J. (1995). *Spreads, Information and Transparency Across Trading Systems*. Chicago: Federal Reserve Bank of Chicago.

O'Hara, M. (1995). *Market Microstructure Theory*. Cambridge, MA: Blackwell.

Stoll, H. (1992). Principles of trading market structure. *Journal of Financial Services Research*, **6**, 75–107.

transaction costs

Joseph Ogden

The buyers and sellers of virtually any asset incur costs in attempting to trade the asset in a public domain. Transaction costs are directly or indirectly associated with efforts to assess the fair value of the asset and to search for a trading counterparty. The size and nature of transaction costs ultimately depend on various characteristics of the asset. In particular, assets whose values can be readily ascertained in relation to other similar assets can be traded with lower costs than assets that have unique characteristics. The size of the trade, as well as the total size of the market (and thus the potential trading volume), also affect transaction costs, due to often tremendous economies of scale in search costs. These characteristics will also determine the type of market structure that will exist to facilitate trading in the asset, or indeed whether a formal market structure for the asset will exist.

Most assets trade in one of four market structures: direct search, broker, dealer, or auction markets. In a direct search market, buyers and sellers conduct their own search effort to find a trading counterparty. Cost and effort incurred by the seller may include placing advertisements in newspapers, placing the asset in a conspicuous public place with a "for sale" sign attached, or other means of drawing the attention of the public. For buyers, efforts may center on locating such advertisements or placing ads indicating an interest in purchasing the asset. Examples of assets commonly traded in direct search markets are real estate, collectables, and used automobiles, though in none of these cases is direct search the predominant market structure.

In brokered markets, either the buyer or seller, or both, hire a broker to conduct a search for a counterparty. For this service, the trader pays the brokers a fee or commission. The amount of the fee in relation to the value of the asset depends largely on the costs normally incurred by the broker. The broker incurs fixed costs for equipment and training (used to monitor the status of potential counterparties and the overall state of the market) that must be allocated to each trade, as well as variable costs specifically associated with a given trade. Examples of assets traded in brokered markets are real estate and fine art, as well as some financial assets such as municipal bonds and large blocks of common stocks.

In a dealer market, the dealer holds an inventory of the asset and stands ready to buy or sell directly against this inventory. Thus, the dealer effectively eliminates search costs and trading delays for both buyers and sellers. In exchange for providing this immediacy of trade, the dealer receives compensation in the form of a spread between the price at which the dealer will purchase the asset, called the bid price, and a higher price at which the dealer will sell the asset, called the ask (or offer) price. Examples of assets that trade in dealer markets are new and used automobiles and financial assets such as secondary markets for US Treasury securities, corporate bonds, foreign exchange, and common stocks traded on the Nasdaq Stock Market and the London Stock Exchange. The difference between the ask and bid prices, expressed as a percentage of the average of these prices, is commonly used as a measure of transaction costs in a dealer market.

Auction markets are characterized by the simultaneous presence of many buyers and sellers in a given location, each monitoring counterparty bids and offers in an active attempt to trade at the best possible price. The auction market structure is best suited for assets with large trading volume. Examples of assets traded in auction markets include fine art and, among financial assets, new-issue US Treasury securities and common stocks traded on the New York Stock Exchange, the Paris Bourse, and the Tokyo Stock Exchange. Trading on the NYSE actually reflects aspects of the broker, dealer and auction structures. Buyers and sellers submit their trade requests to a broker that is a member of the NYSE and is therefore allowed to trade on the floor of the exchange. On the floor, the broker engages in the auction process known as open-outcry, attempting to obtain the best price for the customer. Occasionally, however, there is an imbalance of purchase or sale orders for a given stock, and orders may languish. To avoid this problem, the NYSE assigns to each stock a specialist, a member firm who acts as an exclusive dealer in the stock. The specialist posts bid and ask prices and has a general fiduciary responsibility to facilitate trading in the stock. Brokerage fees paid by customers to the member firms reflect the high fixed cost, and relatively low variable cost, associated with the auction market structure. In addition, when trades are consummated between the customer and the specialist, rather than between two customers, the customer also implicitly pays the specialist for their service as a dealer. For this reason, researchers often estimate transaction costs on the NYSE as the sum of a representative brokerage commission plus the specialists' proportional bid–ask spread.

Bibliography

Garbade, K. (1982). *Securities Markets*. New York: McGraw-Hill.

transition economies

Katherine O'Sullivan

The economies referred to are those which were previously members of the COMECON trading bloc. As this bloc collapsed, the previously centrally planned economies entered a period of transition to a market style of economic organizations. The issues involved in re-engineering the financial and economic systems of these countries, together with the complexities of restructuring the existing social and cultural framework, constitute the economics of transition. Because of the extensive nature of the issues involved in transition, this section will attempt only to deal with the financial sector, and the commercial sectors which are intrinsically related.

The collapse of the centrally planned system created some new, indeed unprecedented, problems. In a command system, markets – and of course market-based prices – are non-existent, with internal allocation achieved through state quotas and external transactions through barter arrangements with the state obtaining its resources by direct ownership of the means of production. The collapse of the communist system left the transitory economies with no fiscal system, no pricing system, no mechanism to provide internal or external liquidity, and no meaningful company, contract, or property law. Transition economies therefore needed to downsize commitments (privatize), create markets, create and capitalize financial intermediaries, and create the infrastructure that Western economies take for granted. As a first step, prompted by the massive overhang of inflation from money supply growth and unspent claims in the banking system, governments introduced harsh fiscal policies, combined with contradictory monetary policies. These policies are typical of those imposed in countries with a high level of foreign debt, the need for financial support, and declining productivity. The "shock therapy" had high social costs, but is now beginning to show itself as successful in controlling inflation and stabilizing exchange rates. The countries which began to move away from the centrally planned approach prior to the complete collapse of the system are showing the strongest signs of recovery (Hungary and Poland).

The legacies of the centrally planned period are similar in most of these countries, but the degree to which they are exhibited is somewhat dependent on the degree to which central planning policies were enforced.

BANKS WHICH HAVE POOR LIQUIDITY

The banks are generally poorly capitalized and have portfolios made up of a large number of non-performing loans, partially as a result of enforced lending to state owned companies and partially due to poor lending decisions post-1989 (Szego, 1993). Private banks have emerged since 1989: however, much of the lending to private companies has not been repaid. As a result, few state owned or private banks are in a position to lend to the new private manufacturing sector for periods of more than one year, and then only on the basis of highly liquid collateral which covers the initial loan plus expected accumulated interest.

Individual banks face problems in three major areas:

1 They are still developing the internal skill base needed to run a bank.
2 There are no performance norms or benchmarks for private companies, thus making pricing risk highly uncertain.
3 The legal system lacks a framework of corporate contract or property law, making it difficult to impose the bank's rights through bankruptcy or seizure of collateral.

In addition to the issues listed above, management in the formerly state owned banks is problematic (Thorne, 1993). The lack of knowledge in the area of bank financial management, combined with the retention of managers in place prior to 1989, has resulted in little change in the structure of the banks. The banks were founded in order to respond to instructions from the center to dispense credits to the state owned companies. Therefore, they have a structure which is highly bureaucratic, heavily overstaffed, and largely unequipped to operate in a market economy. State owned company debt, which is continually rolled over at high interest rates, further hinders the banks' ability to develop their loan portfolio, as much of the capital available is consumed by the interest on these

loans (Saunders and Sommariva, 1993). Given that successful private companies tend to lodge their profit in Western European banks and in hard currency, it is unlikely that the real deposit required for on-lending will increase in the near future.

AN ECONOMIC STRUCTURE WITH FEW COMPANIES OF MEDIUM SIZE

The economies were industrialized through the development of large, vertically integrated firms which had monopolies in their markets (Gibb, 1992). As they were designed to produce in line with a command from the center rather than for profit reasons, they are neither efficient nor market driven, nor did they have much flexibility to exploit opportunities at any intermediate stage. Retention of capital for reinvestment was not a priority for these companies and this has resulted in serious quality problems.

Some of these companies have been broken up and parts sold, with the easiest disposals being companies based in commodity trading with hard currency export potential. However, for those which have not yet been privatized, the structure remains intact and inefficient. As with the banks, the top management of most of these companies has not changed.

The status of the large firms is:

- recently privatized;
- being prepared for privatization;
- partners in joint ventures with foreign investors;
- to be privatized in the future.

PRIVATIZATION

The most attractive firms were the first to be privatized. The privatization method which is often used is the voucher method, with the population (as listed on the voting register) being offered a quantity of vouchers at a nominal price which could then be exchanged for shares of privatized companies through an auction process. While this method may be equitable, it does not relieve the problems associated with the pricing of these firms or with their capitalization. Delays in bringing companies forward to auction and speculative trading in vouchers are major political problems.

Mass privatization has worked well in some of the countries (e.g., Poland); however, it only achieves a change in ownership without restructuring or reform. The companies then need to change the management and financial structures and this may be regarded as the second phase of the process. In many cases, this second phase must be completed in plants which have suffered an output collapse since 1989 (Calvo and Corricelli, 1993). It is remarkable that, almost without exception, the management of the companies has not changed on privatization. This may be attributed in part to the vote of the workers who retain a percentage of the company and tend to vote for their managers to stay on in an attempt to protect their jobs. The maintenance of key management personnel is useful in terms of their knowledge of the other firms operating in the marketplace. However, the lack of turnover of top management in both the state owned (or previously state owned) companies and banks has sometimes been blamed for the slow restructuring of the companies. It may be regarded as in the personal interest of neither the top management of banks nor enterprises to restructure (Frydman and Rapaczynski, 1994).

It is expected that the break up of the state owned enterprises will create a market for supplies and that some of the private companies will be able to compete for this business. However, there is little evidence of this to date.

The private start up and SME sectors are small and relatively new, with mangers inexperienced in operating in a market environment. They have little access to finance, as financiers such as venture capitalists are still relatively inactive and banks are unable or unwilling to take on new, risky loans (Szego, 1993). In a market economy, it would be normal to see high levels of growth in these companies. However, their inability to access affordable funds for long enough periods means that they cannot accumulate capital easily. While they are relatively successful in finding markets in their immediate geographical area, the level of investment needed to succeed on a larger scale is prohibitive. Many managers of small firms have difficulty in pricing their goods, resulting in poor realized value added as compared to the potential. The above factors, combined with high corporate taxation levels,

mean that many of the small companies operate in the informal economy.

The most successful small firms are those which also have an import/export trading branch. The profits from the trading activity feed the relatively newly established manufacturing plant with working capital and investment funding. In addition to the provision of capital, many of the owners of these companies have experience of living and working in market economies prior to 1989. This factor meant that they could successfully enter the market soon after the changes and therefore gain and maintain market share quickly.

While the capital markets are not very active in most of the economies, legislation has been put in place allowing such markets to emerge as the speed of privatization increases. In the economies with capital markets (e.g., Hungary, Poland, and the Czech Republic), there is relatively low turnover. The prices in these markets have fluctuated greatly since their establishment and they remain susceptible to political uncertainty, exchange rate devaluations, poor liquidity, and unpredictability resulting from the inexperience of fund managers. Much of the uncertainty associated with trading has been absorbed by the citizens of the countries as they participated through investment funds using vouchers.

As more companies are privatized, the pricing mechanisms are improving. Liquidity is also improving as regulations are loosened with regard to foreign investors and the experience of the indigenous population increases.

Governments are attempting to put in place legislative measures suitable to a market environment. There has been some loosening of legislation with regard to ownership and investment rights for non-nationals. Foreign investment is protected in most countries.

Legislation is still changing rapidly and some problems remain with regard to its implementation:

- There are long lead times with regard to taking a case to court in most of these countries.
- Corruption in the courts remains a problem, and this is unlikely to change quickly given present institutional structures.

- There are some cultural barriers with regard to collateral redemption.

Under the central planning system, most of the trading between COMECON countries, and with client states such as India and Cuba, was on a barter basis (Grint and Choi, 1993). In many cases the balance of trade was uneven, and the collapse of the communist regime resulted in high levels of debt both between ex-COMECON countries and outside of the bloc. The debt was mostly intergovernmental, and the failure to pay, combined with the currency devaluations in exchange rates, has had serious balance of payments repercussions. Similarly, the reliance on barter means that the mechanisms for the movement of money are weak, and there is no history of private companies raising money in syndicate. This is a continuing problem for the banks given the poor capitalization levels and the fact that many do not have access to international money markets.

Bibliography

Calvo, G. A., and Corricelli, F. (1993). Output collapse in Eastern Europe: The role of credit. *IMF Staff Papers*, **40**, 32–52.

Frydman, R., and Rapaczynski, A. (1994). *Privatization in Eastern Europe: Is the State Withering Away?* London: Central European University Press.

Gibb, A. A. (1992). Small business development in Central and Eastern Europe: Opportunity for a rethink? Occasional paper No. 9241, DUBS.

Grint, K., and Choi, C. J. (1993). *Whither the Embrangled East? Trust and Information in Eastern Europe*. MRP.

Saunders, A., and Sommariva, A. (1993). Banking sector and restructuring in Eastern Europe. *Journal of Banking and Finance*, **17**, 931–57.

Schiffman, H. N. (1993). The role of banks in financial restructuring in countries of the former Soviet Union. *Journal of Banking and Finance*, **17**, 1059–72.

Szego, G. (1993). Introduction. *Journal of Banking and Finance*, **17**, 773–83.

Thorne, A. (1993). Eastern Europe's experience with banking reform: Is there a role for banks in the transition? *Journal of Banking and Finance*, **17**, 959–1000.

valuing flexibility

Alexander Triantis

Flexibility in production allows a firm to switch between alternative "states" of operation in order to respond to uncertainty in input and output product markets. These states may be discrete (e.g., an open or closed plant) or continuous (e.g., operating at different levels of capacity, or selecting different product mixes). The degree of flexibility is inversely related to the size of the switching costs. Recently, sophisticated financial techniques have been developed to quantify the value of flexibility. These techniques are based on contingent claims analysis, which involves replicating the cash flows from the flexible asset with a continuously rebalanced portfolio of underlying traded securities. A martingale, or risk neutral, pricing operator is then employed. Hodder and Triantis (1993) provide a detailed description of this approach for valuing flexibility. They also discuss computational approximation techniques that can be used to value complex compound switching options that arise due to flexibility.

Various types of flexibility have been analyzed using the contingent claims approach. Brennan and Schwartz (1985) and McDonald and Siegel (1985) value the option to shut down and resume production. Trigeorgis and Mason (1987) and Pindyck (1988) examine the options to expand or contract production or plant capacity. Triantis and Hodder (1990) and He and Pindyck (1992) show how to value a production system that has the flexibility to switch its output mix over time. Kulatilaka (1993) shows how to value a dual-fuel industrial steam boiler which allows switching between two inputs in response to input cost changes. Kogut and Kulatilaka (1994) and Mello, Parsons, and Triantis (1995)

value global production flexibility, which allows a firm to change its production location configuration to take advantage of exchange rate fluctuations. Finally, Cortazar and Schwartz (1993) analyze flexibility inherent in a multi-stage production process, and Baldwin and Clark (1993) examine the benefits of modularity in manufacturing.

This literature on flexibility is significant for two major reasons. First, it provides rigorous valuation techniques for evaluating flexibility, thus allowing firms to appropriately weigh the benefits of production flexibility against the significant costs associated with purchasing or developing such flexibility. This is particularly important in light of criticisms that the use of unsophisticated valuation techniques may be leading firms to underinvest in flexible capital. Second, a byproduct of the valuation procedure is the determination of the optimal "switching" policy (i.e., how a firm should optimally use its flexibility). This formal link between production strategy and valuation is important to establish.

Among the specific results that have emerged from the flexibility valuation literature, flexibility has been shown to be particularly valuable under the following conditions: (1) when the underlying uncertainties (e.g., product prices or demands) are very volatile; (2) when the life of the flexible capital is long; (3) when switching costs are low; (4) when more frequent switches are allowed; and (5) when the correlations between the alternative production inputs (or outputs) are low (or negative). The last result concerning correlation indicates that there is an advantage to pursuing strategic diversification in a firm that has flexible capital. The phenomenon of hysteresis is also highlighted in many of the papers in the literature. Hysteresis results when the output price at which one would switch from state 1 (e.g., an open plant) to state 2 (a closed plant) is different than the price at which one would switch from state 2 to state 1. The hysteresis band widens as switching costs and volatilities increase.

Most models in the existing literature on valuing flexibility adopt two key assumptions that are standard in the financial option pricing literature. First, the underlying variables are assumed to be observable and their uncertainty resolution is assumed to follow a diffusion process with constant volatility. Second, the optimal switching (exercise) policy is derived assuming that the objective is to maximize the market value of the flexible asset. These assumptions may be inappropriate for many of the situations in which the theory of valuing flexibility is meant to be applied. These shortcomings of the existing literature on flexibility valuation are discussed further below (along with citations of recent papers that attempt to address some of these problems).

The processes for uncertainty resolution are likely to be quite complicated in practice. Competition in product markets, for example, may result in the product price processes involving stochastic volatility, mean reversion, and/or jumps. These complexities will typically eliminate the possibility of obtaining closed-form valuation formulas. However, the literature on financial options has dealt with fairly general specifications of the uncertainty resolution processes in numerical approximation frameworks (such as lattice approaches). Since most practical applications involving flexibility require the use of numerical techniques anyway due to their complexity (stemming from the American and/or compound option features), future research should attempt to incorporate more general processes to avoid errors from misspecification of the underlying processes.

In some cases, uncertainty resolution may not occur exogenously (simply from the passage of time), but rather may be endogenous, depending on the firm's production strategy. For example, uncertainty about the demand or price of some output may only (or partially) be resolved by producing that output or related outputs. These learning by doing and collateral learning features are incorporated into the investment model of Childs, Ott, and Triantis (1995).

A further complication in valuing flexibility may arise if the values of the underlying variables are not observable. In such cases, costs may be associated with acquiring information in order to decide whether to switch states of production. Alternatively, noisy estimates of the values of the underlying variables may be used. In either case, the resulting effect will be a reduction in the value of flexibility. Determining the magnitude of this reduction in flexibility value is an interesting topic for future research.

The switching strategy for a flexible asset depends on the decision-maker's objective function. This can create problems if the objective of the agent that selects the optimal strategy is not consistent with that of one or more of the principals who hold the switching option. For example, it is well known that agency costs may arise in a levered firm given that management selects an operating policy that maximizes only shareholder wealth. Mello, Parsons, and Triantis (1995) compare first-best and second-best switching policies and measure the resulting agency costs in a levered firm that has global production flexibility. Agency costs may also arise if management tries to maximize its own wealth rather than that of the shareholders (e.g., by continuing to operate when it would be optimal from the shareholders' perspective to shut down operations).

Other factors may cause switching strategies and flexibility values to differ from those identified in the papers cited earlier. The illiquidity of a firm's assets may result in switching strategies that appear suboptimal when compared to those obtained from maximizing value under the assumption of perfect marketability. The structure of the industry in which a firm operates may also significantly affect flexibility value. Kulatilaka and Marks (1988) show that the nature of a firm's contracts with its suppliers can have a significant impact on the value of flexibility. Finally, other "real options" that a firm holds could also affect the value of its production flexibility (on option interactions, see Trigeorgis, 1993).

While there has been significant progress in developing techniques to accurately value flexibility, there remain several important avenues for future research in this area. First, more realistic assumptions need to be introduced into the valuation models, as suggested above. Second, implications of the valuation theory should be tested against empirical data from different industries. Third, since many applications are bound to involve several underlying uncertainties, the search for more efficient computational approximation techniques must continue.

Bibliography

Baldwin, C. Y., and Clark, K. B. (1993). Modularity and real options. Working paper No. 93–026, Harvard Business School.

Brennan, M. J., and Schwartz, E. S. (1985). Evaluating natural resource investments. *Journal of Business*, **58**, 135–57.

Childs, P. D., Ott, S. H., and Triantis, A. J. (1995). Investment decisions for mutually exclusive projects: An options framework. Working paper, University of Maryland.

Cortazar, G., and Schwartz, E. S. (1993). A compound option model of production and intermediate inventories. *Journal of Business*, **66**, 517–40.

He, H., and Pindyck, R. S. (1992). Investments in flexible production capacity. *Journal of Economic Dynamics and Control*, **16**, 575–99.

Hodder, J. E., and Triantis, A. J. (1993). Valuing flexibility: An impulse control framework. *Annals of Operations Research*, **45**, 109–30.

Kogut, B., and Kulatilaka, N. (1994). Operating flexibility, global manufacturing, and the option value of a multinational network. *Management Science*, **40**, 123–39.

Kulatilaka, N. (1993). The value of flexibility: The case of a dual-fuel industrial steam boiler. *Financial Management*, **22**, 271–80.

Kulatilaka, N., and Marks, S. G. (1988). The strategic value of flexibility: Reducing the ability to compromise. *American Economic Review*, **78**, 574–80.

McDonald, R., and Siegel, D. (1985). Investment and the valuation of firms when there is an option to shut down. *International Economic Review*, **26**, 331–49.

Mello, A. S., Parsons, J. E., and Triantis, A. J. (1995). An integrated model of multinational flexibility and financial hedging. *Journal of International Economics*, **39**, 27–51.

Pindyck, R. S. (1988). Irreversible investment, capacity choice, and the value of the firm. *American Economic Review*, **78**, 969–85.

Triantis, A. J., and Hodder, J. E. (1990). Valuing flexibility as a complex option. *Journal of Finance*, **45**, 549–65.

Trigeorgis, L. (1993). The nature of option interactions and the valuation of investments with multiple real options. *Journal of Financial and Quantitative Analysis*, **28**, 1–20.

Trigeorgis, L., and Mason, S. P. (1987). Valuing managerial flexibility. *Midland Corporate Finance Journal*, **5**, 14–21.

venture capital

Charles Schell

Venture capital involves medium-term equity participation in an unquoted enterprise where returns are mainly generated in the form of capital gains realized at the end of the venture.

It variously refers to the application of capital to new or developing unquoted enterprises; the financial support industry which has been built around supplying the capital; or the techniques and procedures involved in the process of screening, evaluating, and investing in enterprises. The term is applied in a variety of business contexts and may refer to a very small investment in a new enterprise start up or a much larger and much more complex structured financing, such as a management buyout (MBO). Depending on who is describing venture capital, the connotation may be positive, with terms like "business angels" used to describe investors, or derisive, with "vulture capital" substituted for venture capital. Even firms which are closely associated with the industry often prefer to describe themselves as development capital or investment capital providers rather than venture capitalists.

So what is venture capital? At its simplest, venture capital is equity investment in new and growing enterprises, but even this definition would not be strictly true. Many investments are a combination of debt and equity investment, and venture capital providers often take a holistic approach to the company's financial structure by carefully balancing the increased risk which additional debt brings with the investor's need for short-term returns. The venture capitalist may not even provide all of the funds, but may only invest a part of the total requirement, and seek other investors on the company's behalf to make up the remainder of the required funds. Banks, pension funds, insurance companies, other institutional investors, suppliers, customers, and private investors may make up the remainder. Even the involvement in new and growing business included in the definition is not always true. Venture capital may be used to restructure failing firms, transfer ownership in a mature firm, or finance a demerger.

Every new venture capital financing seems to expand our definition of what we understand to be venture capital. To understand venture capital we need to look at the types of venture capital applications, the providers and advisors who make up the industry, and the process of placing venture capital.

TYPES OF VENTURE CAPITAL

Since the size of venture capital investment varies from the tens of thousands to the hundreds of millions, business stage from start up to mature, and the industry from high-technology to fast food, it is not surprising that the venture capital industry is fragmented into several distinct types.

For the smallest business, and those which are at the earliest stages of development, there is very little recourse to venture capital funding from commercial venture capital providers, although specialist financial sources, often government supported, may provide some assistance. "Seed capital" funds provide support to enterprises which are still developing a product and may not be able to offer a commercially viable product for at least a year. Likely customers for seed capital are biotechnology and other higher technology companies which may require regular injections of capital over a period of years before a product is clearly defined and its likely market identifiable. While the returns to this type of investment may be very high, most commercial venture capital operations steer clear because of the high risk, the uncertain capital commitments, and the expertise required to assess the proposal.

Once an enterprise has identified a product and market, produced a business plan, and is looking for its first external capital, "start-up funds" may be approached. Unless the business will require at least £100,000 in capital, promises rapid, sustained growth, and stock market flotation within a few years, many of the major venture capital providers will again be less than enthusiastic. This is at least partly because smaller deals may cost nearly as much and take as much effort to put together as bigger deals. Legal and accounting costs for the smallest of equity investments may cost over £50,000, but will rise much less than proportionately with the size of the proposition. Furthermore, a smaller business, even after years of remarkable growth, may still not be large enough to take to the stock exchange. This means that the venture capitalist will face a long-term commitment to a risky and illiquid asset.

Together, seed and start-up funds invest about 6 percent of total venture capital funds in the UK (BVCA, 1992), although this figure may be slightly higher in the USA and the rest of Europe. Far more important in terms of volume are the funds used in business expansion, also referred to as development capital. Investment in unquoted, but established companies may not be considered to be venture capital in the United States, but it appears to be the direction in which the European venture capital industry is headed. Development capital, which accounts for around 30 percent of venture capital financing in the UK, helps family controlled businesses expand beyond the limits set by gearing ratios and reinvested profits, enabling them to prove their ability to establish market leadership and create a reputation which will make them attractive to equity markets. For venture capital providers, this type of investment is attractive because it offers the prospect of a relatively quick and predictable way of cashing in their investment, and the security which the management and firm's well-established track record offer.

While development capital investments rely on growth to build value, management buyouts (MBOs), and buyins (MBIs) establish value through the demerger and eventual flotation of a subsidiary operation. MBO and MBI activity accounts for about two-thirds of venture capital funds invested, but a much smaller proportion of deals, because MBO/MBI deals are typically much larger than other types of venture capital investments. MBOs are usually initiated by existing management of the subsidiary; MBIs involve recruitment of a substantial part of the new management from outside the company. As mentioned above, a management buyout may not rely on growth to create the scale needed for an eventual flotation, and in some cases may involve reducing the size of the spun-off subsidiary's operation, rather seeking to demonstrate previously unrecognized value to potential investors.

Venture capital firms also invest in shares in unquoted companies held by other venture capital providers, a transaction referred to as secondary purchase. Many venture capitalists' portfolios, and a substantial part of certain specialist funds' portfolios, may be made up of turnaround or restructuring investments. These investments may involve buying out existing management and investors and implementing often extreme remedial actions. This type of venture capital investment is very "hands on" or active and is of particular interest to funds which are willing to commit the management resources to the company, as well as the capital.

THE VENTURE CAPITAL PROCESS

Venture capital deals do come in a wide variety of shapes and sizes, but there are certain elements in common. They require a high return to compensate for the risk; they generally have less available collateral than the typical bank loan and hence are more complex and expensive to set up; and they require an exit route in order to recover the fund's capital.

Matching venture capital providers and users is the first stage in the process. Each venture capital fund sets its own criteria for investments, and most have a fairly well defined idea about the minimum and maximum size of investment they are willing to undertake, the length of time they expect to hold the investment, the geographical and industry parameters, the stage of investment, the amount of management involvement they are willing to contribute, and of course, the rate of return they potentially offer. For most venture capital firms the latter may be as high as 40 percent per annum (realized within five years), an amount they consider fair since as few as one in five investments is expected to achieve this target, while twice as many will fail, and the remainder will struggle along without ever providing the target rate of return. Since a 40 percent return on successful investments offers the prospect of a fivefold gain (given compounding) the portfolio offers some prospect of eventually showing a fair return overall, even after the failures. Companies looking for equity funding need to be able to demonstrate the potential for growth that can support the fund's expected rate of return, and perhaps even more importantly, explain how the return will be realized. Most venture capital funds look for an exit route even before the

investment is made – in fact most will require at least two potential exits. Floating the company on a public stock exchange, selling the company to an industry competitor (a trade sale), selling the fund's shares to another venture capital fund (secondary purchase), and selling the shares back to management (an MBO) are all potential exit routes.

Once a match has been found, the venture capital fund will begin its evaluation of the company, usually starting with an assessment of the company's business plan. One venture capital firm reports that it looks at over a thousand plans a year in order to make fifteen investments (Rowan, 1994) and many of the business plans are referred by professionals. For the few companies that pass this first screen, more thorough interviews and investigations will follow, and additional market research and product testing may be required.

After this the company will enter into negotiations with the venture capitalist to determine the amount of equity which the founders or current owners will surrender to the venture capitalist in order to obtain the investment. At the same time, a firm of accountants will usually be engaged to investigate and verify the company's financial projections, particularly the assumptions used to reach the projections, and to look for any other irregularities. This investigation is referred to as due diligence and if satisfactory, agreements are concluded between the venture capitalist, management, and other parties such as banks.

Following the investment the venture capitalist will take a more or less active role in monitoring the investment. Certain firms prefer to maintain a close relationship while others allow management a free hand as long as certain conditions are met. These conditions are usually specified in the agreements, and may provide for the venture capital fund to take control if certain conditions occur. The venture capitalist will often appoint a non-executive director to the board of the enterprise.

Ultimately, the venture capital fund is looking for an exit route and will push for a flotation when the company's growth and market conditions appear suitable. In certain countries a smaller-companies stock exchange such as

Nasdaq in the USA or the AIM in the UK, may allow an easier route to flotation than a full listing, but these markets are less liquid when market conditions are flat. If a full listing is the only option, management may be reluctant to meet the requirements of disclosure, increased public scrutiny, and the high listing costs. Under certain conditions refinancing, secondary purchase, or even a trade sale may seem a better option.

THE INDUSTRY

The venture capital industry was originally established to fill a gap which existed for growing firms which were too small to raise equity from public markets, yet too successful to constrain growth to the boundaries set by bank debt–equity guidelines. Venture capital providers are as diverse in shape as the clients they serve, and range in size from the largest – firms like 3i with £2.5 billion in investments – to the smallest – a three-person office with a handful of small investments.

The industry includes venture capital firms closely associated with or owned by major banks. Insurance and pension funds may also provide funds directly to companies, although they are more likely to invest through specialist venture capital firms.

Companies may also invest in new ventures, and certain larger corporates have specialized units which invest in related new ventures, often with the intention of later acquiring the venture or its new technology, or providing a market for the new firm's product. This type of venture capital is called corporate venturing.

Part of the seed capital and start-up funding not provided by the mainstream venture capital industry is being provided by a new class of venture capitalist, the "informal investor" or "business angel." These investors are often business people who have already sold a business and retired or may be high net worth individuals seeking higher returns than offered by portfolio investment. While the number of business angels is small, it has been suggested that they may be the largest single source of new investment (Harrison and Mason, 1996).

THE FUTURE OF VENTURE CAPITAL

The venture capital industry continues to evolve, and it would be difficult to say what form it will eventually reach or even what name we will be using to describe it. After more than a decade of returns which are probably below the expectations of the institutions which originally provide the funds which the venture capitalists invest, it is certain that there will be changes, and it is just as certain that any retrenchment will create opportunities which others will possibly fill. There is also an increasingly important international dimension to the industry, and the next decade may see venture capital applied in areas currently served by conventional lending products in countries where the banking systems are as yet underdeveloped.

Bibliography

Bhide, A. (1992). Bootstrap finance: The art of start-ups. *Harvard Business Review*, **70**, 109–17.

Bovaird, C. (1990). *Introduction to venture Capital Finance*. London: Pitman.

BVCA (1992). *A Guide to Venture Capital*. London: British Venture Capital Association.

Gregory, A. (1992). *Valuing Companies: Analysing Business Worth*. Hemel Hempstead: Woodhead Faulkner.

Harrison, R., and Mason, C. (1996). *Informal Venture Capital: Evaluating the Impact of Business Introduction Services*. London: Prentice-Hall.

Lorenz, T. (1989). *Venture Capital Today*, 2nd edn. Cambridge: Woodhead Faulkner.

Mason, C., and Harrison, R. (1993). Strategies for expanding the informal venture capital market. *International Small Business Journal*, **11**, 23–38.

Moore, P. (1993). Vultures or venturers? *Director*, **46**, 59–65.

Murray, G. C. (1992). A challenging market for venture capital. *Long Range Planning*, **25**, 79–86.

Ooghe, H., Manigart, S., and Fassin, Y. (1991). Growth patterns of the European venture capital industry. *Journal of Business Ventures*, **6**, 381–404.

Pratt's Guide to Venture Capital Sources (1989). 13th edn. Needham, MA: Venture Economics.

Robbie, K., and Murray, G. (1992). Venture capital in the UK. *International Journal of Bank Marketing*, **10**, 32–40.

Rowan, M. (1994). Are the backers backing Britain? *Finance Director*, June.

Sahlman, W. A., and Stevenson, H. H. (1991). *The Entrepreneurial Venture*. Boston, MA: Harvard Business School.

Sharp, G. (1991). *The Insider's Guide to Raising Venture Capital*. London: Kogan Page.

volatility

Gordon Gemmill

Volatility is the term used in finance to denote the standard deviation of returns on an asset. It is therefore the square root of the variance of asset returns. Given a sequence of n weekly returns, an equally weighted estimate of the weekly variance (volatility squared) would be $\sigma_w^2 = [1/(n-1)]\Sigma_i(r_i - R)^2$, where σ_w denotes weekly volatility, σ_w^2 is the weekly variance, r_i is an individual return, and R is the mean of all returns.

It is customary to express volatility on an annual basis. If an asset price follows a random walk, then its variance grows linearly with time. Hence, the annual volatility is 52 times the weekly variance and the annual volatility may be expressed as $\sigma = 52\sqrt{}\times\sigma_w$. σ will be used henceforth to denote the annual volatility.

A rather simple example of estimating a volatility is given in table 1. Note that more than the ten prices given here would be required to obtain a reliable estimate and the table gives calculations which have been rounded to two decimal places.

Using the table, the weekly variance is then, $\sigma_w^2 = (1/8) \times 329.05 = 41.13$ and the weekly volatility is $\sqrt{41.13} = 6.41$ percent. The annual volatility is then, $\sigma = 6.41 \times \sqrt{52} = 46.25$ percent.

In the example, percentage returns were calculated as $r_t = \log(P_t/P_{t-1}) \times 100$. The reason for using (natural) logs in this calculation is that it is consistent with an asset which has a lognormally distributed price and this leads to returns which are normally distributed. Using such geometric returns has the commonsense feature that an increase in price followed by an equal fall in price gives returns which are equal and opposite, as in the sequence over weeks 2 to 3 (+4.45 percent) and 3 to 4 (−4.45 percent) in the example. Had arithmetic returns been used, the sequence would have given +4.54 percent and −4.35 percent, resulting in a positive average return when the price had not risen.

This simple example of estimating volatility assumed that all observations on returns were equally important. However, it is possible to weight recent returns more heavily than earlier ones, a typical arrangement being an exponential weighting scheme. Yet another approach is to take account of intra-day price movements, by using the day's high and low prices as well as the closing price (see Garman and Klass, 1980).

It is useful to know what levels of volatility typically arise in financial markets. Customary levels would be: shares 25 percent, commodities 25 percent, share indices 17 percent, bonds 14 percent, and exchange rates 12 percent. From a few weeks of observations, it would not be unusual to find a share with a volatility as high as 70 percent or as low as 10 percent. After the stock-market crash of 1987, estimated volatilities for shares exceeded 100 percent in some cases. Volatility for London's FTSE100 Index (estimated from 30-day data) was in the range 8–70 percent over the 1984–94 period. Extreme values do not persist, there being a tendency for volatility to revert towards its long-term mean.

FORECASTING VOLATILITY

Forecasting volatility is extremely important for calculating the fair value of an option. The only unknown in the Black–Scholes options pricing model is the volatility, so that trading in options is effectively trading in volatility. It is possible to solve the model iteratively in order to find that volatility which equates model and market prices, the so-called "implied volatility." This reveals the market consensus for the period to maturity of the chosen option. An interesting feature of implied volatilities is that they tend to be larger for options which are at very low or

Table 1   Estimating volatility

Week	Price	r_i (%)	$(r_i - R)^2$
1	100		
2	110	9.53	56.33
3	115	4.45	19.76
4	110	−4.45	19.76
5	115	4.45	19.76
6	105	−9.10	82.76
7	110	4.65	21.64
8	120	8.70	75.71
9	125	4.08	16.66
10	120	−4.08	16.66
Sum =		18.23	329.05
Average (R) =		2.03	

very high exercise prices, leading to "volatility with a smile." Observed smiles also tend to be skewed to the left, which is consistent with the evidence for some financial assets that volatility rises as the price falls. In principle the implied volatility might be expected to provide a better forecast than an estimate of volatility based upon past returns. Most empirical studies confirm this hypothesis, but not all (Canina and Figlewski, 1993).

Although an asset may be weak-form efficient in terms of prices, with the direction of the next move not predictable from past moves, it is possible to predict whether the next move is likely to be larger or smaller than previous moves. In other words, there are systematic changes in volatility. Time-series models for the variance have been developed, known as ARCH models, which exploit this dependence (Engle and Rothschild, 1992). There is a whole family of such models, some of which allow the distribution of returns to have fat tails and others of which incorporate skewness of the distribution. Despite a large volume of research, the ability of these models to forecast volatility is only marginally better than that of a simple, equally weighted model as given in the example above. Nevertheless, they do confirm that good forecasts require skewness, fat tails, and mean reversion to be taken into account.

Volatility Spillovers

After the stock market crash of 1987, it became apparent that a large price movement in one time zone could spill over into another time zone. Not surprisingly, there is also evidence that an increase in volatility of the US stock market spills over into the European and Japanese markets (Hamao, Masulis, and Ng, 1990). A slightly different kind of volatility spillover is sometimes claimed to occur from futures and options markets to the stock market, to which the response in the United States has been to introduce "circuit breakers": these prohibit further arbitrage between the stock and derivative markets until conditions are quieter.

Excess Volatility

A contentious aspect of volatility in finance is whether it can be excessive. A share's price is fundamentally the present value of the stream of future dividends. Shiller (1981) argued that changes in share prices were larger than could be justified by subsequent changes in dividend payments and he called this excess volatility. Later papers showed that Shiller's argument was not statistically significant and pointed to the potential error which can be made in forecasting dividends. There is also the question of whether investors require a larger risk premium in periods when the volatility is higher, thus affecting share prices.

Volatility of a Bond

In the analysis of bonds, volatility is defined in a rather different way: it is the percentage change in the price of a bond for a 1 percent change in its yield. For example, if the yield rose from 8 percent to 9 percent and the price of a bond fell from 100 to 95, then the bond's volatility would be equal to 5 percent/1 percent = 5. This measure of volatility is related to a bond's duration, as volatility = duration/(1+ yield).

Bibliography

Canina, L., and Figlewski, S. (1993). The informational content of implied volatility. *Review of Financial Studies*, **6**, 659–82.

Engle, R., and Rothschild, M. (eds.) (1992). ARCH models in finance. *Journal of Econometrics*, **52** (supplement),1–311.

Garman, M., and Klass, M. (1980). On the estimation of security price volatilities from historical data. *Journal of Business*, **53**, 67–78.

Hamao, Y., Masulis, R., and Ng, V. (1990). Correlations in price changes and volatility across international stock markets. *Review of Financial Studies*, **3**, 280–307.

Shiller, R. (1981). Do stock prices move too much to be justified by subsequent changes in dividends? *American Economic Review*, **71**, 421–36.

volatility risk pricing

Nikunj Kapadia

In both the academic and popular press, the subject of volatility risk has been an issue of debate. Evidence that stock volatility is both time varying and stochastic has led researchers to ask whether volatility risk is priced in equity stock and option markets. Volatility risk may be said to be priced if the risk premium determining the expected return on the security is a function of volatility.

In the equity stock market, the notion that the expected return is a positive monotonic function of risk suggests that the expected return on the market portfolio should be positively correlated with the market volatility. Although the detailed description of this relationship is not important for pricing individual stocks relative to each other (where one only needs to know the covariance of the stock's return with the market or another posited factor), it is required for understanding the intertemporal changes in prices. There are two questions that have been asked in the literature. First, is there a significant relationship between the expected return and volatility for the market portfolio? Merton (1980) offers some preliminary evidence, noting that the empirical research in examining the relationship between the expected return and volatility is confounded by the fact that the volatility in actual returns is likely to be larger than the volatility in the expected returns. However, the tests of French, Schwert, and Stambaugh (1987) indicate that a positive relationship does exist between expected return and volatility. They decompose the volatility time series into its predictable and unexpected components. Although they do not find a direct relationship between the market return and the predictable component of volatility, they show that the market return is negatively correlated with the unpredictable shocks to volatility. They suggest that this provides indirect evidence of the *ex ante* positive relationship between expected returns and volatility, as a positive shock to volatility would cause an increase in the expected return in the next period, thus decreasing the stock price (and leading to a negative return) in the current period. They confirm this relationship by fitting an ARCH-M model (Engle, Lillien, and Robins, 1987) and showing that the conditional variance is a determinant of the market risk premium.

The second question that has been asked in the literature is whether the changes in the risk premium can explain the time variation in stock prices. Poterba and Summers (1986) examine this question and conclude that the shocks to volatility are not persistent enough to create the magnitude of volatility induced fluctuations in risk premiums required to explain the observed intertemporal variation in stock prices. This conclusion is in line with the general observation in the literature that the volatility of the stock market is difficult to understand in terms of changes in fundamentals. In this regard, it appears that the more interesting and tractable problems lie in other markets, especially derivative markets.

The importance of volatility in determining the price of an option (and thus its expected return) has been well known since the derivation of the celebrated Black–Scholes equation (Black and Scholes, 1973). However, as the option in the Black–Scholes world can be replicated by dynamically trading the underlying stock and bond, there is no additional volatility-based risk premium. For option prices to incorporate a risk premium based on volatility, the option pricing formula has to be generalized to allow for stochastic volatility. Stochastic volatility induces two effects on the option price. First, the underlying stock return distribution is no longer normal; it has fatter tails (kurtosis) and it may also be skewed. The net effect of this on the option price is well understood (Hull and White, 1987; Heston, 1993); the kurtosis reduces (increases) the at-the-money (away-from-the-money) option price relative to the Black–Scholes and positive (negative) skewness increases the price of the out-of-the-money (in-the-money) option price relative to the Black–Scholes.

Second, the incompleteness of markets resulting from stochastic volatility may imply that the equity option price incorporate a volatility-based risk premium. The early literature on stochastic volatility (Hull and White, 1987) made the assumption that volatility risk was diversifiable and thus not priced. However, this assumption is not tenable for the option on a market index (Amin and Ng, 1993). The notion that equity options may incorporate risk premiums is a movement away from the no-arbitrage Black–Scholes world; however, observed anomalies in the option equity markets have attracted attention to such alternative hypotheses. For example, Lamoureux and Lastrapes (1993) provide evidence of the informational inefficiency of implied volatility, which they suggest could be consistent with a volatility risk premium. Unlike the case for stocks, where one might expect a positive risk premium, this may not be the case for stock options. Therefore, researchers have to ascertain both the magnitude and sign of the risk premium. Kapadia (1995) suggests that the index option should incorporate a negative risk premium for the following reason. From the evidence of French, Schwert, and Stambaugh (1987) already cited, stock returns react negatively to positive volatility shocks, while option prices react positively. Therefore, the option acts as a natural hedge to a long stock position. This would indicate that stock options should be priced higher than in the absence of a risk premium. Evidence from Kapadia (1995) suggests that stock options are higher priced than they should be in a Black–Scholes world or in a world of stochastic volatility with a zero risk premium. The difficulty of distinguishing between alternative hypotheses, especially those dealing with the effects of market frictions and alternative distributions for the underlying stock return, still leaves this an open question. Most empirical research has concentrated on the index option markets and it would be useful to test implications in the individual stock option market. If the market volatility risk were priced, it would imply a cross-sectional relationship between individual stock options through the relationship between the individual stock volatility and the market volatility; this could provide empirically testable implications which could supplement the existing results from the index option market. Although empirical research may resolve the direction of the effect of a volatility risk premium (whether the risk premium is positive or negative), the inherent non-observability of the volatility process is likely to make the ascertaining of the magnitude of the risk premium a far more challenging problem.

Bibliography

Amin, K. I., and Ng, V. K. (1993). Option valuation with systematic stochastic volatility. *Journal of Finance*, **48**, 881–910.

Black, F., and Scholes, M. (1973). The valuation of options and corporate liabilities. *Journal of Political Economy*, **81**, 637–54.

Engle, R. F., Lillien, D. A., and Robins, R. P. (1987). Estimating time varying risk premia in the term structure: The ARCH-M model. *Econometrica*, **55**, 391–407.

French, K. R., Schwert, G. W., and Stambaugh, R. F. (1987). Expected stock returns and volatility. *Journal of Financial Economics*, **19**, 3–30.

Heston, S. L. (1993). A closed-form solution for options with stochastic volatility with applications to bond and currency options. *Review of Financial Studies*, **6**, 327–43.

Hull, J., and White, A. (1987). The pricing of options with stochastic volatilities. *Journal of Finance*, **42**, 281–300.

Kapadia, N. (1995). The price of volatility risk. Working paper, New York University.

Lamoureux, C. G. and Lastrapes, W. D. (1993). Forecasting stock return volatility: Toward an understanding of stochastic implied volatilities. *Review of Financial Studies*, **6**, 293–326.

Merton, R. (1980). On estimating the expected return on the market. *Journal of Financial Economics*, **8**, 323–61.

Poterba, J. P., and Summers, L. H. (1986). The persistence of volatility and stock market fluctuations. *American Economic Review*, **76**, 1142–51.

volatility smile

Nusret Cakici

After the 1987 market crash, it became clear that the prices of derivative securities do not exactly follow the model of Black and Scholes (1973). For instance, the Black–Scholes implied volatility is supposed to be constant, but in practice it strongly depends on option strike price and maturity. That effect, commonly known as volatility smile, is in contrast to the basic assumption of the model. Instead of trying to find a more general model based on a specific mechanism, one can simply construct a numerical procedure consistent with the volatility smile. Probably the simplest and most intuitive tools for valuation of derivative securities are recombining binomial (and multinomial) trees. A tree which is consistent with or implied by the volatility smile can be constructed from the known prices of European options. Once the appropriate prices and transition probabilities corresponding to the nodes and links of the tree are calculated, any American or path-dependent option can be priced consistently with the market.

An implied tree should satisfy the following criteria:

- It must correctly reproduce the volatility smile.

- Negative node transition probabilities are not allowed.
- The branching process must be risk neutral at each step.

The last two conditions also eliminate arbitrage opportunities.

The dots in figure 1 represent typical implied Black–Scholes volatilities of the at-the-money and out-of-the-money European options on the S&P 500 index. The index was rescaled to 100. For strikes higher (lower) than 100, the call (put) options are used to deduce the implied volatility.

Apparently, the implied volatility shows huge variations, with the strike price ranging between 10 and 18 percent. Although the tree is built primarily to price American and path-dependent derivatives, one can certainly evaluate any European option on it, just for the purpose of testing the tree. For each European option priced on the tree, implied Black–Scholes volatility is calculated and plotted versus a continuum of strike prices, producing the curve in figure 1. If the method is appropriate, the resulting curve will closely follow the interpolated option prices which defined the tree.

Note that the Black–Scholes formula is used only as a translator between prices and implied volatilities, providing a simpler description of the data.

We are aware of four different approaches to the problem of construction of implied trees. They all deal with computationally simple (i.e., recombining) trees.

Dupire (1994) demonstrates the similarity between the usual problem of finding option prices given the diffusion (in the form of a known volatility and the inverted problem of finding the diffusion process from the given option prices). He sketches a procedure for building a trinomial risk-neutral implied tree which is able to capture both the maturity and strike dependence of the smile. Due to the large number of degrees of freedom of a trinomial tree, Dupire can assign the node prices in advance. The construction of the tree is reduced to the calculation of transition probabilities. Efficiency and stability of the method depend on the details of the algorithm for extracting the Arrow–Debreu profiles from the given option prices.

Rubinstein (1994, 1995) starts building a binomial tree backwards from the expiration date using a set of probabilities assigned to the logarithmically equidistantly spaced final nodes. Following the known European option prices, final probabilities are assigned by a non-linear minimization routine. After that, the method is very simple and easy to program. To obtain a unique (i.e., well defined) algorithm, Rubinstein assumes that the diffusion along any path connecting two given nodes bears the same probability. That assumption guarantees non-negative node transition probabilities, but neglects the actual time dependence of the volatility smile known from the existing options of earlier maturities.

Derman and Kani (1994) proposed an algorithm for a risk-neutral implied binomial tree able to incorporate both the strike price and term structure of volatility. Given the smaller number of degrees of freedom in a binomial tree, the node positions are not known in

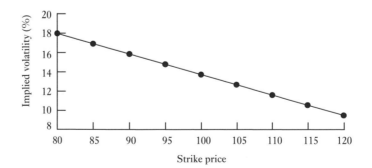

Figure 1

advance. The algorithm of Derman and Kani reproduces the volatility smile accurately in certain circumstances, but fails if the interest rates are high.

Barle and Cakici (1995) introduce important modifications to the method proposed by Derman and Kani (1994). They start from the root at present time and current stock price, so the recombining binomial tree is constructed recursively forward, one level at a time. A new algorithm provides correct treatment of interest rate and dividends, as well as some additional practical improvements. For the purpose of testing, they reconstruct the volatility smile using the new implied tree and obtain excellent results. Their modifications become especially important if the interest rate is high.

The methods of Derman and Kani and the method of Dupire are similar in spirit. They are both able to capture not only the smile, but also its term structure, which is crucial for accurate pricing of American and path-dependent derivatives.

The main purpose of implied binomial trees is to price derivatives consistently with quoted market prices. But they are also useful for analyzing hedging and calculating implied probability distributions.

Bibliography

Barle, S., and Cakici, N. (1995). Growing a smiling tree. *RISK*, 8, 76–80.

Black, F., and Scholes, M. (1973). The pricing of options and corporate liabilities. *Journal of Political Economy*, 81, 637–59.

Derman, E., and Kani, I. (1994). Riding on a smile. *RISK*, 7, 32–9.

Dupire, B. (1994). Pricing with a smile. *RISK*, 7, 18–20.

Rubinstein, M. (1994). Implied binomial trees. *Journal of Finance*, 69, 771–818.

Rubinstein, M. (1995). As simple as one, two, three. *RISK*, 8, 44–7.

warrants

Chris Veld

Traditionally, warrants are defined as rights issued by a company to buy a certain number of "new" shares in this company (during the exercise period against the exercise price). These warrants are nowadays referred to as equity warrants. Around 1980, also bond warrants, giving the right to buy "new" bonds, were introduced. In fact, equity warrants and bond warrants both give the right to buy the (eventual) liabilities of the issuer. Also in the 1980s, other securities were introduced under the name warrant, which give the right to buy gold, oil, foreign currencies, existing shares, and existing bonds. These securities are generally referred to as covered warrants. During the recent past. index warrants also became popular. Because covered warrants and index warrants give the right to buy underlying values, which are existing assets to the issuer, they resemble traded options rather than warrants. This topic will be limited to equity warrants, from now on to be referred to as warrants. Warrants differ from the conversion rights attached to convertibles, in the sense that the warrant exercise price is paid in cash, while the exercise price of a conversion right is paid by redeeming the accompanying bond.

If warrants are exercised, new shares are created. This dilution effect creates a valuation problem. Galai and Schneller (1978) presented the first solution for this problem, by showing that the value of a warrant is a fraction $(1/(1 + q))$ of the value of a call option on the stock of an otherwise identical firm without warrants. The factor q represents the ratio of the number of new shares to be issued upon warrant exercise and the number of existing shares.

However, this solution cannot be used in practice, because such an identical firm does not exist. Building on the Galai and Schneller (1978) result, Crouhy and Galai (1991) and Schulz and Trautmann (1994) derive a dilution corrected version of the Black–Scholes option pricing model. Schulz and Trautmann (1994) also prove that the outcomes of this dilution-corrected option pricing model only marginally differ from the outcomes of the original no-dilution corrected Black–Scholes option pricing model. An important difference that remains between warrants and call options is that warrants generally have a longer maturity. Therefore, a correction for dividend payments on the underlying stock is necessary. One of the few markets in which both warrants and long-term call options are available is the Dutch market. In an empirical study, Veld and Verboven (1995) have shown that, despite the large similarities between these instruments, warrants are valued more highly than long-term call options.

Because of the similarities between convertibles and warrants issued with bonds (warrant bonds), the discussion on traditional and modern motives for the issuance of convertibles is also applicable to warrant bonds. Theoretically, the modern motives are more convincing than the traditional motives. However, from a survey of Dutch companies that issued warrant bonds from 1976 to 1989, Veld (1994) concludes that these companies have mainly been driven by the traditional motives.

With regard to the choice between convertibles and warrant bonds, Veld (1994) concludes that the main motives for the issuance of warrant bonds are (1) the possibility to attract equity while the accompanying bonds remain outstanding; and (2) the possibility to acquire a higher premium for the warrants in relation to the conversion rights, because of the separate trade-ability of the warrants and the bonds. In an empirical study, Long and Sefcik (1990) find that convertibles have an advantage over warrant bonds, because the flotation costs for issuing convertibles are significantly lower.

COVERED AND INDEX WARRANTS

According to Veld (1992), covered warrants are rights to buy existing assets from the issuer. In past issues these assets have included gold, for-eign currencies, oil, existing shares, and existing bonds (for an extensive list of examples, see Duffhues, 1993). Because they entitle the holder to buy existing assets, they are traded more like call options than warrants. The main differences between covered warrants and traded call options are: (1) covered warrants are traded on the stock exchange instead of the options ex-change; thus, the credit risk is not taken over by a clearing organization; and (2) the issuer of covered warrants issues a fixed amount of con-tracts, whereas the number of traded options is flexible. One innovation is basket warrants. These are rights to buy a basket of existing shares of companies in the same branch of indus-try or from the same country.

Index warrants are options on a stock index. They differ from traded options in the same way as covered warrants differ from traded options. On the American and the Canadian markets, Nikkei put warrants have become popular (Wei, 1992). On the European markets a number of index warrants are traded. De Roon and Veld (1996) mention that in the Netherlands index warrants are traded on German, English, French, American, Japanese, and Hong Kong indexes. Wei (1992) has developed a number of valuation models for index warrants.

Bibliography

Crouhy, M., and Galai, D. (1991). Warrant valuation and equity volatility. In F. J. Fabozzi (ed.), *Advances in Futures and Options Research*. Greenwich, CT: JAI Press, 203–15.

De Roon, F., and Veld, C. (1996). An empirical investi-gation of the factors that determine the pricing of Dutch index warrants. *European Financial Manage-ment*, **2**, 97–112.

Duffhues, P. J. W. (1993). Developments in the use of warrants on the national and international capital markets [in Dutch]. In P. J. W. Duffhues et al. (eds.), *Financiele Instrumenten*, Vol. 1. Deventer: Kluwer Bedrijfswetenschappen, 71–93.

Galai, D., and Schneller, M. I. (1978). Pricing of war-rants and the value of the firm. *Journal of Finance*, **33**, 1333–42.

Long, M. S., and Sefcik, S. E. (1990). Participation finan-cing: A comparison of the characteristics of convertible debt and straight bonds issued in conjunction with warrants. *Financial Management*, **19**, 23–34.

Schulz, G. U., and Trautmann, S. (1994). Robustness of option-like warrant valuation. *Journal of Banking and Finance*, **18**, 841–59.

Veld, C. (1992). *Analysis of Equity Warrants as Investment and Finance Instruments*. Tilburg: Tilburg University Press.

Veld, C. (1994). Motives for the issuance of warrant-bond loans by Dutch companies. *Journal of Multinational Financial Management*, **4**, 1–24.

Veld, C., and Verboven, A. (1995). An empirical analysis of warrant prices versus long-term call option prices. *Journal of Business Finance and Accounting*, **22**, 1125–46.

Wei, J. Z. (1992). Pricing Nikkei put warrants. *Journal of Multinational Financial Management*, **2**, 45–75.

Index

Note: Headwords are in bold type